British Writers and the Media, 1930–45

Keith Williams
Lecturer in the Department of English
University of Dundee

First published in Great Britain 1996 by
MACMILLAN PRESS LTD
Houndmills, Basingstoke, Hampshire RG21 6XS
and London
Companies and representatives
throughout the world

A catalogue record for this book is available
from the British Library.

ISBN 0–333–63895–6 (hardcover)
ISBN 0–333–63896–4 (paperback)

First published in the United States of America 1996 by
ST. MARTIN'S PRESS, INC.,
Scholarly and Reference Division,
175 Fifth Avenue,
New York, N.Y. 10010

ISBN 0–312–15820–3

Library of Congress Cataloging-in-Publication Data
Williams, Keith, 1958–
British writers and the media, 1930–45 / Keith Williams.
p.   cm.
Includes bibliographical references and index.
ISBN 0–312–15820–3 (cloth)
1. English literature—20th century—History and criticism.
2. Mass media and literature—Great Britain—History—20th century.
3. Politics and literature—Great Britain—History—20th century.
4. Authors, English—20th century—Political and social views.
5. Great Britain—Politics and government—1936–52.   6. Great
Britain—Politics and government—1910–1936.   7. World War,
1939–45—Geat Britain.   8. Right and left (Political science)
I. Title.
PR478.M37W55   1995
820.9'00912—dc20   96–4326
                                                              CIP

10   9   8   7   6   5   4   3   2   1
05   04   03   02   01   00   99   98   97   96

Printed in Great Britain by
Ipswich Book Co Ltd, Ipswich, Suffolk

This book is dedicated to the patience and support of my wife and children and to my parents' watching and listening.

Contents

Preface   ix

Acknowledgements   xi

Introduction: Obituaries of History and the Thirties
Sublime   1

1   A Twisted Skein: The Media Background   20

2   Refractions: The Media as Subject Matter   48

3   Responses: The Mass Media as Formal Influences   114

4   Involvements: Writing for the Mass Media   151

Conclusions   232

Notes   241

Index   274

Preface:
Mobilising the Medium

In this study of the intertextuality between writing and the media, 'mobilising' is intended in two senses: both the dynamic modernisation of the practice of Leftist writing in the 1930s under the impact of the new mass media, and how that impact featured in the politicisation of writers. Both meanings stem from that decade's accelerated awareness of inhabiting a technological mass-society and -culture, with increasingly complex communications and sophisticated modes of representation. Thirties Leftists were particularly influenced by developments in the early Soviet Union and in Weimar Germany, where the power and forms of the media were eagerly embraced as a modernising influence by avant-gardism with its exhortation toward involvement with modes of production and audiences outside the traditional literary domain. I therefore intend to show how British writers reacted to the mass media, not just negatively – as instruments of mystification, endowing monopoly capitalism and the state with immense new ideological power – but constructively – as a means of political consciousness-raising, as well as a fundamental challenge to the contemporaneity of their own art. In this respect, this study also engages with the cultural fault-lines of the time and its complex negotiations between 'high' and 'low' cultural discourses and genres.

Consequently, the study goes beyond consideration of how the overbearing presence of the forms, assumptions and imagery of the capitalist media were critically refracted in Leftist texts (their mere jeremiad and satire) to examine the formal implications of writers' attempts to subvert and compete with them. It investigates the way newly-privileged technologies of representation, such as radio, photography and cinema, were self-consciously emulated and critiqued by Leftists, but it also explores the practical involvements with the media this often entailed for writers. The final chapter, extending the thirties media experience into the peculiar conditions of the Second World War and immediate postwar Britain, examines the qualified fruition and aftermath of the social-democratic cultural and political consensus that emerged from the period.

Thirties cultural history offers a paradigmatically fractious, but also mutually enriching and potentially liberating, encounter between modern art and the media, which still has powerful implications for today's cultural politics. In order to show this, I intend, for example, to place well-known writers back into this neglected context. For example, Graham Greene's formative literary years were in this period and no writer has been more involved with film 'as critic, scenarist, co-producer, performer, adaptor and adaptee'.[1] Similarly, the epitome of twentieth-century *angst* about the media – *Nineteen Eighty-Four*'s 'Ministry of Truth' – was George Orwell's ironic twist to a phrase from a 1935 study of broadcasting.[2]

While including the background to writers's reactions to the power of the press, I do, however, concentrate on broadcasting and film when examining the media's formal impacts and writers' practical involvements. This is partly because they are specifically modern and technological, but also the sheer volume of Leftist reportage and documentary produced under the influence of the period's journalism merits a separate study.[3] But first I want to introduce my subject by working 'back from the future' to frame it within a Postmodern historical retrospective. For all their characterisation as the decade of naive political commitment, the 1930s were in fact a determining moment in the prehistory of today's debates about Postmodernism and, indeed, can even be seen as initiating some of its key terms (not least in its overtures to popular cultural forms). When we examine Leftist writers' growing scepticism about the possibility of unmediated historical 'truth' this becomes particularly clear. Their encounter with the mass media as constructors of a rhetorically charged and ideologically saturated 'hyperreality', which converts all events into discourse, while appearing to guarantee the literal presence of the facts, was crucial.

K.B.W.

Acknowledgements

Special thanks are due to Professor Stan Smith at Dundee, Professor Jeffrey Richards at Lancaster, Drs Steve Matthews and Michael Brennan at Leeds, Charmian Hearne and John M. Smith at Macmillan, and to all at the British Film Institute and National Sound Archive.

Introduction: Obituaries of History and the Thirties Sublime

The constitution of 'reality' or 'truth' by the performative power of the hyperreal is a familiar topos of today's Postmodern fiction and, equally, of Poststructuralist theory. Graham Swift's photoreporter in *Out of This World* foreshadows Jean Baudrillard's pronouncements on the Second Gulf War of 1991, discussed below: 'it goes without saying that a task force of cameras should accompany the task force to the Falklands. As if without them it could not take place. . . . As if the camera no longer recorded but conferred reality'.[1] In the Postmodern condition, the media do not only inform our perception of events ideologically; for much of the time, reality cannot happen outside their validating gaze. However, writers were already tangling with this paradox in the thirties. The venal journos of Auden and Isherwood's play *The Dog Beneath the Skin* (1935)[2] anticipate Swift's and Baudrillard's point, and it is arguable that thirties media awareness was itself an early symptom of cultural transition to Postmodernity. Indeed, in the purely chronological, if not theoretically-laden, sense, thirties writers were the first Postmodern generation. Their sense of reality was in crisis under the full impact of early twentieth-century technologies, as well as awesome stirrings in geopolitics heralding the globalisation of economic power (postwar corporate multinationalism itself being foreshadowed by the worldwide success of Hollywood). I intend to show that the so-called 'anti-modernism' of the thirties can indeed be read as a transitional phase between Modernism and Postmodernism. As we shall see, the epistemological doubts raised by Modernist art, and at first apparently refuted by thirties writers, were subsequently intensified by their own encounter with media technology and international *Realpolitik*.

Baudrillard's notion of the hyperreal is indispensable, but deeply problematic. Here I take my lead from Christopher Norris's *Uncritical*

1

Theory (1992) which cautions against Baudrillard's reductive view of the role of the 'gigantic simulator of the media' in his pre- and post-Second Gulf War articles: 'The Reality Gulf' / 'The Gulf War Did not Take Place'. As Norris argues, there *was indeed* a true historical event, albeit simultaneously managed for political ends by its 'reality referent' in the media's parallel universe.[3] Baudrillard's articles went a stage too far beyond his own sceptical definition of hyperreality as 'the real's hallucinatory resemblance to itself'. They entered a virtual dimension where the real vanishes at the instant of closest approach, leaving only 'the already reproduced', which simply resembles itself rather than being a trace of something once actually present.[4] Or, to put it another way, the baby turned out to be an optical illusion in the bathwater discarded! Baudrillard seemed to have forgotten Jean-François Lyotard's point that the very idea that the 'performativity principle' is all that counts is part of the recent 'massive subordination of cognitive statements to the finality of the best possible performance'. As Terry Eagleton cautions, Lyotard's theory is a diagnosis of, not a cure for, the dangerous cynicism and paralysis of the Postmodern condition:

> It is not surprising that classical modes of truth and cognition are increasingly out of favour in a society where what matters is whether you deliver the commercial or rhetorical goods. Whether among discourse theorists or the Institute of Directors, the goal is no longer truth but performativity, not reason but power.[5]

This then is the fallacy of relinquishing the enabling notion of 'the real'. Ultimately, it cripples philosophical responsibility and ethical politics. Because we cannot locate any impartial reality beyond discourse or subjectivity, in any absolute sense, this does not automatically negate all possible criteria for relative truthfulness and authenticity. As Julian Barnes qualifies in his Postmodern fiction *A History of the World in 10½ Chapters*:

> when some event occurs we shall have a multiplicity of subjective truths which we assess and then fabulate into history, into some God-eyed version of what 'really' happened. This God-eyed version is a fake. . . . But while we know this, we must still believe that objective truth is obtainable; or we must believe that it is 99 per cent obtainable; or if we can't believe this we must

believe that 43 per cent objective truth is better than 41 per cent. We must do so, because if we don't we're lost, we fall into beguiling relativity, we value one liar's version as much as another liar's, we throw up our hands at the puzzle of it all, we admit that the victor has the right not just to the spoils but also to the truth.[6]

There is a crucial need to maintain a sense of difference between unavoidable discursive transfigurations of events by characteristics of mediation which are inherently ideological, on the one hand, and systematic distortion for politically directed ends, on the other. In 1991 opinion was managed by psychological warfare in which propagandists made deliberate intertextual use of media-informed memory and popular culture, as Philip M. Taylor shows.[7] In the sixties and seventies, US policy was caught out by the dissenting effect on public opinion produced by Vietnam as the first televisual war. Because this unprecedented form of coverage eventually rendered that earlier conflict unthinkable and, hence, unfightable, the Second Gulf War had to be transmitted as a 'prophylactic' or 'safe' conflict in order to make it once again thinkable and to safeguard its fightability. The opening campaign was not targeted at the enemy, but at Western consciousness and at that inevitable first casualty in all wars, truth. By rhetorical inversion of tenor and vehicle, the discourse of this Postmodern war simulated a video game played out on our screens (with 'smart', apparently non-lethal weapons) in which any holocaust was virtual only. Moreover, the integrity of a handful of journalists determined to transgress frames of official reference was never enough to counter the performative power concentrated in the media's institutional compliance.

Half a century before Baudrillard and Saddam Hussein, Orwell wrote of the beginning of the Spanish Civil War (arguably the first fully modern media conflict) that 'History stopped in 1936.'[8] However, the whole irony of Orwell's statement lies in the fact that he knew the conflict manifestly *did not* stop happening for those who experienced it empirically on the ground, even if, like the Second Gulf War, international opinion experienced it mainly vicariously, as a 'reality referent' in egregiously partisan newspapers, newsreels and radio broadcasts. It was because of the political fragmentation and in-fighting of this war, that Orwell realised the 'performative power of the hyperreal', which operated in a virtual dimension, parallel to, if not independent of, the facts, a network of signs that could, nonetheless, interevene in the real conflict and influence its outcome:

> I saw great battles reported where there had been no fighting, and complete silence where hundreds of men had been killed. I saw troops who had fought bravely denounced as cowards and traitors, and others who had not fired a shot hailed as the heroes of imaginary victories; and I saw newspapers in London retailing these lies and eager intellectuals building emotional superstructures over events that never happened. (*Collected Essays*, II, pp. 294–5)

For Orwell and many of his literary contemporaries, the only history genuinely terminated was the Grand Narrative of Truth, the death of naive belief in the 'transcribability' of the actual, in mediation ever giving direct access to objective facts. Hence 1936 is one of the points from which a Postmodern politico-philosophical responsibility has necessarily had to start out.

Simply to ensure the survival of critique and resistance to the performativity principle in the nineties, there has to be a position which negotiates between Baudrillard's extreme cancellation of the real, in which signifier finally divorces referent altogether, and the duplicitous reality-claims of an updated Ministry of Truth. It would be a bad joke of cosmic proportions if Plato's ancient vision of the simulacrum – the identical copy for which no original exists – became the new idealism of our cybernetic and holographic age. However, the 'ironic condition' (to borrow Hayden White's terms)[9] through which we seem to be passing may give rise to a less futile kind of Postmodern theory. Reports of the death of history at the hands of the media in the 1990s will turn out to be as exaggerated as they were in 1936.

For this reason I have used some of Fredric Jameson's key ideas in his *Postmodernism* (1991) to shape my retrospective on the transitional moment embodied in the thirties media crisis.[10] At that time, the objective of representing 'the unimaginable real' of global political relations seemed distinctly possible to writers enthused by a fusion of Marxist theory and new representational technology. For a while there seems to have been a genuine belief that a combination of historical knowledge and 'panoptic' vision would counter the epistemological doubts and representational anarchy unleashed by Modernism. Raymond Williams's notion of 'residual' and 'emergent' kinds of cultural production helps explain attempts by writers to synthesise pre-Modernist realism with some of Modernism's dynamic formal breakthroughs.[11] Their intent, taken as an overview (however unprogrammatic, divergent and contradictory its results) was, in effect, to map a mutated cognitive environment. This new global space, relativised by technology and defamiliarised by Modernism, they hoped, could be inhabited by an adapted human subject, culturally reorientated and politically reactivated. Their method was indeed a neo-realism, taking Marxism's apparent certainties as its unshakeable ideological foundation and emulating the unprecedented 'authenticity' of technological modes of reproduction in its forms. Similarly, in our Postmodern condition it is the 'bewildering new world space of late or multinational capital', with its computer-generated culture of infinitely recessive intertextuality and historical 'depthlessness', that Jameson hopes a politicised form of postmodernist representation might chart.[12] Such an art's critical intertexuality with the media would be fuelled by Guy Debord's argument in *The Society of the Spectacle* that under the technology of contemporary capitalism 'the image has become the final form of commodity reification'.[13] But Debord's idea itself descends from Walter Benjamin's theories about image-fetishism in thirties film and photography and from the discovery of writers like Orwell and Spender that 'vicarious experience, in the latter's phrase, had become 'one of the dominant realities of our time'.[14]

The causes of this thirties media consciousness lay at least partly in developments in continental Europe. After the Great War, sections of the Futurist avant-garde, aligning themselves with the extreme Right or Left, produced competing theories about the politics of art and consequently about how the mass media could be mobilised politically. F. T. Marinetti's endorsement of Fascism and Walter Benjamin's 'modernist Marxism' can thus be taken as opposing horns of the early-twentieth-century writer's dilemma: how to represent the reality of the modern world saturated by what Marinetti called the arts of 'Man multiplied by the machine'. Their positions can also be taken as points of reference in investigating the similar ambivalence and complexities of British writers' responses in the thirties.

In his 1913 manifesto, 'Destruction of Syntax – Imagination without Strings – Words-in-Freedom' (1913), Marinetti proclaimed modern transport and communications were revolutionising human consciousness, a process reflected in Futurism's militantly experimental forms:

Futurism is grounded in the complete renewal of human sensibility brought about by the great discoveries of science. Those people who today make use of the telegraph, the telephone, the phonograph, the train, the bicycle, the motorcycle, the automobile, the ocean liner, the dirigible, the aeroplane, the cinema, the great newspaper (synthesis of a day in the world's life) do not realise that these various means of communication, transportation and information have a decisive effect on their psyches.[15]

According to Marinetti, the technological media were creating 'multiple and simultaneous awareness in a single individual'. On the other hand, in Walter Benjamin's 'Work of Art in the Age of Mechanical Reproduction' (1936), such enthusiasm was radically modified by his suspicion that 'profound changes in the apperceptive apparatus' of humanity brought about by technology meant a new imperialistic power.[16] Benjamin acknowledged the positive potentials of the breakdown of 'aura' with its cultic values, as once-unique works of art were reproduced and disseminated by technology outside the traditional High Cultural domain. But this process was also subject to the commodification Marx diagnosed as the root of the peculiar mystification of the reality of capitalist society. Taking cinema as the most representative modern medium, Benjamin claimed that 'the capitalistic exploitation of film denies consideration to modern man's legitimate claim to being reproduced'. Brecht's question about the theatre was, for Benjamin, more imperative for the new media: 'How can it be divorced from spiritual dope traffic and turned from a home of illusions to a home of experiences?'[17] Benjamin saw the cultural collaboration of the Italian Futurists with Mussolini as the ultimate alienation of the possibilities the mass media offered to consciousness. This he considered inevitable if they were not coupled with a socially just politics: 'Mass reproduction is aided especially by the reproduction of masses' in parades, rallies, sports events and, inevitably, war.[18] The aestheticisation of militarism by the Fascist media, and also (as Benjamin's writings increasingly hinted) Stalinism, was a route to 'modernising' the nation-state without transforming its socio-economic structure according to real collective needs, because surplus value could be wasted by war.

In Britain in the thirties, political developments at home and abroad, such as the establishment of the Soviet state, the Great Depression and the rise of Fascism, broke down traditional disinclination to direct political involvement among middle-class writers and also thrust proletarian writers into the cultural spotlight. On the Left, there was a corresponding reorientation at the end of the twenties away from the perception of Paris as the capital of Modernism and (before the Stalinist cultural reaction and Nazi takeover, respectively) towards Moscow and Weimar Berlin, with the accompanying exhortation that Literature, in order to remain relevant, must adapt to the conditions of the new media and widen its social base. Early Soviet and Weimar avant-gardism, closely linked as they were, developed a programme for modernising culture through forms of art which emulated the forms of the mass-media and, reciprocally, intended to transform mass-media forms into art. The so-called 'anti-Modernism' of the thirties in Britain was, therefore, partly a home-grown attempt to adapt the innovations of English-writing Modernists such as Eliot, Woolf and Joyce to what were seen as more culturally and politically accountable ends, but it was also influenced by Russian Constructivism and German *Neue Sachlichkeit*. The result was a dramatically heightened awareness of the mass-media context, of the contemporary 'force-field', to borrow Jameson's phrase, of economic and technological relations, in which they wrote.[19]

Significantly, it was in a broadcast talk for the BBC's *Youth Looks Ahead* series in 1935 that the poet Cecil Day Lewis used a Joycean metaphor to encapsulate why writing had to keep pace with the mutating consciousness of modernity:

> Life is like Proteus, constantly and bewilderingly changing shape. Literature wrestles with this Proteus till it has him pinned down in a final true form and so compels him to tell his secret. Then, of course, Proteus gets up and begins all over again. Now one has no chance of anticipating the next form that life will take unless one has a firm grasp on its present form.[20]

And central to this was coming to terms with the mass media's influence on contemporary life. British writers realised the scale of their 'colonisation of the mind' with an ambivalent 'sense of shock and excitement', as Valentine Cunningham puts it.[21] But they also tried to develop a constructive agenda to deal with it. Spender declared in 1933 that the 'possibility of a kind of poetry being written which would incite people to action as effectively as the propagandist film' was unlikely.[22] Nevertheless, at least for a time, some writers did believe that, for example, by emulating the devices and motifs of Soviet cinema, they could modernise their writing and mobilise the public for their politics. In the USSR, ironically, Constructivism's programme was eventually suppressed and/or asset-stripped by the Stalinist reaction of the early thirties. In Britain, a coherent programme never fully evolved, as such, but there were diverse experiments which merit reconstructing and historicising.

In Jameson's view, there is now a lag between consciousness and the increasingly complex world system, spanned only by electronic information networks and computerised money-markets. Technology's dizzying advance threatens to leave criticism permanently floundering in its wake: 'there has been a mutation in the object unaccompanied as yet by an equivalent mutation in the subject. We do not yet possess the perceptual equivalent to match this new hyperspace.'[23] His redefinition of the Kantian Sublime is therefore also crucial to my retrospective on the thirties, since a politicised Postmodern aesthetic would include an awareness 'of the limits of figuration and the incapacity of the human mind to give representation to such enormous forces' as the global forcefield of multinational capital. Its art might discover 'some privileged/representational shorthand for grasping a network of power and control' to begin making its, as yet, unimaginable totality comprehensible.[24] Just as in the transitional moment of the thirties, the problem remains the difference between being and knowing, in a reality we have created but which has outstripped our ability to comprehend it: though we already inhabit this vastly more inflected Postmodern hyperspace physically, our thinking remains insufficient to orientate ourselves within it. Equally, in the thirties writers desperately sought to make their own bewildering, media-saturated condition of 'multiple and simultaneous consciousness' politically intelligible, by striving for a form of contemporary sublime that would objectify it.

This 'thirties sublime' was also desired as a way of giving coherence to the legacy of English-writing Modernism, of mapping the chaos of *The Waste Land*. Eliot's poem presented the post-Great War universe, as he saw it. Christopher Isherwood recalled that for his contemporaries Eliot's text (especially as read by I. A. Richards) toured 'in a succession of astounding lightning flashes, the entire expanse of the Modern World', where the traditional certainties of pre-Modernist culture and philosophy lay in ruins.[25] Thirties writers sought an artistic shorthand which might re-equip a politically active subject for life in this modern reality. If new communications technology did not make the ancient fantasy of omniscience feasible in practice, it did temporarily energise hypotheses about the imaginability and accurate representation of global space. Jorge Luis Borges's 'The Aleph' might in some senses offer a more fully Postmodern comment on their quest. His panoptic *camera obscura* 'where, without any possible confusion, all the places in the world are found, seen from every angle' is a cautionary fable about belief in the ultimate medium. Its hero, Carlos Argentino Daneri, is confident the Aleph will enable 'Modern Man' to write an all-including, all-connecting text:

> 'I evoke him,' he said with rather inexplicable animation, 'in his studio-laboratory, in the city's watchtowers, so to say, supplied with telephones, telegraphs, phonographs, radiotelephone apparatus, cinematographic equipment, magic lanterns, glossaries, time-tables, compendiums, bulletins'.... Our twentieth century had transformed the fable of Mohammed and the mountain: the mountain, now, converged upon the modern Mohammed.[26]

However, Borges leaves the Aleph's status as authentic truth or megalomaniac hallucination sublimely unresolved. The promise and failure of the panoptic encyclopaedism, held out by the fusion between Marxism and media technology in early Soviet avant-garde culture, so admired by thirties Leftists, was typified by the documentary film-maker Dziga Vertov's Alephlike plans for 'montage in space and time'. His *kinoki* or 'cinema eyes' would be dispersed around the globe for the purpose of simultaneous, coordinated coverage of reality. By such unrealised projects as *A Day Throughout the World* and *A Minute of the World*, Vertov sought to establish 'a visual (kino-eye) and auditory (radio-ear) class-bond between the proletariats of all nations and all lands on a platform of the communist decoding of world relations'.[27] Like the rest of the Soviet avant-garde's Utopian programme, Vertov's plans for representing modern space were never enacted except in the perverted forms demanded by Stalinism's claim to historical infallibility.

The less organised but equally crucial aspiration to represent global totality in British writing in the thirties took its momentum from the same visionary appeal – the fusion between revolutionary politics and the new media. For example, the panoramic deixis and montage construction of Auden's early verse combine the privileged perspectives of both camera-eyed airman and sovietised Marxist in its bid for a thirties sublime. Hence a whole complex of motifs and susceptibilities – which animated but also, increasingly, troubled Leftist writing during the course of the decade (eventually being rejected by Auden himself) – is already displayed in 'Poem XXX' of 1930:

> Consider this and in our time
> As the hawk sees it or the helmeted airman:
> The clouds rift suddenly – look there
> At cigarette-end smouldering on a border
> At the first garden party of the year.[28]

Note the tension between the contingent positions the reading subject is invited to imagine and the poem's tone of perfectly orientated, Olympian objectivism. Like Borges's Aleph, all its panning, zoom-ins and close-ups metonymically evoke modern space as an intelligible, interconnected wholeness, but one which the cinematic principle of the poem's construction tends to fracture at the very point of asserting it. This makes 'Poem XXX' a provisional and highly unstable solution to the politico-aesthetic crisis. For thirties Leftists (whether social-democratic or, in many cases, Communist) any formula for restoring order and meaning to a world violently mutated into modernity would, to some degree or other, strive to confront new media technologies. Even the liberal Catholic like Graham Greene evolved a method that was at least in part informed by the new media, even if its sanction was ultimately metaphysical: Greene believed his socially critical camera was wielded by the unseen hand of God, rather than by dialectical materialism.[29]

Greene himself noted how the imagination's topography alters with the material advances of the age. The distinctiveness of attempts at an 'anti-modernist' sublime lay not in the discovery of new worlds, so much as in remapping the old, but in media-inflected ways that eventually proved at once both more realistic and more hallucinatory, both diegetic and symbolic. MacNeice's comment about Auden in 1931 could thus stand as a prophetic insight into the ironies of the thirties writers' encounter with the media and *Realpolitik*: 'Mr Auden's mood is that notorious disillusionment of our time which yet goes forward to realise itself – along roads which its own bombs have riddled.' Similarly, in a retrospective at the other end of the decade, MacNeice wrote:

Some of the poets who renounced the Ivory Tower were ready to enter the Brazen Tower of political dogma; where the Ivory Tower represents isolation from men in general, the Brazen Tower represents isolation from men as individuals (witness the typical entowered politician) and also from oneself as an individual.

Believing they had indeed discovered the formula for mapping the modern world system, some of the more politically-committed writers became fatally 'entowered' in their dogmatic perspective. Their camera-eyes lost sight of both the view from the ground and their own common human subjectivity for Stalinism's distant 'historical necessity'.[30] For others, the down-side of their quest gradually emerged as a refigured set of ethical posers.[31] Media hyperreality is, by definition, vicarious reality, at once actual and illusory. As Cunningham notes, the incarceration of consciousness by communications technology had been prefigured in Henry James's 'In the Cage' (1898).[32] This early Modernist short story about a telegraphist, behind her grille, imagining herself on intimate terms with those whose messages she receives only incidentally, plays on 'wire', both a transmitter and barrier. James anticipated the radio-speakers and film-screens which crowd thirties writing, contradictorily barring the human subject off from contact with the world they apparently access. Consider, for instance, Greene's 1934 novel *It's a Battlefield*. Its epigraph, from Alexander William Kinglake's patriotic account of the Crimean War, endorses the idea that individual consciousness and action, though limited as on a fog-bound battlefield ('small numberless circlets commensurate with such ranges of vision as the mist might allow at each spot'), combines on classic *laissez-faire* principles into a historically purposeful pattern. However, this optimism is displaced by the ironies of Greene's text. Paradoxically, although the subjectivities of all the characters in his social cross-section are interlinked, both by physical events and their hyperreal images in the contemporary media, authentic communication between people and their understanding of their place within the social whole remains elusive. *It's a Battlefield* is therefore typical of the transitional moment of thirties *écriture*. Because it attempts to address epistemological and representational questions posed by Modernism it could be justifiably designated 'antimodernist', but, in that it both fails to find answers and complicates the original questions, it is all but Postmodern.

It's a Battlefield's characters are all 'caged' in subjective consciousness, but its bars are rendered deceptively invisible by technology,
giving them the illusion of informed access to a reality beyond their
empirical situation. Greene's Conradian Assistant Commissioner is
first seen at Scotland Yard passing 'down long passages lined with
little glass cells', wired with ringing telephones and buzzers whirring
like cicadas – a jungle of communications systems, more tangled
and sinister than the one he remembers as an ex-colonial officer.[33]
Narrative events are both constantly monitored and reshaped by
their selective representation in the media, which are themselves a
false barometer of an overall situation, manipulated by politicians.
This 'partialness' of communications is symbolised by the fact that
Jim Drover (the 'ordinary man' who kills a policeman at a protest),
though nominally at the centre of events, is a voiceless cipher. The
glass cell of his bus-driver's cab is merely replaced by the glass-cell
of a prison visiting booth, in which 'you couldn't speak and look at
the same time', where language and image never fit together and
make a complete reality: 'A look through the glass. A word through
the wire' (p. 66).

By 1937, Rex Warner was voicing erstwhile Leftist technology-
enthusiasts' growing ambivalence, paranoia even, about the hyperreal, capitalist or otherwise. In his satirical fantasy *The Wild Goose
Chase*, sublime panopticism had already been converted into an
instrument of surveillance and repression, not something by which
the subject can orientate itself in Modernity, but by which s/he is
mystified and subjected – a totalitarian version of the Aleph and a
prototype for Orwell's 'telescreen':

> By manipulating the appropriate controls I can throw on that
> screen a picture, something like a cinematograph picture, of events
> taking place in any part of our territories. It is a question of being
> able to control the light waves. We have a similar installation
> which enables us to hear any conversation which we wish to
> hear. . . . [34]

Michel Foucault used the Panopticon, Bentham's model prison with
its special mode of surveillance, to epitomise how ways of seeing
and being seen are internalised as ways of policing the self.[35] As
Cunningham comments, though the resurgence of diegesis in the
thirties 'was undoubtedly an effort to assert authority, knowledge,
command of experience, the capacity to muster typologies',[36] the

decade's course increasingly problematised 'Poem XXX''s superficially confident mapping. In the end, liberating, media-informed readdressing of reality didn't dispel epistemological doubts raised by Modernism about the paradoxes of representation and the represention of consciousness. If anything they were reinflected and intensified in thirties texts, as writers themselves became progressively entangled with the mass media and with the consequences of ideologies of the mass. Such responses characterise the course of thirties writing and highlight its transitional post/modern condition.

Whatever became of the programme of the avant-garde under Stalinist coercion, without equivalent state resourcing, British writers were inevitably limited to *ad hoc* forays in a capitalist marketplace. Jameson's view that in the Postmodern nineties we have no choice but to think of multinationalism dialectically 'as catastrophe and progress all together', again derives from what we might call Benjamin's 'catastrophic optimism',[37] but in turn it re-illuminates the dilemma of thirties Leftists, who sought to practise their art in contemporary technological and economic conditions without either merely ignoring or submitting to them.

The vicarious experience of *Brave New World* was only a satirical step away from scientific feasibility, according to Lance Sieveking, one of broadcasting's pioneers. The ' "Smellies" or the "Tasties" ' hadn't yet arrived, but 'the attenuated "Hearies" and "Lookies" ' were already available in the radio-play and the film.[38] To Day Lewis, the advent of television (the BBC began an experimental service as early as 1929) meant the age's 'virtual reality' technology was advancing so rapidly that cinema itself, let alone Literature, might conceivably be culturally anachronistic in the near future:

When television is perfected – and possibly Mr Aldous Huxley's 'feelies' introduced – they will provide us with an unreality far more unreal or a realism a hundred times more devastating than the most frenzied ambitions of the entertainment writers can rise to. I can even envisage the day when we shall put a book onto a mechanism as now we put on a gramophone record, and the whole thing will be enacted for us. Sitting in our armchairs at home, we shall see hear and smell the author's characters. But whether this performance could be called 'literature,' or our share in it 'reading,' are questions quite beyond my reeling imagination.[39]

Only a year later Greene reviewed Dallas Bower's ideas for post-television theatre: a kind of holography in which a cylindrical translucent screen with overlapping projectors would display apparently solid moving figures. Day Lewis did see a positive side to all this, because it 'is very soon going to compel literature to decide what its real job is', what print could do that other media couldn't.[40] As Orwell put it in 1938, the individual writer could no more escape this force-field of economic and technological conditions, than the corner shop-keeper could 'preserve his independence in the teeth of the chain-stores' (*Collected Essays*, I, p. 373). Jameson cautions the nineties that 'some fundamental mutation of the sphere of culture in the world of late capitalism' has resulted in the loss of the 'semiautonomy' which gave art its 'critical distance' from the socio-economic base and enabled it to resist transformation into merely another commodity fetish.[41] But this mutation was arguably already underway in the thirties. On the one hand, the erosion of the high cultural status of literature by the forms of the new media could be a liberating experience for writers in a class-system. On the other, their own migration into media projects, notably film, by definition mortgaged them more closely to contemporary capitalism.

Serious theoretical discussion of the mass media was initiated in the thirties by the Leavises and Christopher Caudwell, at opposite ends of the politico-critical spectrum. It came to feature regularly in the *Criterion's* Broadcasting Chronicle, in *Left Review*, and later in essay collections such as *The Arts Today* (1935), edited by Geoffrey Grigson, and *The Mind in Chains* (1937), edited by Day Lewis. Significantly, Charles Davy in *Footnotes to the Film* (a popular 1938 symposium, in which progressive authors hobnobbed with directors, producers, critics and actors) argued the cultural inadvisability of ignoring the media's impact, as exemplified by cinema:

> The millions of people who fill these cinema theatres receive constantly a stream of emotional suggestions from the screen; their ideals, opinions, tastes are all more or less affected by the films they see. . . . Not to know something of how and why and where such films are made and circulated, something of the men and women who make them and of the audiences who pay to see them, is to remain blind to one of the major forces which for good or evil is shaping the civilisation of to-day and to-morrow.[42]

In the course of the thirties, F. R. Leavis's neo-Arnoldian *Mass-Civilisation and Minority Culture* split[43] was rediagnosed on the Left as itself a symptom of, not a cure for, the ills of the political and cultural order. Hence the widespread and diverse attempts to turn popular media 'narcotics' into stimulants, by examining their effects and adapting their forms. By outmanoeuvring and subverting the mass media, Leftists hoped, as Cunningham puts it, 'to capture the mass-audience for good writing and art, to discover their own mass-appealing subject-matter and, the ultimate challenge and goal, seek to transform bourgeois art and aesthetics in the process, creating new, non-bourgeois kinds of art for the awakened masses'.[44] This was classically dialectical thinking, with the media as thesis, committed writing as antithesis and the new art as synthesis. The media's redeemable 'mass' features appeared ripe for exploitation, as Charles Madge argued in his 1937 essay 'Press, Radio and Social Consciousness'. Simultaneously, the pressure of middle-class unemployment forced artists both into closer identification with the exploited masses and into employment by the mass-media who exploited them. Writers had to confront the elusive identity of the *Massenmensch* – a particularly influential hypothesis about the 'average' subject of modernity – from a perspective of ambivalence and tension. Leftists like Madge rightly felt that the real answer to Ortega y Gasset's question 'What is he like . . . and why is he like it, that is, how has he been produced?' was complicated by the fact that 'the mass is already largely what it has been made by the Press and the rest of capitalism'.[45]

That is not to suggest all Leftists became involved with the mass media for politically clear reasons. Their motivations were often muddled and contradictory, if not sometimes naive or plainly mercenary. Other claims on their cultural allegiances could be divisive and complex. Americanisation was considered as much of a threat to the transcendent values of the cultural establishment, from which many bourgeois writers were trying to defect, as radical politics, and Hollywood cinema was its main conduit. The newest of the three Englands discovered by Priestley on his *English Journey*, of 'motor coaches, wireless, hiking, factory girls looking like actresses' was peculiar 'far more to the age itself than to this particular island. America, I supposed, was its real birthplace.'[46] Ironically, The transatlanticism of popular culture could induce a meshing of attitudes between Right and Left about mass culture sponsored by capitalism on the transatlantic model which:

could offend both the anti-materialism of the public-school and Oxbridge tradition and those sectors of left opinion which saw mass culture as a debased substitute for popular culture or indeed as a conservative form of social control governed by capitalist production.[47]

In retrospect, the inherent contradiction of the Leftist cultural position was between élite cultural standards and mass-appeal, even if many did not fully objectify it at the time. The dilemma was how to adapt popular forms (though some went further down the popularising road than others, as we shall see) and make them consciousness-raising, while avoiding the authoritarianism epitomised by Q. D. Leavis's *Fiction and the Reading Public* with its fear of cultural levelling by the effects of the mass-media and nostalgia for a mythical time when

> the masses were receiving their amusement from above (instead of being specially catered for by journalists, film directors, and popular novelists, as they are now). They had to take the same amusement as their betters, and if *Hamlet* was only a glorious melodrama to the groundlings, they were nonetheless living for the time being in terms of Shakespeare's blank verse. . . . Happily they had no choice.[48]

or the similar position of the early BBC, as stated by Lord Reith in 1924: 'It is occasionally represented to us that we are apparently setting out to give the public what we think they need, and not what they want, but few know what they want, and very few what they need.'[49] Given a choice the public overwhelmingly preferred Tom Mix to Shakespeare, or, more frustratingly for Leftists, Douglas Fairbanks to Eisenstein, even in the Soviet Union.[50] Writers barely began to understand at the time that it was not a question of what they felt the masses *might* want in an ideal free state, but what people actually read, listened to and watched, when, where and under what circumstances. The new subjectivity mass-media discourses made available was very complex and, potentially at least, politically multivalent. It was culturally and linguistically heteroglot, and could also be gendered and generational. Elsie, the Carne's maid, in Winifred Holtby's *South Riding* (1936), for example, 'was trilingual. She talked BBC English to her employer, Cinema American to her companions, and Yorkshire dialect to old milkmen like

Eli Dickson.'[51] Claude Cockburn recollected that the popular force of Americanised speech lay not in any alleged 'vulgarity' or debasement of the national culture, but in its democratic appeal – a point confirmed by media historians such as Paddy Scannell and David Cardiff. The reality was 'always more indicative of threatened class attitudes and postures'. American entertainment simply did not treat working people as second-class citizens.[52]

Writers were justly concerned by the blatant escapism of Hollywood features, but above all questioned claims by the modern 'actuality' media to give privileged access to global facts. Sir Stephen Tallents, who ran the Empire Marketing Board and first realised the propagandist potentials of documentary by employing John Grierson in the late twenties, told the Institute of Journalists in October 1937, 'This is an Age of News. All over the world they seem to be turning from fiction to reality.'[53] Conversely, Leftist writers became increasingly worried that an 'Age of News' had unprecedented potential for marketting fiction in the guise of fact. But if such distinctions could not be stabilised along a boundary between true and false, between 'invented' and 'uninvented' content, then neither could they be stabilised by simplistic formal criteria. Walter Lippmann discussed the 'fictions' of real events disseminated through media reporting (a point which influenced both Grierson's film documentarism and Mass-Observation's investigations of the formation of popular opinion).[54] For Leftists capitalist-sponsored documentary films and newsreels did not give unmediated access to truth, so much as their own distinctive, hyperreal construction of the world. Insidiously, here was a technological point at which fantasy and actuality film merged in a kind of virtual reality. Opposites in theory, Hollywood fictions and factual films overlapped as sign systems in practice. Both acted to position their consumers in imaginary relation to their actual conditions of existence.

A crucial aspect of our ineluctable media-dependence, therefore, might be termed 'else-awareness': i.e. the individual's consciousness of *elsewhere*, of diverse events simultaneouly unfolding outside his/her immediate, empirical experience to which s/he can have no unmediated access, by definition. The cult of reportage, written or visual, among thirties Leftists was symptomatic of this, but often self-consciously reflective rather than an expression of any naive confidence in the truth-value of reported facts. Leftists came to realise media 'else-awareness' positioned the subject in a global informational order that was not simply real, in the empirical sense, but also symbolic, the prototype of Baudrillard's hyperreal. Media which seemed to record history *sur le vif*, whose signs seemed transparently identical with their referents, carried a powerful ideological alibi, which Leftists were anxious to expose. As Auden and Isherwood's 1938 play *On the Frontier* put it, 'Truth is elsewhere': i.e. never fully self-present, but diffused through a complex web of communications, whose signifying operations tend to efface their own processes.[55] Thus in trying to stimulate alternative kinds of else-awareness that would connect with and demystify the subject's mundane conditions in the here and now, writers attempted to keep open a breach for imagining how the truth might be otherwise.

However, thirties Leftists were slower to recognise that although the domestic and foreign events they tried to focus public attention on were not in themselves mythical, their representation on Radio Moscow or in *The Daily Worker* also needed ever more vigilant scrutiny. Confusing 'official' anti-capitalist mediation with the real, in some ways afforded more insidious scope for ideological displacements than did Hollywood features or Gaumont-British newsreels, as Orwell discovered in Spain. The most obvious testimony to this is the wish-fulfilling cult of Stalinist Russia, by which few writers were totally unaffected. Similarly, Stephen Spender recollected that his else-awareness of events in Nazi Germany involved a highly inflected and problematic transaction between real and vicarious experience, between mediated facts and unconscious investments:

> In a curious way the crimes committed by the Fascists became my own personal life, vicariously lived. Every morning I searched the newspapers for the German news. If I read of a fall in the German markets, or of some act which seemed to indicate that a spirit of defiance still existed in Germany, or even of the arrest of an anti-Nazi. I felt an almost sobbing satisfaction. External things over which I had no control had usurped my own deepest personal life, so that my inner world became dependent on an outer one, and if that outer one failed to provide me with its daily stimulus of crime and indignation, I often felt a kind of emptiness.

And in 'To A Spanish Poet' Spender wrote, 'reading the news, my imagination breeds/The penny-dreadful fear that you are dead./ Well what of this journalistic dread?' Learning to identify and separate the objective and subjective factors in that media-informed 'journalistic dread' proved an increasingly necessary and often *angst*-ridden process.[56]

Reconstructing the moment of the thirties sublime might provide some pointers and warnings for an ethical Postmodernism. In some small way, it may make the intellectual adaptation necessary for catching up with the dizzying economic and technological mutation of our current condition at least more conceivable by evaluating the promises and failures of this neglected transition in cultural history. From the early thirties British writing became saturated with references to the mass media, in Cunningham's words:

> Going to the cinema, listening to the wireless, reading newspapers, were abruptly taken for granted as stock activities of fictional characters. Newspaper reports, newspapers tycoons and film moguls, radio announcers and film stars became obligatory to the up-to-the-minute novel or drama. Nor, if they wanted to be alert and socially observant, must poems miss out on such phenomena.[57]

It was in this period that 'already reproduced' fragments from the mass media began to feature as documentary materials in intertextual montages. Writers also began to emulate and investigate the techniques of film in their form, and to employ the jargon of the movie editor in their theory. In Chapter 1, I now want to sketch out the 'force field' of technical developments, economic conditions and social effects of the mass media in which thirties Leftists wrote.

1

A Twisted Skein:
The Media Background

Philip M. Taylor has pointed out that twentieth-century total war mobilises 'the entire resources of the nation – military, economic, psychological' and has developed the weapons of 'censorship, propaganda and psychological warfare'.[1] Keith Middlemas and others have shown how the Great War's Ministry of Information created a direct link between central government and mass opinion through the media 'whose consequences were ultimately as significant as the expansion of suffrage itself'.[2] Similarly, British success in wearing down American neutrality became the model for future propagandists' international use of the media, as Hitler acknowledged in *Mein Kampf* (1924). The rise of totalitarianism in particular 'concided with the related technological revolutions of the sound cinema and the radio', which revolutionised the potential for influencing mass-audiences.[3] Perhaps the acme of hyperreal spectacles between the wars was Hitler's aerial touchdown at the Nürnberg Parteitag in 1934. As witnessed by Ambassador Sir Nevile Henderson this involved building a literal castle in the air, then reproducing it for the vicarious participation of millions by the state-of-the-art resources of Nazi broadcasting and Leni Riefenstahl's film *Triumph des Willens*:

> His arrival was theatrically notified by the sudden turning into the air of the 300 or more searchlights with which the stadium was surrounded. The blue tinged light from these met thousands of feet up in the sky at the top to make a kind of square roof, to which a chance cloud gave added realism. The effect, which was both solemn and beautiful, was like being inside a cathedral of ice.[4]

The technical developments, economic conditions and social effects of, the mass media after the Great War form a complex background, to which the saturation of thirties texts with media images was the sign of a complex literary response. The media were becoming an ever more powerful ideological force for channelling social consciousness; for constructing the nation's self-image in terms of hegemonic consensus; for standardising language and culture; for soaking up precious leisure time on the one hand, and narcotically mitigating the limbo of unemployment on the other.[5] Then as now, Britain's mass media functioned, in effect if not intent, as a mechanism for political and cultural '*dis*proportional representation'. Madge's essay 'Press, Radio, and Social Consciousness' (1937) argued that so-called media of mass-communication were actually media for *one way* mass-publication. Though 'listeners are legion . . . the voices which speak are few'. The 'full blast of the written and spoken word' had been loosed on the population coupled with the persuasiveness 'of music on the air and of giant pictorial images'. This weave blent 'instruction, entertainment, propaganda, advertisement in such a way that it is impossible to disentangle the twisted skein.'[6] It is the main ideological and technical threads in the intertextuality of this 'twisted skein' which I want to unravel in this chapter, before examining writers' entanglements in them.

James Curran itemises the main traditions of conceptualising the function of the media: in classic liberal theory, they are representative institutions exposing governments 'to the full blast of public opinion'; another tradition reverses the flow 'with governments skilfully using the media to manage public opinion'; a third, more complex, model views them 'as an arena in which a plurality of political opinions and social values, derived from a variety of influences, is contested or negotiated'.[7] This last, Gramscian model seems to correspond most closely to the dialectical views of thirties Leftists, typified by Madge, that the British media, though mortgaged to the establishment, also had complex characteristics ripe for radical exploitation.

THE PRESS

A. J. Cummings, of the *News Chronicle* and other papers, who made his name reporting the Soviet Metro-Vickers trial, wrote in *The Press and a Changing Civilisation* (1936) that newspapers had become 'almost as much a part of our daily lives as the houses we live in'.[8] In his own terms he recognised hyperreality was not so much something the subject entered at will, but an ideological dimension intersecting empirical experience. British newspaper sales mushroomed in the early thirties, but press claims to be 'The Voice of the People' were treated with unanimous suspicion by Leftist commentators. Cummings recognised it was not a question of *direct* government control (although measures like the Sedition Bill were certainly repressive), but ownership. Britain's press-baronage was itself a much more effective system of *indirect*, economic, censorship:

> the two paramount objections to the millionaire newspaper-proprietor are (1) that the gramophone voice as an expression of public opinion is often a fantastic and dangerous illusion, and (2) that millionaire proprietors are not prone to champion sincerely and consistently causes which do not appear to be in the selfish interest of great wealth.[9]

In Spender's view, press freedom was 'one of the most profitable of democratic illusions'. Newspapers were more properly the ear, not the voice, of the people, 'through which the bosses shout their propaganda, though, in theory, they are given facilities to express themselves, should they ever be in position to do so'.[10] Lord Northcliffe's henchmen were first to stake their claim that 'ministers should do the bidding of a Press which claims to be the voice of the people'. However, Arthur Calder-Marshall asked, 'Are, in fact, Lords Beaverbrook and Rothermere "the masses"?'[11] Conversely, the political coincidence of owners and state in a decade ruled by a Tory-dominated coalition from 1931 made direct government interference particularly unnecessary, according to Cummings, while fostering apparent independence:

> It is only necessary for the Foreign Minister or the head of the Government to appeal to the patriotism of the newspaper proprietors and the newspaper editors and to assure them with solemn head-waggings that the country will be in peril unless the country's diplomacy is supported in the national Press, for the majority of proprietors and editors to sing their patriotic chorus.[12]

Despite largely operating in the 'national interest', as defined by the National Government, the press's public image was still overcast in the thirties by its role in stirring jingoistic frenzy in the recent past (both Beaverbrook and Northcliffe had also directed the Ministry of Information and its Enemy Propaganda Department, respectively, during the Great War). 'It is a platitude', noted Cummings, 'that the War produced the worst excesses of racial animosity, of continuous lying, of Government-inspired propaganda, of mass-hysteria.'[13] He reminded his readers of the *Kadaververwertungsanstalt* story, disseminated by the 'quality' *Times*, alleging the Germans recycled corpses as munitions. Ironically such fabrications provided grounds for the disbelief which later greeted the actual atrocities of the Nazi *Endlösung*. Leftist suspicions of the press are confirmed by their predominantly Rightist ownership (though in the thirties the press was not so overwhelmingly owned by the Right as it is today)[14] and by the pro-Appeasement lines of *The Times* and the *Observer*, owned by the Astor family, and especially by Northcliffe's brother and heir, Viscount Rothermere. The fact that only one major daily criticised Chamberlain's Munich agreement with Hitler testifies to the degree of proprietorial solidarity with Government policy.[15] A 1939 readership survey found 69 per cent of the population over 16 read a national daily paper and 82 per cent a national Sunday. Those who didn't were mostly illiterate. In these conditions, wrote Cummings, without much exaggeration, the Labour Press was 'as a candle wick to a powerful system of floodlighting'.[16]

The populist *Daily Mail*, founded in 1896, represented the views of the lower middle-class, as Alfred Harmsworth, later Lord Northcliffe (the original megalomediac who died insane in 1922) saw them. Its influence declined under Rothermere and competition from its rivals, the *Daily Express* and the *Daily Herald*. The *Mail*'s constitution of the nation 'was defined by exclusion as well as inclusion'.[17] No distinction was made between constitutional Labour politics and Bolshevik treason, typified by the notorious 'Zinoviev Letter' of 1924. Rothermere estimated the *Mail*'s stunt gained the Tories 100 seats at the general election (though the BBC also failed to be even-handed and to treat its authenticity as unproven).[18] Richard Griffiths shows 'the only major British daily to taken a consistently pro-Nazi line' was equally hysterical in support of Mussolini and Franco. As Orwell wrote, 'the *Daily Mail*, amid the cheers of the Catholic clergy, was able to represent Franco as a patriot delivering his country from hordes of fiendish "Reds" '.[19] Rothermere's agitation for the extra-parliamentary solution of the British Union of Fascists (founded 1932) extended Northcliffe's undemocratic gerrymanderings. Rothermere's *Sunday Dispatch* also threw the backing of its million-and-a-half readership behind Mosley, offering cash prizes for reasons 'Why I Like the Blackshirts'.[20] Although his papers backed off to a certain extent after Fascist violence at Olympia in June 1934, the *Mail* headed the press pack's wartime campaign for indiscriminate internment of 'enemy aliens', including anti-Nazi refugees.

Cummings believed that the press, 'besides confusing news with views, mingled facts with propaganda' and by 'elimination, suppression, positioning and tendentious headlines was able to distort an argument, a policy or the facts of a political situation'.[21] Orwell noted as early as 1928 that advertising revenue, not sales, now constituted proprietors' real income, inducing cut-throat competition and making editorials subserve vested interests. (See *Collected Essays*, I, p. 34 and IV, pp. 59–60.) As Cummings put it, 'The opinion often expressed by persons with no experience of newspaper organisation that a well-run paper can succeed on the grand scale even if it consistently flouts the supposed interests of the advertising class is founded upon a grotesque illusion.'[22] Similarly, subscribers were bribed with commodities like 'free' life and health insurance, silk stockings, crockery and sets of Dickens. Both the Labour *Daily Herald* and Conservative *Daily Express* boosted their circulations above two million by such means. As Stevenson comments, 'In the absence of commercial radio or television, and with roadside hoardings as the only main competition, it was the newspapers which provided the main channel for the new age of mass consumerism.'[23] The arrival of the easily-digested 'tabloid' format made the popular daily an even more effective marketing vehicle. The *Mirror* adopted it first in 1934 (on the advice of the American advertising agency J. Walter Thompson, to its new editor, Guy Bartholemew, who also reorientated it politically). A year later Rothermere sold it, inadvertently midwifing the most successful left-of-centre paper of the time. Before long others were featuring similarly huge headlines and telegraphic sentences, shrinking text in inverse proportion to photographs and strip cartoons, breaking neat columns into the 'staggered jigsaw' layout.

MacNeice caught the paradox of vicarious intimacy which the transfiguration of events into the selective discourses of the press often provided for its readers. In his view, stories coalesced into an unconscious, ceaselessly reinforced pattern, causing the subject to withdraw from the actuality with which they seemed to hold out virtually tangible contact:

firstly, the newspaper heroes, sportsmen or politicians, are for them dream-figures, *though they know they are real people*; secondly, the repetition with variations of their performances (Mr Ramsay MacDonald . . . Mr Ramsay MacDonald . . .) builds up a vast and gentle rhythm in the back of the mind, hypnotising us into an escape from reality. . . .'[24]

BROADCASTING

Between the wars, radio became a vastly powerful medium for propaganda, despite Marconi's belief in his invention's potential as 'the greatest weapon against the evils of misunderstanding and jealousy',[24] monumentalised in the BBC's motto, 'Nation shall speak peace unto nation'. Radio played a specially belligerent role in the European Civil War of the twenties and thirties between Fascism and the Comintern. Limited neither by literacy nor geography, radio enabled one nation's propagandists to speak directly and immediately to large numbers of people in another, undermining borders in a way the press never could, and making Europe 'begin to resemble a single polity – the site of struggle between various super-national ideologies'.[25]

Cummings rightly concluded that 'The monopoly of the so-called Press Lords is as nothing compared with the gigantic monopoly, real and potential, of the great State wireless organisations of the world.'[26] As A. J. P. Taylor put it, 'The Englishman still belonged to a community' but became 'shut up in a box listening to a tinier box.'[27] That tinier box informed the listener's conception of, and relationship with, the nation as a whole with both negative and positive consequences. As Scannell and Cardiff show, the BBC treated its audience not as a mass, but as 'a constellation of individuals positioned in families' with a range of cultural needs. The menu would be as broad as possible. Besides entertainment, the private, domestic life of the 'listener-in' would be enfranchised and enriched by linking it to the discourses of the public world, 'broadening horizons, extending informally the education of family members and providing them with new interests and topics of conversation'.[28]

Radio was the new 'deity of the hearth', but its rapid spread indicated that for the first time production had created a surplus above and beyond bare necessity for the majority. The first mass-produced set was the 1935 Philco, a little Bakelite equivalent to the Volkswagen, the contemporary German 'People's Car'. Upmarket ones sported art-deco styles like Pye's sunrise motif. As the most advanced items of domestic consumer hardware, forms and materials emphasised their role as 'mediators of modernity' while conditions of listening brought with them a whole host of new social rituals and habits.[29]

Regular British broadcasting began in 1922 and the BBC became a corporation in 1926. By the Second World War, three-quarters of families possessed sets, paying nine million ten-shilling licence fees. Radio grew from enthusiast's pastime to national habit in less than two decades, literally part of the furniture in most homes. However, broadcasting's hours and activities were tightly restricted. The BBC's Charter gave nominal independence from the government of the day, but still made it effectively a state monopoly. Paradoxically though, this also left it indirectly vulnerable to commercial pressures. Right up until the Munich crisis in 1938 the BBC obligingly broadcast no news bulletins before 7 p.m., because of political lobbying by the Newspaper Proprietors' Association who feared its competition. On the 'Reith Sunday', no programmes, weather forecasts excepted, were transmitted before 12.30, not to distract listeners from Christian observance. Even afterwards they were limited mainly to religious topics and 'serious' music. The BBC carried far fewer plays, features and outside broadcasts than today.

In *Broadcast over Britain* (1924), Sir John Reith, Director-General until 1938, set out his principles of public service broadcasting. Radio would bridge the dissociation between the mass of individual citizens and an increasingly complex society, enabling them 'to make up their own minds on many matters of vital moment, matters which formerly they had either to receive according to the dictated and partial versions and opinions of others, or to ignore altogether'. Tied neither to commerce nor state, the BBC's non-profit-making monopoly would ideally be animated by high standards and available throughout the nation.[30] Influenced by Walter Lippmann's theories of modern public relations and civic responsibility, the Reithian BBC aspired to be the disinterested 'integrator for democracy', by informing and enlightening public opinion, keeping all members of society in touch and actively responsible for collective processes.[31] But from the outset there was a fundamental conflict between Reith's idea of a democratising national utility and its inception by the state, leading to confusion, in moments of crisis, between duty to the public good and to the national interest, as defined by government, and to the compromising of BBC independence. It was this which made Madge conclude the BBC was 'an idol of quite illusory impartiality'.[32]

The dilemma – in the last resort, whose interests did it serve? – confronted the newly-formed BBC immediately during the General Strike. Anxious to prove its 'responsibility' and begin a news service with Fleet Street silenced, Reith, in effect, sided with the Government. In the words of his own memorandum: 'Since the BBC was a national institution, and since the Government in this crisis were acting for the people . . . the BBC was for the Government in the crisis too.'[33] This set a precedent hamstringing the BBC in future crises. However, as Scannell and Cardiff point out, The BBC's hands were tied by Government anyway. Lack of radio publicisation of the causes of the strike, as Asa Briggs notes, was probably as much down to ignorance about 'the straight facts of working-class life' as conscious bias. Either way, it put paid to confidence in BBC impartiality among sections of the Left and the working-class, who dubbed it the BFC, 'British Falsehood Company' from that point.[34]

Since the early BBC didn't conduct proper audience research, governmental pressures, often covert, tended to be those felt and responded to (combined with well-orchestrated Right-wing press campaigns), rather than public opinion. But it received continuous accusations of propaganda bias from both Left and Right, although the Left were not really in much of a position to influence its policy at a structural level, whatever the inclinations of individual programme-makers. The crossfire of denunciation climaxed during the Spanish Civil War, but actual bias was less advertent than *de facto* and institutional. The way the BBC had been constituted made it a 'governing institution', with aims and functions delegated by Parliament.[35] It was in practice, like the rest of the thirties media, prone to cooperate with and be subtly manipulated by ministers, less interested in informing than managing democracy. Legitimate on-air electioneering was far outweighed by new techniques for orchestrating opinion, censorship and control, sytematically developed and applied.

However, it is a myth that the BBC always pusillanimously eschewed contentious topics in the thirties. Reith kicked strenuously against the traces, especially the ban on political, industrial and religious controversy in the BBC's Charter. Though it was officially lifted in 1928, attempts to open the field were subsequently thwarted by the 'immediate advantage and self-interest' of Government.[36] The evolution of BBC news exemplifies how politicians combined with vested interests to baulk his ambitions – a proper news department was not established until the end of 1934. Bulletins always carried a tone of public authority and objectivity, even though Reith privately believed news could also be 'the shock-troops of propaganda'.[37] News was always compiled on the principle that it was far more sensational to hear of a crime or disaster in a broadcast than to read it in a newspaper, because the spoken word was somehow assumed to have a more unmediated relationship with the reality, although the BBC modelled the sobriety and structure of its format on the establishment *Times*. It also tended to get its facts from press agencies and government departments, rather than live correspondents on the ground. Moreover, the BBC's early function in 1926 as a means of overriding the General Strike-bound press set its pattern of institutional, if not party political, conservatism, making it the primary mouthpiece for statements by statesmen and the monarchy, which in turn boosted its oracular status: Edward VIII broadcast his abdication message personally; Baldwin made frequent transmissions explaining National Government policy; most famously, Chamberlain declared war on the air not through the headlines. Subsequently, the BBC was subject to Ministry of Information censorship and largely dependent on it for data, becoming a major instrument for shaping 'national morale', broadcasting Churchill's speeches, listened to by 70 per cent of the population in 1940.

Political pressure caused 'self-censorship, increasing caution and a retreat to safer ground' in the thirties BBC.[38] This is exemplified by the history of the Talks Department. Under Hilda Matheson and, from 1932, Charles Siepmann. Talks made documentary programmes pioneering both in their subject matter and the methods by which they presented social problems to a sharply divided public. This was especially the case with two series about unemployment, during the period when it peaked (i.e. 1932–34), and one on the slums, which predate much literary and film documentary on the same subjects. The 1933 series *S.O.S.* by S. P. B. Mais, was followed by Howard Marshall's *Other People's Houses* and in 1934 by Felix Greene's *Time to Spare*, the first two based on eye-witnessing and statistical evidence, the third on the unemployed speaking for themselves. Intended more as appeals to the nation's dormant conscience than political interventions, nevertheless, their timing and techniques 'undercut their professed neutrality'.[39] *Time to Spare*, in particular, provoked a Press and Commons row about the reality of unemployment subsistence and the Means Test. Reith, in a rare display of genuine independence, refused MacDonald's covert request to terminate the series: he would stop it only at the price of broadcasting the Government's intervention. However, this progressive trend was halted when Sir Richard Maconachie became new Talks director in 1935. In practice, the continuing taboo on 'controversy' tended not so much to produce balance, but to have a conservative weighting.

Institutional complicity led to a crisis for broadcasting and nation alike: 'The muffling of open debate, the silencing of dissent . . . created a vacuum at the heart of public life.'[40] There is strong evidence that surveillance was kept on overseas coverage, as part of Appeasement policy, in deference to Nazi complaints about Germany's representation in the British media, and especially because foreign governments assumed the BBC was the voice of HMG.[41] It is also more than coincidence that Reith was transferred to Imperial Airways in June 1938 when the whole question of distinguishing between duty to the people and Government-defined national interest was reaching flashpoint with the need for access to vital facts for the nation's survival.[42] Public opinion was 'managed' into accepting the dismemberment of Czechoslovakia by temporary concealment of the cost of 'peace for our time'. Chamberlain proved equally good at cultivating the microphone as he had the newsreels. 1938 was, therefore, the measure of the failure of public service broadcasting, the legacy of the political cat's cradle binding BBC and state:

> If it was a conspiracy, then . . . it was one into which the BBC was drawn unwittingly. But there was no grand strategy behind it. It was rather the cumulative effect of precedents established and powers imposed piecemeal by central government in the decade following the lifting of the ban on controversy.[43]

The situation typified what Mass-Observation called the 'gulf – of understanding, of information and of interest' which the thirties media perpetuated and deepened between rulers and ruled.[44] Only slowly and painfully did broadcasters realise the establishment's power to define political realities, as Scannell and Cardiff note: 'The struggle to make politicians answerable and accountable to the electorate through broadcasting was not joined until the establishment of commercial television and the new forms of broadcast journalism' of the late fifties.[45]

The BBC held a moratorium to determine its future loyalties, after Munich following the startling reversal of public opinion when the consequences became known: should it now tell the whole truth about the inevitable drift to war and prepare the population with the full facts despite the Government? An immediate consequence was that the BBC at long last began building up its own team of foreign correspondents. There had been little use till then of on-the-spot commentary. The BBC's first aural scoop was the 1936 Crystal Palace fire, which Richard Dimbleby reported from a phone box. This lagging behind was partly explained by the relative primitiveness of its mobile sound recording technology compared to German and American systems. Ed Murrow and William Shirer's live link-ups covering the Austrian *Anschluss* and the Munich Crisis from key European cities for CBS showed what broadcast journalism could achieve with the right equipment and without political interference. As Scannell and Cardiff put it, 'For the first time history had been made in the hearing of its pawns.'[46] In Britain, the sound of things to come was heard only at the beginning of 1939, when Dimbleby covered the fall of Spain to Franco and the flight of Republican refugees. For the first time listeners heard the actual gunfire and bombing over Dimbleby's live, unscripted commentary that would soon become routine background. Wartime's spontaneous commentaries on aerial dogfights would typify the immediacy of the changed conditions, demanding quick reactions and new methods.

Public service was a missionary concept, evolved under Matthew Arnold's influence by the Victorian middle class for the betterment of the lower orders. Consequently, Reith committed the BBC to a regime of cultural, moral and educative uplift designed 'to carry into the greatest number of homes everything that was best in every department of human knowledge, endeavour and achievement', through music, talks, drama and entertainment.[47] However, the BBC's definition of 'the best' often tended to marginalise cultural plurality and dissent. Most ironically, 'public service' broadcasting was founded on monoglot (in Bakhtin's sense)[48] stigmatisation of the demotic speech of the vast majority of the public as 'unclear' and, by implication, 'bad', English. Regional accents and dialects were 'extreme variants' (so was upper-class drawl) and rejected for the 'Received Pronounciation' Southern Standard English of BBC announcers, referred to not as middle-class, but 'educated English'. The selection and training of announcers was partly directed by Professor Arthur Lloyd-James (secretary of the BBC's Advisory Committee of Spoken English). He was, therefore, also partly responsible for linguistic pseudo-science muddying the BBC's genuinely educative function. The 'national culture' was shaped in a patrician discourse assumed by Lloyd-James to be a linguistically 'neutral' and 'classless' ideal which would 'level up' the speech of the masses by example. This is not to say that there wasn't high-echelon internal dissent from this view. R. W. Postgate's *Listener's Commentary* pointed out in 1930 that 'The etiolated voice of the BBC announcer has become a regular joke for the hard-up music-hall comedian, rating after mothers-in-law and gorgonzola.' Though admitting he spoke it himself, he found 'by experience that it is apt to annoy those who do not possess it, and it might be wise to adulterate the pure Oxford liquor with some provincial accents. Mr Herbert Smith, the ex-president of the miners, has a very fine Yorkshire accent, but I do not suppose there is much hope of hearing him.'[49] The thirties ether was, consequently, largely monopolised by politicians., writers, actors and public figures with the right accent, leading to widespread alienation among non-standard audiences. Even when Wilfred Pickles was allowed to read news bulletins in a Yorkshire accent from 1941, this was arguably a concession to the necessity of gaining the confidence of working-class people for the war effort at a desperate time, rather than linguistic democratisation: it was hoped a regional voice might give bulletins greater credibility. The BBC did not invent bias against the demotic, it merely perpetuated one with ancient roots in literary convention, which, as Ian Rodger points out, presumed matters of state could not be discussed in 'language only spoken by simpletons, social inferiors and comic characters'.[50] Early BBC drama, likewise, indiscriminately collapsed fine gradations of local accent into three radio dialects: Cockney, Mummerset and Northern.

Because it brought a national audience into being, the BBC also had the function of creating a 'national culture', but this was shaped in ways, of which language was but one example, that were disproportionately representative of particular sectional interests. The pastoral myth that the essential identity of a highly industrialised, largely urban/suburban, multi-cultural society like Britain consisted in Southern English rurality was reinvented by the interwar media, but especially by broadcasting. Cardiff and Scannell argue that the

BBC created that 'we-feeling' of belonging to an abstraction, 'the nation', precisely by fostering a feeling of communal identity among dispersed audiences, linking them to a symbolic heartland by regular 'ceremonies of the air', employing techniques specific to the new medium. Even actuality recording, though rare, tended to be used to authenticate this myth of 'a *settled* community with traditional roots'.[51] It was too problematic, for example, to incorporate the unemployed and deprived in such broadcasts. Like Griersonian documentaries and jingoistic features like Noël Coward's *Cavalcade*, broadcasts about Empire Day glossed over rifts such as Ireland and India. In practice the BBC did not so much transmit national reality as a 'one big happy family' vision of a paternalistic state and commonwealth. This metaphor characterised George V's Christmas messages. Similarly, elaborate international relays sought to give it concrete expression through cross-sections of voices from all over the country and the Empire. Such idealisation also rapidly overlaid this modern technological medium with the 'patina of tradition'. By the end of the thirties, 'It seemed as entwined with immemorial ivy as Oxbridge.'[52]

Though the BBC was much more sensitive to accusations of mandarinism and metropolitan bias than is often assumed, given its ground rules and assumptions, radio's possibilities as either a popular or progressive artistic medium, let alone a combination of both, were limited in thirties Britain. But broadcasting genuinely did bring enormous leisure benefits to ordinary people, gradually helping to erode social and cultural boundaries simply because its national audience necessitated the development of a spread of programme styles that had to be accessible enough to appeal to all. Nowhere is this truer than in Music and Variety, which gradually humanised Broadcasting House from the mid-thirties, partly as a response to competition from commercial Radio Luxembourg. As Scannell and Cardiff note, broadcast entertainment became more socially inclusive as it became more culturally inclusive with the jazz of Henry Hall's BBC Dance Orchestra, crooners and popular comedians: 'Classless in manner, democratic in their identification with the audience, such performers were to come into their own during and after the Second World War.'[53] Comics were particularly important in breaching BBC stuffiness. Patrician language experts might be 'unaware in their social isolation' that their own dialect was 'a huge joke' among the majority,[54] but radio comedians continuously guyed it as the only regular broadcasters not speaking

it themselves. Attempts to produce 'radiogenic' entertainment cul-
minated in the innovative and immensely popular *Band Waggon*. As
with cinema, US commercial radio was a democratising influence:
the original idea for this 'continuity series' came from an eponymous American show (no doubt, screwball comedy was a factor
too). Its comedians Arthur Askey and Richard Murdoch were so
'resident' their act evolved around occupying an imaginary flat at
the top of Broadcasting House. *Band Waggon* typifies how, by the
late thirties, this monument to Reithian sobriety, as Scannell and
Cardiff point out, was turning into 'a house of fun'.[55] The programme's surreal zaniness drew on diverse elements in popular
culture but also extended the principle of parody and burlesque as
essential features of radio entertainment, even drawing the po-voiced
announcer into their non-standard banter, in a carnivalesque subversion of discursive hierarchy. It's interesting to compare this situation with Leftist writers' largely hostile or indifferent attitudes to
Britain's cinema comics (see below, Chapter 2). With rare exceptions there was perhaps even less consciousness among them that
this kind of radiogenic entertainment might have the potentials for
fusing the radical with the popular.

In 1930, *The Listener*'s editor, R. S. Lambert, put up a stout defence of broadcasting against accusations that its effects meant
debasement. On the contrary, it was regenerating cultural life:

> What broadcasting, the motor-car and the cinema have done is to
> blow this antiquated concept of things out of the water. Youth
> has to-day marvellously extended powers of using the faculties
> of sight, hearing and motion, and correspondingly less depend-
> ence upon teaching and elders for gaining experience. This is the
> way in which democracy has come to the young.[56]

But his editorial's title, 'Are We Becoming Vulgar?', characteristically begged the question who 'we' and who 'the vulgar' might be.
By the end of the thirties, however, the BBC had tentatively begun
a more genuinely reciprocal relationship with audiences. This was
assisted by the Listener Research Department, set up in 1936 (a
direct consequence of the appointment of Sir Stephen Tallents as
Controller of Public Relations, with his EMB and GPO pedigree),
which gave more accurate understanding of audience tastes to
programme-builders. Its feedback provided some kind of way

through the Scylla of 'culture from above' and the Charybdis that 'market preferences' were the only true democracy, and thus played a great part in future cultural and political history, especially during the war, when attention to those needs and wants became imperative for maintaining national morale.[57]

Though from the mid-thirties, Britain's radio and public life became 'stifled at the centre', it 'continued to flourish in the margins'.[58] The BBC National Programme was supplemented by the Regions, the most innovative of which, from the point of view of both popular programming and radical literary possibilities was the Northern, based in Manchester. Its largely working-class audience affected the character of Manchester's broadcasting, which reflected the identity and accents of the region. Manchester 'OBs', outside broadcasts, were particularly progressive, with its 'flying squad' of sound engineers, inspired by Midland's 1934 *Microphone at Large* series.

Northern Region produced much of the period's most important work in drama and features, but airtime for literary culture of any kind, let alone one with radically dissenting views, was limited. Asa Briggs shows that in 1930, drama constituted 1.49 per cent of BBC output and poetry and prose readings, 0.64 per cent – a minuscule amount, though by 1938, the percentage for drama had risen to 3.03.[59] The first specially-written radio play, Richard Hughes's *Danger*, broadcast in January 1923, was about a mining disaster, but there was little chance for such controversial subjects in the thirties. The scope of the play of ideas was strictly limited because of continuing taboos. Though not subject to the Lord Chamberlain's theatrical veto, the BBC had its own system of 'amber warning-lights at the cross-roads of Sex, Religion, and Politics', as Val Gielgud put it.[60] The taboo against adultery almost scuppered a 1932 production of *Othello*! L. Du Garde Peach's narrative dramas ran into censorship problems when they got too contemporary. His 1933 play about Great War veterans on the dole, entitled *Three Soldiers*, after Dos Passos, was only just acceptable, but *Gold*, which analysed the role of the markets in the inflation crisis, was postponed for six months until it was less burningly topical. R. F. Delderfield had his *Experiment in Futility* on the Abyssinian war rejected in 1935 and his 1938 *Spark in Judea*, which viewed the events of the Crucifixion from the perspective of Roman soldiers, was 'too realistic'.[61] Given this background the career of radio-writers, especially on the National Programme, could be very precarious, as Rayner Heppenstall's exemplifies. Between 1936 and 1938, Heppenstall scripted encyclopaedic features on 'frozen meat, unicorns, the lost continent of Atlantis, explorers (Sir John Franklin and Ludwig Leichhardt), Malta, the industrial North a hundred years ago'.[62] His November the Fifth programme risked a topical parallel with the Reichstag Fire Trial frame-up, substituting Lord Cecil for Goering. But Guy Fawkes under torture, 'heard off-stage, like the tenor in *Tosca*', drew letters to *The Times* protesting about the subversiveness of portraying even royalty's remote ancestors as political gangsters. Heppenstall's subsequent refusal to alter a script on astrology terminated his involvement with prewar radio.

Early technical conditions also affected radio's possibilities for drama. As Gielgud put it. 'Broadcasting began in little more than the rôle of universal eavesdropper – just as Television began as the universal eye-at-the-keyhole.'[63] The movement away from merely listening in at the theatre to the development of studio construction and acting techniques was gradual and difficult. Although the 'blind nature of the medium' offered dramatists a much wider field of possibilities beyond the confines of stage naturalism, they were not widely exploited. Plays were generally broadcast live rather than 'canned', so writers were able to exploit editing techniques more akin to film only relatively late in the medium's history, even though a sophisticated Dramatic Control Panel to coordinate action and effects from different studios had been operational since 1928 with Lance Sieveking's *Kaleidoscope I*.[64] Val Gielgud, Productions Director with responsibility for drama from 1929, sponsored a wide repertoire of broadcast plays, but mostly adapted pre-radio texts. In 1934, for example, there were five Shakespeares, two Chekhovs and two Ibsens, five classic and contemporary novel adaptations, with just six plays specially commissioned. Only two by the particularly radiogenic modern Bertolt Brecht were broadcast in the whole decade.[65] In this respect, the BBC's dilemma was the same one that exercised the Left, i.e. how to create forms peculiar to the new medium that would also be popular. An *Experimental Hour* ran briefly in 1937, modelled on the *Workshop* of the American Columbia Broadcasting System, but was, symptomatically, discontinued for lack of public interest.[66] Radio drama tended not to be 'easy listening', precisely because of the imaginative cooperation demanded of the audience in creating illusions. This took concentration even with traditional forms, and even more so for assembling narrative order from more 'montage' productions. The contingency of radio drama's popularity became clear when the visual medium of television became nationally available after the Second World War.

Similarly, the documentary possibilities of radio were limited by both technical and political factors. Reith insisted in *Broadcast Over Britain* (1924) on live transmission, so that what is heard might be considered real, because of the virtual instantaneousness of its reception. Recorded programmes, inserts or effects might compromise this rigorous standard. In its early days, the BBC went to absurd lengths, like keeping a microphone permanently on standby at Bournemouth so the genuine sea sound might be on tap.[67] But this defining of authenticity in purely temporal terms discounted the essential similarity of reproduction by mechanical means in both live and recorded transmissions. On the other hand, this tended to limit 'life' to the studio, unless it was in an OB, requiring much cumbersome technical organisation. Actuality material did offer a new kind of hyperreal verisimilitude but the scope for obtaining 'candid' subjects in the field and bringing them back to the studio was very restricted. Discs had been pioneered by the Germans during the Great War, but still by the mid-thirties BBC recording was possible only in London studios, almost exclusively for 'bottling' examples of significant broadcasts. Films were streets ahead in location recording. The BBC's first actuality feature, the rather Orwellian *'Opping 'Oliday*, made in Kent by Laurence Gilliam in 1934, used a recording van hired from a film company (it interviewed pickers in the fields and pubs, caught their singing on the train, and even used a locally-accented mediator). Moreover, only by D-Day did BBC correspondents have their own portable disc recorders (the Germans were already using tape). The routine use of dramatisation in radio features – 'live' speech being, generally simulated in the studio by scriptwriters and actors – paradoxically, reflected both these technical conditions and unremitting suspicion of spontaneous utterance, lest it be unvetted and controversial. Partly because of these limitations on actuality material, features themselves were eventually to prove a more innovative area for radio dramatisation than the play, because they always had to be given a definite shape. This was also true of their social accountability. As Scannell and Cardiff put it, the feature's initial developments 'ranged from avant-garde aestheticism to more plain-spoken direct forms of social documentation and reportage',[68] but the conditions of the thirties meant that the kind of pioneering work into 'pure radio' features carried out by Sieveking became inappropriate.

CINEMA

Logie Baird first publicly demonstrated the transmission of television pictures in 1926, the year before the first 'talkie' arrived in Britain, but although the world's first regular TV service was opened by the BBC from Alexandra Palace in 1936, it remained experimental, reaching only 20 000 sets in the Greater London area until after the war. Otherwise this most virtual form (as it then was) of 'the real's hallucinatory resemblance to itself'[69] would undoubtedly have enhanced the status of the photographic media in the thirties even further. As a *Listener* Editorial, 'The Real Thing', on the first televisation of the Cenotaph Service put it:

> the television camera is a privileged spectator. No one is likely to stand in its way, no policeman will tell it to pass along. It is an impressive thought that last Thursday's broadcast may have enabled stone deaf invalids, living many miles from London, to take an active part in the Cenotaph Service for perhaps the first time since the annual convention began.[70]

Sieveking accurately predicted the future of actuality broadcasting as 'a pefect balance between what is seen and what is heard'. Television's illusion was of seamless, simultaneous, coordinated access to global reality: 'fading up first outside the Houses of Parliament, then the face of the Prime Minister, then a glimpse of the members listening, then a flash of the subject of the reported speech – the industrial north – ships in the ports of England – the face of the German Foreign Minister – fitting the pictures to the announcer's words'.[71] But between the wars it was primarily the explosion of photomagazines, newsreels and Griersonian documentary's primary association with film, which gave the photographic image the status of most privileged technological medium of hyperreal representation. Hence its objective status and claims to unmediated recording of facts was most extensively emulated and investigated by writers. Commercial newsreels purveyed Baudrillard's paradox to the widest audience. Documentary, though lauded among an intellectual minority, rarely reached the masses.[72] In 1934, according to Paul Rotha, 18 000 000 Britons were going to the cinema each week, overwhelmingly to see features, generating £40 000 000 in revenue for the box offices.[73] The most frequent cinemagoers tended to be young, predominantly working-class, urban and female. Above all movie culture leaked out of the picture houses, through conversation and magazines, deep into the life of the time – into the naming of children, the scripting of desires.

A. J. P. Taylor described cinemagoing as 'the essential social habit of the age'.[74] Film had unprecedented reach as *the* mass medium, requiring neither literacy nor maturity for consumption. Hence the power of the movies was both more fascinating and disturbing to writers than press or radio, offering Leftists the most exciting possibilities and difficult challenges. For Benjamin, film technology was the key to more genuinely proportional political and cultural representation, but the effect of commercial cinema was primarily as an instrument of control. This was because, as Miles and Smith point out, whereas older arts were 'not directly reliant on money', in film 'finance was from the very start a quite basic issue'.[75] As Alexander Korda wrote in 1938, 'Circumstances have turned the impresario into the industrialist'.[76] Moguls liked to argue that the movie industry was the most effective example of market democracy that had ever existed, always led by consumer pleasure – 'In no other sphere has the people so great a power of veto' – that it was a Utopian space in which the masses not the élite decided what constituted cultural value, the ultimate embodiment of the Utilitarian ideal:

> In a world in which artists, actors, musicians and writers abound (all by tradition and in their own reckoning arbitrators, not arbitrated upon), the voice of the people, of the man and more particularly of the woman in the street is, for all practical purposes, the voice of God; and the philosophy to be held, on pain of bankruptcy, is that of the greatest happiness of the greatest number.[77]

The movies, to be a global industry, according to Korda, had to appeal to the universal in human nature: 'When a film has reached out . . . to the Lowest Common Multiple – or, in more flattering phrase, to the Highest Common Factor – in human emotion, then it will succeed all over the world.'

It is certainly true that, as Davy admitted, that the 'most obviously new capacity of the cinema, as a source of entertainment' meant universality of sorts: an omnivorous appetite for subjects and ability to ransack any time or place for them. But, whether produced unconsciously by market forces, designed by vested interests, or a combination of both, the 'universal' values projected by features had a distinct ideological tendency:

> Most films preach the worship of success and teach that success is the reward of virtue. They teach that life's supreme felicity consists in the winning of a desired woman. They teach that good intentions plus muddled thinking are lovable and will do no harm. They teach that our present society will bring the best man to the top. They teach that luxury is an art and art a luxury.[78]

In the mid-thirties the British industry went through an upturn as the result of government intervention and the enormous popularity of *The Private Life of Henry VIII* (1933), which enabled Korda to build the massive new Denham studios for London Films. But the Cinematograph Act of 1927 had already inevitably led to the involvement of big business in all the major aspects of the industry: production, distribution and exhibition. 'The inevitable consequence', as Jeffrey Richards puts it, 'was the creation of huge, complex, interlocking empires run by movie moguls every bit as powerful within their industry as their Hollywood counterparts.'[79] Two combines, the Ostrers' Gaumont-British Picture Corporation and John Maxwell's Associated British Picture Corporation dominated the decade, although increasingly challenged by Oscar Deutsch's Odeon circuit. The links between politicians and producers worked both ways. They advised the Conservative Party Film Association on propaganda and regularly promoted nationalistic values in their features, with the cooperation of military and imperial authorities. Korda, especially, was involved in projecting the image of Neville Chamberlain (himself ex-secretary of the Party's Research Department responsible for developing its use of film and newsreels). Isodore Ostrer even made a secret agreement in 1935 to place his entire organisation at the Party's disposal.[80]

Making films upholding the *status quo* was not just a question of profit, because producers were anxious to maintain government protection for the industry to enable it to compete with Hollywood and be seen as part of the establishment: 'It was for these reasons that they set up and operated the censorship system and depicted themselves as playing a vital role in the projection of Britain.'[81] Lack of direct intervention in the detailed and strictly enforced cinema code in the thirties was therefore, just as with the Press Proprietors' Association and the BBC, not an indication of the autonomy of the industry, but its very opposite. Censorship was especially tightened through the practice of script-vetting.[82] Indeed, it's impossible to explain the nature of British cinema in the thirties without first understanding the role of the British Board of Film Censors (BBFC). Arguably it was also as influential in shaping writers' attitudes to and involvements in the medium as the Ministry of Information (MoI) would later be to shaping their wartime media work. As Clive Coultass puts it, through virtually the whole decade, there was 'a massive silence from the British cinema on political and social questions'.[83] The BBFC worked in cooperation with the trade association of film distributors, who agreed not to handle films it did not license. For this reason, the films not shown or unmakeable in the thirties are just as culturally and politically revealing as those that were. Nominally independent, but closely in touch with the Home Office and with a president appointed by the Home Secretary, in practice, the BBFC provided the National Government both with an effective means of close control over cinema *and* an alibi similar to that operated in the case of press 'D notices'. Not funded by Parliament, BBFC decisions were, conveniently, not fully subject to democratic scrutiny and debate.

Far from being a bunch of barmy old duffers and maids, as they were often caricatured, many of the Board's personnel were public relations professionals, adding weight to the argument that its policies were calculated, not simply blimpish. For example, Lord Tyrrel, BBFC President from 1936, also chaired the British Council: 'Combining as he did responsibility for both censorship, i.e. negative propaganda, at home, and for positive, 'cultural' propaganda for overseas, he could be said to have come as close as the niceties of the British constitution allowed in peacetime to being a Minister for Propaganda.'[84] Similarly, the Board's secretary, Joseph Brooke-Wilkinson, controlled Great War film propaganda to allied and neutral nations.

The BBFC's paternalism, embodied in rules known as 'O'Connor's 43' (after T. P. O'Connor, the original chief censor) deemed the public incapable of responsible choice. Its own pamphlet 'Censorship in Great Britain' laid out 'the broad principle that nothing will be passed which is calculated to demoralise', based on its hypothesis of 'the average audience which includes a not inconsiderable proportion of people of immature judgment'. According to its critics, such as Forsyth Hardy, if the public's mentality were fixed at this retarded level, 'How can the British cinema ever grow up?'[85]

Hardy also objected to the stupidity of working solely by category, without due consideration of the meaning and purpose of a film. Decisions taken on public order or moral grounds also tended to have political implications, as in notorious cases like Herbert Wilcox's *Dawn*, Eisenstein's *Potemkin*, the three-minute short on 'collective security', *The Peace of Britain*, numerous newsreel items and *March of Time* editions, like 'Inside Nazi Germany'. The BBFC was supplemented by *de facto* censorship exercised by local authorities, using fire regulations to ban films considered 'inflammatory' for other reasons. Most often the Board's grounds for banning a film as 'controversial', were themselves controversial, or raised the suspicion the term itself was code for viewpoints diverging from National Government consensus. Banning both extreme Left and Right-wing dissent, criticism of foreign countries and attacks on established institutions, couldn't have had anything but the net effect of maintaining hegemony by suppressing debate. Similarly, there was no room in BBFC policy for radicalised thrillers like Greene's: though crime films were one of the decade's staples, 'the Board made it clear that they must be about the detection and punishment of crime', with no criticism of the system, sympathy for the criminal and, in effect, questioning of social norms.[86] The history of the film *Love on the Dole* demonstrates BBFC policy towards social and economic problems most clearly. Although already a highly successful novel and play, Gaumont-British's script was rejected on 15 March 1936 because 'There is too much of the tragic and sordid side of poverty . . . and the final incident of Sally selling herself is prohibitive.' If the script had been revised along these lines Greenwood's narrative would have been gutted. The BBFC also objected to 'coarse' language and mob confrontation with the police. Remarkably all it found objectionable in the thirties was included in the version eventually filmed in 1940. As the *Sunday Pictorial* commented, 'what a difference a war makes!', exposing the class double-standards that existed about the content of a public, mass, as opposed to private, literary medium in the thirties.[87] This confirms that cinema was more stringently censored precisely because it was *the* popular medium. As Hardy put it, 'The platform and the pulpit, books and plays, can be used with comparative freedom by any one with something new and vital to say about religion, politics or the relations between men and women: but censorship would deny this right to the screen.'[88] *Love on the Dole* was acceptable only when conscripted into the MoI's wartime propaganda campaign explaining 'Why We

Fight'. Industrial disputes, class conflict, and so on, were certainly depicted in thirties features, but reduced to a clash of personalities, or backgrounded by 'love interest': the BBFC 'banned or discouraged films which confronted these subjects head on', but 'positively welcomed' the preaching of class harmony and cheery acceptance.[89]

The Board also obligingly toed the general foreign policy line of Appeasement. It banned the film *Thaelmann*, which protested against the German Communist leader's imprisonment without trial by the Nazis, and *March of Time*'s number on Abyssinia. However, the Board could be (relatively) evenhanded: there was no special policy against anti-Fascist films: the depiction of all foreign countries avoided offence by eliminating any hostile depiction, guided by the weather-eye of the Foreign Office.[90] The Board seemed terrified of giving any exposure to Russia at all, as in the cases of both the pro-revolutionary *Potemkin*, and the anti-Soviet thriller *Sabotage* which denounced the Metro-Vickers affair as a show trial. Anti-Nazi propaganda was perceived as a public order issue, which might provoke disturbances of the Olympia/Cable Street type. Covert criticism or topical allegory had to be very subtle to slip past, as in the case of Gaumont's *Jew Süss*. Not until the outbreak of hostilities were explicitly anti-Nazi films permitted, when the BBFC came under the MoI, as in the case of Louis Golding and Gordon Wellesley's *Freedom Radio* script, approved as early as October 1939. Released in 1941, it included a long montage sequence retrospectively rushing through the brutalities of Nazism, as if the censors were trying to make up for lost time. In the thirties themselves, as Richards argues, the Board's attitude to the controversialness of 'abroad' 'could only encourage the view among the cinema-going public that all foreign countries were far-off places of which we knew and indeed wanted to know very little'.[91]

Hollywood domination of British film culture was one form of foreignness that could hardly be ignored, although attempts to restrict it, as in the case of the 'quota quickies', spawned by the 1927 Cinematograph Act, had a dire effect on the reputation of British films among home audiences from which they never fully recovered, even during the wartime 'renaissance'. BBFC policy was, at least to a certain extent, anti-American, though whether it derived from the ideological fear that democratic ideals might infect the English class-system, or nationalistic cultural prejudice, cannot be ascertained. Nevertheless, the chauvinism/anti-semitism of the Right was sometimes a uncomfortable mirror-image of

Leftist calls for more British films, as was the panic of contemporary moralists about the allegedly corrupting effect of cinema (compare the postwar period and TV). Paradoxically, though, the Government was content to leave promotion of the Empire to commercial features after the dissolution of the EMB Film Unit in 1933, because Hollywood did a grander job. Nothing illustrates the extent of this colonisation of British filmgoing better than the fact Hollywood even dominated this area! The BBFC's willingness to see empire-building romances as 'apolitical' naturalised the ideology such films promoted.

Early Nazi attempts at propaganda features failed miserably at the box-office, because they were too explicit, causing Goebbels to switch to 'pure entertainment' – musicals and adventure movies – more effective, because implicit. BBFC policy was not dissimilar: its most approving term was 'harmless', indicating the presence of propaganda under certified innocence. D. A. Spencer and H. D. Waley recognised the accessory function of such films in 1940 as 'aids to day-dreaming', that, like the tabloids, compensated the average human being for the lack of fit between their reality and desires.[92] An indispensable aspect of this was the star cult, with its projection and transference. Stars accomplished 'the difficult task of being both ordinary for the purposes of identification and extraordinary for the purposes of admiration. The great success of such British stars as Gracie Fields, George Formby and Jessie Matthews lay in the achievement of this elusive blend.'[93] This process might outlast the film for individual members of the audience. Above all, the star cult celebrated conspicuous consumption and the myth of success: the October 1935 issue of *Picturegoer* article about Barbara Stanwyck was symptomatically titled 'The Drudge Who Reached the Stars'. The stars' behaviour sanctioned bourgeois individualism, resolving social and economic problems at the personal level of charisma.

The explanation for the smaller number of British stars lay in the differences between Britain's class-system and the (in some ways at least) more democratic tones of Hollywood. Mainstream British films were all too often too English and socially-marked to be identified with by ordinary people. The view of British talkies 'over there' was not dissimilar. RP could be effete and uncharismatic for American audiences too. Korda's US film distributor predicted of *Things to Come* (1936), 'Nobody is going to believe that the world is going to be saved by a bunch of people with British accents.'[94] Filmed

West End farces, full of Charlie's auntics and cut-glass accents, seemed more foreign to working-class and Celtic audiences than Hollywood products. Consequently, British stars came mainly from stage and music hall, rather than legitimate, bourgeois theatre, with exceptions like Laurence Olivier and Robert Donat. Even rare anti-establishment films, such as the adaptation of R. C. Sherriff's play *Journey's End* (1930) (cinema's British equivalent to *All Quiet on the Western Front*, though made in Hollywood), endorsed a social view 'in which on the whole it was the upper classes who experienced the noble and serious emotions in life and the working classes who supplied the comic relief'.[95] Between the two types of debonair gentleman hero and sentimental working-class clown, only American films supplied a spectrum of 'ordinary' types which working people readily identified with: professionals like pilots, oil-men, reporters, gumshoes and gangsters.

The socially disproportional national image projected by the indigenous industry was mockingly summarised by Russell Ferguson in 1937: 'The majority of us move in society. One thing is quite clear. We don't work in coal pits or iron foundries.' Major national problems, in thirties features, were never the chronic ones of industrial decline, systematic unemployment and endemic poverty, but marginal and aberrant. In this continous ripping yarn, any threat to bourgeois tranquility was represented by spies and fanatics, threatening 'to blow up London, or to bring down all the machines at Hendon with death rays', and never fascist expansionism.[96] And if Britain's present was subjected to movie censorship and displacement, so was the past, glorifying the establishment, to the exclusion of everyone else's. It's a cliché that the historical consciousness of a generation was more effectively moulded by the cycle of hagiographic films following *The Private Life of Henry VIII* (1933) than by schooling. History was ransacked for parallels with current moods and events: the sequel to *Victoria the Great* (1937), for example, *Sixty Glorious Years* (1938) aimed to restore national confidence around the Munich débâcle. Historical films also clearly indicate BBFC's double standards over 'controversy', since they assumed fundamental state structures were not political at all.

For the vast majority of audiences, hyperreal contact with current events was limited to commercial newsreels, which is what made them a primary shaper of the age's 'else-awareness'. Any contemporary reputation for objectivity is belied by their editing of the facts and political affiliations. As mentioned, in 1935 Isidore Ostrer formally agreed to place his *Gaumont-British*, one of the most widely distributed newsreels, at the National Government's disposal. Similarly, the owners' cartel, the Newsreel Association of Great Britain (NRA) aided Chamberlain particularly at election times. Nicholas Pronay shows that the newsreel companies covertly cooperated in the second half of the thirties to push rearmament, by reviving the Great War's image of the goosestepping Hun, while the Government was publicly pursuing the directly contradictory policy of Appeasement.[97] This duplicitous strategy could not have been effected through newspapers or radio, because of the maverick qualities of press barons, and because the BBC was, as a *de facto* state monopoly, perceived by Goebbels as the voice of HMG (aside from the fact that such a party-political issue would have given the Opposition automatic right to airtime balance). In effect, the newsreels waged a black propaganda campaign for 'psychological rearmament', in Sir Robert Vansittart's phrase. Public opinion was softened up cumulatively by 'facts', to convince it of the reason and necessity for policy shift in advance.

Though not under BBFC jurisdiction, the newsreels' freedom 'rested upon custom only and it was clearly understood that the government could have chosen to ignore it if the newsreel companies behaved "irresponsibly".'[98] Newsreels had to cooperate because of dependence on government agencies. This indirect political pressure was exemplified by what happened to *Paramount News* when it ignored instructions not to film the 1932 National Unemployed Workers' Movement (NUWM) Hunger March. Close-up footage of mounted police batoning crowds was politically damaging. Within 48 hours Paramount was refused permission to film the Lord Mayor's Show and never broke ranks again. Consequently, companies regularly consulted the Home Office before deciding what would be news.

As Pronay points out, we need to understand the *modus operandi* of the newsreel to understand its ideological effects. Its primary technique was not argument, but, like press editing, 'communicating through the selection, headlining and juxtaposition' of events. Not a 'quality' medium, 'it was expected by its "popular" audience to explain as well as present',[99] which is did very much in the Northcliffe tradition (Rothermere, in fact owned one of the companies). It was this which enabled the newsreel to play an instrumental role in maintaining Government credibility, 'as men who shared the feelings of the people about war', against accusations of militarism.

The key to the projection of 'Chamberlain, man of peace' lay in collaboration with film advisers like Korda and, during the Munich crisis, even with the Nazi state newsreel company, covering the German end of negotiations. The obvious contradiction of this apparent 'pacifist' ruling the World's largest Empire was simply never raised. The newsreels' unofficial appearance and vulgar populism was the perfect alibi for the Government to disassociate itself publicly from its own machinations. Marketing rearmament as the answer to unemployment began in the newsreels and may, therefore, also be seen as the precursor of 'People's War' reconstruction propaganda, MoI policy for all media from the Blitz onwards.

In the twisted, intertextual skein of thirties culture, the media constantly fed off and reinforced one another, in content or in form, in ideology or technique. A radio *Newsreel* commentary programme was broadcast weekly in 1933–34 and just as newsreels were modelled on tabloid editorials and political authorities, spoke Janus-voiced through radio and screen. Reporting and, especially, broadcasting became popular subjects in a number of film genres (in features like *Death at Broadcasting House, Radio Parade of 1935. Radio Lover*, as well as documentaries like *BBC: Voice of Britain*). This negotiation and its hegemonic effect was flippantly, but, nonetheless, tellingly depicted in the Society comedy *Wedding Rehearsal* (1932), which inverted Sam Goldwyn's ideal Hollywood scenario that 'starts with an earthquake and works its way up to a climax'. At the opening of the film, a tabloid press-run announcing a volcanic disaster is stopped so a celebrity hitching can grab the headlines instead.[100]

Given the context of the thirties, any so-called 'laws of the market' are historically helpful only as evidence of a kind of cultural unconscious. As Arthur Marwick puts it, 'the bigger its commercial success, the more a film is likely to tell us about the unvoiced assumptions of the people who watched it. It is the tedious documentary, or the film financed by political subscription, which tell us least.'[101] My justification for this account of the intertextuality of thirties Leftist writing and the mass media is what it uncovers about a crucial transitional (post/modern) phase in the relations between cultural formations like literature and 'popular entertainment'. Though statistically, as Richards and Aldgate argue, 'the films of Gracie Fields . . . are more likely to be more valuable to the social historian than the poems of W. H. Auden',[102] the encounter between movies and poetry is highly revealing as cultural history, especially since their separation at the time came to be seen by writers them-selves as an increasingly artificial and undesirable state of affairs. The impact of the media is a defining characteristic of the writing of the time, as the next chapter will show.

2

Refractions: The Media as Subject Matter

The mass media were never passively reflected as subject matter in thirties Leftist writing, but always critically 'refracted', in ways ranging from po-faced Jeremiad, to satire and subversive parody. In this Chapter I want to examine refractions by both bourgeois and proletarian Leftists across a representative range of texts and genres.

THE PRESS

Aldous Huxley's *Brave New World* (1932) satirised the contemporary press as well as cinema. Whereas the 'feelies' are open to all, newspapers are stratified in line with the novel's troping of social as genetic engineering. Elite Alphas take the *Hourly Radio* (i.e. *The Times* or the *Telegraph*) while the lowest orders consume the *Delta Mirror*. Similarly, in Greene's *It's a Battlefield*, press discourse divides by social positioning: 'Men stood in their doorways and read the *News of the World* and spat. In Wardour Street and Shaftesbury Avenue they were reading the *Sunday Express*: in the almost empty Circus Conder bought an *Observer*' (p. 136). Huxley's answer in his 1936 essay 'Writers and Readers' to the conundrum of how the press could be overwhelmingly Rightist and yet also read by millions whose politics inclined otherwise showed a curious blindspot for a writer so informed about conditioning. He took it as proof that 'most people choose their daily paper, not for its opinions, but for its entertainingness, its capacity to amuse and fill the vacancies of leisure'. Propaganda was far less 'efficacious than the habits and prejudices, the class loyalties and professional interest of readers'.[1] It did not occur to Huxley that an ideological agenda might be expressed other than in the 'macropolitical' forms of editorials and news reporting – could be immanent in a paper's *Weltanschauung* – and that the tabloids might negotiate with 'habits, prejudices and

48

even class-loyalties' to achieve 'micropolitical' influence over those not consciously Conservative. Conversely, it was the linchpin of Charles Madge's explanation about the hegemonic success of the Tory press *even among* Labour voters.

Madge argued that social consciousness was unavoidably founded on 'exchange of information and ideas', but in Britain this was conducted largely through capitalist newspapers. The press manipulated subconscious repressions, social jealousy and criminal tendencies to compensate a 'habit-bound, automatist population' with 'vicarious experience of what is denied them in real life'.[2] People were sceptical about reporting, yet unavoidably influenced for lack of alternative, more objective sources to narcotic sensationalism. Madge quoted the *Daily Mirror*'s 'true story' of 26 October 1936, the 'Human Mole', to show how the idea of the reporter, 'the anonymous and impersonal "I" who tells the story', was exploited to confuse 'the real world with this world of poetic fantasy'.[3] Hence the rise of popular papers like the *Daily Mail* represented a compromise between subversion and control, constructing a plausible account of social reality but at the same time keeping democracy out of touch with itself. Press barons had to satisfy 'the requirements of the mass' as much as their own, although, self-fulfillingly, 'the mass is already largely what it has been made by the Press and the rest of capitalism'. Most importantly, the press inverted 'the proportion of class interests in the population of the country' and even the Labour *Daily Herald* depended on capitalist advertisers, who would hardly subsidise a paper seriously intending radical change. Though it was difficult to estimate, Madge was confident that the 'full scope of the demand for genuinely working class news' was potentially enormous.[4] It was this demand Mass-Observation (M-O) would try to satisfy. Cummings also argued that, like the BBC, the popular press had positive features which 'in part justify its claim to broaden and deepen the basis of human interests'. Consequently Madge and M-O tried to devise a dialectical programme to exploit these features and mobilise a new, radical reporting medium.[5]

Arthur Calder-Marshall agreed with Spender that the press constituted 'the ear', not the voice, of the people and that its freedom was an alibi for more effective control:

It speaks not for, but to, the people. It tells them not what they think, but what they should think. The Press is not the mirror of the public, but the public is the mirror of the Press. The myth is preserved of its popularity, because it has been found to be a valuable myth, financially and politically. The difference between the muzzled fascist Press and the fangless English Press is essentially a difference of myth rather than freedom. In fascist countries they know what is in the papers is merely an official version of the truth. In Great Britain, they don't.

He also concurred with Orwell's view that this agenda operated through mass-circulation economics not direct censorship. Profits made from newspapers which cost two to three times more to produce than sell were indirect – the buying of the public's confidence that they were forming their own opinions from reliable facts: 'A person paying a penny for a paper feels that he has paid for the information which it contains. The newspaper is a news-service supported by him and people like him. That is his view. Therefore he can trust the contents of the paper.'[6]

This abuse of the public trust invested in print was a constant Leftist theme. Madge's essay is perhaps the most coherent and comprehensive theorisation of it, but assumptions of mass-circulation lying and trivialisation were common to writers politically disparate as Louis MacNeice in *Autumn Journal* (1939) and Evelyn Waugh in *Remote People* (1931) and *Scoop: A Novel about Journalists* (1938). In *Autumn Journal* XIX, the 'file of sandwichmen/Carry lies from gutter to gutter'; they peddle the voices of the powerful at the expense of their own, being 'doll-dumb'. In *Remote People*, 'anxious journalists' despatch reports 'well before the event' to reach the Monday editions.[7] Consequently, caricatures of megalomaniac proprietors abounded: Lord Rothermere became 'Lord Monomark' of the *Daily Excess* in Evelyn Waugh's *Vile Bodies* (1930); Beaverbrook, 'Lord Copper' of Megalopolitan Newspapers' *Daily Beast*, in *Scoop*. They were similarly rife in Leftist writing: Beaverbrook is conflated conspiratorially with Rothermere as 'Beethameer, bully of Britain' in Auden's 'Diary of an Airman' from *The Orators* (1932) and subjected to wish-fulfilment revenge by disabused readers:

They shall turn on their betrayer when the time is come.
The cousins you cheated shall recover their nerve
And give you the thrashing you richly deserve.

The inescapable reach of 'Beethameer's' influence was particularly distasteful to Auden:

In kitchen, in cupboard, in club-room, in mews,
In palace, in privy, your paper we meet
Nagging at our nostrils with its nasty news . . .

But the precedent for their undemocratic political meddling was set
by Lord Northcliffe, caricatured by Auden as 'Heathcliffe':

I'm the sea-dog, he said, who shall steer this ship;
I advertise idiocy, uplift, and fear,
I succour the State, I shoot from the hip;
He grasped at God but God gave him the slip.
(*English Auden*, pp. 86–7)

Consequently the Right-wing '*Courier*'[8] is target number one in the
airman's surrealist campaign to subvert bourgeois hypocrisy. An
interpolated leading article accusing prominent citizens of everything from arson and coining, to onanism and piracy on the high
seas 'is on the table of every householder in time for late breakfast'
(*English Auden*, p. 92).

Following Auden, 'Bimbo' in *The Magnetic Mountain* (1933) was
another version of Beaverbrook, unmasked as a social disease by
Day Lewis:

We can see the spy through that painted grin;
You may talk patriotic but you can't take us in.
You've poisoned the reservoirs, released your germs
On firesides, on foundries, on tubes and on farms.
You've made yourself cheap, with your itch for power
Infecting all comers, a hopeless whore.

Lewis warned the 'Scavenger barons', with their 'pimping press-
gang', that 'We'll make you swallow your words at a gulp/ And
turn you back to your element, pulp', and served notice on these
'Closet Napoleons'.[9]

Though such menacings were rhetorical fleabites compared to
the Juggernaut of circulation figures, Leftist fear of the press undermining the democratic process was clearly grounded in historical
fact. Hitler told Goebbels the Nazis' greatest asset was induced
forgetfulness. Similarly, Leftists felt stunts like the *Mail*'s Zinoviev
Letter were likely to recur because media-shortened public memory
easily loses its sense of contradiction. In *The Ascent of F6*, Lord

Stagmantle's papers doublethinkingly suspend their routine jingoism to smear an elected Labour Government with an imperial atrocity:

> STAGMANTLE (*beginning to laugh wheezily*). British General Butchers Unarmed Mob! Children Massacred In Mothers' Arms! Murder Stains The Jack!
> JAMES (*hastily*). Yes, yes. . . . The nauseating clichés of gutter socialism –
> STAGMANTLE. Socialism my foot! Why, that's out of the *Evening Moon*! Splashed it all over the front page – nearly doubled/ our sales that week! No offence, General. We were out to smash the Labour Government, you know: and by God, we did! Your little stunt came in handy: any stick's good enough to beat a dog with, you know!

In Stagmantle's book truth-telling and Left-wing subversion are synonymous and have to be similarly suppressed. In response to Lady Isabel's naive belief that honesty is the best policy, Stagmantle replies that lying is a patriotic duty and telling the truth tantamount to treason: 'The truth is that we're under-garrisoned and under-policed and that we're in a blue funk that the Ostnians will come over the frontier and drive us into the sea . . . you want me to tell that to the public! What do you take me for – a bolshevik?'[10]

If British press barons were 'closet' Napoleons, continental dictators had stormed out of theirs wielding the papers' psychological potentials with unapologetic ruthlessness. F. L. Stevens's *On Going to Press* defined news as 'not only what happens but what is being thought'.[11] Brunsatz, Minister for Propaganda, in Hillel Bernstein's allegory *Choose a Bright Morning* (1936) boasts of his power to create 'news' in the latter sense:

> Propaganda is our first line of defence. . . . Let the generals wear their uniforms and quarrel about tactics, about infantry or artillery. The army at my command is more powerful than any of theirs. If I decide to-night that the people of Bidlo must have a certain thought in their heads at 9.45 a.m. tomorrow, I give the word, exactly at 9.45 a.m. Tomorrow there will not be a head in Bidlo to which my thought has not yet penetrated.[12]

A state-controlled press sustains real crypto-Fascist Austrian Chancellor Dollfuss as 'Our wet dream dictator, our people's president,/

Printed in papers and cut out with scissors', in Spender's *Vienna* (1934), and in John Lehmann's *Evil Was Abroad* (1937) a nightmare prophesying the crushing of Austrian democracy is set in a newspaper office:

> many people were seated at desks all round the walls, correcting proofs and shouting down telephones to make themselves heard above the din of the printing machines. These machines . . . looked to Peter more like tanks than linotypes, heavily armoured and emitting jets of fire, and the workers whose hands were on the levers seemed to be dressed in unmistakeably military uniform.[13]

Spender also recollected the Nazi *Der Angriff* trying to shove the tottering Weimar Republic over the psychological edge at the time of the the Darmstädter National Bank crash with the headline 'Alles bricht zusammen', 'Everything is collapsing'.[14]

Some writers even blamed devaluation of words themselves on the papers: 'language suffers from exhaustion and from the feverish delirium of the yellow Press', argued Day Lewis.[15] By similar means, totalitarian press agitprop and capitalist escapism collaborate subliminally to subvert German democracy by inflating the fears and desires of desperate people in Isherwood's *Mr Norris Changes Trains* (1935):

> The vocabulary of newspaper invective (traitor, Versailles-lackey, murder-swine, Marx-crook, Hitler-swamp, Red-pest) had come to resemble, through excessive use, the formal phraseology of politeness employed by the Chinese. The word *Liebe*, soaring from the Goethe standard, was no longer worth a whore's kiss. *Spring, moonlight, youth, roses, girl, darling, heart, May*: such was the miserably devaluated currency dealt in by the authors of all those tangoes, waltzes and fox-trots which advocated the private escape. Find a dear little sweetheart, they advised, forget the slump, ignore the unemployed.[16]

The international effects of the press made writers anxious for the fates of both Britain and Europe and gave prominence to warmongering megalomediacs in topical fiction. In Christopher Caudwell's thriller *Fatality in Fleet Street* (1933), Affiliated Publications director, Lord Carpenter (with his closet Napoleonesque profile and 35 563 271 circulation), literally manufactures news by fomenting war against

Russia over the head of Parliament. His campaign is foiled only by assassination.[17] The scenario is given a different twist in Auden and Isherwood's *On the Frontier* (1938) where Valerian plays profiteering brinkmanship with Armageddon: 'Do you seriously imagine that wars nowadays are caused by some escaped lunatic putting a bomb under a bridge and blowing up an omnibus?' Valerian pins his cynical faith on media-shortened public memory and tolerance for sensation where even international crises quickly lose their impact: 'It will end in itself. In ten days there will be a new distraction – an international football match or a girl found murdered in her bath.'[18] However, having reported the pseudo-event for so long, his media cannot douse it when it actually combusts.

To thirties writers old enough to have served in the Great War who could not forget anti-German hysteria whipped up by the likes of Horatio Bottomley, it was difficult to regard press patriotism as anything but John Bull. Thus leftish veteran J. B. Priestley wrote in his *English Journey* that visiting Blackburn's slums felt like being 'a comfortable newspaper proprietor who has just inspected a front-line trench (in a safe sector) and is now leaving the brave boys to it, thank God!' (pp. 264–5). Press coverage of international sporting events sometimes seemed a continuation of the Great War by other means. In the summer of 1936 a British climbing team's attempt on Nanda Devi in the Himlayas was jingoistically reported in papers like the *Mail*.[19] Consequently. *F6*'s expedition is also sponsored by Stagmantle as a media fiction to sublimate a depressed public's desires and discontents. A whole national ideology is at stake in the race against Ostnia's team, as the 'typical' member of the public unconsciously grasps:

> You see? The foreigner everywhere,
> Competing in trade, competing in sport,
> Competing in science and abtract thought:
> And we just sit down and let them take
> The prizes! There's more than a mountain at stake.
>   (pp. 89–90)

The promotion of a round-the-world air-race in John Sommerfield's *May Day* (1936) is likewise exposed as wish-fulfilment for the masses, to distract them from the forthcoming demonstration against industrial speed-up: FORCED LANDING IN SIBERIA: WORLD FLIERS BEAT RECORDS; THOMPSON FLIES ON heroic headlines blare throughout the novel. Prince's Travel Company coordinates press, radio and cinema publicity for similar aerial stunts to glamorise a poor African country for tourism in Holtby's *Mandoa, Mandoa!* (1933).

The integrity of journalists who collaborated with proprietors' dubious agendas was also widely impugned. Crime reporter Conder in *It's a Battlefield*, trading inside information on the Communist Party in return for police leaks, knows only too well what he does and what it's worth:

> 'Take this to the subs,' he said, and watched his exclusive story disappear in the hands of a messenger down the stairs; soon it would be leaden type and soon a column of print, and twenty-four hours later it would be pulp. It did not seem fair to Conder that the products of his brain should be condemned to the same cycle as his body. . . . He began to write, again without thinking: 'Reds clash behind locked Doors'. No story left his hands with the truth unheightened. Condemned to the recording of trivialities, he saw the only hope of posthumous immortality in a picturesque lie which might catch a historian's notice as it lay buried in an old file. (p. 85)

Conder's venality contrasts with the naive optimism of Conrad Drover, the condemned man's brother:

> 'Spot the Stars', he read. 'Are you Insured? Mr MacDonald –' There was a photograph of the Prince of Wales opening a new hostel for the unemployed; he was surrounded by men in frock coats carrying top hats: women in fur coats pressed round the edge of the picture gazing at the golden key. An officer and his bride stepped out of St Margaret's into the blaze of publicity under arched swords. A shabby woman with a cameo brooch seemed out of place on the same page: 'Mrs Coney, wife of the murdered police constable.'

Conrad believes this 'voice of the people' will provide the same publicity to safeguarding justice for the common man, not suspecting that professionals like Conder misinform society precisely to make it manageable for the rich and powerful: '"Go and see her," Conrad said. "If she'd sign the petition the news would be in every newspaper. Something would be done"' (pp. 64–5).

On a global scale, the hacks in Auden and Isherwood's play *The Dog Beneath the Skin* know all the 'dope' about multi-national

manoeuvrings but keep mum, because, in the Chorus's words.
'They're in the racket too!'

> 2nd J (*singing*).   The General Public has no notion
> Of what's behind the scenes.
> They vote at times with some emotion
> But don't know what it means.
> Doctored information
> Is all they have to judge things by;
> The hidden situation
> Develops secretly.
>
> 1st J.   To grasp the morning dailies you must
> Read between the lines.
> The evening specials make just nonsense
> Unless you've shares in mines.
> National estrangements
> Are not what they seem to be;
> Underground arrangements
> Are the master-key.[20]

But there were more subtle forms of journalistic bad faith. Mrs
Coney isn't just traumatised by crime: ' "Are you the Press?" The
eyes, bewildered and hunted, peered over Milly's shoulder, flinched
in dread of a battery of cameras, of tripods, of microphones' (*It's a
Battlefield*, pp. 94–5). To the victims of the Nazi coup in Isherwood's
Mister Norris newshound Helen Pratt is 'as relentless as their tortur-
ers': 'What would happen to them afterwards frankly didn't interest her. She was out to get facts' (p. 180). Ascertaining what's news
is fatally unproblematic to her. She is the privileged fly on every
wall, but oblivious to the tragic human dimension of events: 'To
hear her talk, you might have thought she had spent the last two
months hiding in Dr Goebbel's writing-desk or under Hitler's bed.
She had the details of every private conversation and the lowdown
on every scandal.' Pratt's ghoulish objectivity contrasts with William
Bradshaw's tardy 'inside-knowledge' through personal involvement
with the victims behind the headlines: 'The temptation to fill out
the gaps in her story, or, at least to betray my knowledge of them,
was considerable. Thank goodness, I didn't yield to it. She was
no more to be trusted with news than a cat with a saucer of milk'
(pp. 185–6). Later in his joint reportage with Auden, *Journey to a
War* (1939), Isherwood satirised an actual American journalist, who

although he had 'been on the *Panay* at the time of the incident' had
a similarly opportunistic conception of the newsworthy:

> he was bored and tired – homesick, weary of China and the war.
> He was giving Canton its last chance. If a real story didn't break
> within a fortnight, he'd do his best, he said, to get sent back to
> the States. We retired, not wishing to bother him further, and
> viewed him from a respectful distance with awe. A disillusioned
> journalist is the Byron, the romantic Hamlet of our modern
> world.[21]

Even the motivations of well-intentioned journalists were questioned in Anthony Powell's *Venusberg* (1932). Lushington had perhaps been led by 'some hereditary flaw in his character' into
becoming foreign correspondent in 'a country on the Baltic, the
name of which he could never remember. He was a serious young
man with a pink and white face who believed implicitly in eventual
progress on a scientific basis.'[22] The likely end of Lushington's green-
horn liberalism might well be Minty, feckless, Old-Harrovian hack,
in Greene's *England Made Me* (1935). Minty survives by 'translating
into Swedish all the dope he could discover in the movie magazines' about Garbo, until he gets the chance to blow the whistle on
criminal industrialist Krogh, not out of public interest, but petty
revenge.[23]

Press agents were even lower life than hacks. In Bernstein's *Choose
a Bright Morning* Larry Mulden 'once created a pacifist lobby on
behalf of munitions manufacturers', so 'they could put up a patriotic
fight' against it, though his attempt at a Red Scare lacks conviction,
because even he can't 'believe in Santa Claus anymore' (pp. 23–4).
Journey to a War features a Kuomintang Government press officer
who might be the original of *Animal Farm*'s porcine propagandist
'Squealer':

> The daily news-bulletin was read by Mr T. T. Li, the official mouth-
> piece of the Government. He resembles the most optimistic of
> Walt Disney's Three Little Pigs. The word 'defeat' has no place in
> his mouth. Every Japanese advance is a Chinese strategic with-
> drawal. (p. 44)

In the thirties the press was a major regulator of how and what
facts were admitted to public consciousness. In *The Dog Beneath the
Skin* it does not record the reality of events, but confers it on them:

Dozens of things occur every day, curious, embarrassing, shocking incidents: but how few of them happen! The Press disregards
them: therefore they cannot have taken place! the Press is an
artist: It has a certain picture to paint. Whatever fails to harmonise
with that picture, it discards; regretfully perhaps, but firmly. . . .
(p. 177)

The reality conferred could be very different from the experience,
as Milly Drover finds on comparing Mrs Coney to her press photo:

Milly looked at her with astonishment and saw now the cameo
brooch, the grey hair pulled back from the forehead, the black
high-necked dress, but what the newspapers had failed to indicate was the smallness of the scale; she was no more than an
imitation in miniature of the harsh and unbearable woman. (*It's
a Battlefield*, p. 94)

Proletarians, and those from the regions in particular, felt especially liable to press misrepresentation. In Lewis Grassic Gibbon's
Grey Granite (1934), the *Evening Runner's* reporters manufacture anti-
working class coverage by catalysing violence at a Scottish NUWM
protest:

the news went humming into the south about the fight in the
Royal Mile, pitched battle between unemployed and police, how
the reds had fought the bobbies with bottles, battering them from
their saddles with volleys of bottles: would you credit that now,
the coarse brutes that they were? The poor police had just tried
to keep order, to stop a riot, and that's what they'd got.

Grey Granite also shows the 'micropolitical' effect of an ever-
lowering common denominator of tabloid sensationalism: even Communist pickets bunk off to get 'the racing news and the story of a
lassie raped, bairned, killed, and fried up in chips – Ay, fairly educative, the Scottish newspapers.' Reinforcement of linguistic hegemony was particularly galling to dialect writers: the *Tory Pictman* is
'full of dog Latin and constipated English, but of course not Scotch'.[24]
In Walter Brierley's *Sandwichman* the tabloids help crack the solidarity of the working-class family unit. The tension of the Means
Test interview scene, which forces Arthur Gardner on the streets, is
heightened by the father's concealment behind a newspaper until

his rage at the shame brought on the family by his 'layabout' son reaches flashpoint.[25]

The survival of the few genuinely oppositional press voices was always jeopardised in a market system, then as now. According to Calder-Marshall, even the radicalism of the *Daily Herald*, organ of Official Labour, had been progressively diluted since the twenties when Odhams obtained the majority share and developed it into a popular paper.[26] Similarly, Miners' Federation Secretary, James Cameron, in Harold Heslop's novel *Last Cage Down* laments how the *Daily Herald* had rotted its teeth on mass-circulation economics and tabloid gimmicks by 1935:

> To-day, it was a daily complete with a crossword puzzle, insurance scheme, prize gift schemes, other kinds of schemes, and a vast circulation. He had known it when it was a struggling journal before the War. He had read it as a weekly and then through those hard years following the War when, as a Left journal, it was the miracle of Fleet Street. Now it was respectable, full of circulation stunts and pen portraits. He regretted the passing of the old writers, Gadfly and Lance Matteson. . . .[27]

The *Daily Worker*, despite its small circulation, was undoubtedly a potent force among the working classes and fellow-travelling writers, but in East-Ender Simon Blumenfeld's *Jew Boy* (1935) rich bohemians in a workers' café sport it as an accessory to posing: 'Communism apparently was becoming fashionable. To them carrying about a *Daily Worker*, was not a sharing of the bitter struggles of the proletariat, but a sign of the highest intellectualism.'[28]

At the other end of the political spectrum, the press fostered the kind of climate in which political violence in Europe happened to far-away minorities, disconnected from Britain's internal problems. *Jew Boy* comments on publicity for anti-Fascism, before the Battle of Cable Street between East Enders and Mosleyite marchers made it unignorable in 1936. Sweatshop cutter Alec, returning from a mass protest against Nazi persecution knows, frustratingly, how its impact will be diminished: 'To-morrow in the morning papers there would be one blurred photograph of the demonstration and a small paragraph saying ten-thousand Jews had marched to Hyde Park' (p. 54). The press often forestalled understanding of the implications of political violence, particularly abroad, for their reader's own futures, and failed to alert them to insidious dangers.

John Cornford warned in 'At Least to Know the Sun Rising Each Morning':

> At the Street corners they were selling papers
> Told us what teeth were broken in what riots,
> Where fighting on the frontier is unsuccessful
> But causes as yet no panic in the city.
> Think. Rome felt not otherwise than this
> Who, dying slowly, is spared defeat,
> Suffers, perhaps, greater humiliation.[29]

As mentioned in Chapter 1, the mainstream press also had extensive links with organisations further Right than the National Government. Rothermere's own editorial in the *Daily Mail* (15 January 1934) ran:

> At this next vital election Britain's survival as a Great Power will depend on the existence of a well-organised Party of the Right, ready to take over responsibility for national affairs with the same directness of purpose and energy of method as Mussolini and Hitler have displayed. . . . That is why I say Hurrah for the Blackshirts! . . . Hundreds of thousands of young British men and women would like to see their own country develop that spirit of patriotic pride and service which has transformed Germany and Italy. They cannot do better than seek out the nearest branch of the Blackshirts and make themselves acquainted with their aims and plans.[30]

His support for Mosley is parodied in the *Evening Moon*'s 'disinterested' reporting of the Lads of Pressan Ambo, started by the vicar in *The Dog Beneath the Skin*:

> 1st JOURNALIST (*helpfully*). 'Standing outside all political parties and factions, for Church, King and State, against communism, terrorism, pacifism and other forms of international anarchy, to protect Religion and succour England in times of national crisis.' Is that right, sir?
> CURATE (*surprised*). Why, those are almost exactly the Vicar's own words. However did you know? (p. 160)

In 1943, Orwell recollected such Rightist fellow-travelling in 'Who Are the War Criminals?', an essay which shows how much the political *volte-faces* and Doublethink of *Nineteen Eighty-Four* derive from prewar criticisms about the press common among Leftist writers (*Collected Essays*, II, pp. 363–9). The crucially different factor in Orwell's case was his prescient realisation, as his Spanish Civil War reportage puts it, that reporting by Stalinised sections of the Left-wing press 'could be every bit as spurious and dishonest as that of the Right' when they deemed it politically expedient.[31]

BROADCASTING

The oracular reputation of the BBC exercised Leftist texts in the thirties as much as the blatant tendentiousness of the press. Calder-Marshall believed 'that great voice of the public, was really the still, small voice of a privileged class', whose ideology and accent were 'amplified in the control room'.[32] However, this did not mean that Leftists did not believe the BBC had redeemable features if it could be made more genuinely representative, as we shall see in Chapter 4.

Exemplified by royal occasions, transmitted 'live' by pre-rehearsed commentators (the Coronation of George VI in 1937 was the first on both television and radio)[33] broadcasting's power to transmit Lipp-manesque 'fictions', giving mass audience's vicarious participation in events was second only to the newsreels. Calder-Marshall pointed out that

> a chosen sequence joined to chosen sentences and the audience feels that it has really 'experienced' something. . . . Even the word 'relay' . . . has taken on in the public mind a wider meaning. A superstitious belief, like that concealed in the boast of the news-reel that 'brings the world to the world,' exists that the *actual event* is being sent over the ether. This belief is of course rejected as soon as it rises to consciousness; but in most people, it does not reach consciousness.[34]

That atavistic superstitiousness could be part of the credibility invested in a modern, 'scientific' medium was notoriously evidenced by the mass-hysteria broadcast by Orson Welles's production of Howard Koch's treatment of *The War of the Worlds* for CBS in 1938. This simulated the immediacy of a live news commentary on an extraterrestrial invasion for Hallowe'en.[35]

Calder-Marshall came as close to Baudrillard's concept of hyper-reality as anyone in the thirties, when he concluded of radio that 'The material world has given place to the etherial.' The perform-ativity of BBC broadcasting made the establishment's definition of reality appear identical with reality itself; its discourse, 'the plain, wholesome truth'. This impression was assisted by the use of ex-perts on the air: 'even though we may know that the speech has been blue-pencilled before it was delivered and that it represents not what the expert wants to say, but what the officials of the BBC will allow him to say. . . . They are, in fact, not hiring his brain, but his name.'[36]

As with the press, Leftist criticisms of broadcasting grew through-out the thirties. A 1932 Auden poem features Lord Reith himself – 'like a blasted tree/ Was the gaunt director of the BBC' – pretend-ing aloofness from the chimps' tea party where Rothermere and Beaverbrook brawl over bananas ('A Happy New Year (to Gerald Heard)' *English Auden*, p. 448). Most Leftist texts agreed with Madge and Calder-Marshall about such vaunted disinterest.[37] BBC discourse differed from the press in methods, not aims. In Auden and Isherwood's *F6*, for example, Stagmantle switches smoothly from tabloid demotic to Reithian RP when before the mike – 'From such pioneers, the man in the street may learn to play his part in the great game of life, small though it may be, with a keener zest and daring' – just as Beaverbrook actually did in Empire talks (*F6*, pp. 40–1).

Radio construction of the newsworthy rivalled the press's. 'There is no news tonight', the BBC's announcement, when nothing was deemed reportable, might well have reassured audiences history was temporarily suspended (whatever underlying crises continued unabated) though it was ridiculed by the newspapers for doing so on Good Friday 1930.[38] Similarly, in MacNeice's verse play *Out of the Picture* (1937) radio, like press reporting, renders the atrocious merely sensational, trivialising it into a consumable commodity, while at the same time ignoring the implications of mundaner actualities:

The news that blows about the streets
Or vibrates over the air
Whether it is rape, embezzlement or murder
Seems frivolous, if not farcical without dignity.
Whereas the actual fact before it becomes news
Is often tragic even when commonplace.[39]

The City in Warner's *The Wild Goose Chase*, broadcasts 'All-you-need News' for the impoverished peasants outside its privileged environs, strenuously denying rumours of political and economic crisis, and reporting opposition from a slanted perspective.[40] Calder Marshall argued that 'The essential difference between a "sport" and a "state" relay is that the commentator of sport does not know beforehand what is going to happen or what attitude he must take up, whereas the "state" commentator knows almost exactly what will happen and quite exactly what attitude he must adopt.'[41] However, Warner lampooned BBC fair play and political balance by inverting Calder-Marshall's distinction. In *The Wild Goose Chase*, the murderous result of a rugby match is broadcast in advance and its rules are surrealistically stacked – the red-shirted 'Pros' are kitted with boots; the 'Cons', with machine guns and an armoured car. Leftists' science-fiction visions of how radio might shape the future were always cautionary. The Twenty-Seventh century Nazi Empire in Katherine Burdekin's proto-*Nineteen Eighty-Four*ish *Swastika Night* is a post-literate society. A bare minimum of the subject races are permitted to read, but then only technical manuals and the Hitler Bible, because 'News was always broadcast.'[42]

Although Storm Jameson believed 'The novelist must be a receiving station for the voices coming from every corner of the society he lives in',[43] literary anxieties about wireless 'monoglossia' and propagandism stuck so deep they shaped Isherwood's conception of the writing process much more negatively. In his review of *The Grapes of Wrath*, intrusive didacticism is troped as a kind of 'interference', jamming both textual plurality and readerly autonomy: 'there are moments at which Ma Joad and Casey – otherwise such substantial figures – seem to fade into mere mouthpieces, as the author's voice comes through, like another station on the radio'.[44] The BBC voice was particularly pilloried for amplifying and transmitting ruling-class language and history and, hence, repressing the 'heteroglossia' of demotic English (it was this that made Greene feel the title of Grierson's documentary on the BBC, *The Voice of Britain*, simply *had to be* ironic.)[45] Glaswegian James Barke's *Major Operation* (1936) even insisted rookie announcers could be brainless as long as they could pronounce 'Wethah fawcaust'.[46] Aping the BBC manner could raise working-class hackles, even when well-intentioned. At the craft centre in *Sandwichman*, the secretary runs through the itinerary: ' "Tea at six, and then at half-past seven the evening programme begins." ' The unemployed 'laughed with him, either humorously because of the wireless touch, or cynically for other reasons' (p. 165). Before Wilfred Pickles' broadcasts during the Second World War, dialect news broadcasts were merely surreal fantasy in poems like Roger Roughton's 'Animal Crackers in Your Croup'.[47]

But radio's intrusiveness, even more ineluctable than the tabloids', could produce surreal incongruities of its own, precisely because it was becoming so normalised. As Greene wrote, 'in the inn the radio played continuously. You couldn't escape it: with your soup a dramatised account of the battle of Mons, and with the joint a Methodist church service.'[48] In *I Crossed the Minch* (1938), MacNeice encapsulated the grotesque disproportionality between BBC claims to provide a National Service and BBC exclusiveness as it sounded in the regions:

> I listened to the voice of London enunciating facts for the masses with a soi-disant impartiality. I heard my late landlord in Birmingham, a professor of economics, discuss the industrial midlands. I heard an art critic whom I know discuss the portrait of a writer whom I know. And the glorious fact dawned on me that really I knew everybody. I knew hardly a soul in the Hebrides, but that's not where everybody lives. How lovely to belong to that wider civilisation – how lovely to belong to that clique![49]

The National Service resembled Swift's 'flying island' of Laputa, beamed everywhere, yet obscuring local identities under its *haute-bourgeois* cultural shadow. MacNeice, of course, became a full-time inhabitant of this etherial island from 1941, although he certainly helped break down some of its insularity by his own brand of broadcast innovation, as we shall see in 'Involvements'.

The BBC disapproved of 'background listening' and expected audiences to use its broad menu 'selectively and with an open mind'.[50] But Calder-Marshall argued that mass radio-dependence was less likely to raise the kind of discerning consciousness that was the Reithian ideal, than to foster indiscriminate, unreflective consumption:

> Housewives cook and make the beds and dust to music: and not music only. They have now got to be oblivious to subject. Music or talking, it is all the same. These radio-bibbers drink-in Cosmo Cantaur or Stainless Stephen, Beethoven or Irving Berlin with the

same half-conscious thirst. They are like babies to whom the nipple has become the milk, lying contented sucking at their dummies.[51]

There's no doubt radio brought people into contact with realities elsewhere, but it also sometimes put them out of contact with their own. This was literally the case with the ticklish reception quality of the early sets, necessitating headphones and endless retuning. In Henry Green's *Living* (1929), 'Mr Craigan put wireless earphones over his head. "You and yer wireless", Gates softly said, "it's enough to make anyone that lives with you light 'eaded, listening like you might be a adder to the music." '[52] And proneness to fiddling with this new mechanical toy was a gender divider too. In Walter Green-wood's *His Worship the Mayor* (1934), Mrs Evans regards the radio habit as an infantile compulsion: ' "He's sekkled for the night, thank God,' she said: 'I've left him trying to get Moscow or whatever he wants on wireless. And his tea what he was shoutin' about goin' stone cold on table. That's a man all o'er for y'. Conterairy, conterairy. Twiddlyitis on wireless, that's his latest craze." '[53]

Proletarian writers expected the BBC to represent working-class voices and culture even less than the press. In *Grey Granite*, Chris Colquohoun finds Scottish Regional programming nauseatingly irrelevant to her daily darg:

And you'd listen to talks on ethics and cocktails and how to go hiking on the Côte d'Azur, minding the baby, copulation in catkins, and the views of Jacob P. Hackenschmidt on Scotland and Her Ancient Nationhood: and you'd switch the thing off, lost, that was better, worth paying a licence to keep the thing quiet. . . . (p. 20)

For Jim Cameron, in *Last Cage Down*, it's *Children's Hour* which epitomises Reithian patronising: 'it was the most fatuous balderdash he had ever heard. They were busy doing a play, and he wondered if the child of modern times, even in the Darlstone pit villages, had any time to spare from their play to listen to this terrible mush of humour and sentimentality.' But he considers its adult fare hardly more edifying: 'as he was not so learned in the programmes of the British Broadcasting Corporation he could not ask for the alternative, which in all probability would be a jazz band, blaring and "putting in the obscene dirt" of muted trumpets and trombones and so forth' (p. 194).

Radio furnishes a literal bromide for terminally-ill Lily Sawdon in Holtby's *South Riding*, 'It was dangerous to sew or move about much; she might startle to life the sleeping pain. But voices came to her out of the silence, singers and jesters and actors from Broadcasting House. She acquired favourites and enemies' (p. 354). James Hanley gave the most pathetic example of widespread working-class radio-dependence. A paraplegic ex-collier, altogether lost in ethereality after eleven, bed-ridden years, 'always enjoyed the talks on it, and he was generous in his praise of those who spoke through its medium. "You know, you get the feeling that they are really talking to you, and for you, and, after all, it's fine to feel that, isn't it?" '[54] Radio is a constant intrusion in the cramped home-life of Arthur Gardner, Walter Brierley's 1930s 'Jude the Obscure' in *Sandwichman*, trying to get through a part-time University scholarship. His brother croons along while he slogs for exams on the kitchen table. When he retreats upstairs to escape cricket, he is branded snootily anti-social: ' "'E might as well 'ave said, 'Shut the bloody wireless off', as do that,' the father burst out angrily. "Does 'e think the damned 'ouse is made for 'im and 'is studyin'?" ' (pp. 8–9 and 78–9). But Sommerfield went furthest in portraying broadcasting as part of a fully-orchestrated capitalist communications conspiracy. In Cunningham's words, as 'the BBC represses the voice of the masses, so the crowd-opposing police in *May Day* are the ones equipped with radio'.[55]

Occasionally, albeit grudgingly, Leftists represented broadcasting more democratically, as a potentially subversive force even. Brierley's Gardner wants to stay in for Beethoven, but his girlfriend drags him off to Fred and Ginger at 'the Hipp'. Blumenfeld's Alec hungrily appreciates the cheap set as a redistributor of cultural wealth, like classical concerts, hitherto monopolised by the rich, and both of them use it for horizon-broadening information. (See, for example, *Jew Boy*, pp. 251–2.) Sommerfield featured fictional crashing of broadcasts as a form of protest the media could not ignore – 'the loudest instruments in the orchestra of suppression were forced to echo the undertone of a working class motif', while M-O analysed real incidents of the same.[56] The BBC could also be by-passed for alternative sources like Soviet stations. Communist Joe Frost in *Last Cage Down* is 'one of that new breed of men, who read diligently, who owned a radio'. Frost learns all about the propaganda machine Party hero Dimitroff is up against, but remains undaunted: ' "That chap Goebbels is always bawling on some

German radio. . . . It's a wonder somebody doesn't ram a loud-speaker down his throat . . . him and his . . . Fuehrer"' (pp. 42 and 106).

Marconi's belief that radio was an automatic aid to international understanding was not shared by writers. In *It's a Battlefield* mealy-mouthed Mr Surrogate insists the League of Nations must 'broadcast' universal brotherhood. Crabbe takes his metaphor literally, but finds peace signals drowned by more powerful transmitters: ' "I've heard Moscow," Crabbe said, "I've heard Rome, I've heard New York, but I can't get Geneva" ' (p. 91). Within the nation, the BBC's Charter supposedly provided airspace where opposing interests could debate in a balanced and civilised manner. Veteran commentator A. G. Gardiner wrote in 1931, that radio communications appealed to 'the individual reason rather than to the crowd emotion'. As Briggs notes, widespread belief in radio's 'rationalising' effect on politics persisted right up to 1939 in 'blissful ignorance of hidden persuaders and public relations techniques'.[57] However, in Hitler's ranting, writers detected revealing echoes of the disproportional representation on their own nation's airwaves and the danger implicit therein. MacNeice's *Autumn Journal* XVIII sees radio's potential for political obfuscation and bad faith, rather than informed democratic choice:

No wonder many would renounce their birthright,
The responsibility of moral choice,
And sit with a mess of pottage
Out of a square box from a mad voice –
Lies on the air endlessly repeated
Turning the air to fog. . . .
(Collected Poems, p. 139)

In Bernstein's *Choose a Bright Morning*, sets must be on to receive propaganda broadcasts on pain of execution, anticipating Orwell's inescapable, twenty-four hour telescreens. Similarly, another Warner allegory, *The Professor* (1938), set in an unnamed *mitteleuropäisch* country, is a topical conflation of events in Austria in which internal broadcast propaganda played a major role, assisted by Goebbels' prior invasion of the country's ether: firstly, the attempted *Putsch* by Austrian Nazis in July 1934, when Dollfuss was assassinated, heralded by seizure of the Vienna radio station; secondly, the *Anschluss* of March 1938, when his successor Schuschnigg tried to forestall another coup by broadcasting a call for a plebiscite. This led to his replacement by the pro-Nazi Seyss-Inquart, who used the medium to invite the Wehrmacht into Austria, allegedly to save it from a Communist uprising. Since the chancellorships of both Dollfuss and Schuschnigg were themselves already progressive stages in clerical dictatorship, the liberal professor is also an hypothesis about a Britain under threat from external and internal authoritarianism. Symbolically, in Chapter IX, 'The Broadcast', as the professor thinks he is using the intellectual clarity and reach of wireless to safeguard democracy – 'in hundreds of thousands of homes families were gathering around radio sets in large or small rooms, staring at the instruments, whether home-made or expensively manufactured, as though those arrangements of wood, glass and wire were oracles, gods, or idols' – National Legion chief, Colonel Grimm, jams his speech and hijacks its key terms: ' "The Interim Government offers you three things, Peace, Discipline, and absolutely Fair Play." '[58] The professor's understanding of radio's psychological impact demonstrates the vulnerability of Reithian principles:

> when the person of the speaker was invisible all inessentials and vulgarities were removed and the path of communication from mind to mind was clear. On the one hand the speaker could not bolster up a bad argument by a display of histrionics, and on the other hand the audience were not as a rule subject to those irrational storms of irrelevant emotion that so often overwhelm people when they are gathered together under one roof in a public meeting. (pp. 185–6)

Ironically, the professor is soon fleeing from the irrational mob stirred up by Grimm. Appropriately, CBS's William L. Shirer reported that after capturing Schuschnigg, the Nazis tortured him 'by keeping the radio in his room on night and day'.[59]

As Ernest H. Robinson wrote in his *Broadcasting and a Changing Civilisation* (1935) 'Naturalness must be simulated by methods which are really unnatural. The successful speaker before the microphone must be a master of voice production and elocution.'[60] Advised by the chief announcer that ' "Above all ... a good presence is essential" ' The Professor employs the 'cool and level' voice of the 'lecture room' (p. 188). But radio was used more successfully for broadcasting a whole gamut of more emotive 'absent presences' in the thirties, from Baldwin's gentleman-farmerly reassurance and

Roosevelt's cosy 'fireside talks' with the American nation, to Hitler and Mussolini's manic manifestations. In Auden and Isherwood's *On the Frontier* this is parodied in a séance – ' "Mrs Veigal says it was perfectly wonderful. She could hear Bob's voice just as if he were in the room." ' A warning about delusions by 'an evil spirit' is, tellingly, ignored (p. 165).

Writers increasingly felt totalitarian networks did not give access to reality, so much as construct mutually exclusive versions of it. In *On the Frontier*, the border splitting the Ostnian–Westland set is dominated by portraits of the Leader on one side, the King on the other – a visual embodiment of Orwell's paradox that modern communications shrank geographical distances between nations while simultaneously expanding ideological ones.[61] The wireless sets beneath give complementary half-accounts of the same atrocity:

> WESTLAND RADIO. Maria Kinderheim, the six-year-old child injured in the bomb outrage at the Iron Bridge, died in hospital this evening. This brings the number of the Westland dead up to nineteen.
> OSTNIAN RADIO. Peter Vollard, the eighty-year-old labourer injured in the bomb outrage at the iron bridge died in hospital this evening. This brings the number of Ostnian dead up to twenty. (p. 142)

Eventually, the antagonistic radio rhetoric of respective heads of state fatally interlocks, as Cunningham puts it, in 'the same warmongering direction'.[62] No wonder the Chorus warns broadcast voices ' "commit treason/ Against all truth and reason/ Using an unreal aggression/ To blind you to your real oppression;/ Truth is elsewhere./ Understand the motive, penetrate the lie/ Or you will die" ', insisting news presentation is informed by, and on behalf of, fatally unrepresentative interests (pp. 147–8 and 153).

Broadcasting also inevitably shaped writers' forebodings about the cultural effects of the forthcoming war. In MacNeice's *Autumn Journal* VII, the radio mingles with the Chekhovian sounds of anti-aircraft preparations:

> Hitler yells on the wireless.
> The night is damp and still
> And I hear dull blows on wood outside my window:
> They are cutting down the trees on Primrose Hill.

MacNeice expressed their common fear that the British media would be subjected to the kind of *Gleichschaltung* ('forcing into line') imposed in Germany, destroying the minimal freedoms writers' qualified support for the British war effort was intended to defend, in the interests of 'official' truth: 'And must, in order to beat/ The enemy, model ourselves upon the enemy,/ A howling radio for our paraclete' (*Collected Poems*, pp. 113–14). Such fears proved exaggerated, but the very real and complex pressures of wartime expediencies (both from the MoI, and from the internal self-censorship of writers themselves) on the radio involvements of MacNeice and others will be discussed in detail in Chapter 4.

THE CINEMA

In 1937 Greene wrote that statistics for film-audiences dwarfed the mass-circulation of the *Daily Express*: 'The voice of Mr Paul Muni has been heard by more people than the radio voices of the dictators' ('Ideas in the Cinema' repr. in *Reflections*, pp. 48–9). Similarly, Priestley's *English Journey* concluded: 'Soon we shall be as badly off as America, where I could find myself in large cities which had not a single living actor performing in them, nothing but films, films, films. There a whole generation has grown up that associates entertainment with moving pictures and with nothing else' (p. 118).

MacNeice's *Autumn Journal* XXIV granted film's virtual idols equal status with major thinkers as influences over the history of the time: 'Sleep quietly, Marx and Freud,/ The figure-heads of our transition. / Cagney, Lombard, Bing and Garbo,/ Sleep in your world of celluloid' (*Collected Poems*, pp. 151–2). In Greene's *It's a Battlefield*, Central London grinds to a halt because '"This is a State occasion. The Queen's going to a talkie."' After she's gone in, 'It was like the end of the two minutes' silence on Armistice Day', another key 'ceremony of the air', as we have seen (IAB, p. 106). Cinema, for these and many other reasons, was undoubtedly the new medium which obsessed thirties writers most, drawing both their most concentrated enthusiasm and flak. *Brave New World* set a pattern for refractions of cinema's ideological manipulativeness and the anaesthetic tendencies of the mass media in general. The *hypnopaedia* of Huxley's dystopia was reinforced by the 'feelies', emphasising the vicariousness and fetishism of consumer response to the potentials of virtual-reality technology:

The house lights went down; fiery letters stood out solid and as though self-supported in the darkness. THREE WEEKS IN A HELICOPTER. AN ALL-SUPER-SINGING, SYNTHETIC-TALKING. COLOURED, STEREOSCOPIC FEELY, WITH SYN-CHRONISED SCENT-ORGAN ACCOMPANIMENT.

'Take hold of those metal knobs on the arms of your chair,' whispered Lenina. 'Otherwise you won't get any of the feely effects.'

The Savage did as he was told.

Those fiery letters, meanwhile, had disappeared; there were ten seconds of complete darkness; then suddenly, dazzling and incomparably more solid-looking than they would have seemed in actual flesh and blood, far more real than reality, there stood the stereoscopic images, locked in one another's arms . . . 'Aa-aah. Ooh-ah! Ooh-ah!' the stereoscopic lips came together again, and once more the facial erogenous zones of the six thousand spectators in the Alhambra tingled with almost intolerable galvanic pleasure.[63]

Winifred Holtby's *Mandoa, Mandoa!* (1933) quickly reversed Huxley's scenario, bringing the movies to the 'savage'. This black comedy of cultural dislocation also satirises 'advanced society': the tribal leader's infatuation with technology, especially cinema, questions its benefits to Westerners, since the screen's sensual paradise is no more authentic for them than for Safi Talal who takes it literally: 'He was homesick for a civilisation that he had never known.'[64] The remote Mandoans capture a Hollywood location-unit making *The Siren of the Swamps*. Forced to surrender their apparatus as ransom, they grant Mandoans and their slaves 'the inestimable benefit of the Talkies.' Modernity is consequently mediated to Mandoans entirely through the specimen reels *Hollywood Parade, Diamond-set Divorce, College Girls Must Love* and *Red Hot Momma*. They are the ideal audience because they can relate what they see to experience even less critically than Western audiences: 'They sat in composed and dignified acquiescence, sucking in pleasure, accepting novelty, disconcerted neither by magic nor mechanics' (pp. 23 and 153). Movie culture rapidly colonises them: every village boy wise-cracks in 'the best Chicago *patois*'; sacred processions reverently chant "'Oh, Dinah!/ You're the belle of Carolina!/ There's not a girl that's finer!/ Sure thing'"; Gish and Pickford are, literally, deified (pp. 24 and 39). Most ironically, the civilising intentions of Western missionaries are baulked because Talal's slave-owner's vision of Mandoa's future is only too compatible with the dystopian possibilities of Western culture. He prefers the sinister futurism of Fritz Lang's *Metropolis*, to the West's official ideals, for his Brave New World.

In his essays, Huxley suggested the movies' tranquilising project was consciously orchestrated. 'Dreamland', the name of a Margate picture palace, 'implied a whole social programme, a complete theory of art', so that cinema now replaced religion as 'the opium of the people'. Hollywood represented the 'Fordisation' of images. Its cult of the rich, glamorous and powerful furnished 'imaginary compensations' for 'poverty and social insignificance': 'Hence those Don Juans, those melting beauties, those innocent young kittens, those beautifully brutal boys, those lascivious adventuresses.'[65] Huxley's cue was eagerly followed by Marxist theorists who diagnosed popular cinema as the inevitable pseudo-culture of commodity-production, alienating artists and consumers alike. Thus Christopher Caudwell in *Illusion and Reality* (1937):

> Because art's rôle is now that of adapting the multitude to the dead mechanical existence of capitalist production, in which work sucks them of their vital energies without awakening their instincts, where leisure becomes a time to deaden the mind with the easy phantasy of films, simple wish-fulfilment writing, or music that is mere emotional massage – because of this the paid craft of writer becomes as tedious and wearisome as that of machine-minder. Journalism becomes the characteristic product of the age. Films, the novel and painting all share in the degradation.[66]

Cinema was likewise refracted as a new opiate for the people in poems such as Auden's 'A Communist to Others' (1932):

> Brothers, who when the sirens roar
> From office shop and factory pour
> 'Neath evening sky;
> By cops directed to the fug
> Of talkie-houses for a drug
> Or down canals to find a hug
> Until you die . . .
>   (*English Auden*, pp. 120–2, p. 120)

Even Dylan Thomas, more surrealist than socialist, joined the chorus. Vicariousness and the phantasmic distort desire in 'Our Eunuch Dreams':

In this our age the gunman and his moll,
Two one-dimensioned ghosts, love on a reel,
Strange to our solid eye.
And speak their midnight nothings as they swell;
When cameras shut they hurry to their hole
Down in the yard of day.

They dance between their arclamps and our skull.
Impose their shots, throwing the nights away;
We watch the show of shadows kiss or kill.
Flavoured of celluloid give love the lie.[67]

Calder-Marshall's contribution to *The Mind in Chains*, on 'The Film Industry', drawing on his own experience as a reader for MGM, argued that, like tabloid newspapers, 'films are made by the very rich to be shown to the very poor . . . celluloid now gives them the relief from present trouble and the resignation to future servitude that they got formerly from the Bible and the confessional'. He wrote elsewhere, though, that the movies were a symptom, not cause of a social reality where the majority 'are so downtrodden and depressed that any happiness they achieve must take the form of fantasy'.[68] Any pretension by Hollywood to be dealing with real-life problems resulted in escapism more insidious than Disney or the Marx Brothers. *Mr Deeds Goes to Town* (1936) collapsed economic into moral questions, and moral questions into heroic 'personality' in a typical distraction strategy: 'the individual is used to plead the general case specially. This tendency, implicit in the capitalist approach to social questions, has led to the star-system . . . the interest shifts even from the individual portrayed, to the individual portraying.'[69]

But the sheer size of cinema's audience posed an almost insuperable challenge to the relevance and modernity of Leftists' writing. Victor Small in *Left Review* felt they had to begin by facing up to apparent audience indifference to the lack of relevance in what was watched:

[N]o one is less interested in the fate of what might well be a social asset than the eighteen millions of British citizens who pour their odd cash into cinema box offices each week. Let us be quite clear on this: the extent to which a product supplies or creates a social demand affects any criticism of that product . . . it would seem our film companies will never touch subjects of social significance.[70]

One way writers rose to this challenge was by becoming professional film critics, as, most notably, in Greene's case. As David Parkinson argues, Greene's first juvenile movie article in the *Oxford Outlook* (February 1925) already displays preoccupations that would recur throughout the 1930s: the comparison of cinema with the Elizabethan stage, belief that aesthetics and popularity were not inimical, an attack on sexual censorship. (See *Mornings in the Dark*, pp. xiii and 385–6.) In his first notice, 'At the Super-Cinema', which appeared in June, he began theorising 'poetic cinema's' responsibility to the real. (See *Mornings in the Dark*, pp. 3–4.) John Grierson considered Greene 'the best critic we had', precisely because of his rigorous scrutiny of its aesthetic potentials and ethical entailments.[71] Alternatively, Greene considered the typical reviewer's discourse as self-publicisation for the industry:

> One day he is required to write a fulsome interview with a visiting star at the Savoy, the next to criticise a film in which she appears. The double role is too much for the reviewer, and his criticism reads like an extended interview, gossiping little paragraphs about the stars, an inaccurate sketch of the story, no mention of the director unless he is, like Capra or Clair, world-famous, and no mention at all of the film as a film, that is to say, sequences of photographs arranged in a certain way so as to get a certain effect. (*Sight and Sound*, Autumn 1936; *Reflections*, p. 44)

As early as 1929, Greene, like Benjamin, identified economics as the chief brake on film's potentials. By the time artists awoke to them, 'a great barrier of financial success had been erected', reversing the normal history of an art form's evolution (*The Times*, 19 March 1929; *Mornings in the Dark*, p. 395.). Greene's reviews attempted to determine what cinema's lost 'first principles' might be. For the purpose, he reformulated Ford Madox Ford's literary distinction between serious novels and 'nuvvels', because of the 'parallels between the flat, easy photography' and popular prose style, which wasted countless feet or pages without picking 'out of the mass the sharp detail that puts the characters in *our* world.' Such movies weren't films, he argued but " 'pictures", one picture after another.' (*Spectator*, 26 July 1935; *Mornings in the Dark*, p. 12).

A passionate reader of *Close-Up* and especially Pudovkin's articles on montage,[72] Greene did a four-and-a-half-year stint reviewing for the *Spectator* (July 1935–May 1937 and again June 1938–March 1940) and for the short-lived *Night and Day* (July–December 1937). His attitude to the industry's volume output was scathing. In his first eleven months' *Spectator* reviewing, out of a gross of films, 'only 13 conveyed any kind of aesthetic experience and another 48 were reasonably entertaining: the other 63 films were trash' (*Mornings in the Dark*, p. 108).

Like Calder-Marshall, Greene derided openly escapist products less than those screening ideological agendas behind alibis of historical credibility: 'The thirties . . . were a period of "respectable" film biographies – Rhodes, Zola, Pasteur, Parnell and the like – and of historical romances which only came to a certain comic life in the hands of Cecil B. de Mille . . . I preferred the Westerns, the crime films, the farces, the frankly commercial.'[73] He also felt 'pure entertainment' was often as not, pure consumerist hype. *The Great Ziegfeld* hoved irrelevantly into view like an over-inflated advertising blimp (see *Spectator*, 18 September 1936; *Mornings in the Dark*, p. 139). But, conversely, Greene was no high-cultural snob and probably went further than virtually any other left-leaning commentator down the popularising road: the cinema's mass-appeal had to be treated 'as a virtue' ('Subjects and Stories' (1938); *Reflections*, p. 63).[74]

In effect, much of Greene's writing was taken up with squaring this post-Leavisian circle. He believed cinema held the key to a literary form that would be both representative of the political interests of ordinary people and be representative of popular tastes in a way that the novel had long ceased to do:

> Mr Priestley or Mr Brett Young represent the people about as much as do the prosperous suburbs of Balham and Streatham . . . *The Texas Rangers* is nearer to popular art than *Anna Karenina*. I admire a film like *Song of Ceylon* more perhaps than anything else I have seen on the screen, but I would rather see the public shouting and hissing in the sixpenny seats. (*Reflections*, p. 46)

If the standard of what passed for popular cinema was aesthetically unworthy, its morality was unedifying, ironically, *because* it was so impeccable: 'the huge public has been trained to expect a villain and a hero . . . it's no good thinking of drama as the conflict of ideas: it's the conflict – in terms of sub-machine-guns – between the plainest Good and the plainest Evil' (*Reflections*, pp. 48–9). Though he despised glib sentiment ('Handkerchiefs pushed up through the dark all round me like mushrooms in a cellar') (*Spectator*, 20 September 1935; *Mornings in the Dark*, p. 30). Greene denied emotional excitement would always take audiences away from depressing political realities into a world of wish-fulfilments, because 'if you excite your audience first, you can put over what you will of horror, suffering truth' (*Reflections*, p. 65). His aspiration, then, was to find, or perhaps become, the 'Dickens of the screen' who could do it (*Mornings in the Dark*, p. 513). However, BBFC policy meant in practice that serious subjects could not be given popular treatment at all, let alone from a radical perspective:

> We cannot treat Human Justice truthfully as America treated it in
> *I am a fugitive from a Chain Gang*. No film which held the provin-
> cial J.P.'s up to criticism or which described the conditions in the
> punishment cells at Maidstone would be allowed. Nor is it pos-
> sible to treat seriously a religious or political subject. (*Reflections*,
> pp. 66–7)[75]

Greene also realised that, paradoxically, the spell of licensed movies was largely libidinal. Hints in his novel *The Confidential Agent* (1939) came closer to the truth of their institutionalised ambiguity than the hard-core blatancy of Huxley's 'Feelies':

> 'You seem to see a lot of Emily.'
> He blushed. He said, 'Oh, we're good friends. We're both
> Groupers, you see.'
> 'Gropers?'
> 'No, no, Groupers, Oxford Groupers.'
> 'Oh yes,' Rose said, 'I know – house parties, Brown's Hotel,
> Crowborough . . .'
> . . . .
> Fortescue brightened. His old-young face was like a wide white
> screen on which you could project only selected and well-censored
> films for the family circle.[76]

Mainstream cinema provided a publicly acceptable face for pruri-ence, a 'screen' for entertaining forbidden thoughts, as in Freud's definition of censorship, not for suppressing them as such. This double-standard was also personified by Holtby in Mrs Brimsley, of *South Riding*, watching 'the big romance':

> Lovely she thought it. It filled her with vague longings. She looked at the languishing lady on the screen and saw sinuous movements, hips slim as a whiting's, wet dark lips and lashes luxuriant as goose-grass in a hedge bottom. She thought: I'm a back number. Nobody wants me. The boys are sick of me. She remembered her square uncompromising reflection in the polished mirror above her chest of drawers.
>
> The star on the sofa lent back to receive her lover's passionate embrace.
>
> Well now, that's not what I call nice, criticised Mrs Brimsley. If I caught one of my girls carrying on like that, I know what I'd do to her. (pp. 396–7)

Mrs Coney in *It's a Battlefield* is similarly both scandalised and tittilated: 'They brought great noisy cameras and told me to speak to them. They said they were going to put me on the films.' Mrs Coney said with pale astonishment, thinking of campuses and cocktail parties and orgies in Imperial Rome' (p. 96).

Consequently, Greene fought a running battle against the BBFC's Victorian hypocrisy. Reminding his readers that they had tried to classify Disney's *Snow White* for adults only, he declared it long overdue 'that this absurd committee of elderly men and spinsters . . . was laughed out of existence' (*Spectator*, 9 February 1940; *Mornings in the Dark*, p. 371). Greene had earlier fallen foul of the system himself by trying to point out that the movies could pander to the most dubious forms of sexuality under their alibi of certified innocence. As his own editor on *Night and Day*, he didn't pull punches. The result was the infamous case against his *Wee Willie Winkie* review. The prosecution reduce Greene's psychological point to the crass allegation 'I had accused Twentieth Century-Fox of "procuring" Miss Temple "for immoral purposes"', and the judgement upheld the BBFC definition of censorship, not Freud's: 'The fact that the film had already been licensed for universal exhibition refuted the charges which had been made in the article.'[77] The case may not have been a concerted plot by the industry to shut him up, although Twentieth Century-Fox did menace *The Spectator* not to re-employ him. (See *Mornings in the Dark*, p. 554.) A sidelight on the ethos of the case occurs in Blumenfeld's *Jew Boy*. Frustrated Alec expressly *wants* cinema to sublimate his libido, deliberately choosing the most grimly respectable programme. But the dimmed environment seems charged with inescapable eroticism. Even Disney's Minnie Mouse becomes suggestive with her 'long legs in the thick high-heeled shoes and the absurd little lace-trimmed drawers', while the improving documentary is full of soft-porn close-ups of barebreasted natives (pp. 100–1).

Perhaps the movies' most potent cocktail mixed sex with success. *The Confidential Agent* showed its recipe for mixing libidinal displacement with socio-economic wish-fulfilment:

> It was a musical play full of curious sacrifice and suffering: a starving producer and a blonde girl who had made good . . . everybody's name went up in neon lights – the producer's too: the girl's, of course, was there from the first. There was a lot of suffering – gelatine tears pouring down the big blonde features – and a lot of happiness. It was curious and pathetic; everybody behaved nobly and made a lot of money. . . . He felt her hand rest on his knee. She wasn't romantic, she had said; this was an automatic reaction, he supposed, to the deep seats and the dim lights and the torch songs, as when Pavlov's dogs salivered. It was a reaction that went through all social levels like hunger. . . . (pp. 64–5)[78]

In Anthony Powell's *Agents and Patients* this Pavlovian reaction causes gormless Blore-Smith to disgrace himself with an unwelcome pass: 'all at once his feelings for Sarah became clear to him. It was a revelation. Something transcendental.'[79]

Movie seductiveness worked on a split-subject. As Miles and Smith put it, such transference 'involves a complex psychological paradox, the voyeuristic pleasure of looking combining with the narcissistic pleasure of looking at oneself'.[80] In Isherwood's *Goodbye to Berlin* (1939), only between star-struck affairs does Sally appreciate the irony of this: 'they were showing a film about a girl who sacrificed her stage career for the sake of a Great Love, Home and Children. We laughed so much that we had to leave before the end.' But Hollywood glamour later provides a literal alibi for conartist, 'George P Sandars' – " 'He said they were looking out for an English actress who spoke German to act in a comedy film they were going to shoot on the Italian Riviera." ' He literally seduces Sally with the auto-suggestiveness of movie culture: " 'I suppose they *could* have been things he'd read in fan magazines, but some-how I'm pretty sure they weren't" '.[81]

Elizabeth Bowen's account of star-gazing was more first-hand and sympathetic, perhaps because it wasn't inhibited by a stand-ardised political response. She knew it appealed to a contradiction in herself, but felt *consciously* giving in to erotic fantasy did not threaten her intellectual judgement. It was

> A sort of sensuous gloss: I know it to be synthetic, but it affects me strongly. It is a trick knowingly practised on my most fuzzy desires: it steals a march on me on my silliest side. But all the same, in being subject to glamour I experience a sort of elevation. It brings, if not into life at least parallel to it, a sort of fairy-tale element. It is a sort of trumpet call, mobilising the sleepy fancy.

She saw nothing unhealthy in vicarious contact with the object of desire: 'I enjoy sitting opposite him or her, the delights of intimacy without the onus, high points of possession without the strain. This could be called inoperative love.'[82]

The increasingly baroque luxuriousness of the dream-palace chain styles were architectural extensions of movie escapism, as in *The Confidential Agent*: 'They sat for nearly three hours in a kind of palace – gold-winged figures, deep carpets and an endless supply of refreshments carried round by girls got up to kill' (p. 64). Sim-ilarly, in *South Riding*, Lily Sawdon slips into sensual reverie by internalising the opulence of the cinema tea-room:

> Marble pillars swelled into branching archways. Painted cupids billowed across the ceiling. Waitresses in green taffeta tripped between the tables; from some hidden source a fountain of music throbbed and quivered. . . . The beautiful Blue Danube. She used to waltz to that with Tom when she was courting. A lovely waltz. Their bodies melted together. One will, one impulse moved them. She lay back in her chair. It was richly padded. The tea was good. The toast was hot, dripping with butter. (pp. 257–8)

Again Bowen was unusual among writers for objectifying her own, rather than an unsophisticated character's, hedonistic pleasure in the whole cinema-going rite:

> like a chocolate-box lid, the entrance is still voluptuously pro-mising: sensation of some sort seems to be guaranteed. How

happily I tread the pneumatic carpet, traverse ante-rooms with their exciting muted vibration, and walk down the spotlit aisle with its eager tilt to the screen. I climb over those knees to the sticky velvet seat, and fumble my cigarettes out.[83]

Surprisingly, Stanton Griffis, chairman of Paramount, agreed with Calder-Marshall that the workers' celluloid habit was not so much a cause as a symptom of their social conditions, when interviewed by John Danvers Williams: 'Men and women, working all day at machines and ledgers, find the superficial entertainment created by Hollywood a very necessary antidote – a means of helping them to forget the boredom of their lives.'[84] MacNeice's *Autumn Journal* XVII encapsulated how this 'antidote' worked on the dispossessed:

The luxury life is only to be valued
By those who are short of money or pressed for time
As the cinema gives the poor their Jacob's Ladder
For Cinderellas to climb.
(Collected Poems, p. 135)

The top rung of the ladder was Hollywood's myth of itself, as projected in self-reflexive features about ascent to stardom. MacNeice pointed out in *Zoo* (1938) that this was a particularly widespread form of media-encagement:

The Zoo . . . bristles with pathetic fallacies and false analogies. One never goes . . . without hearing someone say that something is almost human. . . . I think that many of the two million do feel themselves at home there – just as they feel themselves at home in the bedroom of Loretta Young or the racing car of James Cagney or a Shanghai Express or a garden of Allah or a Lost Horizon.

Although MacNeice, like Bowen, wasn't too politically correct to admit being an inmate himself: 'I get from the Zoo a pleasure not essentially different in kind from what I get when going to sports or to the movies.'[85] The line he took in 'Ode' (1934) on the 'frivolous nostalgia/ . . . film-fans feel/For their celluloid abstractions', as a purely imaginary home-sickness, diverting their potential for more critical else-awareness, softened as the thirties went on (*Collected Poems*, p. 54). Sasha in Jean Rhys's *Good Morning Midnight* (1939) warns 'For God's sake watch out for your film mind' and Anna in her *Voyage in the Dark* (1934) stands out from the film-minded crowd by finding the delinquent femininity of the villainness 'Three-Fingered Kate' an uplifting rôle model.[86] But although many Leftists believed cinema posed as a kind of counterfeit, collective uncon-scious, few went as far as MacNeice, in admitting they had film-minds of their own and acknowledging empathy with the 'frivolity' of the masses:

> Four or five times a week we went to the cinema, going solely for entertainment and never for value, holding hands like a shopgirl with her boy-friend. The organist would come up through the floor, a purple spotlight on his brilliantined head, and play us the 'Londonderry Air' and bow and go back to the tomb. Then the stars would return close-up and the huge Cupid's bows of their mouths would swallow up everybody's troubles – there were no more offices or factories or shops, no more bosses or foremen, no more unemployment and no more employment, no more danger of disease or babies, nothing but bliss in a celluloid world where the roses are always red and the Danube is always blue.[87]

MacNeice was also aware, as he admitted in a December 1937 BBC talk, that it was the socialisation of the bourgeois male Leftist that, ironically, prevented him admitting 'he is merely a bit of the crowd: the crowd are always the other people'. Intellectual con-tempt for mass-modes of consumption, while it drew sanction from anti-capitalist credentials, was uncomfortably close to more con-ventional kinds of snobbery. MacNeice's charlady 'who never went to the excellent suburban cinema at her door, but always took half-an-hour's tram ride to the centre of the town – to see exactly the same film in an almost identical cinema – because, she said, there was much more class in the audience' – was comparable to the radical film-society buff, who 'goes to the pictures – not that he *calls* them the pictures – for the ideas and the photography, particularly in films German or Russian'.[88]

MacNeice's own sense of the potential of British popular features is summed up with Auden in the 'Last Will and Testament' section of *Letters from Iceland* (1938). While mocking insincerity and avoid-ance of controversial topics, they saluted artistry where it was due and sympathised with both *émigré* and British-born directors' frus-trations in the face of the industry's restrictions:

We hope one honest conviction may at last be found
For Alexander Korda and the Balcon boys
And the Stavisky Scandal in pictures and sound

We leave to Alfred Hitchcock with sincerest praise
Of *Sabotage*. To Berthold Viertel just the script
For which he's waited all his passionate days.[89]

Writers prepared to experience popular features unprejudicially were more sympathetic and penetrating about ordinary filmgoers' responses and came closer to formulating that all-important concept of pleasure, so conspicuously and puritanically neglected by Leftist intellectuals at the time. Bowen, for example, treated the predominantly female audience with a respect lacking among her male contemporaries which suggested a misogynistic, as well as class, tendency in their highmindedness. 'In Why I Go to the Cinema', she listed her own reasons as 'wish to escape, lassitude, sense of lack in my nature or my surroundings, loneliness (however passing) and natural frivolity'. Writers were not disembodied Olympians, she insisted; they needed relief from work that was just as exhausting as more humdrum occupations: 'my reasons for cinema-going are not unique or special: they would not be interesting if they were . . . like everyone else. I slough off my preoccupations there. . . . I judge the film as I judge the bottle of wine, in its relation to myself, by what it does to me.'[90] Tastes and IQs might differ, but the objective – pleasure – was the same. She relished immersion in the crowd and its communicated sensations. Beneath her flip tone was a sketchy but serious attempt to explore cinema's complex appeal and the diverse, socially-situated needs of its consumers, matched at the time only by Mass-Observation's research on Bolton's cinema audiences and anticipating the inclusive models of postwar Cultural Studies: 'To reject as any kind of experience a film that is acting powerfully on people round seems to me to argue a poverty in the nature. What falls short as aesthetic experience may do as human experience: the film rings no bell in oneself, but one hears a bell ring elsewhere.' Bowen was capable of broaching the question the other way round. The motivations behind the revulsion of politically-aware intellectuals were also, 'complex and interesting'.[91]

Another *Footnotes* contributor, Sidney L. Bernstein, showed greater confidence in the maturity of taste and judgement among ordinary people than either the BBFC or many Leftist commentators. They were emphatically *not* a monolithic, undiscriminating mass. The genuine film fan was

> the graduate, as it were, of the picture-going school. His critical faculty is developing, he can distinguish between good and bad photography and knows something of the technique of film-making. Sometimes he can even differentiate between the good and bad acting of his favourite stars. He is acquiring some degree of articulateness in the correspondence columns of his fan magazines and is eager for pertinent information.
>
> The film-fan is not to be confused with the hero-worshipper, who is completely 'gaga' in his appreciation.... His interest is not critical. His approach to the film is one of identification.[92]

Bowen and Bernstein suggested individuals did not necessarily compliantly occupy 'subject positions' constructed by film-makers. They might occupy them critically, or even a plurality of overlapping and contradictory positions.

Some Leftists would eventually plunder their own 'film minds' to write commercial scripts (with or without thought about politico-cultural circle-squaring, as we shall see in Chapter 4). For example, 'the Danube is always blue,' even during the Vienna Uprising, in Isherwood's confessional novel, *Prater Violet* (1946), though his actual thirties scripting was by no means as tacky as its fictional counterpart. Similarly, Gordon Comstock in *Keep the Aspidistra Flying*, the jaundiced poet *manqué*, is an indirect admission even the austere Orwell felt the cravings features assuaged:

> He yearned to go inside, not for Greta's sake, but just for the warmth and the softness of the velvet seat. He hated the pictures, of course, seldom went there even when he could afford it. Why encourage the art that is destined to replace literature? But still, there is a kind of soggy attraction about it. To sit on the padded seat in the warm smoke-scented darkness, letting the flickering drivel on the screen gradually overwhelm you – feeling the waves of its silliness lap you round till you seem to drown, intoxicated, in a viscous sea – after all, it's the kind of drug we need. The right drug for friendless people.[93]

It was a sign of the times that E. W. Bakke's classic study, *The Unemployed Man* (1933), took into account the effects of cinema culture on the jobless. One of them told him, 'The pictures help you live in another world for a little while. I almost feel I'm in the picture.'[94] Blumenfeld's *Jew Boy* depicts the acting-out of a once-a-week fantasy to sustain you through the rest as a well-established tradition in the working-class. At the Contessa ballroom, Alec encounters youngsters from the sweat-shop: 'Couples pushed past him unceremoniously, Clark Gables, and Marlene Dietriches, and Tallulah Bankheads', and nostalgises, 'In his day, the boys had all been Valentino's, with sleeked hair, and centre partings, and long sideburns' (p. 171). In *The Road to Wigan Pier* (1937), Orwell was in a better-informed position to sympathise with how and why the system's casualties imagined themselves as its ideal beneficiaries: 'You can always get a seat for fourpence, and at the matinée at some houses you can even get a seat for twopence. Even people on the verge of starvation will readily pay twopence to get out of the ghastly cold of a winter afternoon.' After the show, Wiganites understudied the stars on their own internal screens: 'You may have three halfpence in your pocket and not a prospect in the world, and only a corner of a leaky bedroom to go home to: but in your new clothes you can stand on the street corner, indulging in a private daydream of yourself as Clark Gable or Greta Garbo, which compensates you for a great deal.'[95]

The most deprived districts of Britain had the highest concentration of cinemas and most frequent cinemagoers. However, as Miles and Smith point out, 'The success of Hollywood, in fact, rested on the successful disguise of its motivating ideology', as opposed to the cruder integration propaganda of the British film industry.[96] The star-system inevitably seemed fairer and more democratic than the class-system, which had reasserted its linguistic stigma on the soundtrack. Greene found it almost scuppered the casting of his first practical involvement (*The Green Cockatoo*) in 1936 when he tried to depict the British underworld. Even actors 'with appallingly tough faces' all had Oxford accents. (See *Mornings in the Dark*, pp. xxxv–vi.) While the myth of log-cabin-to-White-House individualism made American conservatism dynamic, the snobbery of British movies often cost them the minimal saving graces of foreign features, according to Greene. Even the 'low life' in Hitchcock's innovative crime films were portrayed 'with the "amused" collector's air of a specialist in sensation', while the worst French films were relatively class-free and 'the cafés and the dance-halls are of the kind familiar to the majority of the audience' (*Spectator*, 6 December 1935; *Mornings in the Dark*, pp. 52–3).

Rare serious attempts to examine the media's construction of actuality, like *Sensation*, the story of a village murder exploited by a swarm of Fleet Street locusts, were themselves, ironically, infected by the 'curious air of unreality' endemic to home-produced features (5 February 1937; *Mornings in the Dark*, p. 172). Bowen shared Greene's views about their movies' social and historical unrepresentativeness: 'All over this country, indoors and out, a photographable drama of national temperament is going on, and every object has character.' The immense diversity of rural and industrial culture was reduced to a clutch of 'little Englandland' clichés: Westminster Bridge, gables and oak beams, Oxford Colleges 'drearily reappear to give English films their locality'.[97] What was true of locality was also true of social types, reducible, according to proletarian playwright Ewan MacColl, to 'inane caperings of actors got up to look like butlers disguised as Claude Hulbert or Jack Buchanan' or 'leading ladies who delivered their lines like well-brought-up children intent on pleasing nanny'.[98]

British film-making also suffered from Hollywood's homogenising effect on the world market, which overrode lived cultural and historical differences between the identities of national audiences. Alternatively Greene hoped for a 'national public' for British features based on 'trench kinship which isn't a matter of class or education, but of living and dying together in the same hole' ('Ideas in the Cinema', *Reflections*, p. 49). His popularising ambition, was, arguably, only realised to a certain extent in the extraordinary circumstances of the Second World War, as discussed in Chapter 4.[99] The situation in thirties popular cinema largely remained as depicted in Henry Green's 1929 novel *Living*, where the movies abolish national divisions and incite social aspiration, but principally through a universalised American dream of personal gratification rather than cultural redistribution or social progress. Factory-boss's son and factory-worker share common pleasures, but also imposed ideological horizons:

A great number were in cinema, many standing, battalions were in cinemas over all the country, young Mr Dupret was in a cinema, over above up into the sky their feeling panted up supported by each other's feelings, away, away, Europe and America, mass on mass their feeling united supported, renewed their sky. (p. 59)[100]

As Tennessee Williams's *The Glass Menagerie* (1945) pointed out, movies were a dynamic medium, but kept thirties audiences still and in place: 'People go to the *movies* instead of *moving*! Hollywood characters are supposed to have all the adventures for everybody in America, while everybody in America sits in a dark room and watches them have them! Yes, until there's a war. That's when adventure becomes available to the masses!'[101]

Greene wrote that *Victoria the Great* showed not only Americans could be ignorant of British history and identity (*Sight and Sound* (Winter 1937/38); *Mornings in the Dark*, p. 426), but Hollywood was often only too eager to collaborate in the view of Englishness the establishment wanted to project. In 1933 Holtby reviewed Noël Coward's round-up for Fox Films of the twentieth century so far, *Cavalcade*, noting Hollywood's power to transfigure events into its own discourse, rendering them more emotionally intense even for those who actually experienced them and 'successfully exploiting those memories that now, after so many years, release the tears we could not shed when they were part of our lives – not shadows on the screen'. She deplored how this 'entertainment' film was billed with *Round the Empire*. Like BBC ceremonial broadcasts, the 'educational' short toured a commonwealth of peoples ' "all cherishing the same ideals" ', but not its rifts.[102] *Round the Empire* even alluded to *Cavalcade* as a patriotic dramatisation bearing out its own picture of consensus. *Cavalcade*, according to Holtby, also demonstrated how Hollywood happily endorsed native generic-social bias, if it were profitable:

> There are, apparently, two kinds of Englishmen – the Dignified Gentlepeople, whose partings and deaths and sorrows are tragic – and the natives below stairs – cooks and mothers-in-law and housemaids and the like – whose goings-on are invariably comic. When Diana Wynyard as Jane Marryot said 'Goodbye' to Clive Brook, her gallant and loving husband, we bit our lips and blinked our eyes in sympathy. When Una O'Connor as Ellen Bridges said 'Goodbye' to her equally gallant and loving husband, Alfred, we giggled in appreciative amusement . . .

The film fostered nostalgia for a Britain 'in decline'. Its representation of society was, Holtby hinted, both highly selective and somewhat at odds with Coward's sexual orientation and prior career: 'Personally, I do not really think that the Edwardian era had quite so many advantages as he believes over our present one. Nor do I think that the Cowardesque glimpses of night-club life, homosexual fondlings and twentieth-century blues with which the film ends, present an entirely adequate picture.' Holtby's last novel, the feminist panorama *South Riding* (1936) was, consequently, an attempt to dramatise the contemporary reality of mundane Britain that *Cavalcade* so glibly omitted, where anonymous lives and inconspicuous organisations continuously meshed in the vital web of local government (see Chapter 4).

Greene also noted that working people were usually represented in British features, with patronising tokenism. Though there were notable exceptions like the Lancashire farces Priestley wrote for Gracie Fields, such as *Look Up and Laugh*, which had both 'pleasant local flavour' and 'genuinely provincial' plots. Though sentimental, this comedy in which Gracie saves local market stallholders from both chain-store and local bureaucrats was distinguished by a sense that Priestley's 'observation and experience, as well as his invention, has gone into its making' (*Spectator*, 9 August 1935; *Mornings in the Dark*, p. 17). However, that 'one ray of hope' had been captured and formulated by *Shipyard Sally* which superimposed Gracie's features carolling 'Land of Hope and Glory' over a launching by the Queen, confusing values and making the liner 'the background to the face'. Greene concluded that all Fields's pictures seemed 'designed to show a sympathy with the working class and an ability to appeal to the best circles', eradicating unemployment and industrial unrest with sentimental songs and keeping dividends 'safe for democracy' (*Spectator*, 18 August 1939; *Mornings in the Dark*, pp. 321–2).

Greene's hunch that Fields's increasingly fairytale roles were actually at the heart of Depression politics, was confirmed by her newsreel appearances as star guest opening new factories, etc, but this was only part of the greater intertextual pattern. As Miles and Smith put it, 'escapism had a distinct habit of re-appearing as realism: "stars" were also "news". The ephemera of cinema culture, with movie magazines contending that stars were the same people in real life . . . worked to take cinematic ideology out of the cinemas and into the streets.'[103]

Fields became Britain's highest-paid star, with ships named after her. 'Our Gracie's' wholesome 'Lancashire lass/working-class Britannia' image made her the ultimate common-denominator of the culture.[104] The opening of *Sing As We Go* (1934) shows cotton-looms suddenly grinding to a halt, after a newspaper headline announcing 'Mills Forced to Close Down'. But Gracie is determined the factory gang show will go ahead even if they have to practise in the dole queue, because 'If we can't spin, we can still sing'. Not for nothing did the title-song become Britain's anthem of the Depression (America's politically hardhitting 'Brother, Can You Spare a Dime?', on the other hand, was popularly credited with sinking the Hoover adminstration in 1932). Similarly, not for nothing did Robert Graves dub Priestley 'The Gracie Fields of Literature'.[105] Priestley's novelistic celebration of consensus-through-entertainment, *The Good Companions*, filmed in 1933, anticipated Fields's appeal, just as his patriotic wartime pastoral *Let the People Sing* showed the effect of working with her.

It's impossible to say to what extent this ex-mill girl hung on to her, actually semi-genteel, Rochdale accent and lifestyle out of egalitarian loyalty to her roots or because, in the RP-strangulated context of British talkies, they became phenomenally marketable assets (a sort of cinematic hypostasis of the Lancashire tradition of choosing a mill-operative as 'Cotton Queen'). The key to Fields's mythic status was her very ordinariness and 'naturalness', which meant her Cinderella success-story merged with the plots of her films. For her proletarian audiences, she merely appeared to be playing herself. But her endorsement of the success ethic, though 'talent' and 'hard work', as Richards points out, 'probably also explains her success with middle-class audiences, enabling her to eventually make the transition from a sectional to a national symbol' and to sustain consensus in a class-system pretending to meritocracy (tokenism, as ever, being the exception that disguises the rule).[106] Gracie's social chameleonism had become all too explicit by *Shipyard Sally*. As an affected musical-hall artiste's daughter, her accent is correspondingly RPed, although she immediately slips into Rochdale and stage-Scots to woo working-class Clydesiders. When the Slump hits, she becomes a kind of Ellen Wilkinson without the accompanying marchers, exiting with the Great War number 'Wish Me Luck as You Wave Me Goodbye'. In the course of gaining access to the head of the Committee of Enquiry to present the workers' petition, Gracie becomes an upper-class tranvestite and also impersonates an American starlet, altering accent and style to suit her circumstances. Because Lord Randall hates jazz, she finally switches to Northern Irish to win him over with 'Danny Boy'. Illusory resolution of class- and cultural-divisions this may have been, but it's cynical to blame

Fields for the needs she appealed to and soothed, though her message was undoubtedly more popular for not coming in the accents of a Government Minister: 'They've been loyal to their country and their country should be loyal to them.' Gracie's role was, specifically, as a mediator between, and reconciler of, labour and capital, magically solving unemployment in the cotton (*Sing As We Go*, 1934) and shipbuilding (*Shipyard Sally*, 1939) industries. Hence 'a potential symbol of working-class discontent was subtly subverted', with Priestley's help.[107]

Loved by the people, loathed by most intellectuals who wanted to liberate them, Fields also symbolised the virtually unbridgeable gap between radical and popular culture in the thirties. Bowen, again, showed insight into this question. According to her, it was impossible to evaluate Fields's films outside their peculiar social and cultural locality: 'I would not willingly see, for its own sake, at my nearest London cinema, a film in which she appeared. But I should feel I had missed something if I missed seeing a Gracie Fields film in the Gracie Fields country.'[108] Richards argues radicals were 'wholly out of touch with the popular mood', besides lacking either the programme or resources to take on the mainstream industry. As Peter Stead notes, the alternative film culture of the thirties was mainly limited to 'a national film institute, a network of film societies, a number of intellectual film journals, a whole tradition of documentary film-making and close links between those interested in film and educationalists, especially those engaged in adult education,' although research by Bert Hogenkamp and Stephen G. Jones has subsequently extended this to cover more radical networks like the Workers Film and Photo League.[109] However, the vivacity of Fields's films could be revealing about the truth of working-class life in ways impossible in earnest documentaries and without the puritanism that handicapped much Leftist criticism.[110]

Dialectical attempts by writers to locate and exploit progressive potentials in the popularity of working-class stars were regrettably rare, although Orwell had some interesting hunches. Richards rightly detects a parallel between the films of George Formby, Gracie's male counterpart, and Orwell's belief in the subversiveness of working-class humour.[111] Orwell even took the title for his Wigan reportage from the music-hall joke popularised by Formby's Wiganite father, but the fact that Formby's Lancashire laddish *double-entendres* could also be seen as one of the roots of today's reactionary comedy suggests a blindspot in his attempts to analyse the micropolitics of 'mass' culture. Just as Fields helped defuse class-conflicts by giving expression to discontents in such a way as to absorb them into the framework of National Government consensus, Formby's films were a celluloid saturnalia, over which George presided with all the 'certified innocence' of a BBFC licensed Lord of Misrule, packaging an otherwise unruly eroticism and verbal ambiguity in terms privileging masculine immaturity. This seems distinctly comparable to Orwell's notorious remark that the comic genius of music-hall and seaside postcards 'is entirely masculine. A woman cannot be low without being disgusting, whereas, a good male comedian can give the impression of something irredeemable and yet innocent, like a sparrow' ('The Art of Donald McGill', *Collected Essays*, II, p. 191, note). Orwell thought such gender-specific humour a necessary mechanism of resistance by what he called the 'unofficial self'. But this apparently Rabelaisian voice of the proletarian unconscious subverting the censorship of an authoritarian culture, far from being unequivocally liberating, has proved susceptible to ventriloquism. For example, the way that postwar tabloids constructed 'popular' sexuality in sexist terms exemplifies today's libidinally-saturated culture of 'bed and circuses' as Angela Carter put it.[112] However, *The Sun* and Bernard Manning were a long time off (a mutation explored in Trevor Griffiths's play *Comedians* (1977)) from Formby's early films. These were arguably potentially subversive, although as they went on, any exposure of snobbery usually managed to defuse audience resentment, by its presentation as exceptional not systemic (the standard pattern in thirties features involving class).[113] Similarly, we can't blame Orwell for not knowing Bakhtin whose concepts of carnival and dialogics, though contemporary, were only introduced to the West by Julia Kristeva in the sixties, because of their marginalisation by Soviet Socialist Realism.

The proletarian writer who got tantalisingly closest to Bakhtin's ideas, under Joyce's influence, was probably James Barke. In the Chapter of *Major Operation*, 'Red Music in the Second City', which has a particularly heteroglot style and carnivalesque subject matter, Barke asked the leading cultural question, but, unfortunately, did not fully answer it: 'Ah, Mae West! Sex! Taboo! Wonder what Mrs Bloom would have thought about Mae West? Or Mae West about Marion Bloom?' (p. 122). It was a momentary recognition that avant-garde writing and the modern popular culture epitomised by cinema could talk to each other and might have created a synthesis with the potential to truly break down social and cultural hierarchies.[114]

The equivocal possibilities of 'working-class' stars notwithstanding, it was overwhelmingly true that screen entertainment was both big business itself and made workers docile for big business in turn. In MacNeice's *Out of the Picture*, Clara de Groot rivals Mary Pickford as 'the World's Sweetheart' and sets the work-tempo of modern times:

> I should like to give my name to something.
> To have a liner called after me –
> Where in the engine-room
> The great cranks plod their Assyrian feet
> Saying Clara de Groot, 2, 3 –
>   (pp. 41 and 91)

The star-cult also ameliorates soul-destroying mass-production in *It's a Battlefield* (1934), where Greene's Battersea match-factory girls mimic their idols:

> Between the lines of machines the girls stood with tinted lips and waved hair, fluttering an eyelid, unable to talk because of the noise, thinking of boys and pictures and film stars: Norma, Greta, Marlene, Kay. Between death and disfigurement, unemployment and the streets, between the cog-wheels and the shafting, the girls stood, as the hands of the clock moved round from eight in the morning until one (milk and biscuits at eleven) and then the long drag to six.
>
> Two hundred match-boxes moved upwards to the drying-room; the hands of the clock pointed to five minutes to seven. Greta put a hand to the left. Norma a hand to the right, Marlene pressed down her foot, Kay Rimmer tried to draw her own image in the dusty stale air . . .

Although Kay goes to a Communist meeting instead of the big feature, her commitment is undermined anyway, because its romance runs in her unconscious as she flirts with a Party intellectual, 'smiling and pouting, a faint evocation of a famous film actress' (pp. 29 and 49).

When the press weren't misreporting miners, cinema was busily sublimating their discontents, as in Hanley's account in *Grey Children*:

'it was exciting, full of colour; it transported one from a kind of grey monotony to a fantastic world of make-believe, brazen and alluring, false and glittering, the whole pattern of life poles apart from that lived by the now silent onlookers of the film'. But the trick didn't always come off, as the same audience's response to a royal short showed, in the wake of the Prince of Wales's unfulfilled promise to the Rhondda that 'something must be done': 'the film brought forth a series of cat-calls and boos, the like of which I have never heard' (pp. 73–4).

Leftist poets and playwrights also attempted to demystify the movies for their audiences. Auden's 'Poem XVI' of 1933 features 'Gaumont theatres/ Where Fancy plays on hunger to produce/ The noble robber, ideal of boys' (*English Auden*, p. 142) and in *The Dog Beneath the Skin*, the Chorus re-directs the audience's distracted attention from 'the cinemas blazing with bulbs: bowers of bliss/ Where thousands are holding hands', to 'Look left' at what the movies distracted them from, 'locked sheds, wharves by water' (p. 54). Benjamin considered the movies substituted the unique aura of the person, for the 'spell of the personality, the phoney spell of a commodity'.[115] Thus 'personality' is objectified as the absurdest of fetishes in *The Dog Beneath the Skin*. 'Miss Lou Vipond' played by 'a shopwindow dummy, very beautifully dressed' and audience fantasies of reciprocal arousal exploded: ' "Goodness knows what she can see in a chap like me!" ' (pp. 141 and 137, respectively).

The Workers' Theatre Movement also lampooned this two-dimensional Land of Cockayne. Thom Thomas's 1932 piece *Their Theatre and Ours* asks 'When have you seen the workers' life, as you know it – on the stage music-halls or films?' Typical Hollywood treatment of poverty is designed to neutralise the drudge's capacity to detect economic double-standards:

GIRL: (*as film actress, runs in and flings her arm round 4th's neck*) (*in languishing tones*). Oh, I want to get away from this terrible wealth and luxury.
HE: (*nobly*) Money's never brought anyone *real* happiness.
GIRL: Oh to be poor once more, and happy, to get away from the burden of money . . .
HE: How well you understand! Let us go away together!
SHE: (*naïvely*) Do you think my husband would mind – much?
FILM DIRECTOR: (*enters*). That'll do for now, Miss Greater Garbage. And here's the cheque I promised you.

SHE: (*looks at cheque in disgust*) You're a mean skate. Mr Griffiths. Ten thousand bucks is no good to me. I'm having a midnight supper party tonight!

The gangster genre was similarly unmasked as a mere displacement of institutionalised larceny: 'GIRL: (*runs on screaming*) Oh! So it's you, the Squirt! Alias the Slosher! Alias Charlie Chaplin! Alias the Archbishop of Canterbury! Give me back my jewels and my honour!'[116]

Leftist novelists particularly wanted to detoxify working-class movie-addicts. A maid's cinematic reveries are exposed in Summerfield's *May Day* as literal parentheses in reality:

(She was young and lovely: she saw herself at the cinema, always triumphant, young and lovely, undergoing a thousand miseries and misunderstandings, but always winning the rich young man in the end, and fading out in a misty, haloed kiss and the wedding music playing. But when she came out into the open air afterwards she knew very well that the world was not so, that rich and handsome young men might look kindly on her but the embraces proferred in their eyes would bring her no triumph. She dreamed, but she also knew . . .) 'Where are you, Jean . . .' wailed the cook in a voice of despairing irritation. 'Coming,' she called back sulkily, and went downstairs. (pp. 14–15)

Barke's *Major Operation* scrutinised cinema as just one strand from the skein of pop-culture. Barke fully sympathised with alienated Scottish workers' motives for identification and escapism, but nonetheless deplored its global colonialism:

New times, new machinery. Mass production, mass culture, mass gutter journalism – what could Loch Lomond mean? The bonnie banks had had their day in the consciousness of the drawing-room ballad writers. The world isn't a drawing-room any more for the Gentlemen of Culture. But thousands haven't even a bit of a room to themselves: and the drawing-room for them is also the kitchen and the coal cellar. Holding up the corner of the street palls like any other job. A sixpence gets a packet of fags and leaves enough for a seat at the cinema. The wise-cracking of Hollywood gets into the brain and the blues rhythm gets into the blood for there's nothing else to keep them out. So America

becomes the cultural centre of the world. Even the Jap can tell
you about Charlie Chaplin and Greta Garbo. . . . And Garbo, the
Swede, is somebody, while Flora MacDonald might be a skivvy
in Milngavie. In fact that's what Flora is. (pp. 108–9)

In Greenwood's *Love on the Dole*, the unpoliticised Helen Hawkins
nevertheless spurns compensation for squalid homelife by 'shadows flickering on a screen':

> Dully, insistently, crushing came the realisation that there was no
> escape, save in dreams. All was a tangle: reality was too hideous
> to look upon: it could not be shrouded or titivated for long by the
> reading of cheap novelettes or the spectacle of films of spacious
> lives. They were only opiates and left a keener edge on hunger,
> made more loathsome reality's sores.[117]

Other proletarians created exemplary working-class characters who
controlled their celluloid habit by maintaining critical detachment.
In *Major Operation*, bourgeois adulteress Mabel Anderson is seduced
by the 'The Modern Man of Fiction: of Hollywood', but Jean, stead-
fast wife of Big Jock MacKelvie, NUWM organiser

> was not enamoured of the sophisticated love-making of the fool-
> ish Hollywood puppets. Nor did she enjoy the fantastic exploits
> of the celebrated Slim M'Gurk. But for nearly two hours she was
> able to forget she lived in Walker Street . . . able to forget its
> sounds, smells and meannesses. This constituted a break in her
> weekly darg: her seven-day battle with existence. (pp. 35 and
> 94–5)

Chris Colquohoun grasps the duplicity of Hollywood's Cinderella
myth in *Grey Granite*. Grassic Gibbon achieved a brilliantly dialogic
effect, emphasising the remoteness of Hollywood discourse from
Chris's actuality by translating it into her dialect. The feature's
heroine was a poor, but respectable New York 'lassie' who nonetheless lived

> in a place like a palace with a bath ten feet in length and three
> feet deep, and wore underclothes that she couldn't have afforded,
> some childe had paid for them on the sly. But the picture said

No, through its nose, not her, she was awful chaste but sore chased as well, a beast of a man in her office, the manager, galloping about the screen and aye wanting to seduce the lassie by night or by day.

But instead of 'taking him a crack in the jaw', she kept coming home tearfully to do a lot of undressing and bathing, though always 'hiding her breasts and bottom, fair chaste'. Predictably, virtue is rewarded with a break to stardom when she sings 'that the skies were black and she was blue, and something rhymed with that, not spew' and sending all the audience wild 'not with rage, but joy, they'd been dropped on their heads when young'. When she is apotheosised into a famous actress, 'the film did a sudden close-up of her face with a tear of gratitude two feet long trembling like a jelly from her lower eyelid' (pp. 93–4). Bernard Bergonzi calls Garbo 'a metonymic emblem of the star-system or even of the cinema itself' in the writing of the time.[118] But her cultic value gets short-shrift from Chris: 'Greena Garbage had been right fine, cuddled to death and wedded and bedded' (*Grey Granite*, p. 197).

Continental movies also drew both enthusiasm and flak from thirties writers. These could be as cynically commercial as Hollywood and Denham's blockbusters. *Agents and Patients* (1936) (for which Anthony Powell drew on his own film-scripting experiences from 1935–36) sends up the venal cosmopolitanism of Berlin's Universum Film AG (Ufa). The *Niebelheimnazionalkunstfilmgesellschaft* uses a trilingual soundtrack to clean up the market. As the hero lies dying at the mercy of the advancing cannibals:

> the German says: '*Muth verloren, alles verloren. Da wär es besser nicht geboren.*' The Frenchman says: '*J'irai loin – bien loin, comme un bohémien, par la Nature, heureux comme avec une femme.*' The Englishman says: '*Play up and play the game.*'. . . While the oncoming cannibals croon the refrain of the 'Boating Song' from the jungle, over which night is falling. (p. 122)

However, the films of European and, particularly, Russian, avant-gardists were inspirational to many thirties Leftists. Domiciled in Central Europe well before the Auden gang, Alick West was politicised by *Battleship Potemkin* in Zürich at the time of the British General Strike. Throwing events at home into international relief, it left him with 'a permanent memory of the crawling carcases that were the sailors' food, the relentless tread of the Czar's soldiers and the perambulator bumping down the steps before them, and the sailors' unyielding will and courage. Outside the cinema there were two young men selling a paper. *Die Rote Fahne*.'[119] Time and again, early Soviet films such as Eisenstein's *Potemkin* (1925), *October* (1928), *The General Line* (1929), Dovzhenko's *Earth* (1930), Ekk's *The Way into Life* (1931), Pudovkin's *The End of St Petersburg* (1927), *Mother* (1926), *Storm Over Asia* (1928), and Vertov's *The Man With the Movie Camera* (1929) appear in writings from and about the period. Spender's sense of the whole history and tragedy of the thirties unreels from memories of watching them with Isherwood, Auden and Upwood:

> These films, which form a curiously isolated episode in the aes-
> thetic history of this century, excited us because they had the
> modernism, the poetic sensibility, the satire, the visual beauty, all
> those qualities we found most exciting in other forms of modern
> art, but they also conveyed a message of hope like an answer to
> *The Waste Land*. They extolled a heroic attitude which had not yet
> become officialised; in this they foreshadowed the defiant indi-
> vidualism of the Spanish Republicans. We used to go on long
> journeys to little cinemas in the outer suburbs of Berlin, and there
> among the grimy tenements we saw the images of the New Life
> of the workers building with machine tools and tractors their
> socially just world under the shadows of baroque statues reflected
> in ruffled waters of Leningrad, or against waving, shadow-
> pencilled plains of corn.

The comparable imagery of the last verse of Spender's 1930 poem 'The Truly Great' was also pastiched from such films.[120] He de-picted the Sovietised film-mindedness of the Weimar *Sonnenkinder*, of which he and Isherwood in particular saw themselves as honor-ary members, as an integral expression of their generational self-awareness in his reworked 1929 novel, *The Temple*.[121] This enthusiasm cut across class and ethnic boundaries among Leftists. Blumenfeld's Jewish East Ender Alec complains that in 'the capital of the world', there was not one film to 'sit through without leaving his intelli-gence outside', since 'the brains were kicked out' of the German industry by the Nazis. But it's particularly ironic that London's bourgeois film societies, showing Soviet agitprop banned from gen-eral release, are beyond his worker's means: 'who had guineas for membership and three and sixes for seats?' (p. 98). MacColl recalls that the more affordable Salford Workers' Film Society's season of Russian and Weimar avant-gardism 'started me on the road I was to travel for the next twenty years'. Even Elizabeth Bowen wryly conceded watching Soviet films was a superior, cerebral indulgence, suspending her desire to smoke: 'the supreme test'.[122]

Some Leftist writers even tried countering the seductiveness of capitalist movies by borrowing motifs from Five Year Plan films which made the modernisation of Soviet agriculture and industry seem epic. Spender's poem 'The Express' evoked the Futuristic energies of Turin's *Turksib* and his 1933 poem 'The Pylons' was galvanised by filmic allusions to Soviet electrification:

There runs the quick perspective of the future.
This dwarfs our emerald country by its trek
So tall with prophecy.
> (*Collected Poems*, p. 58)

Such 'quick perspectives' of an imagined future were common in Leftist poetry and indicate the extent to which some writers were enthralled by the subject matter and scale of Soviet films. Tom Wintringham's embarrassing 'Immortal Tractor' is an example of such cinematic seven-league-boot borrowing:

Lenin is speaking. All who hear him know
Here, too, a Tractor's building, and will grow;
Here, in the cities where the cold fog kills,
In the ploughless valleys, on the blank, bare hills,
'Mid the famine of the mines and the pthisis of the mills,
We are moulding, forging, shaping the steel of our wills
Into pinions, into pistons, crankshaft-web and crankshaft-throw
We are building Lenin's Tractor. It will grow.[123]

When the Auden gang weren't playing imaginary extras themselves they were busy casting one another. Spender thought of 'Chalmers' (i.e. Edward Upward) as 'the smiling young Comsomol hero who saves the boys in the reform school in one of our favourite films – *The Way into Life*',[124] despite Day Lewis's scoutmasterly warning in his 'Letter to a Young Revolutionary':

Cut out that personal religion; those enervating dreams; visions of tractors advancing over the skyline and hedges between fields and men going down; phantasies of yourself in Russian blouse and peaked cap, persuading the English to give up their possessions and plough for others to reap. It won't pass. If you join the Communist Party you'll have to wear a stiff collar and get down to some hard labour.[125]

Bowen put her finger on the displacement underlying this Boy's Own group fantasy. The Russians might have scrapped bourgeois-romantic 'sex-appeal as an annexe of singularising, anti-social love. But they still treat with glamour; they have transferred it to mass movement, to a heroicised pro-human emotion'.[126]

More worryingly, Grierson pointed out how Soviet cinema had been divorced from Soviet conditions since Stalin relegated Vertov to newsreel work and Eisenstein recanted his 'Formalism'.[127] Greene agreed that such ideal projections concealed the increasing repressiveness of Russian reconstruction. The dehumanising factory in Chaplin's *Modern Times* did not suggest 'his little man would be more at home at Dniepostroi'. Similarly, his review of *Lenin in October* concluded that the Communist film was politically exhausted, condemned to remaking its own history for the new leadership: 'What is left is the excitement of melodrama handled with the right shabby realism . . . most agreeable of all the unconscious humour of the re-arrangement – the elimination of Trotsky and the way in which Stalin slides into all the important close-ups' (*Spectator*, 14 February 1936 and 25 November 1938; *Mornings in the Dark*, pp. 74 and 274–5). Greene even suggested Mikhail Romm's film would have to be continuously re-edited to match the course of the Show Trials. But the final irony was the film of Friedrich Wolf's anti-Nazi play *Professor Mamlock*, released *after* the Molotov–Ribbentrop Pact. History had outrun it. Despite characters earnestly debating as if at a meeting of the Left Book Club, it was already a grotesque anachronism because the rationale for the Popular Front it advocated had collapsed (see *Spectator*, 1 September 1939; *Mornings in the Dark*, pp. 325–6). Consequently, in 'The Winter War: Finland' (1940), Greene used early Soviet movie titles as poetic shorthand for the mutation of Communist Utopia into totalitarian aggressor:

The portraits of Stalin wilted on the windscreen,
And we carried films called *Earth* and *Mother*.
But the rifles jammed and the boots let in the snow,
And the tanks stopped.

(*Reflections*, pp. 82–3)

The documentary was a minority category of British film that Greene relished for its social, rather than Socialist, realism. And this view survived the thirties, as confirmed by a 1941 radio talk. The directors of the numerous small documentary companies still lived 'the common life', drawing imaginative material from 'the street and the house next door', without the insulation of vast salaries, chromium offices and convenient memory loss (*Mornings in the Dark*, p. 515). According to him, true cinematic realism was permeated 'as with a juice, by awareness of a purpose', rather than a goggling, passive observation of reality. Good poetic cinema could never be made from mere form, only 'arty cinema', as in Flaherty's figures against the skyline in *Man of Aran* which substituted picturesque effect for the truth about a way of life and taught the islanders shark-fishing to create drama. Such calculated pastoral could not stand against the genuine poetic insight into the relations between exotic subjects and imperial consumers in Basil Wright's *Song of Ceylon* which closed 'with the revolving leaves . . . as if he were sealing away from us devotion and dance and the gentle communal life of the harvest, leaving us outside with the bills of lading and the loud-speakers' ('Subjects and Stories' in Davy (ed.), *Reflections* pp. 61–3).

But the independent outfits spawned by Grierson's protégés did not generally raise controversial subjects so much as promote matters of commerce. In *Letters from Iceland*, Auden and MacNeice ironically bequeathed to the GPO Film Unit 'a film on Sex', and to Grierson 'something really big/ To sell' (p. 246). All too often documentaries omitted facts like scandalous working conditions in the industries or Government departments they publicised. As Auden noted, the prickly question of financial support frustrated the medium's ethical potential: 'truth rarely has advertisement value'. He remained sceptical about whether industry or Government were disinterested enough to ever 'pay for an exact picture of the human life within their enormous buildings' (*English Auden*, pp. 355–6).

Calder-Marshall felt the net effect of the Griersonian method was to muzzle progressive tendencies 'not by complete suppression, but by semi-expression'. Documentaries sponsored by vested interests and/or the National Government prevented pressure for reform becoming revolutionary by appearing to do something: 'The general public is distracted from the contemplation of present affairs, or if not distracted, misled and cheated in their interpretation.'[128] When it came down to it, 'Mr Grierson', he wrote, 'is not paid to tell the truth, but to make more people use the parcel post.' His reservations about Rotha were similar: 'To judge by the contrast between his films and his books, his bosses, if they don't tell him what to put in, at least tell him what he's got to cut out.' The technological romance exemplified by the commentary in *The Future's in the Air* (1937), written, ironically, by Greene himself (see Chapter 4), claimed a universality belying real conflicts of interest:

> The epic sense of man's conquest of the earth and sky and sea wouldn't sound so like stage thunder, if one could feel more certain 'what man?' . . . The man who designed the aeroplane; the men who built it but will never fly it; the professional pilot who is paid as much as a lorry-driver; the people who can afford to travel in it; the people who derive their income from aviation stock; or the man who looks up, shading his eyes with his hand, and takes a rest from his work till it disappears behind a cloud?[129]

Nevertheless, Calder-Marshall pinned his hopes for the future of British film to the realisation of documentary's full potentials, 'not as some critics maintain, because documentary is a superior, purer or more creative branch of the film, but merely because the makers of documentary have more technical knowledge of the film as a medium and more liberty of expression'.

Greene shared Calder-Marshall's reservations, in theory if not always in practice. Equally, it seems unlikely that the subtext he read into the GPO's *The Voice of Britain*, publicising the BBC, was intentionally satirical of the huge economic and techological investments (ranks of transmitters and enough bureaucracy to run a totalitarian regime) made in broadcasting to achieve, what was in Greene's view, such a patronising underuse of it potentials: 'Miss Nina McKinney singing "Dinah", Henry Hall's Dance Orchestra playing "Piccadilly Riot", a spot of pleasure, a spot of dubious education, and a spot, just a spot, of culture when Mr Adrian Boult conducts the Fifth Symphony' (*Spectator*, 2 August 1935; *Mornings in the Dark*, p. 14).

Documentary's claim to objectivity was widely suspected to be a way of recruiting credulity. Powell's *Agents and Patients* links it with confidence trickery. Chipchase and Maltravers persuade Blore-Smith to fund their bogus life-study *Oedipus Rex*. Documentary's reputation as scientific and unmercenary is the perfect alibi: 'The films would, at present at least, have no commercial value whatever. But they would be of immense use in spreading an understanding of psychology if privately shown.' Technical jargon like 'cutting' and 'juxtaposition of sharp contrasts' is part of their act. Shoot 'quite fortuitously' and, hey presto, '*Montage* will do the rest' (pp. 49 and 165–6).

As with radio, writers felt film's propaganda potentials might well make it a repressive medium in wartime. In *Journey to a War*, Isherwood and Auden got a foretaste of features that might soon be the norm:

> The big picture was about a Chinese weakling who turned traitor to his country and agreed to make signals to Japanese aircraft in exchange for cocaine injections given him by a fiendish Jap doctor. He was shot, of course, and the audience clapped. And then the avenging Chinese troops captured the town – and everybody clapped still louder. We both wondered how long it would be before we were applauding similar trash, only a shade more sophisticated, at all the London cinemas. (p. 174)

Similarly, it wasn't just in Soviet cinema that Greene detected documentary techniques glossing over political *volte-faces* to remake history and shorten public memory. Now 'the war of nerves' was on. *Confessions of a Nazi Spy* presented retrospective versions of events like Munich which the BBFC passed without demur, as if they in no way contradicted how the British cinema constructed them at the time. As he sardonically, pointed out, this 'picture of methodical violence and treachery', even got a 'U' certificate, refused to most Westerns. In Greene's view, the BBFC's belated antifascism was the final nail in Appeasement's coffin. But Anatole Litvak's pastiche of fiction, voice-over commentaries, maps and newsreel excerpts confirmed the suspicion Greene shared with other Leftists, that the else-awareness sponsored by screen reporting all too often made no connection with the intimacy of the viewer's everyday existence. The picture imposed a kind of reality – that of 'news' – one in which hardly anybody believed very deeply because it 'is concerned only with the big events, the march of an army corps and the elimination of a people' (*Spectator*, 23 June 1939; *Mornings in the Dark*, pp. 304–5).

Footage-faking in *Waugh in Abyssinia* (1936) and Huxley's narcotic 'Feelietone News' show that anxiety about cinema's power to distort history was certainly not exclusive to Socialists or Communist fellow-travellers. But, because of the massively disproportional representation in the British media, the Left were particularly motivated to expose falsities and omissions about chronic social and economic crises and international events like the Spanish Civil War. Understandably, the form of factual film most often attacked was the newsreel, because of the extent of its control over public access to hyperreality. Cinematic attempts by groups like the Socialist Film Council and Federation of Workers' Film Societies to expose 'What the Newsreels Do Not Show' were intertextual with Leftist writing.[130]

George Barker claimed in *Calamiterror* (1937) that 'The horror facts, the humans in the horror' were never shown by 'blackout Paramount'.[131] Moreover, it wasn't just a question of what commercial newsreels omitted, but what they included and how it was edited. Calder-Marshall considered them a kind of 'anti-montage', the opposite of revelatory Vertovian cutting: 'Rallies, tattoos, garden parties, marches past, races of all sorts, sporting events and fascist jamborees are the mainstay of the newsreels. They give no pictures of the world. The audience is faced by a multiplex and incomprehensible series of events, without significance.' Newsreels shared the function of the gutter press, 'to distract and bewilder with unrelated events' and conceal 'the injustice and incompetence of capitalism'.[132]

Calder-Marshall argued that the agenda of the newsreel cartel combined anti-Popular Front propaganda with a projection of National Government policies as domestically moderate and internationally disinterested. The newsreels' method was the most pernicious example of how the camera 'always selects and distorts', yet gave an impression of actuality rivalled only by the BBC: 'the audience is prepared to swear that it has seen with its own eyes what the commentator tells it it has seen'.[133] He evidenced the notorious 'atrocity' footage of Republican troops gunning a statue of Christ, in which the commentary omitted to mention their bribe. Similarly, he berated the way British editions of *The March of Time* were subject to BBFC interventions, tacitly accepted by Griersonian documentarists who contributed material to it.

The Workers' Theatre Movement also highlighted the newsreels' selective conferment of reality: Tom Thomas's *Their Theatre and Ours* again, skitting 'a day in the life of the Prince of Wales', and suggesting what such anodyne reporting excluded:

> In the morning he reviewed the Puddleton Boy Scouts and opened the new bridge, which 500 men have been building for two years. We see him being welcomed by the mayor and corporation.

(*Player who plays the mayor sticks his stomach out at this – and gravely shakes hands*)
We see him receiving the cheers of the 500 men who finished up today
(*Mayor claps his hands faintly*)
who thus express their appreciation of the splendid work he is doing.
(*The players representing the workers blow raspberries.*)
VOICE: (*continues*) The Prince, though naturally fatigued by his exertions, after a sumptuous lunch provided by the Town Council, reviews a parade of the police force
(*rest of players line up while he 'reviews' them*)
who have distinguished themselves recently by a baton charge against unemployed demonstrating to the Town Council against the Means Test.
(*On this they draw imaginary batons and use them.*)
                    (Samuel *et al.* (eds), *Theatres of the Left*, pp. 141–2)

Given such assumptions, Day Lewis's poem 'Newsreel' (1938) was the *gatherum* of a decade's suspicions that Hollywood fantasies and cinematic reporting worked together to position moviegoers in a hyperreality that anaesthetised critical else-awareness:

Enter the dream-house, brothers and sisters, leaving
Your debts asleep, your history at the door:
This is the home for heroes, and this loving
Darkness a fur you can afford.

The poem warned that the audience's failure to connect the violence of far-off events with their mundane existence would be breached by experience. Such 'exotics' would soon spring up in their own backyards:

Grow nearer home – and out of the dream-house stumbling
One night into a strangling air and the flung
Rags of children and thunder of stone niagaras tumbling,
You'll know you slept too long.
                    (*Complete Poems*, pp. 171–2)

It's instructive to compare 'Newsreel' to the last page of *Homage to Catalonia*, published the same year. Orwell too felt the 'deep, deep sleep of England, from which I fear we shall never awake, unless jerked out of it by the roar of bombs' was largely media-induced.

As we have seen, writers were tremendously excited by the profound changes in consciousness cinema brought about. But they were also rightly troubled that the new standard of realism promised by photographic images was partly a new illusionism. MacNeice's *Zoo* features the following exchange: 'Reader: The Camera cannot lie. Writer: Neither can it discriminate. The camera is much too glib. The realism of the camera is not *the* realism.' MacNeice thought the photograph's mass-reproducibility encouraged visual prejudices (the French term for a photographic negative is *cliché*), rather than closer perception: 'and the moment you got into the Rhinoceros House, up came the old preconceptions like a film between you and the rhinoceros' (pp. 17 and 18). More optimistically, in *Letters from Iceland*, Auden emphasised photography's potentials for democratic representation in his observation of masses and of masses observing themselves: 'Go down by chara' to the Sussex Downs,/ Watch the manoeuvres of the week-end hikers/ Massed on parade with Kodaks or with Leicas.' According to him, 'any ordinary person could learn all the technique of photography in a week. It is *the* democratic art, i.e. technical skill is practically eliminated' (*Letters from Iceland*, pp. 52 and 137). But in 1938 he wrote a wry recollection of the legendary war-photographer Robert Capa which emphasised the image's 'hazardousness' and voyeuristic opportunism: 'The journalist Capa plays dicing games,/ He photographed Teruel town in flames' ('Passenger Shanty', *English Auden*, p. 233). If the camera affected the way collective reality was validated, it also problematised how writers viewed and discriminated personal experience. Spender, for example, whose brother Humphrey had also lived and worked in Germany and was strongly influenced by *Neue Sachlichkeit* photography, was always on the look-out for telling images, as if through a mental viewfinder, or projecting them on an internal screen. But in *Journey to a War*, Isherwood, whose narrative persona in *Goodbye to Berlin* (1939) disarmingly pretends to camera-eyed neutrality (discussed in Chapter 3), recoiled from a snap-happy Englishman who had merely become an optical tourist of others' misery: 'Everything thrilled him – bomb-craters, pagodas, stomach-wounds, the faces of old beggars: he was perpetually whipping out his camera for a photograph' (p. 67).

On one hand, the photograph might feature as the ultimate document. In Burdekin's *Swastika Night*, it challenges the organised disappearance and reinvention of the facts of the past in a proto-Orwellian manner. The O'Brien-like Knight von Hess proves to the Englishman Alfred, by means of the single surviving print, that Hitler was not actually the Wagnerian demi-god of countless propaganda icons. Instead this virtual fragment of history shows him short, paunchy 'face hairless as a woman's except for a small black growth on the upper lip'. But the bigger shock is its proof that women were not always the sub-human creatures to which they have been reduced by centuries of gender *Endlösung*. The long-haired blond 'boy' next to the Führer, who 'looked . . . more noble, more German, more manly, despite his youth', is actually a 1930s Hitler *Mädchen* (pp. 66–7). On the other hand, the photograph was very much suspected as 'the real's hallucinatory resemblance to itself'. In Dylan Thomas's 'Our Eunuch Dreams', its 'lying likeness . . . is married to the eye,/ Grafts on its bride one-sided skins of truth' (*Collected Poems*, p. 14). MacNeice's *Out of the Picture* hints that dubious interventions take place during the processing of transitory reality into static image. Dr Spielmann says, 'A negative is a positive in psychology, you know. In fact it is just like photography. *You* take the photographs; we develop them' (p. 33).

Writers refracted the already-reproduced reality of the photograph as an equivocally vicarious experience. For example, Spender's 'War Photograph', beginning 'I have an appointment with a bullet', is said to be a response to Capa's famous shot of a dying (or tripping?) Republican militiaman. The poem makes death itself a kind of photographic reflex, instantaneous yet historically transfixing: 'I am that numeral which the sun regards,/ The flat and severed second on which time looks,/ My corpse a photograph taken by fate' (*Collected Poems*, p. 202). In this way, mediated events became subjects of further representations, as in George Barker's 'Elegy on Spain' (1940), 'dedicated to the photograph of a child killed in an air-raid on Barcelona', which emphasises the virtual tangibility of photographic 'truth':

O ecstatic is this head of five-year joy –
Captured its butterfly rapture on a paper:
And not the rupture of the right eye may
Make any less this prettier than a picture.
O now my minor moon, dead as meat
Slapped on a negative plate, I hold
The crime of the bloody time in my hand.
(*Collected Poems*, p. 114)

Sometimes it worked the other way other way round too: Bill
Brandt admitted following Orwell's writing to photograph the 'other
country' of *The English at Home* (1936) and *A Night in London* (1938)
and Priestley's *English Journey* drove Rotha north for his film *The
Shipyard*. It's a matter of regret, though, that there was no full-
blown British example of intertextual collaboration between photographer and writer to match that between James Agee and Walker
Evans in the States.[134]

MEDIA IN GENERAL

Leftist refractions of the media in the thirties are striking in their
recurrent themes and motifs and the overall consistency of their
criticisms. In Central and Eastern Europe, 'the elimination of voices/
That contradict official faces', as Spender's *Vienna* (p. 22) puts it,
was carried out openly, with unprecedented technical ruthlessness,
supplementing media control with the extremest censorship –
murder – and terror. Similarly, Hollywood's epic budgets were
dwarfed by the resources of media spectacles like Nürnberg for
what Benjamin called the 'reproduction of masses'. Propaganda
Ministers could transform whole nations into sets of themselves,
whole populations into extras. In *Choose a Bright Morning*, Brunsatz

> just puts in an order for the whole country and it's delivered . . . he
> teaches us all a lesson in the quality of bigness. Half a million
> supers as mob atmosphere and you don't even have to pay them
> or tell them when to cheer. Five miles of bunting. Five million
> words over the radio stations. All the bonfires and special street
> lighting he wants, and if he's keen for a really good blaze he even
> orders a couple of buildings burned down . . . In Bidlo the press
> agent has come to heaven. (pp. 97–8)

The everyday reality of Bidlites is rendered utterly plastic by
media campaigns. Like all good totalitarian regimes Bidlo needs a
scapegoat, but since it has not got the necessary racial minority to
persecute, they have to be invented. It is decreed the duty of every
tenth person to assume a Jewish identity. Anyone refusing is shot
for treason anyway. Conversely, cosmetic representation of Bidlo's
concentration camps causes a stampede to get places in these luxury
resorts. *Choose a Bright Morning* reaches the conclusion contemporary

Realpolitik is a surreal tragi-farce modelled on Disney or Low, rather than the other way round:

> all these strutting heroes, dictators and sub-dictators ... are simply comic strip ... characters who have broken loose from their appointed confines, have taken on life, size and power, and are overwhelming the world. It is, in short, a revolution of clowns ... who rule according to their orthodox principles that a club and a beating solve all problems. (pp. 200–1)

Leftists were in general agreement that Britain's media also kept its population in a misinformed condition. *Autumn Journal* XVII anticipates Poststructuralism's 'mystified subject' as 'The doped public sucking a dry dug' (*Collected Poems*, p. 138). In this way, they believed, hegemony kept democracy ideologically *out* of touch with itself, to reverse Grierson's phrase.[135] Opposition was an affordable luxury precisely because the nation's media were so disproportionally representative, according to Calder-Marshall: 'While vested interests believe in the efficacy of their own propaganda, they don't mind a few dissentient voices, because they know they'll be drowned in the babble.'[136] Auden summed up this feeling that the media gave purely imaginary resolution to the contradictions of a disunited kingdom in 'Letter to Lord Byron II' – the brave new consumer society of the South and the deprived, consoled North: 'To those who live in Warrington or Wigan', it constituted 'not a white lie, it's a whacking big 'un.' (*Letters from Iceland*, p. 50) Likewise, in Warner's *The Wild Goose Chase*, Government power rests 'not so much on the ability to act but on the ability to persuade people to allow them to act' (p. 263). For Calder-Marshall, the media prolonged the distracting mental ethos of the Great War by other means:

> Newspapers, news films, speeches are filled with prophecies, scares and reassurances. And in the interests of one party, the nation is called upon to sink its differences, to turn from contemplation of the existent hardship and injustice within the country towards a greater, but as yet non-existent, evil outside. It is the old trick of saying suddenly 'Look over there,' and landing your opponent one on the jaw as he turns away.[137]

Whatever its specific variations, this integration propaganda theme was the principal one. In *Wigan Pier*, for instance, Orwell argued media-technology promoted the myth of capitalist progress as an alibi for changes in production 'to meet the demands of underpaid, underfed people', who, paradoxically, lived in a world where information was co-ordinated globally, minute-by-minute (p. 82). *Nineteen Eighty-Four*'s 'prolefeed' derived from such misgivings. Consequently, it was a small step from Orwell's condemnation of capitalist publicity in the thirties to his postwar satire of the totalitarian media: he represented both serving the same repressive ends: yoking populations to socially-inverted priorities and legitimating unaccountable power.

The tendency of the media to appropriate and promote authoritative discourse, to create an orthodox hyperreality as if it were unmediated, was satirised in Holtby's 1934 short story 'The Voice of God'. A shy genius creates an apparatus that can listen in to speeches from the past. His invention is made public only by accident and exclusive rights are greedily snatched up by a media baron. The scoop of all time will be live radio transmission of the sermons of Jesus, with transcripts in the *Daily Standard*. The scheme founders, however, when The Word turns out not to be the purity of RP, but the ancient obscurity of Aramaic. The Almighty's literal meaning then quickly fractures into a Babel of translations and exegesis by rival scholars and interest groups.

The thirties media both served the ends of dubious politics and simultaneously mystified their machinations. Chamberlain as head of the Conservative Party Research Department first realised the importance of cinema for political propaganda. This served the MacDonald–Baldwin Government well at the 1935 election through its National Publicity Bureau. When Chamberlain became Prime Minister, he cultivated a colloquial, avuncular presence for the newsreels, giving audiences the impression of a personal, face-to-face explanation for policies, entirely distinct from his parliamentary image as the 'undertaker from Birmingham'. The first real TV pictures, demonstrated by Baird to the Royal Institution mixed images of a real human face with a ventriloquist's dummy.[138] In this respect, R. C. Sherriff's 1933 treatment of H. G. Wells's *The Invisible Man* stands as a brilliant *tour de force* of the metonymic devices of the photographic media and an implicit deconstruction of the personae contemporary politicians projected. The Invisible Man, played by Claude Rains, only appears for the last 30 seconds of the movie. He is quite literally an absent-presence for the rest of it, a mere outline delineated by bandages and clothes or the objects he manipulates. These visual tropes suggest an anti-fascist subtext by cross-referencing other media. For example, rendered megalomaniac by his transparency drug and ability to strike anywhere, without warning, the Invisible Man plans world conquest. A key close-up shows a wireless announcing his latest act of terrorism. As the speaker expands to fill the screen the parallel with another invisible voice is arresting: two kinds of technological disembodiment and ubiquity, with the potential to broadcast hysteria, symbolically converge. Another contemporary version of this 'invisible man' theme is the *The Fall of the City*, Archibald MacLeish's radio parable play (originally broadcast by CBS, but also by the BBC (see Chapter 4)) about the bad faith of masses, panicked into accepting 'irresistible' dictatorial power through propaganda. At the climax, the conqueror advancing on the prostrate citizens is revealed as an animated suit of armour. He is literally a hollow sham, an 'empty signifier', filled only by their amplified repressions and wishful thinking. By means of the play's eyewitness correspondent narrating events, broadcasting both creates and then unmasks this false agency, simultaneously baring its own devices. The same duality in the potentials of film is implied in Whale's movie.

Leftist writers tried to disseminate critical consciousness of phoney public faces. In Spender's *Vienna*, the butchers of the Austrian workers, Dollfuss, Fey and Stahremberg 'Appear frequently, shaking hands at street corners/ Looking like bad sculptures of their photographs' (p. 19). In *Journey to a War*, Auden and Isherwood initially found Chiang Kai-shek unlike 'the cloaked, poker-stiff figure of the newsreels'; however, at the first photo-opportunity, the Kuomintang leader immediately struck his familiar posture (p. 58). Similarly, in their *On the Frontier* Westland's Leader 'plays very stiffly, like a newsreel photograph of himself. His Platform voice is like a trance-voice, loud and unnatural.' Stahl says of him 'Why he isn't a man at all! He's a gramophone!' – a mass-reproduction without any original at all, casting doubt on political simulacra in general and on the authenticity of their causes. (See Character Notes and p. 124.) Bertolt Brecht's *Life of Galileo* (1939) points out that it's not the land lacking heroes which is pitiable, but the one needing them.[139] Similarly, in *On the Frontier* the Führer is essentially a mechanism for transference and sublimation, purging and ennobling 'by proxy': 'The Leader, you see, is our national martyr . . . we need someone to do our suffering for us' (p. 124).

The interaction of publicity techniques with mass perceptions endowed politicians with a heroic aura Carlyle scarcely dreamed of. *Choose a Bright Morning*'s Winsatz 'radiated fame, authority and all kinds of destiny . . . the overwhelming cumulative effect of so many photographers, so many journalists, mass meetings, parades, speeches, tourists' (pp. 46–7). In *It's a Battlefield* the same spell effaces the authentic presence of the parliamentary private secretary completely. Carrying 'the glamour and consciousness of innumerable photographs', he is window-dressing only:

> His face was like the plate-glass window of an expensive shop. One could see, very clearly and to the best effect, a few selected objects: a silver casket, a volume of Voltaire exquisitely bound, a self-portrait by an advanced and fashionable Czechoslovakian. (p. 9)

Writers also traced the transmission and multiplication of compelling images of actualities elsewhere through the media's twisted skein. Symptomatically, Spender argued Picasso's *Guernica* mural, displayed in the Spanish pavilion at the 1937 Paris World Exhibition, incorporated a reaction to the 'already reproduced' as well as to an objective event:

> it is not a picture of some horror which Picasso has seen and been through himself. It is the picture of a horror in the newspapers, of which he has read accounts and perhaps seen photographs.
> This kind of second-hand experience, from the newspapers, the news-reel, the wireless, is one of the dominating realities of our time. . . .[140]

A point Republican propagandists were only too aware of, as Robert Hughes notes: 'Guernica did not need to be a specific political statement. The mass media supplied the agreement by which it became one, and Picasso knew exactly how and where to insert his painting into that context.'[141]

The solution for Leftist writers, then, did not consist in discovering some mythical form giving unmediated access to the real or to authentic history (as hardline Socialist Realism claimed to do),[142] but in striving to disseminate alternative perspectives on events. Otherwise, as *On the Frontier* warns, the media's concerted jamming of global danger signals would prove fatal:

The drums tap out sensational bulletins:
Frantic the efforts of the violins
To drown the song behind the guarded hill:
The dancers do not listen; but they will.

Eric Thorvald and Anna Vrodny, the Westland–Ostnian Romeo and
Juliet, eventually break through the play's ideological barriers to
encounter each other in a neutral 'good place', beyond the reach of
propaganda. 'Where the air is not filled with the screams of hatred/
Nor words of great and good men twisted/ To flatter conceit and
justify murder' (Epigraph and p. 150). But this was pious Utopianism
by 1939, because any space of absolute truth, uncontaminated by
the post/modern informational struggle, had proven illusory.

In Spender's play *Trial of a Judge* (1938) the fight for justice around
a political slaying becomes a question of media 'performativity',
not objectivity. The account established by the liberal-democratic
judge is overborne by more powerful propaganda:

FIRST BLACK PRISONER. Our martyrdom
Blazoned on a million sheets of paper
Is a trumpet blowing
Millions to the cause
Oh heroes who warn the people's enemies
With this exemplary, just, horrible death.

And after the judicial process has been hijacked, comes the Fascist
campaign of 'organised forgetting' in which the audience are
metadramatically implicated by internal censorship of their own
memory:

THIRD BLACK PRISONER . . . Destroy all photographs taken and
all reports of speeches in this Court. The last ten minutes are
wiped out. *They never happened.*
BLACK TROOP LEADER [*advancing to the front of the stage*]. If
your imaginations
Invent and publish any picture of this scene.
Remember that the lines cut by the memory
Into the brain may cut so deep
They kill life altogther.
Delete those lines. Make your brains blank.[143]

In 1935, E. H. Robinson's *Broadcasting and a Changing Civilisation* still hoped technology's truth-telling possibilities would be realised in the future – 'The microphone might so easily be used for the immediate good of the public as a whole that it is a pity that its potentialities are largely wasted. Why has no government yet thought of setting up a "Ministry of Truth"?'[144] – but Orwell's ironic twisting of his idea in 1949 derives from thirties Leftists' incipiently Postmodern scepticism that such a project could ever be more than a fantasy or political alibi.

There is no doubt that the 'full blast', as Madge called it, of the early twentieth-century media irrevocably altered the consciousness of writers at the most fundamental levels. Cinema seemed to rupture the very fabric of the space–time continuum. Like a literal embodiment of Modernist *mémoire involontaire*, the past could now burst back at any moment. Greene's movie writings exemplify this, but push it beyond the secular into the uncanny. Rewatching Valentino's *Son of the Sheik*, Greene commented, was like a dream from J. W. Dunne's *Experiment with Time*: 'The man is moving on the screen and at the same time he is dead and magnificently and absurdly entombed. No acting can quite preserve the presence of that awful and simultaneous future.' This revival of the dead and disappeared past was apocalyptically magnified in footage from the Great War (BBC talk, 29 August 1937; *Mornings in the Dark*, pp. 511 and 516).[145] Watching silents evoked similar imagery on the eve of the next war in Greene's short story 'A Little Place Off the Edgware Road' (1939). The psychological displacements of this text gather all Greene's preoccupations with the 'buried life' of the cinema in the thirties: its role as a collective, cultural unconscious; its fundamental ambiguousness as a medium of absent presences; its 'haunting', both by what it represses and what it preserves. Greene's metaphysics of sin and guilt battened on film. His revival house is in Culpar (*culpa*) Road and resembles a nightmare of being 'alone in the huge dark cavernous burying ground of all the world'. For Greene the very token of modernity was eerily atavistic, its bleached ghosts generated not from ectoplasm but material effects, always about to 'dissolve altogether into dots and flashes and wiggly lines'.[146] 'Edgware Road' also foreshadows the catacomblike Viennese sewers in Greene's screen masterpiece, *The Third Man*, home to blackmarketeer Harry Lime, another corrupted comeback form the land of the dead.

For most Leftists the cultural crisis remained essentially secular.

At one level, the media might have liberated serious writing from the obligation to be popular entertainment, but this freedom also threatened it with irrelevance. As Day Lewis argued in his radio talk, 'Until fifty years ago, reading verse was a widespread mental recreation: Shakespeare, for instance, got his poetry across under the guise of entertainment.' To embrace Modernist formal 'difficulty' as an end in itself meant abandoning the majority to the 'laws of the market' and irrevocably fixing the gulf between writer and people. According to Day Lewis this option was not open to the politically-committed, because the 'ever increasing flood of false art . . . – the gutter-press newspapers, dope-fiction, sentimental and unreal films' was weakening 'the workers' responses to the emotional effect of genuine art'.[147] Consequently, in 1937, Edgell Rickword's 'Culture, Progress, and the English Tradition' attempted to quell writers' post-Leavisian fears about cultural standards under threat from 'mass-civilisation':

> He is fearful of the radical transformation of society by the proletariat, because he thinks that the artistic and intellectual values he cares about will be swamped by the products of Hollywood, Fleet Street and Elstree. He does not realise that it is capitalism which is making those values meaningless.[148]

Rickword argued that only through Socialism and Socialist art could society incorporate change in the technologies of representation in a genuinely democratic and enlightening kind of way. Consequently, in the next chapter, I want to go beyond Leftist writers' criticism of the capitalist media, to examine the formal innovations of their own attempts to subvert and compete with them.

3

Responses: The Mass Media as Formal Influences

The output of Leftist cultural production obviously could never equal that of the press, broadcasting and cinema. Even networks like the Workers' Film and Photo League, the Left Book Club or Mass-Observation never had access to a fraction of the media's resources or technology. Mass-Observation's vision of itself, for example, as a 'nationwide intelligence service' incorporated the idea of a truth-telling alternative to the BBC, allowing the nation to 'listen in to the movements of popular habit and opinion'. It certainly posed some kind of challenge to the conventional media in the late thirties, but it could never hope to rival the scale and regularity of their coverage, despite its boast that 'The receiving set is there, and every month makes it more effective.'[1] However, the influence of media techniques on the formal structure of thirties writing was undoubtedly enormous. They were major impulses behind the widespread use of different kinds of textual montage, which in turn were often used to subvert or demystify their power. Perhaps the most convenient way of dividing up this pervasive media-influence on the forms of thirties texts, since montage has interrelated broadcasting and cinematic derivations, would be broadly by literary genre, beginning with drama and moving to verse and fiction.

DRAMA

Charles Davy argued that the Modernist 'poetic' novel was closer to cinema than was drama. The reason was that in 'theatre everything must happen in real space and time, whereas the cinema and the novel are alike free . . . to mould both to their own needs.'[2] However, his account, like Allerdyce Nicoll's *Film and the Theatre* (1936) was based on traditional notions of theatrical construction and overlooked contemporary experiments. The epic theatre developed by Piscator and Brecht in Germany incorporated technological devices like slide projection, moving films and animated cartoons in its spatio-temporally fluid, montage style. Consequently, the Workers Theatre Movement (WTM), active from the mid-1920s through a network of groups like Red Radio and Red Megaphones, and the magazine *Red Stage*, sought to absorb such influences from the mainland and the USA into their own agitprop (imported American plays which used epic structures and cinematic effects, like Clifford Odets' *Waiting for Lefty* (1935), on the New York taxi drivers' strike, and Irwin Shaw's proto-absurdist *Bury the Dead* (1936), which featured mutinying corpses in the Great War, became national standbys in the WTM repertoire). H. B. 'Thom' Thomas, a North London stockbroker's clerk, developed the WTM's satirical pantomime/revue format in *Malice in Plunderland, Strike Up* (1929), and *Their Theatre and Ours* (1932). Thomas rejected Naturalism because it failed to reveal underlying socio-economic connections, using instead what he called 'the X-ray dialectical realism of montage' for rapid cross-cutting in material staged by WTM groups all over the country.[3] This spawned in turn the topical-montage method of Montagu Slater's documentary play on the South Wales mine sit-ins *A New Way to Win* (1936), as well as a whole host of agitprop scripts on issues like Nazi rearmament (*Dr Krupps*) and the Reichstag fire-trial (*For Dimitrov*).

However, as Ewan MacColl, one of the Red Megaphones' founder-members, recalled, how could 'the propertyless theatre of a propertyless class' ever obtain enough modern equipment to compete seriously with the capitalist media?[4] Breakthroughs like Theatre Union's production of *The Good Soldier Schweik*, which used a back-projector made by sympathetic Metropolitan-Vickers scientists (refugee actors said it was better than Piscator's) were rare indeed. The WTM also used popular culture to recapture an audience who 'had stayed away from the theatre in large numbers ever since the Elizabethan age'. It could not shirk the fact that, whatever its political unsoundness, 'For most working people the basic form of entertainment was the Hollywood film' (Goorney and MacColl (eds), *Agitprop to Theatre Workshop*, pp. xlviii–xlix). Hollywood succeeded with mass audiences precisely because it produced stars like James Cagney and Jean Harlow who could act working-class roles convincingly. Consequently, MacColl and his contemporaries regarded its lack of social-marking as a liberating example – 'In our theatre, we said, an actor will be able to walk into a steel foundry and pass as a puddler, our actresses will be able to stand at a loom and look like any other Lancashire mill-girl' (p. xlix) – a determination that paid off in the dynamic regionalism of Theatre Workshop.

The principal documentary form used by WTM groups was the 'Living Newspaper', pioneered by the Russians during the building of the Turksib Railway (itself turned into a cinematic icon by Turin). Soviet travelling shows explained Party projects and policy to illiterate audiences. Later Hallie Flanagan's American Federal Theatre adopted the form to publicise Roosevelt's New Deal in 1936 with *Triple A Plowed Under* and *One Third of a Nation*. However, WTM groups had already been lampooning the media on stage and street with a repertoire of satirical sketches like *Suppress, Oppress and Depress* long before the form arrived in Britain via the States and often using devices drawn from the media themselves. Manchester Theatre of Action's *John Bullion* (1934) presented a conspiracy to inflate armaments shares, featuring 'Deafen'em' of the *Daily Excess*, 'a big noise in the press', a BBC Northern Programme microphone voice and a 'mutograph' showing newsreels, eventually taken over by striking anti-war workers (repr. in *Agitprop to Theatre Workshop*, pp. 2–11). But the most successful of WTM media sketches was *Newsboy*, adapted from the script of New York's Laboratory Theatre by novelist Simon Blumenfeld (repr. in Samuel *et al.* (eds), *Theatres of the Left*, pp. 14–20).[5] Its action is continually intercut by the newsboy's shouted headlines about events around the world (Sacco and Vanzetti, Thomas Mooney, Scottsboro, Torgler and Thaelmann), which are then dramatised by the other characters. Finally, the action turns back on his 'conversion' to *Daily Worker*-seller after being, literally, pressganged into experiencing the unreported human significance behind the news for himself.

The first all-British Living Newspaper was performed in 1938 by North London's Unity Theatre (founded in 1936), based on the 1937 Coronation bus strike, the largest industrial dispute since 1932 and sign of a new stage of struggle, specifically between transport workers' union boss Ernest Bevin and the militant London 'Rank and File' movement's resistance to the new industrial policies of speed-up and increased hours. Arthur Arent, author of *Triple A Plowed Under*, visited Unity to share the American experiences, stressing that topicality ought not to mean slapdash aesthetic crudity. The result was *Busmen*, a collaboration between John Allen, Montagu Slater and taxi-driver Herbert Hodge.[6] Unity wanted 'to emulate on stage the effect of *The March of Time* newsreel documentary', as Chambers puts it. Bus workers provided information, checked on the naturalness of dialogue and authenticity of costumes; Slater wrote the verse and Hodge prose scenes between bus driver and wife 'reminiscent of Odets', while Allen edited the whole package by scissors and paste.[7] They inserted minutes and transcripts of court and TUC hearings and also followed Mass-Observation's recent method in their Coronation Day Survey *May the 12th* (1937) of using comments overheard in the street. Statistics were projected in graphs and its scenes linked by the choric-commentating 'Voice of the Living Newspaper', in the flies. *Busmen's* 24 episodic sequences covered the whole dispute and provided a socio-economic cross-section from Commons to Aldgate bus queue, intercut by the way the dispute was reported in the media. Scene 8 exemplifies how the Living Newspaper presented the limitation of public perception of events by news coverage:

BUSMAN'S WIFE (*from previous scene*): You'd do much better if you took the queue and demonstrated outside the Passenger Board's offices. Make 'em put more buses on the road, provide proper accommodation and shelter. I don't know how you people stand it.
WINTERBOTHAM: Blimey, I'm doing the best I can, ma. I've even gorn so far as to have photographs of the queue taken to show people 'ow we're being messed about.
BUSMAN'S WIFE: Well, and what did you do with them?
WINTERBOTHAM: I sent 'em up to the Daily Press. And what did they do with them? They appeared on the back pages among the pictures with the 'eading 'Starving Russians lining up for their Dog Biscuits'.[8]

But Rotha's criticism of *Busmen* in *World Film News* also recognised how the Left's shortage of technical expertise and equipment limited the impact of its counter-productions.[9]

Another Living Newspaper, Theatre Union's *Last Edition*, dramatised events leading to the Munich Pact. Its fast-moving anthology style derived from everything Joan Littlewood and MacColl had learned, showing how the flexible montage form of Living Newspapers could incorporate mass-declamation, satirical agit-prop, dance-drama, constructivist and expressionist elements, juxtaposition of song and dramatised actuality (MacColl recalled the depiction of the recent Gresford pit-disaster was particularly effective, as open scene and courtroom drama with actual newspaper excerpts (see Samuel *et al.* (eds), *Theatres of the Left*, pp. xiv and xliv). The theme connecting all this was unemployment, hunger marches and industrial conditions. *Last Edition* also cannibalised Hollywood musicals like *42nd Street* and *Fox Movietone Follies* and pre-empted Brecht's *Resistible Rise of Arturo Ui*, by drawing on gangster and Marx Brothers movies to burlesque Appeasement. In the sketch 'Who Killed Johnny the Czech?' Hitler became mob boss 'Siggy', with Italian side-kick, 'Muscle In'; and Chamberlain, 'Lance the Umbrella Man', with 'Eddy his echo' Daladier, who cover *Realpolitik* with international respectability:

Siggy. Aw, cut the sob stuff. You gotta go, Johnny.
Lance. Sure and after you, Joe the Red.
Eddy. I'm afraid so, Johnny. It is destiny.
Muscle. That's very good worda.
Johnny. Okay, okay. But don't forget, you birds, that Siggy'll double-cross you. He'll two-time ya. Then you'll be on the spot.
Siggy. Shut up! Okay, boys. Give him the works.
All four draw their pistols.
Lance. Hold on a minute.
He opens his umbrella and covers the four guns. They fire. (repr. in Goorney and MacColl (eds), *Agit-Prop to Theatre Workshop*, p. 33)

Unity's planned Living Newspaper 'issues' on Spain, crime and housing were abandoned when war supervened, though an important aspect of the Left Book Club's documentary activity was its Unity-inspired Theatre Guild, launched in April 1937.[10] Similarly Unity's grandiose plans to collaborate with film-maker Ralph Bond and Mass-Observation to produce more Living Newspapers didn't come off (although a Unity Group did appear in the Communist Party film *Peace and Plenty*).[11] Unity's only other Living Newspaper, *Crisis*, was on Czechoslovakia. Hectically assembled by Slater, Randall Swingler and Roger Woddis, with other writers including a Czech, it opened on 29 September 1938 in time for Chamberlain's notorious flight. Using the full range of techniques and materials, inserting broadcasts and speeches showing National Government duplicity, later 'editions' were continuously updated to incorporate new developments (some of which appeared more quickly than in the papers). However, its public life was curtailed by the Lord Chamberlain's ban.[12] Despite that, Montage drama on topical issues continued to evolve. Jack Lindsay, for example, who wrote mass-declamations for Unity like *Who Are the English?*, carried the Living Newspaper formula to the Army Bureau of Current Affairs, for scripts on *Lendlease*, invasion preparations (*The Japanese Way*) and questions about the postwar world (*Where Do We Go From Here?*). It also descended into MacColl's postwar Radio Ballads, via the anthology format of *Johnny Noble*, his saga of a 'typical' fisherman's life, set amid the key events of the thirties and forties. Similarly, Rotha's *World of Plenty* and Jennings's *The Silent Village* show how the Living Newspaper fed back into film, one of its own origins.

A kind of climax to the media-responsive drama of the thirties was Unity's *Babes in the Wood*. Robert Mitchell's 1938 topical agit-pantomime became a news-event itself. The (mostly hostile) press coverage it generated was rivalled only by *Last Edition*'s termination by MacColl and Littlewood's arrest. It was an example of the way Leftist theatre could attract wider audiences by assimilating popular forms, in this case, pre-cinematic. It opened on 15 November and became an instant circle-squaring hit, giving up-to-the-minute feedback to counter the reporting of events. The Babes represented Austria and the Czechs; the Wicked Uncle, Chamberlain, with accomplices Hit and Muss; Robin Hood and Maid Marian were the Popular Front and the public. It certainly wounded Chamberlain's projection as a 'man of peace'. Geoffrey McKeeman deliberately played him against his newsreel persona as Low's caricature. This new stage image actually got international exposure as *Time*'s picture of the week. Similarly, the Fairy Wishfulfilment, obligingly circulating illusions and disinformation, lampooned Fleet Street and the press-baronage. *Babes* also parodied the much-publicised sky-journey, whenever the Wicked Uncle entered, in Chambers's words, 'to the sound of an aeroplane in a comic descent', and contrasted salvationary myth-making with the Government's dismal economic record in lyrics like Geoffrey Parsons' 'Love on the Dole'. Stage caricature of a living PM was unprecedented and Tory MPs tried to close the show.[13]

For obvious reasons, writers actually had to write for the sound medium of radio to explore its dramatic possibilities, since these depended on performance and could not be easily reproduced on the page. (Therefore, plays and features by the few radical writers that were broadcast in the thirties belong in Chapter 4.) Non-theatre texts by Leftists were limited to mimicking the experience of 'listening-in' rather than appropriating them more directly. Dial-twiddling in Greene's *England Made Me*, as the doomed Anthony Farrant unwittingly gambles his last, is one of the best examples of this:

> 'Half-past nine,' Anthony said. 'The last news in London.' Kate turned the pointer. 'A depression advancing from Iceland,' a smooth anonymous voice said and was cut off. 'Good old London.'
> 'There's Moscow,' Kate said, swinging the pointer; 'there's Hilversum, Berlin, Paris. . . .'
> Aimer à loisir,
> Aimer et mourir,
> Au pays qui te ressemble.'
> 'The Duke of York, opening the premises of the Gas Light and Coke. . . .'
> The Voices went out one by one like candles on a Christmas cake, white waxen, guttering in the atmospherics over the North Sea . . . a whistle on the ether. (pp. 176–7)

In a novel about ruthless multinationalism and moral deracination, it's appropriately atmospheric that radio evokes a global context for imminent murder.

Symptomatic of the peculiarity of broadcasting's influence is the fact that there was such a thing as the cinematic- but not radio-novel in the thirties, though radio was certainly a model for the use of recorded echoing 'voice-overs', to express characters' thoughts and memories over stage action, as in the play of Barke's *Major Operation* (1940). 'Radiogenic', like cinematic, techniques existed in literary and, particularly, dramatic form long before the medium itself. A good example is the way in which the 'radiogenic' potentials of Ibsen's play *Peer Gynt* or Strindberg's *Ghost Sonata* influenced a strand of the Modernist novel which developed in parallel with broadcasting, through Joyce's Modernist 'play for voices', the 'Circe' chapter of *Ulysses* (1922), in turn imitated by Orwell's most 'experimental' piece of writing, the Trafalgar Square section of *A Clergyman's Daughter* (1935), and finally merging with broadcasting itself as the postwar script *Under Milk Wood* (1954), aided by Dylan Thomas's own experience as a radio scriptwriter, poem-reader and actor in plays and features from 1937. *Under Milk Wood* also drew on a narrative structure pioneered in thirties radio drama.

The formal problem of creating radio drama, rather than just drama-on-the-wireless was intertextual with literature on the one hand and cinema on the other. The most avant-garde precedent was Lance Sieveking's 1928 *Kaleidoscope I*. Subtitled 'A Rhythm Representing the Life of Man from Cradle to Grave', its words, effects and music were montaged with the technical assistance of the recently developed 'dramatic control panel'. According to Peter Black, Sieveking opened radio up to Modernism and enabled it to reproduce the fluidity of cinema.[14] As John Drakakis has commented, it was henceforth possible to dissolve temporal and spatial boundaries, extending radio's powers of aural suggestion, and 'offering parallels in sound' to epic theatre.[15] The montage and 'stream of consciousness effects' Sieveking initiated were soon explored more fully in Tyrone Guthrie's *Squirrel's Cage* (1929) and *The Flowers Are Not For You To Pick* (1930). Thus, as Drakakis put it, 'a basic grammar of radio production' was formulated from literature, drama, and psychology, but especially film, with terms like 'fade-in', 'fade-out' and 'cross-fade'. Even sound-effects could now be seen as 'aural transformation' of 'camera angle and focus'.[16] On the whole, though, and with notable exceptions like D. G. Bridson (discussed in Chapter 4), the innovative possibilities of radio plays and 'dramatised' features were barely exploited by Leftists until the very different political circumstances of the Second World War. The intertextuality of radio and theatre also remained largely one-sided. Broadcast stage drama remained the norm, so much so even the new medium of television picked up the habit, Priestley's *When We Are Married* being the first theatre performance televised directly in November 1938, although in its earliest days BBC TV had also been rather more experimental (Pirandello's *The Man With the Flower in his Mouth* had been adapted for transmission from the studio in 1930). The 'middlebrow' microphone serial was also conceived in 1938, making radical drama far less characteristic of thirties broadcasting than were the *The Archers'* ancestors.

Nevertheless, MacColl and Littlewood were brought together by features work for the Northern Region in the mid-thirties, particularly for D. G. Bridson (see Chapter 4). Jimmie Miller, as MacColl was known at the time, also presented eye-witness radio documentaries like Olive Shapley's *Homeless People* (6 September 1938) and wrote the historical feature *The Chartists' March* (13 May 1938) for producer and radio poet, John Pudney. Littlewood suggested using Engels' *The Condition of the Working Class in England* to compare with the present for Shapley's *The Classic Soil*. Littlewood and MacColl put their broadcasting experience to good use on stage. Ian Rodger in *Radio Drama* goes so far as to argue that 'even if they had never heard of Brecht', it would have determined Theatre Workshop's style and approach: 'The mixture of song, of direct statement to the audience, of narrated dramatic scenes, is a formula familiar to the radio feature of the thirties.'[17] During the Spanish Civil War, for example, their Theatre Union staged dramatic interludes and pageants for Medical-Aid, strongly influenced by the polyphonic radio-montage style developed by Archie Harding and Bridson. As MacColl recalls, spotlighted workers would make testimonal speeches, between songs and passages from the *Flaming Poetaster*: 'The effect produced by juxtaposing the flat Lancashire accents . . . against the soaring voices of the choir, the rich velvety bass-baritone of Paul Robeson, or the stinging hail of MacDiarmid's poetry, was riveting.' Abrupt formal contrasts and radiophonic location changes became integral to the Theatre Workshop style and MacColl's postwar radio-ballads, 'those BBC documentaries in which the form and spirit of folk-music and recorded actuality strive to become a single entity'. Similarly the Spanish sequence of their *Last Edition* used another device introduced by A. E. Harding in his feature *Crisis in Spain*, to coordinate separate events and locations, which became standard in radio. An uncharacterised 'microphone voice' 'would repeat a phrase at intervals or would read out a list of names or a group of statistics or a catalogue of dates' between each Naturalistic scene (Goorney and MacColl (eds), *Agit-Prop to Theatre Workshop*, p. xlvi; for Harding's influence, see Chapter 4).

Radiogenic montage was also commonly used to subvert the power of broadcasting itself in the experimental drama of bourgeois Leftists. 'Mr and Mrs A' in *F6* are saturated by radio as well as press propaganda. They are very much a parody of the 'average' member of the public envisaged by programme builders. The *Radio Times* 'Listeners' Own' number for April 1938 imagined 'Mr and Mrs Listener' with their four children and Fido the dog.[18] Throughout, the epic technique gradually reveals a jingoistic agenda behind official broadcasting, climaxing in a surreal radio 'question panel', a format established in the thirties and reaching its apotheosis in the *Brains Trust* in 1941. Auden and Isherwood's mock-experts are unmasked because the questions posed to them articulate the ordinarily unconscious investments in the relationship between broadcaster and public. The answer to the tediousness of work, money worries, the decay of love and the mystery of mortality, is the same distraction and consolation by vicarious adventure: 'Think of those climbers up on F6. No decent food. No fires. No nice warm beds. Do you think *they* grumble? You ought to be ashamed of yourself (see *F6*, pp. 89–90). The action of MacNeice's *Out of the Picture* is similarly intercut throughout by a pantomimic Announcer and Listener-In.

MacNeice's writing shows that his eventual move to the BBC in 1941 was inevitable. Both Christopher Holme and Barbara Coulton maintain that MacNeice's reportage set an important precedent for his features work,[19] but his talents as a dramatist, so restricted by the conditions of the thirties, blossomed in wartime. Similarly, R. D. Smith has pointed out that MacNeice had long been practising radiogenic poetic techniques like 'internal monologue, the swift, sharp-cut cinema reel of a life flashing through the mind of a dying person, sound effects verbally placed and primed, music as function not decoration', exemplified not just by *Out of the Picture*, but also his translation of Aeschylus's *Agamemnon*, performed by the Group Theatre in 1936. The classical chorus would become an especially important aspect of his broadcast style. As Walter Allen commented, MacNeice turned his already essentially public poetry into 'what might be called an applied art'.[20]

MacNeice had outlined the dilemma of the innovative playwright in the thirties, caught between smug-bourgeois naturalism, whose public came not to be challenged, but to 'break bread with society', and artless didacticism, as sometimes offered by Left Theatre revues: 'the complacent reverence of the audience was painful to contemplate. Shoddy writing, production, and acting were uproariously applauded, under the aegis of Mr Gollancz and the shadow of Spain.'[21] Advising his contemporaries in 1938, he pointed to his own eventual way out. For writers of dramatic verse, radio was the medium offering the greatest challenge (though, citing Auden's GPO work, he also felt verse 'more suitable than prose for a commentary on certain types of film'). Broadcasting offered the opportunity not just of collaboration with other artists, but with a vast public, whose requirements and criticisms could largely only be guessed at. However, he was confident that not only could a creative relationship be built up, but that interaction with popular demands would enable the poet to discover resources outside his traditional cultural isolation.[22] The degree of his success will be examined in Chapter 4.

VERSE AND FICTION

Photographic, rather than radiophonic, montage was the principal media influence on the form of thirties verse and fiction. Francis Klingender's essay in *5 on Revolutionary Art* had praised John Heartfield's photomontage for the way it reassembled visible reality[23] and many Leftist writers were excited by the contribution such techniques made to the visual agitprop produced by the political struggle in mainland Europe. The montage described in Auden's 1937 essay 'Impressions of Valencia' resembles the topographical format of his poem 'Spain' (see *English Auden*, pp. 360–1 and 210–12, respectively). MacNeice too recalled the striking juxtapositions of Republican posters.[24] The portable camera was also an essential aid for many writers and photographic materials were widespread on and between book covers, while the pervasiveness of cinematic terminology in their discourse corresponded to writers' attempts to emulate and investigate the formal properties of motion film.

Just as the movies were the medium most refracted in Leftist texts, so they had the most dynamic influence on textual form, especially since many writers felt cinematic techniques might modernise their own medium without forfeiting political clarity. In the course of attacking the capitalist media many thirties writers developed their own types of montage. Collisions between different kinds of factual representation and/or imaginary events provided perspectives which challenged the notion of unmediated realism and its assertion of univocal truth. Cinema promised a new kind of factual authenticity, but its cultural status was problematic. The subjectivity of 'camera-eyed' witnesses, as much as their objectivity, was foregrounded in thirties texts, undermining any universalised norm of human perception or technological reproduction. Writers, following Brian Howard's interests in Weimar avant-gardism, undoubtedly began to conceive of the 'camera eye' as a kind of standard for observational accuracy and Mass-Observation's founding pamphlet of 1936 talked of its volunteers as 'subjective' cameras, whose individual bias would be edited out by the correlation of images. Isherwood typified this tendency and almost certainly knew *Kino Glaz* and other Vertov films (whether he got his own literary 'camera-eye' via Dos Passos' short story or not). But he was also typical in his increasing suspicions about the privileged objectivity of filmic discourse. His own creative 'fixings' of fact in *Goodbye to Berlin*, as we shall see later in this chapter, are not only based on editing, but acknowledge that the camera-eyed witness is always part of the reality he reports, in explicit or displaced form. Virtually every member of the Auden-gang seemed to view their experiences, especially in central Europe, through the semi-detachment of an avant-garde lens. To take a much less-known example, in John Lehmann's *Evil was Abroad* Rudi, the unemployed Viennese youth moves 'in the strange, numbed manner that made Peter think of a figure in a slow-motion' and 'just as if he were watching a film . . . he saw a figure cross this common with head averted'. (The working-class Rudi's own cinematic outlook, by ironic contrast, to the narrator's is Hollywoodised.) Similarly, the face of a correspondent, fresh from the Reichstag arson, 'seemed to be changed by what he had just been through, darkened and older, while at the same time it was keener: like two shots in a film that fade into one another' (pp. 5, 32 and 173).

This tendency to reach for cinematic effects became almost automatic, a stylistic cliché of the period in itself. Spender's 'Poem 6' of his 1930–33 collection is a particularly gimmicky example: 'I was on a train. Like the quick spool of a film/ I watched hasten away the simple green which can heal/ Sadness' (*Collected Poems*, p. 24). But cinema undoubtedly fostered an enormous range of energising metaphors for proletarians as well as bourgeois Leftists. In *The Last Cage Down*, Jim Cameron's premonition about the unsafe mine roof is as vivid as a movie. Consequently, his vendetta against the boss (in defiance of Party warnings against personalising politics) parodies the 'man's gotta do' heroics of Western showdowns: 'he had seen it written in the future as clearly as if it had been cast upon the screen in a cinema. He had not anticipated that the victim would be his own brother.' *The Last Cage Down* also considers transatlantic political ethics in feature terms: ' "I reckon when they start making a revolution over there there'll be an awful lot of blood spilt," Elsa had said, "Why, I once saw a picture of them gangsters . . . it was awful. They must be wicked, Jim, don't you think?" ' Jim replies, ' "I reckon we have our gangsters over here, Mother" ' (pp. 258 and 237–8, respectively). However, it was one thing borrowing cinema imagery for popular intertextual appeal and quite another incorporating its grammar into textual structure, as we shall see.

Verse

The influence of cinema in thirties poetry was undoubtedly boosted by Auden's keen interest. MacNeice linked Auden's observational alertness with the camera in 1938: 'He admires the cinema's unrivalled capacity for rapportage'. But MacNeice also acknowledged Auden derived this from their High Modernist predecessors. Eliot 'cuts quickly . . . by juxtaposing shots of the contemporary world with shots which he has deliberately hoarded and selected from his world of books or culture'.[25] Greene also argued that Raymond Spottiswoode's definition of montage as 'irruption of natural continuity' could easily apply to *The Waste Land* (see *Spectator*, 27 September 1935; *Mornings in the Dark*, pp. 484–5). Moreover, MacNeice's post-thirties revaluation of Eliot's masterpiece admitted that his generation's politically-committed adaptation of its techniques had failed to answer its pessimism about the evasiveness of reality and epistemological doubt: 'The cinema technique . . . would naturally intrigue the novelty-mad adolescent . . . but that the total complex of mood-and-meaning remains for me now, for all its enrichment by experience and study, qualitatively the same as it was then, strikes me as astonishing.'[26]

As we saw in the Introduction, early Auden provided a kind of template for the visual awareness and mobility of thirties poetry, but Auden's own valuation of cinematic form became more sceptical as the decade unfolded. 'Poem XXII' of 1934 begins breezily as if leaving through a photo sequence of the day's events and impressions (see *English Auden*, p. 152). Later in 'Letter to William Coldstream, Esq.' (1937), Auden posed as both documentary cameraman and editor:

Let me pretend that I'm the impersonal eye of the camera
Sent out by God to shoot on location.
And we'll look at the rushes together.

                              (*Letters from Iceland*, p. 223)

But objective visualisation is already problematised, since, a few lines further back, Auden quoted Coldstream's belief that the artist is more rightly both perceiver and teller, spy and gossip. Consequently, the poem presents images from 'the rushes', but also foregrounds subjective impressions and symbolic associations which could not be represented in austere, deictically-undisrupted documentary footage. This mischievousness epitomises the growing critical tension between textual performance and strictly-emulated film technique:

Face of an Icelandic Professor
Like a child's self-expression in plasticine
              A child from the bottom form.

Then a lot out of focus.
Now a pan round a typical sitting-room
Bowl of postcards on the table Harmonium with Brahm's Sapphic
Ode
Pi-picture – little girl crosses broken ravine bridge protected by
angel.
Cut to straddling ponies – close up of farmer's hands at a girth
strap
Dissolve to long shot of Reykholt school
Corbusier goes all Northern.
Close up of Gynaecologist Angler offering me brandy
In the next war he said
There'd be one anaesthetist to at least four tables.

Not surprisingly, the poem finally makes explicit the widening differences it has implied all along, by admitting one medium's techniques
cannot be literally employed in another: 'The novelist has one way
of stating experience,/ The film director another/ These are our
versions – each man to his medium' (*Letters from Iceland*, p. 227). 'I
Am Not a Camera' would be Auden's final conclusion about impersonal cinema poetics in the eponymous postwar poem.[27]

'Poem XXII' of 1934 also contains a 'newsreel' verse coordinating
hyperreal events with intimate experience, and cleverly suggesting
the effect of enlargement and foreshortened movement on the screen:

Ten thousand of the desperate marching by
Five feet, six feet, seven feet high:
Hitler and Mussolini in their wooing poses
Churchill acknowledging the voters' greeting
Roosevelt at the microphone, Van der Lubbe laughing
And our first meeting.
                              (*English Auden*, p. 153)

Other writers followed Auden's formal cue in this respect also. As
we have seen. Day Lewis's 'Newsreel' was itself constructed as a
kind of news montage, but with a subversive commentary designed
to objectify the latent subtext of conventional screen-reporting and
its effects on the audience. Similarly, in Orwell's *Coming Up for Air*,
fear of repression in the next war (shaped by Orwell's persecution
by a totalitarianised media and police in Spain) suddenly unspools
like an uncensored newsreel from a nightmare future. As George
Bowling warns:

It's all going to happen. All the things you've got at the back of your mind, the things you're terrified of, the things that you tell yourself are just a nightmare or only happen in foreign countries, the bombs, the food-queues, the rubber truncheons, the barbed wire, the coloured shirts, the slogans, the enormous faces, the machine-guns squirting out of bedroom windows.[28]

In 1949, MacNeice wrote that 'since *Autumn Journal* I have been eschewing the news-reel and attempting a stricter kind of drama which largely depends upon structure.'[29] His own 1943 poem, 'The News-Reel', was therefore crucially transitional – a revisiting of the informational confusion of the thirties in an ironically revised version of one of its characteristic forms. The poem thus encapsulated MacNeice's own struggle to disentangle a politically enabling meaning from the cumulative snarl of hyperreal images and personal memories since Munich: 'A tangle of black film/ Squirming like bait upon the floor of my mind/ And scissors clicking daily' (*Collected Poems*, p. 203). Mere montage seemed no longer adequate to the task. The poem resisted the urge to pick out and connect isolated images and expressed the hope that a more complete and satisfactory pattern of values would emerge over time out of this 'blind drama' from the editing suite of history.

Fiction

Film technique came into its own as a new principle of poesis in the thirties novel. 'It is the cinema which has taught a new habit of narrative', as Evelyn Waugh put it in a review of Greene's *The Heart of the Matter* (1948), recalling his literary contemporaries' schooling in its craft:

> it is as though, out of the indefinite length of film, sequences have been cut which, assembled, comprise an experience which is the reader's alone, without any correspondence to the experience of the protagonists. The writer has become director and producer ... he controls the action, and moves freely about it, but he is not part of it. His camera is like the eye of God, seeing all, but withholding judgement.[30]

But Grahame Smith misrepresents the thirties generation's apprenticeship to Modernism when he claims that even Greene's 'best

work has reached a large public because he avoided 'the experiments in fiction associated with the names of Joyce, Faulkner and
Virginia Woolf', and chose to model his technique instead on 'the
major popular art of the twentieth century'. Joyce, Faulkner and
Woolf were the very novelists Raymond Williams regarded as 'film-
makers manqués'.[31] The cinematic novel in the thirties is as much
a question of developing certain pioneering Modernist interests as
resisting others.

As early as 1929, Greene himself linked Joyce with directors such
as Cavalcanti and Ruttmann: *Ulysses* and *Rien que les Heures* had
much in common in their representation of one day (see *Mornings
in the Dark*, p. 4). In 1938, in the same collection of movie essays
featuring Greene's 'Subjects and Stories', Charles Davy considered
cinema and the Modernist poetic. Using section two of Woolf's *The
Years*, '1891', Davy argued that her narrative's distinctly multiple
and simultaneous consciousness 'could be used without much
change as the shooting script of a film'. Like camerawork and editing, argued Davy, Woolf's method avoided 'description of a single
scene from a single fixed viewpoint', but instead scattered them
through space and coordinated them in time to construct 'a new
unity'. It was 'from a precisely similar selective approach to
nature . . . which breaks down and chooses and rebuilds – that the
cinema derives its own creative power'.[32]

In 1928 Greene paralleled film's evolution from the stage of action to that of thought with the novel's. Technical advance was
culturally relative. Hollywood, for example, was stuck in anachronistic realism, comparable to the novels of Defoe. Alternatively,
German Expressionist films like *Warning Shadows*, 'with its strange
removal of action to the second hand' had reached the early Modernism of James and Conrad (*The Times*, 9 April 1928; *Mornings in
the Dark*, pp. 387–90). But film was 'still the limping Pegasus of the
arts' precisely because it had the potential to catch up with and
outdo literary narrative. Echoing Woolf on Modernism and psychology, he argued its mobile images could give a much closer
impression of 'the flashing inconsequence of human thought' ('A
Film Technique: Rhythms of Space and Time' (1928), *Mornings in
the Dark*, pp. 390–2, and 396–7).

Cinematic intertextuality was a hot political as well as aesthetic
issue in the thirties. In September 1937, the *Daily Worker* featured
Dos Passos's short story 'The Camera Eye' as a model for popular
Leftist fiction, complete with advice on how to read it: 'remember

that this is the verbal equivalent to the inclusive technique of photography, registering apparently irrelevant and even distracting
details for the sake of achieving a complete atmospheric approxi-
mation of reality'.[33] In the days before recanting his 'Formalism',
Eisenstein saw no incompatibility between his projects for filming
Ulysses and *Das Kapital*. Despite Karl Radek's subsequent denunciation of Joyce's *Ulysses* at the 1934 Soviet Writers' Union Congress
as 'a heap of dung, crawling with worms, photographed by a
cinema-apparatus through a microscope', many British Leftists
followed Joyce's interest in film in their quest to find a suitably
modernised neo-realism.[34] The Modernists associated cinema particularly with the dynamic totality of urban society. Ezra Pound
wrote in 1922, 'The life of a village is a narrative. . . . In the city the
visual impressions succeed each other, overlap, overcross, they are
cinematographic.'[35] Similarly, Alick West's *Crisis and Criticism* (1937)
focused on the cinematic aspects of *Ulysses*, arguing that it was
indeed a 'reflection' of a real social and historical context, though *in
a complex, mediating sense*. Joyce's montage coordinated 'the individual action within the totality of relations existing at that moment'. *Ulysses* broke the 'traditional unity' of Naturalist narrative,
but constructed a panorama of the city of Dublin 'growing out of
its social basis':

> there is not only a continual jumping from one line of action to
> another, between which on the old basis there is no connection
> whatever; there is also a change in the conception of individuals
> performing these actions. They are also conceived in terms of
> relation, not of distinct demarcated consciousness.[36]

Calder-Marshall countered the hardline Socialist Realist argument
that such techniques disrupted narrative structure and distorted
actuality. They were an appropriate alternative, he insisted, because
conventional realism was itself politically regressive:

> Because the subject matter of a capitalist film is fantastic, the
> treatment must give the appearance of naturalism. The camera
> and the microphone are used like a natural eye and ear, reproduc-
> ing what is seen and heard. The possibilities of the film medium,
> which are broader and more fluid than those of any other art-

form, must be limited to a fraction of their capacity. Yet there is no aesthetic justification for this practice, naturalism in the studio being as artificial as any other means of expression.[37]

Basil Wright agreed that cinematic realism was inherently illusory and 'achieved by a constant interference with natural forces'. Furthermore, according to Allardyce Nicoll, it could, paradoxically, endow representations of both actuality and fantasy with equivalent plausibility.[38]

Greene reviewed that breviary of cinema technique, Raymond Spottiswoode's *A Grammar of the Film*, in 1935.[39] Greene felt Spottiswoode struck a sane balance in recognising film's possibilities without overinflating them, unlike canting ethusiasts, among whom Greene now regretfully included old masters like Eisenstein and Pudovkin. Greene was also sceptical about montage. As the artistic buzzword of the time, its method was 'so vaguely apprehended that its very existence has been denied and its particular meaning has been swallowed up in the meaningless general term, "constructive cutting"' (see *Spectator*, 27 September 1935; *Mornings in the Dark*, pp. 484–6). Spottiswoode's elaboration cleared the matter up: 'the production of a concept or sensation through the mutual impact of other conceptions or sensations; in its structural aspect, the juxtaposition of shots, series and sequences in such a way as to produce this impact'.[40] Greene felt the whole point of such technical rules was that they were descriptive, not prescriptive, and could be creatively broken. Though he was confident that if montage could be extended beyond Russian films and English documentaries, and that the standard of features would immediately improve beyond the 'potted play', he was wary of its overuse. Relentless cutting from one point of 'high tension' to the next, was 'close to melodrama' because it lacked fidelity to the merely routine which made up such a large part of reality (*Mornings in the Dark*, p. 486).

Despite Greene's reservations, montage was virtually talismanic for thirties novelists. Part one of Anthony Powell's *Afternoon Men* (1931) is glibly entitled 'Montage'. Calder-Marshall's experimental *Dead Centre* (1935) simply juxtaposes fifty fragmentary perspectives on a fatal sports accident and leaves the reader to interconnect them by imaginative effort. Montage 'cross-sections' of the modern big city, as in the films of Vertov and Walther Ruttmann were particularly influential. Philip Henderson's *Events in the Early Life of Anthony Price* (1935) contains an account of Ruttmann's day-in-the-life-of-

Berlin documentary *Sinfonie einer Großstadt* (1927). The protagonist relishes the satirical collisions of candid images:

> As night fell lights came out all over the town, electric signs dazzled the eyes and advertisements for beer, cigarettes, toothpaste and scurf-destroyer sprang to magnified, flickering life on the sides of buildings, Regiments of cars waiting in the traffic-block took their human loads to their evening pleasures. Wine lists were scrutinised, waiters bowed, men gazed in women's eyes, the lips caked with rouge in mock-voluptuousness. Brimming glasses of wine were raised. Orchestras struck up and jazz conductors pranced and punched the air among the palms. Everyone began jigging and revolving, just as the machines in the factories jigged and revolved. Huge clowns appeared, absurdly tragic or fatuously grinning, spun and dived through paper hoops, the crowds applauded and emptied their pockets of the money earned during the day. A starving man threw himself into a canal.[41]

A *Left Review* advertisement proclaimed the similarly panoramic scope and cinematic mobility of John Sommerfield's *May Day* (1936) as 'A cross-section of the social pyramid, from the factory to the managing director's luxury flat. It's three days of life today, and it *moves* – it's got technique.'[42] Sommerfield owed much to the fascination the dynamics of film held for Modernists like Dos Passos, Joyce, Jules Romains and Woolf, as well as actual film-makers like Vertov and Ruttmann.[43] *May Day* was a radical cinematic adaptation of the formal templates of novels like *Ulysses* and *Mrs Dalloway* – both fictionalised cross-sections of one June day – which revealed the collectivity of mundane social and economic relationships. *May Day* unfolds from morning, 29 April, to early afternoon, 1 May, 'a few years hence', and its characters and events are meant to be 'typical' of an average year between 1930 and 1940 (see Sommerfield's 'Author's Note').

Andy Croft points out that *May Day* was simply 'one of the best of several' such cinematic *romans fleuves*.[44] Others included (with varying degrees of Leftism and artistic success) James Barke's *Major Operation* (1936), Walter Allen's *Innocence is Drowned* (1938), Anthony Bertram's *Men Adrift* (1935) and *The King Sees Red* (1936), Arthur Calder-Marshall's *Pie in the Sky* (1937), Storm Jameson's *A Day Off* (1933) and *Here Comes a Candle* (1938), and, of course, Graham Greene's *It's a Battlefield* (1934). Many attempted panoramic perspectives like *May Day*'s and often used montage and camera-eye techniques. Dot Allan's *Hunger March* (1934) has topical affinities with both *May Day* and fellow Scot James Barke's *Major Operation*, whose techniques of simultaneity and coordination also recall *Ulysses'* 'Wandering Rocks' chapter. As Croft puts it.

> Panoramic pictures like these, both detailed and generalised, static and moving, strained to convey an adequate sense of the scale and complexity of contemporary urban life. Their bird's eye perspectives reveal the collective working routines, the necessary working patterns of the modern city, its collective functions, moral geography, mass pleasures and visible sociology.[45]

As Stuart Laing shows, *May Day* demonstrates the cross-fertilisation between avant-garde writing and film in its departure from conventional narrative structure. Vertov, Ruttmann and Sommerfield all used 'totalising images of the city as a network of communication system'[46] and *May Day* opens with a panorama of London's complex and mystified organisation, where lives are consumed in alienated labour: *'Let us take factory chimneys, cannons trained at dingy skies, pointing at the sun and stars, and blinding their aim with their own exhalations: towering more than church spires, their long shadows leaning across lives more heavily than did the medieval darkness of the hand of God'* (p. 3, Sommerfield's italics). But the 'normally invisible connections', as Laing puts it,[47] of the social and economic system are troped by Sommerfield with London's material communications: 'shining tarred roads', 'geometries of telephone wires and tramlines', skies oozing 'soot and aeroplanes' and railways writhing 'like worms under the clay, tangled with spiderwebs and mazes of electric cables, drains and gaspipes' (pp. 3–4). Griersonian documentary's more heroicised vision of civic interdependence largely played down the frictions between different economic interest groups, but the following description from *May Day* of factory machinery under the new 'speed-up' policy seems to imitate the Griersonian 'romance of industry' only to exhume its controversial roots in questions about who benefits from technological progress:

> Sweating oil and weeping streams of soapy water they clash insatiable metallic jaws with a machinegun rattle that drowns their motors' electric whining and slavering. The bright metal peels away in delicate helices, a golden rain of dust drowns in greenish oil. The chucks come round and round in turn with

eager exactness, with the same monotonous inevitability of movement as the girls' hands, only faster, ever so much faster. There
is no weariness to spoil their work, no fallible mind to guide
them. And they never bleed. One man could look after the lot of
them. All he has to do is to see that they get a regular diet of
metal rod and strip. And he could be eliminated if it was cheaper.
(p. 29)

Sommerfield's attempt to construct a cross-sectional view of the
modern metropolis also raises radical questions about the politics
of 'panoptic' media perspectives on society. The police gyroplane
monitoring the workers' march has a literal view over the 'living
map of London' (p. 209) rivalled only by the imaginative cooperation between the narrator's Vertovian 'camera-eye' and the reader.

May Day used 'phrases at once compressed and highly suggestive', in Storm Jameson's terms, for displaying the paradoxically
intimate relations 'between things (men, acts) widely separated in
space or in the social complex'.[48] Greene's *It's a Battlefield* (discussed
below) also used montage to (in Helga Geyer-Ryan's terms), reconstruct human subjectivity and 'meet the demands of cultural modernism', but dissolved pessimistically into isolated, individual
viewpoints. In contrast, *May Day* confirmed 'the capacity for political action'[49] by not making the reader share the characters' sense of
alienation. It puts him/her in the position to construct an overall
political pattern across the suggestive intervals between the images
it coordinates. For example, while out riding, Peter Langfier, son of
the manager of the carbon works on which the action centres, passes
'George Everdene, gasfitter, 47' unemployed: an ironic juxtaposition of two kinds of 'leisure' based on class difference. Later, Martine
Seton, worried her husband John risks the sack if he joins the
forthcoming demonstration, sees some graffiti publicising it at the
same time as the Earl of Dunbourne, on his way to the directors'
meeting to decide the factory's fate. As the Earl then drives past the
Park Lane Office of Amalgamated Industrial Enterprises. Sir Edwin
Langfier is just leaving it, depressed by the fascistic industrial tactics of the director Sir William Gilray, who in turn observes him
walking across the Park. Gilray is planning how to win the confrontation provoked by the Consortium's speed-up policy while a taxi
passes with a loud-speaker, calling 'all out on May Day' (see pp.
45–50).[50]

Cinema's influence also filtered into the structures of more tech-
nically adventurous proletarian texts. Ewan Tavendale's police in-

terrogation in *Grey Granite* features in flashback: 'And across his memory there swept again, picture on picture, an obscene film, something they'd stick in him while he writhed, a bobby's hand' (p. 161). Greenwood expresses *His Worship the Mayor*'s fear of exposure as a slum-landlord ripping-off the Public Assistance Committee by overcharging his unemployed tenants as a cinematic insert: 'A holy terror stirred in his heart. Streamer headlines of future issues of the newspapers appeared in front of his mind's eye: "Grave charges against Two Cities' Councillor." Lor!' (p. 301). Blumenfeld wove a whole knot of movie associations into *Jew Boy*. Paul Robeson-like American Communist sailor 'Jo-Jo' persuades Alec of his duty not to emigrate to the Soviet Union by alluding to *Potemkin*: '"We gotta stay heah. We don't scuttle from de hold like rats cause de ship is sinkin'. We'se de crew, we'se got responsible jobs. We'se got to chuck de officers overboard an' save de ship . . . cause it belongs to us. Yes sah!"' The novel's climactic scene also works through another popular screen motif: 'He had no desire for sleep, so many things had happened to him to-day, and the events were still playing themselves out in his head, like bits from a newsreel' (pp. 343 and 347).

On a grander scale Barke's *Major Operation* coordinated images to suggest a panorama of Glasgow in the opening section 'SUNSET OVER THE SECOND CITY', representing the reactions of all classes to apparently auspicious changes in the literal and economic climate during the Slump. Later a democratising Saturday-night supper ritual brings together classes all over the city in the chapter 'RHAPSODY OF FISH AND CHIPS'. Ken Worpole argues that *May Day*'s success determined Jim Phelan's choice of the 'big city' cinematic style in his *Ten-A-Penny-People* (1938), but another Jewish East Ender, Ashley Smith, wrote what was, in many ways, the culmination of thirties panoptic metropolitan cross-sections, *A City Stirs* (1939). Smith dispensed with conventional narrative altogether, by cutting synchronically between places, persons and activities, and interconnecting social and economic extremes.[51] Indeed Grierson's own description of Ruttmann's *Symphonie* could have served as a blueprint for Smith's treatment of London, detail by detail, from the visual rhythm of the train entering through the suburbs right down to the afternoon shower:

Wheels, rails, details of engines, telegraph wires, landscapes and other simple images flowed along in procession, with similar abstracts passing occasionally in and out of the general movement.

There followed a sequence of such movements which, in their total effect, created very imposingly the story of a Berlin day. The day began with a procession of workers, the factories got under way, the streets filled: the city's forenoon became a hurly-burly of tangled pedestrians and street cars, there was a respite for food: a various respite with contrast of rich and poor. The city started work again, and a shower of rain in the afternoon became a considerable event. The city stopped work and, in further hectic processional of pubs and cabarets and dancing legs and illuminated sky-signs, finished its day.[52]

The cinematic novel form had become highly self-conscious by 1939. Smith described the new London day as if it were itself a hyperreal illusion with the sun 'a great projector' screening its images on the earth. And like Vertov and Sommerfield, he used the motif of weaving for social interconnections, as in his 'footage' of morning commuting:

They are being packed tighter towards the centre, by the charged concentrated influx of the crowded trains. There is the reassuming of a million tales of pain and happiness; the threads are being picked upon their manifold interwoven shuttles of intrigue; the interdependent woof and warp of their close-meshed lives; bound together like vetch grass; treading each other's heels like ants. They are hurrying into the tremendous tale they are making, into the never-ceasing shaken kaleidoscope of their unending story.

However, Smith's camera-eye had a less politically-preprogrammed sense of the underlying historical pattern of this collectivity than Sommerfield's, albeit unorthodox, Communist text: 'Over the ethos, the spirit, the psyche of the city no man or organisation has any control . . . The symphony that is played is no lilting melody, no coordination of cadence and rhythm, but something spontaneous, tangled and gigantic, created by itself, integral with its own life and movement.'[53]

Perhaps the most thoroughgoing and subtle attempts to emulate and investigate movie form among thirties novelists were made by Greene and Isherwood. The young Greene, as Parkinson notes, left good films convinced that he was going to produce good writing. His confidence derived in particular 'from the communal response to the ultimate popular art-form'. After watching Feodor Ozep's

The Crime of Dimitri Karamazov in 1932, Greene completely 'recast' the heroine of his own breakthrough novel, *Stamboul Train*. Greene recalled in a 1969 interview that such influence long predated his actual work for cinema, as in the case of *It's a Battlefield*, his only deliberate attempt to narrate in purely cinematic terms, though, ironically, also one of his few novels never filmed (see *Mornings in the Dark*, pp. xv and xviii, also 524–30).

Greene hinted how the poetic possibilities of montage had shaped the social and/or international cross-sections of these early novels in *The Lawless Roads* (1939):

> There is something dauntingly world-wide about a ship, when it is free from territorial waters. Every nation has its own private violence, and after a while once can feel at home and sheltered between almost any borders – you grow accustomed to anything. But on a ship the borders drop, the nations mingle – Spanish violence, German stupidity, Anglo-Saxon absurdity – the whole world is exhibited in a kind of crazy montage.[54]

In *It's a Battlefield*, Greene sets 'close-ups' of individual actions within his panorama of what Croft calls the metropolis's 'moral and economic geography'.[55] Consider the following passage at the end of Chapter One, as the Assistant Commissioner and Parliamentary Private Secretary leave Drover's prison:

> The man who tears paper patterns and the male soprano were performing before the pit queues, the shutters of the shops had all gone up, the prostitutes were moving west. The feature pictures had come on the second time at the super-cinemas, and the taxi ranks were melting and re-forming. In the Café Francais in Little Compton Street a man at the counter served two coffees and sold a packet of 'Weights'. The match factory in Battersea pounded out the last ten thousand boxes, working overtime. The cars in the Oxford Street fun-fair rattled and bounced, and the evening papers went to press for the last edition. . . . At each station on the Outer Circle a train stopped every two minutes. (pp. 22–3)

This not only evokes a whole social context by juxtaposing short sequences, but also deploys a clutch of cinematic effects to maximise their poetic associations. Take for example, the generalised, anonymous movement – raised shutters, migrating prostitutes, or the 'accelerated motion' of the blurring taxis – set against 'close up' individual actions in exact locations. Visual hints, anticipating narrative strands that will later be connected with the main plot, are flashed at the reader: Drover's sister-in-law Kay works at the match factory: café-proprietor Jules will lead her to betray his cause by accidentally burning the petition in a moment of frivolity. At the end of the passage, a rapid sequence of newspaper headlines (a cliché, of course, in thirties films) underlines how the novel's events will become incestuously entangled with their hyperreal refractions in the media, like the closed circuit of the Underground itself.

It's a Battlefield is almost meta-fictional in its intertextuality with film and Greene's fondness for foregrounding the screen itself as an ambiguous symbol of un/consciousness (as we saw with *The Confidential Agent* in Chapter 2) can be traced back to it. Conrad Drover, for example, resorting to blackmail to obtain money for a gun, 'noted with pleasure a faint unease touch the wide white face' of his victim 'like the shadow of a man crossing the empty screen' (p. 156). Above all, Greene had a popular director's eye for the memorable device. The moment of a slaying, shown in flashback as the murderer is apprehended, is pure Hitchcock:

> The Assistant Commissioner . . . saw for a moment not the brossed hair and the fat desperate face, but an old woman, who had been too close with her money, raising her hands and screaming, while the steam from Paddington Station rose across the window and a goods train plodding down to Westbourne Grove hooted on a higher note than she could reach, so that no one heard her. . . . (p. 83; see also the discussion of Greene and Hitchcock below.)

Similarly, the final paragraph anticipates Greene's greatest *coup de cinéma*, the 'temptation scene' on the Big Wheel at Vienna's Prater funfair in *The Third Man* (1949). The Assistant Commissioner evades existential *angst* about human justice by absorbing himself in forensic details. Conversely, Harry Lime cynically disregards the mere 'dots' below who just might be future casualties of his adulterated penicillin. Both moments of bad faith are characterised by dehumanising, cinematic shifts in perspective: 'Then without warning, from his dissatisfaction and self-distrust and shame, his spirits rose; all that worried him dropped away, like the little figures running back from the landing ground as an airship lifts' (p. 202). The metaphor which describes the policeman's elation also ironically echoes contemporary newsreel footage of the launch of the ill-fated R. 101 in 1930.

Few thirties writers explored the possible intertextuality between the two mediums as far as Greene, though some occasionally pushed it into openly surreal disruption of deictic continuity, as in *The Wild Goose Chase*. Warner's satirical narrative is so cinematically fluid it renders both geography and duration entirely relative. His allegorical 'other' country is both just over the frontier and impossibly remote. Similarly, the same event lasts days or years, depending upon how it is viewed. Among the totalitarian City's intellectuals, this elasticity reaches the apogee of sophistry and moral evasion. The hero is seduced by a woman whose body and mind can move simultaneously on opposed planes at will. In effect she can perceive reality like a film run backwards, 'undoing' her act of adultery and enjoying it conscience-free. By such means thirties writers used cinema to extend Modernism's preoccupation with the paradoxical nature of space–time and consciousness. In this way, they anticipate the fully Postmodern ironies and ethical conundrums of novels like Kurt Vonnegut's *Slaughterhouse Five* and Martin Amis's *Time's Arrow* where historical causality can be completely reversed.

Early Soviet anti-Naturalism was all but suppressed by the late thirties, but occasionally Russian films could still show writers that the way ahead was 'poetry expressed in images', as Greene put it evidencing Yefim Dzigan's *We from Kronstadt*, in which the camera cut poignantly back and forth between the heavy rocks round the necks of condemned prisoners to the weightless wings of circling gulls (*Spectator*, 26 February 1937; *Mornings in the Dark*, p. 180). But Greene insisted commercial movies also had something to teach the artist. While deploring myths of 'market democracy', he recognised their potential for helping Literature off its pedestal to reach a wider public: 'popular taste' might be a dictatorship, but 'awareness of an audience is an essential discipline' (*Spectator*, 20 December 1935; *Mornings in the Dark*, p. 57). Stalinist hijacking of Soviet cinema also qualified Greene's opinions about British censorship. Paradoxically, the suppression of anything 'controversial' was potentially a creative asset as much as a handicap. It saved serious filmmakers from the glib didactics of Socialist Realism – 'the lifeless malice of

Pudovkin's capitalist automatons, that dreadful shadow of Victorian progress and inevitable victory'. The challenge was to make psychological virtues out of taboos – 'It is for the artist to show his cunning now', intending 'cunning' in the double-sense of the subversive skill needed to circumvent BBFC duplicity (*Reflections*, pp. 65–6). The adapted thriller might provide a formula for features that could be both popular and radical at once and explains why it became such an important form for writers especially in Greene's own film work during and after the war.

Fritz Lang's films had always been at the heart of Greene's precocious interest in cinema,[56] but by 1937 he was holding up *The Spy* and *Fury* as models imbuing 'all the old excitements at their simplest and most surefire' with 'poetic drama' (*Mornings in the Dark*, p. 417). He reserved special praise for Lang's protégé Peter Lorre's performance as the child-murderer in *M* – 'There was nothing of the bogey, the lighted turnip, the Karloff about his performance' – recalling 'the expression of despairing tenderness he turned on his small victim, the hapless struggle in his face against a habit he could not break'. Lorre also portrayed the very image of involuntary compulsion in Karl Freund's *The Hands of Orlac*. It's possible to see Lorre's morally equivocal case studies as screen-prototypes for Greene's psychically maimed, obsessional thirties hero-villains like Raven and Pinkie, especially with the following passage in mind: 'Those marble pupils in the pasty spherical head are like the eyepieces of a microscope through which you can watch the tangled mind laid out flat on the slide . . . his very features are metaphysical' (*World Film News*, July 1936; *Mornings in the Dark*, pp. 403–4.). Equivocal links between vulnerability and brutalisation, innocence and corruption were both Lorre and Greene's stock in trade. Indeed Lorre's acting under Lang's direction might well have provided a model for other thirties writers. Katherine Burdekin's psychopath in *Proud Man* (1934) is likewise no monster, but motivated by a similar paradox: he murders his pre-pubescent victims to preserve them from consciousness of the world of adult sexuality by which he was prematurely traumatised.[57]

Creative ambivalence to Hitchcock's thrillers would also be a major factor in Greene's development. He continually berated the 'tricksiness' of Hitchcock's devices – 'The murderer's button dropped on the baccarat board; the strangled organist's hands prolonging the notes in the empty church' – for his failure to prolong such moments into structurally integral conceits, like Basil Wright's bell-startled bird tracked across the landscape of *Song of Ceylon* (*Spectator*, 15 April 1936; see *Mornings in the Dark*, p. 102). But as Grahame Smith has suggested, Greene's antipathy for the British director was probably rooted in his own penchant for similarly ingenious shocks arising from 'the eruption of pain and terror in the everyday'.[58] This seems to be confirmed by another example Greene fixed on in *The Thirty-Nine Steps* (1935) in which the scream of a charwoman discovering a corpse cuts to the sound of the *Flying Scotsman*, which is tellingly close to the drowning of a dying scream by a train whistle in *It's a Battlefield*, as noted above (*Fortnightly Review*, March 1936; *Mornings in the Dark*, p. 399).

In his autobiography, Greene admitted *Stamboul Train* was largely inspired by the early thirties train-feature vogue, because he couldn't afford an actual Orient Express trip. The genre also disciplined his dramatic economy so that key scenes

> consisted of isolating two characters – hiding in a railway shed in *Stamboul Train*, in an empty house in *A Gun for Sale*. It was as though I wanted to escape from the vast liquidity of the novel and to play out the most important situation on a narrow stage where I could direct every movement of my characters. A scene like that halts the progress of the novel with dramatic emphasis, just as in a film a close-up makes the moving picture momentarily pause.[59]

Although *England Made Me* was 'the only occasion when I have deliberately chosen an unknown country as a background and then visited it, like a camera-team, to take the necessary stills',[60] the cinematic influence is more structurally fundamental than mere use of 'location shots'. The 'editorial' complexity of a sequence depicting Krogh's *Citizen Kane*ish megalomania, which tracks the proliferation of Krogh's monogram through rapid changes of location and scale – from in-door close-up to panorama – is an excellent example:

> He rose and his coat caught an ash-tray and spun it to the floor. His own initials were exposed, E.K. The monogram had been designed by Sweden's leading artist. E.K. – the same initials endlessly repeated formed the design of the deep carpet he crossed to the door. E.K. in the waiting-rooms; E.K. in the restaurants; the building was studded with his initials. E.K. in electric lights over

the doorway, over the fountain, over the gate of the court. The letters flashed at him like the lights of a semaphore conveying a message over the vast distances which separated him from other men. It was a message of admiration; watching the lights he quite forgot they had been installed by his own orders. E.K. flickering across the cold plateau a tribute from his shareholders; it was as close as he got to a relationship. (p. 34)

Greene believed the movie method of imbuing narrative with simultaneous poetic subtext was vital to novelists. In view of their postwar collaboration, it was prescient of him to write in 1936, that in Carol Reed's screen version of Priestley's *Laburnum Grove* the camera 'acts with a kind of quick shrewd commentary', as if its picture of suburbia were taken 'stereoscopically' from two angles (*Spectator*, 31 July 1936; *Mornings in the Dark*, pp. 125–6). Above all, Greene recognised the chief problem shared by screenplay and novel was 'the dark backward and abysm of time' (7 February 1936; *Mornings in the Dark*, p. 73), to which, as *England Made Me* shows, they might find similar solutions. Through concatenating 'flash-backs', Kate Farrant's night thoughts slip in and out of affluent Stockholm present and dodgy London past, reality and dream, in a restless textual interplay of conscious and unconscious meanings suggesting Greene's double debt to the language of Modernist internal monologues, like Joyce's 'Penelope', as well as the imagery of cinema:

Don't be afraid. Don't hesitate. No cause of fear. No bulls on this exchange. The tiger bright. The forests. Sleep. Our bond. The new redemption. And we rise, we rise. And God Who made the lamb made Whitaker, made Loewenstein. 'But you are lucky,' Hammond said that day in Leather Lane, 'Krogh's safe. Whatever comes or goes people will always have to buy Krogh's.' The market steady. The strand, the water and street between us. Sleep. The new redemption. No bulls, the tiger and the lamb. The bears. The forests. Sleep. The stock is sound, the closing price. We rise. (p. 61)

Film also played a vital role in adapting Modernist form for more politically upfront purposes in Isherwood's writing. In *Christopher and His Kind*, he recollected seeing G. W. Papst's *Kameradschaft* (1931) (also the subject of a Randall Swingler poem) in Berlin with Spender, in which French and German workers transcend recent enmity to collaborate during a disaster: 'Christopher told Stephen that, when the tunnel caved in and the miners were trapped, he had thought: "That makes Virginia Woolf look pretty silly." '[61] However, in his foreword to the reissue of his first novel, *All the Conspirators* (1928), he acknowledged his indebtedness to Joyce, Woolf and Forster.[62] The disarming 'I am a camera' aspect of Isherwood's thirties writing, which problematised the 'objective' reporting of the new visual medium, was also inherited from the High Modernists.

As we have seen, Spender recalled their joint keenness for Russian movies distributed by Willi Muenzenberg's KPD company, Prometheus, which had 'all those qualities we found most exciting in other forms of modern art, but . . . also convened a message of hope like an answer to *The Waste Land*'. Similarly, Paul Piazza has itemised Isherwood's methodical borrowings from early German cinema – his suggestively abrupt cuttings between scenes, allusion and paralepsis.[63] In *Goodbye to Berlin*, for example, the increasingly hallucinatory quality of the visit to the TB sanatorium climaxes in a symbolic focus that owes much to Expressionistic film. People and things become displaced so that the patients, 'muffled in shawls and blankets', turn into spectral dummies:

> They all thronged round us for a moment in the little circle of light from the panting bus, their lit faces ghastly like ghosts against the black stems of the pines. This was the climax of my dream: the instant of nightmare in which it would end. I had an absurd pang of fear that they were going to attack us – a gang of terrifyingly soft muffled shapes – clawing us from our seats, dragging us hungrily down, in dead silence. (p. 141)

Such sequences may well have been inspired by films like Wiene's *The Cabinet of Dr Caligari* (1920), F. W. Murnau's *Nosferatu* (1922) or Fritz Lang's *Doktor Mabuse* (1922). Isherwood also admitted the naked proletcultism of *Kameradschaft* stimulated more than his politics. No doubt his own portrayals of homosexuality, of Berlin's *Halbwelt* and slums derived from Richard Oswald's *Anders als die Anderen* (1919), Josef von Sternberg's *Der Blaue Engel* (1930) Pabst's film of *Die Dreigroschenoper* (1931), and Brecht's own *Kuhle Wampe* (1932).

Isherwood relished film's potential for psychoanalytic as well as socio-economic revelations. Benjamin believed it defamiliarised 'our field of visual perception' in the same way Freud's *Psychopathology of Everyday Life* (1901) had revealed the subtext of mundane language: 'The camera introduces us to unconscious optics as does psycho-analysis to unconscious impulses.'[64] Isherwood used cinematic inter-textuality for making complex associations:

> I was, and still am, endlessly interested in the outward appear-ance of people – their facial expressions, their gestures, their walk, their nervous tricks, their infinitely various ways of eating a sau-sage, opening a paper parcel, lighting a cigarette. The cinema puts people under a microscope: you can stare at them, you can examine them as though they were insects.

From this standpoint, 'the stupidest film may be full of astonishing revelations about the tempo and dynamics of everyday life' and the cinematic novelist could project his scenes 'on to an imaginary screen'.[65] Isherwood's point is backed up Charles Davy who argued that, paradoxically, it is precisely because the cinema is a 'vigorous poetic language' rather than an objective one that it can afford to take its subject matter from the quotidian.[66]

David Lodge has argued that literary synecdoche/metonymy – symbolic use of 'detail of appearance, behaviour, dress, possessions etc.' – naturally long predates film, but was 'used by writers of the 1930s with an economy and visual flair' intensified by it.[67] Isherwood epitomised this tendency in that he was primarily interested in filmic structure as a highly efficient method of packing literary realism's apparent *oratio recta* with subversive 'unconscious' mean-ings, and of activating the reader's psychological complicities. Again this derived as much from popular features as avant-garde experi-ments by Pudovkin, or special effects such as *The Invisible Man's*. Alfred Hitchcock discussed metonymic use of objects as a peculiar cinematic way of dramatising powerful emotions by displacement, giving the example of close-ups, repeatedly shuttling back and forth between a knife and the Verlocs' faces, in *Sabotage* (1936), his ver-sion of Conrad's novel *The Secret Agent* (1907). This method of building up tension makes the knife the signifier of Winnie's mur-derous intent, as well as its instrument.[68] Similarly, in *Goodbye to Berlin's* 'Sally Bowles', synecdochic close-ups imply judgements with-out pausing for explicit comment, as with Sally's fingernails 'painted emerald green, a colour unfortunately chosen, for it called attention to her hands, which were much stained by cigarette-smoking and as dirty as a little girl's'. It is appropriate that Sally, aspiring to UFA's celluloid pantheon, should be repeatedly focused on this way, her nails' grotesque artificiality suggesting the psychic damage behind her *blasé* façade. Developing the same motif, later in 'The Nowaks', a working-class tuberculosis victim is implictly compared with Sally – 'When she talked and became excited her hands flitted tirelessly about in sequences of aimless gestures, like two shrivelled moths' (pp. 31 and 137). Likewise. Otto has visions of a disembodied hand, like a cross between Belshazzar's Feast and Karl Freund's *Orlac*. This macabre living synecdoche threatens his life and symbolises his own alienated potentials, as one of Weimar Berlin's doomed youth.

Brian Finney argues that Isherwood's 1933–34 stint as a Gaumont-British scriptwriter helped him capitalise on his film-mindedness, forcing 'him to visualise his scenes to a much greater extent than before, ruthlessly to prune his prose and to treat his dialogue with a dramatist's economy'.[69] Many of the sudden and disorientating changes in perspective and location in Isherwood's novels emulate camera angles and editing to suggest the narrator's subjective state. In the intoxicated Sylvesterabend sequence in *Mister Norris* the visual effect is whirling and dismembered:

> My glance reeled about the room, picking out large or minute objects, a bowl of claret-cup in which floated an empty matchbox, a broken bead from a necklace, a bust of Bismarck on top of a Gothic dresser – holding them for an instant, then losing them again in general coloured chaos. In this manner, I caught a sudden glimpse of Arthur's head, its mouth open, the wig jammed down over its left eye. I stumbled about looking for the body and collapsed comfortably onto a sofa, holding the upper half of a girl. (p. 31)[70]

Similarly, in *Goodbye to Berlin*, at the beginning of 'The Nowaks', the mobility of the narrative imitates a roving camera, passing through the city gate and down the street, recording symptomatic details of impending political apocalypse on walls and pavements, then jerking vertiginously upwards:

> The entrance to the Wassertorstrasse was a big stone archway, a bit of old Berlin, daubed with hammers and sickles and Nazi crosses and plastered with tattered bills which advertised

auctions or crimes. It was a deep shabby cobbled street, littered with sprawling children in tears. Youths in woollen sweaters circled waveringly across it on racing bikes and whooped at girls passing with milk jugs, the pavement was chalk-marked for the game called Heaven and Earth. At the end of it, like a tall, dangerously sharp, red instrument, stood a church. (p. 108)

Such camera-eyed effects certainly present an implicit 'quick shrewd commentary' on experience (to borrow Greene's phrase about Carol Reed) and are intensified in the episodic structure of the second 'Berlin Diary (Winter 1932–3)'.

Perhaps the most subtle documentary novel of the thirties, *Goodbye to Berlin* also epitomises writers' attempts to emulate and investigate cinematic form. Isherwood's 1939 'Author's Note' emphasised its six fragments were 'cuts' from the footage for an unfinished epic. It's as if *Goodbye to Berlin* is the 'readerly text' on the page, and *Die Verlorenen* (Isherwood's original title) or *The Lost* is the 'writerly text', constructed from poetic implications by the reader's imaginative interaction with its montage. By this method oblique thematic intermeshings bind all its characters together in consciousness, as Isherwood put it, 'of the mental, economic and ideological bankruptcy of the world in which they live'.[71] *Goodbye to Berlin* also fits the general pattern of anti-Nazi novels by contemporary British writers, deeply concerned by the way fascism was being constructed. They strove to transgress the barriers erected by Appeasing media between everyday consciousness and atrocities elsewhere, as in Sally Carson's *A Traveller Came By*:

Things about Germany felt unreal. You read the papers, went to meetings . . . English and distant and comfortable, you could not comprehend hatred of the Jew anymore than you could visualise his terror: you could not associate the hectic moments of gangster films – the shot in the night, the blood in the dark, the waiting terror behind closed doors – with this serene life in England, with its slow, expensive traffic, its courteous, good-looking policemen, well-lit, well-ordered streets. You could hardly imagine it, let alone feel it.

As Croft points out, such novels centred 'around the experience of an innocent Englishman abroad'.[72] The notorious camera-eyed 'neutrality' of the first-person narrators in Isherwood's Berlin books was a similar strategy to increase the reader's sense of shock through the outsider's apparent lack of reaction.

Goodbye to Berlin demonstrates the fallacy of presenting the self as an innocent I-witness and, hence, the impossibility of reporting experience in an ideologically uninflected way in literature or film. As Paget argues, only when camerawork is 'interrogated closely does the univocal cultural "I" behind the camera', the subject with whom the spectator identifies as a norm of perception, 'stand revealed'.[73] The neutrality of Isherwood's autobiographical persona was, therefore, deliberately problematised through a hierarchy of consciousnesses, narrated, narrating and authorial. This only gradually comes to light, because the reader is initially encouraged to identify with an apparently objective and undivided perspective on reality. Isherwood was far less straightforward in his adaptation of radical film documentary than, for example, Sommerfield. By the time Isherwood came to make his apparently confident reference to the 'objectivity' of the camera-eye at the beginning of 'A Berlin Diary (Autumn 1930)', it was after a decade of scrutinising cinematic intertextuality: 'I am a camera with its shutter open, quite passive, recording not thinking. Recording the man shaving at the window opposite and the woman in the kimono washing her hair. Some day all this will have to be developed, carefully printed, fixed' (p. 11). Superficially this asserts the 'artlessness' of the medium, but it also suggests the processes which are invisible in its final, edited product, thus questioning cinematic simulations of reality and their concealed linkage. As Samuel Hynes points out, the pretence is 'to be, not the photographer, whose consciousness selects and focuses, but the camera, the photographic mechanism itself'. This is a fallacy because, in Piazza's terms, the eye behind the viewfinder is a 'sentient observer'.[74] Objectivity is the most self-deceiving of the mind-games 'the lost' play to evade their own responsibility for Berlin's dangerously decaying social reality.

Vertov's films also made the camera-wielding subject into the *object* of his reporting by continuously superimposing his image over those he constructed, as well as allowing others to notice the camera, approach it, interact with it. Isherwood seized on Vertov's placing of his camera-eye in its own focus, but coupled analysis of its visual dynamics with his own psychological preoccupations, to achieve a similar, but more oblique self-reflexivity, by subtle sidelights catching the 'impersonal' perceiver in a kind of peripheral vision. To adapt Storm Jameson's words, the camera-eyed witness fails to 'keep himself out of the picture'.[75] Telling complicities about sexuality, violence and fear of 'otherness' materialise indirectly, as if by parapraxis, despite his strenuously detached descriptions. For example, in the sanatorium visit discussed above, the narrator's irrational perception underlines the exploitation of suggestibility by Nazi propaganda. The concentration camps were repositories for projected fear of difference, just as the horror of infection momentarily obliterates the narrator's sense of common humanity with the patients. They become effaced by their condition, disease personified. By such transference, victim becomes scapegoat; the cure, extermination.

Isherwood also used a cinematic perspective on ominous historical events to undercut his characters' bad faith. As Sally finally seems about to clinch a rich patron who can launch her stardom and fulfil the narrator's own vicarious desires, the funeral of ex-Chancellor Hermann Müller passes under the hotel balcony. Müller resigned in March 1930, after the Wall Street Crash, dying a year later. Hindenburg's subsequent appointment of Heinrich Brüning, secretly supported in military circles, began the fatal slide towards dictatorship:

> Ranks of pale steadfast clerks, government officials, trade union secretaries – the whole drab weary pageant of Prussian Social Democracy – trudged past under their banners towards the silhouetted arches of the Brandenburger Tor, from which the long black streamers stirred slowly in an evening breeze.
> 'Say, who is this guy, anyway?' asked Clive, looking down. 'I guess he must have been a big swell?'
> 'God knows,' Sally answered, yawning. 'Look Clive, darling, isn't it a marvellous sunset?'
> She was quite right. We had nothing to do with those Germans down there, marching, or with the dead man in the coffin, or with the words on the banners.

This leads the 'narrated I' into a Faustian suspicion that they are on the verge of forfeiting 'all kinship' with the mass of humanity 'who earn their living, who insure their lives, who are anxious about the future of their children' (p. 56). The procession signifies the passing of Weimar itself, and its symbolism is particularly effective because of the aerial vantage point, the camera-eye zooming in for close-ups on faces, banners and coffin, then receding into a distance shot of the Brandenburger Tor, which, despite solemn excrescences paying lip-service to democracy, signals the imminent victory of Prussian authoritarianism. The observers are detached from these ominous events as if watching a newsreel of a foreign country, impatient for the escapist feature. Aptly, the original cover was Humphrey Spender's photograph, 'Berlin Lützowplatz 1933', showing Isherwood observing the street below. Thus Isherwood brought together the complementary myths sponsored by commercial cinema and mainstream documentary. Sally's seduction by Hollywood fantasy is no more insidious than the camera-eyed narrator's belief in his own detachment. As we have seen, in the thirties 'aerial' perspective could suppress common humanity in the name of panoptic, hyperreal fictions of 'historical knowledge and certainty', in Cunningham's phrase. *Goodbye to Berlin*'s method subtly rejects such power exercised from a privileged position and the 'attitudes cognate' with it.[76]

According to Eisenstein, cinema plays auto-suggestively on our preprogrammed habit of supplying conceptual links, so that film 'understood dynamically, is just the process of arranging images in the feelings and mind of the spectator'.[77] However, like Auden's poetry, Isherwood's prose manipulated the intertextuality of visual and verbal media, rather than literally importing techniques from one into the other, and Isherwood came more and more to recognise its critical limitations. For example, *Lions and Shadows*' description of a flat arranges objects to imply an 'absent-presence' metonymically, not unlike the technique of *The Invisible Man*:

> that pathetically neat room, as I now picture it, seems to cry out for the disorderly human traces of cohabitation – the hairbrush discovered among the papers in the drawer, the unfamiliar queer-feeling garments in the dark cupboard, the too small slipper you vainly try to pull on when half awake, the wrong tooth-brush in your glass, the nail-paring in the fender and in the tea-cup the strange lustrous single hair. But the room, as long as I occupied it, remained virgin, unravished. . . . (p. 137)

The image of desire is constructed through these detailed close-ups which could only be transcribed to film by destroying the text's tactical ambiguity, activated in the mind of the reader. As Keith Cohen argues, the mental image (signified) is elicited by a verbal sign . . . in no way a substitute for the mental image, but rather a vehicle toward it. In the film, on the other hand, signified and signifier are identical (the sign for a table is a table); hence the ease with which the filmic image becomes a substitute for the spectator's fluctuating mental image.[78]

If Isherwood's flat were actually filmed it would produce the dilemma of specification – hairbrush, garments, slipper, etc. are strategically *ungendered* in the text. His alibi of 'questionable heterosexuality', would either be blown or fitted to the norm.[79] Such self-protective ambiguity might not be a necessity now, but indicates the ingenuity gay writing needed to get round the censorship at the time.

Having demonstrated the manifold structural effects that new media like radio and film had on virtually every genre of thirties texts, from drama, to verse and the novel, I now want to follow the inevitable migration of Leftist writers into the media themselves, which climaxed in wartime propaganda work, and consider how culturally and politically radical their involvements actually were.

4

Involvements: Writing for the Mass Media

The logic of Leftists' refraction of the mass-media in their texts and the dynamic effects that radio and especially film montage had on their techniques inevitably led to many incursions by writers themselves into broadcasting and the cinema. However, the pattern of motives and involvements was both complex and unprogrammatic, lacking a fully coherent theoretical and organisational basis. It was also inevitably conditioned by the technological and institutional conditions of the respective media, especially the collective nature of their products and the basic question of finance. Leftist writers, therefore, would have to wait for the unique circumstances of the Second World War, as we shall see, for the opportunity to intervene in any numbers and the chance to implement their notions about modernising form and politically progressive content in practice. For the purposes of this comparison. I have therefore divided this chapter into separate sections on writers' pre- and post-1939 involvements.

THIRTIES BROADCASTING

Because broadcasting is a predominantly verbal medium, writers had, in some way or other, been involved in radio since its inception. Greene's account 'Poetry by Wireless' showed his characteristically precocious interest in its literary possibilities. Greene took part in a broadcast with, among other undergraduates, Harold Acton and Bryan Howard. In 1925 the microphone experience was still unfamiliar enough for the fetishism of talking to an inanimate apparatus, supposedly accessing the national consciousness, to be obviously bizarre: 'As Earl Harold at William's court spoke over the casket of saints' bones, I spoke over this box that I hoped contained the great heart of the British public. The box did not deign a smile, not a glimmer of a glance' (*Oxford Chronicle*, 30 January

151

1925; *Reflections*, p. 15). Greene's encounter anticipated the way thirties Leftists hoped to use radio to reach and radicalise a wider audience. It was also prescient in its suspicion about commitment to a medium whose workings could be mystifying and whose effects on the public were distant and largely unguessable.

Modernists and contemporary critics certainly tried to infiltrate broadcasting with notions of literary culture, both high and radical, in the thirties, though the resulting programmes were a trickle not a flood. Wyndham Lewis, T. S. Eliot, Ezra Pound and F. R. Leavis all appeared on or wrote for the BBC. Even *Brave New World* was broadcast in 1937, with Huxley himself as narrator, though by CBS's experimental Workshop.[1] The younger Leftist writers also got a limited toehold. Along with the script for *Hadrian's Wall* produced by the poet John Pudney, 25 November 1937, which featured the famous 'Roman Wall Blues', Auden selected bad verse for *Up the Garden Path*, and Britten, bad music. But Day Lewis ran into trouble with the Talks Department for politicising literature overtly in 1935. His attempt to convince the BBC's audience that writers were unavoidably faced with the choice of aligning themselves 'more or less consciously with one of the larger world-movements based not on the individual but on the masses – with Communism or Fascism', outraged its taboos on controversy and unconstitutional politics.[2] Nevertheless *The Listener* became an important platform for Leftist writing, despite Reith's reservations about the 'suitability' of avant-garde art. As Cunningham puts it, the sympathetic editor Janet Adam Smith made its literary pages 'almost the house organ of the Auden group'.[3]

As far as the medium itself was concerned John Grierson's complaint about the way the BBC's conservatism stifled formal innovation was only slightly exaggerative:

> Its producers have used the microphone very much as the early film makers used their camera. They have accepted it as an essentially immovable object to which all action or comment must be brought. . . . A few simple deviations there have been in the so-called 'actuality' programmes (in this borrowing from our documentary example), but they have been so tentative and ill-equipped, that for all its years of work and national fields of opportunity the BBC has created no art of microphone sound, and in its own technique, not a single artist.[4]

A factor that may have put writers off involvement in the thirties was what Lance Sieveking called the 'ghastly impermanence of the medium'. As Scannell puts it, 'A thing of beauty might might well be a joy for ever in the shape of an urn or a poem, but a radio feature was written on the wind.' Besides its evanescence, broadcasting represented a daunting erosion of formal and cultural boundaries. It was not just radio's mechanical reproduction that destroyed 'the aura of the aspiring art object', but the voracious 'ebb and flow of a varied output', its lack of a sense of occasion and ritualised space 'set apart from the routines of everyday life'. All this, plus bureaucratic pressures, as biographies of the period testify, tended to diminish creative flair.[5] Leftists had the additional problem of political unacceptability. One of the trailblazing exceptions who did establish himself was D. G. Bridson, staff writer and producer for the Northern Region from 1935. Bridson recollected his situation in the allegorical terms of Eric Gill's statue of Prospero on Broadcasting House, whose servant Ariel's Calibanesque genitalia were censored with a chisel on its hierarchy's insistence in 1932. Bridson was particularly concerned to resist BBC stigmatisation of the otherness of regional and working-class speech, derided in the contemporary parody of its motto as 'Nation Shall Speak Posh unto Nation'.[6]

The first radio play, Richard Hughes's *Danger* (1923), in which three Welsh miners confronted a pit disaster, opened a potential new dimension of 'virtual reality'. It was so unprecedented the announcer warned it might frighten the children. But in effect it was little more than an ethereal extension of the transparent 'fourth-wall' theatrical principle, as if the listener were 'eavesdropping on an actual event'.[7] Its Naturalism was enhanced by the fact that the first radio playwright was a novelist, so that *Danger*'s characters spoke as if 'overheard' rather than in declamatory stage dialogue. If *Danger* established one early broadcast drama tradition, a rival Modernistic one was started by Tyrone Guthrie at the end of the 1920s. In the 1931 BBC *Handbook*, Guthrie argued that faithful transcription of real life was a recipe for dullness. His *Squirrel's Cage* (1929), on the other hand, used short stylised scenes and choric interludes to depict the entrapment of a social archetype – a young clerk – in the alienation of his daily routine. Similarly. *The Flowers Are Not For You to Pick* (1930) dramatised the death by drowning of a frustrated young missionary in a series of radio flashbacks from his past life. Guthrie's third radio play. *Matrimonial News*, used a stream of consciousness technique to 'listen in' to the private thoughts of a disillusioned middle-aged woman, awaiting a potential lover. However, Guthrie's work was regarded as too 'abstract' by Val Gielgud, who became head of BBC Drama in the thirties. Brother of John, Gielgud came from a traditional theatrical background and lumped Guthrie's approach, unfairly, with Sieveking's *Kaleidoscope* features.

Guthrie, like many contemporary film-makers, talked about exploiting the purely 'symphonic' possibilities of the medium.[8] But broadcast drama also had Modernistic potentials which were 'inherent in neither the film nor the stage'. Its impressionism, though limited, was 'highly concentrated in quality': 'Deprived of sensual sops to Cerberus . . . the mind of the listener shapes and expands these into pictures. . . . Playwright, producer, and actors combine to throw out a sequence of hints, of tiny clues, suggestions.' He felt radio shared the advantages of both a mass and intimate medium with an audience dispersed in individual homes, able to receive 'The minute pulsations of feeling, the delicate gradations of thought which each member of the crowd experiences when alone.'[9] But early BBC dramatists did not, in Rodger's words, have 'the benefit of theories of radio drama. Writers, producers and actors were still finding their way.' As Hughes put it, the 'stuff of radio' was still unformed, 'in the crucible: blazing, volatile, as yet innocent of the mould.'[10] The rare occasions when new technical resources were exploited to the full on thirties radio did not succeed in tapping mass-audiences. Judging from listener feedback, 'A play labelled "experimental" might as well have been labelled "poison" ', according to Gielgud. Original pieces might well be hits with critics, but 'it was the – too often flat-footed and ham-handed – adaptation of a good old stage favourite that was popular'.[11] The first play, for example, on the short-lived 'Experimental Hour' was MacLeish's *The Fall of the City* (1937), one of the two CBS productions (the other was documentarist Pare Lorentz's *Job to Be Done*) imported by the BBC in the thirties. Its Modernism and right-on politics bombed and the 'Experimental Hour' was ditched for more Microphone Serials in 1938. Though he subsequently abandoned his radio career, Guthrie's innovative model was developed much more in Features, especially after it became a separate section under Laurence Gilliam, in 1936 (see below). Features was less inhibited about 'causing offence' and more populist in spirit than Drama.

Guthrie's early broadcast plays were groundbreaking in several other important respects, more conducive to popular consumption. Their abandonment of literary Naturalism and individuated 'bourgeois' psychology brought them, as Rodger points out, 'closer to the much earlier dramatic form of the morality play', in parallel with the contemporary work of Brecht, 'which featured similar archetypal figures . . . involved in a debate about their conditions and their dilemma'. Conversely, developments such as Epic theatre were partly 'due to the writer's response to the problems created by the enlargement of the audience in radio and film'. Awareness of a mass public encouraged radio writers to return to a commonplace of ancient literature – matching words to the 'natural cadence and manner of . . . normal speech'. Later some of the writers who actually cut their teeth in radio work, transferred their new skills to novel, stage and film, helping 'to bring about a revolution in dramatic diction and structure and . . . improve the quality of film dialogue'.[12]

Another radiogenic development was the evolution of a distinctive style of narrative drama. It was conventionally employed on the BBC in adaptations of popular and classic novels, but had socially-committed parallels in the work of dramatists like Brecht who used it for didactic purposes. The 'random audience' of radio, largely unused to theatre-going, also needed instruction and guidance. Guthrie's plays employed many 'Brechtian' devices, like choric commentaries, though MacLeish was credited with innovating radical narrative drama on radio by Erik Barnouw. In the Preface to *Fall of the City*, MacLeish stated 'The eye is a realist, the ear is already half a poet.' He believed radio 'had developed tools which could not have been more perfectly adapted to the poet's uses had he devised them himself'.[13]

The social mix of radio's new national audience also affected the direction of British drama in the thirties, especially in terms of subject matter and linguistic register, helping to redraw established cultural boundaries, even if it didn't dismantle them. Before broadcasting, British play audiences, as Rodger puts it, were 'socially limited and culturally homogeneous'. Suddenly scripts had to be written for one 'which might include coal-miners, farm labourers or fishermen'. Whereas the Mandarin theatrical tradition tended to depict the excluded working-class and their diversity of demotic speech as comic/moral stereotypes only, they were now, as listeners, in a majority, requiring voices with which they 'could easily identify and associate'. The logic of the medium inevitably, albeit gradually, demanded writers and actors who represented idiom and dialect with 'insight and respect'.[14] This democratisation of diction had to confront particularly entrenched artistic and social prejudices. (Sieveking complained bitterly about the difficulty of obtaining actors who could accurately impersonate a range of voices and social groups for programmes like his *Intimate Snapshots* (1929), which featured dialogue between a lift-conductor and charlady.)[15] It got underway in the thirties, but was not really achieved until the fifties.

Radio's 'random audience' also had a crucial bearing on the contest between traditional and Modernist poetics in the medium. There was an apparent incompatibility between two aims: bringing art within everyone's reach and innovating distinctive radio forms. *The Listener*'s letter pages in the thirties featured an ongoing debate about this question. For example,

> Your correspondent, Mr Littlewood, complains that modern poetry puts 'a strain on the intelligence,' and he deplores it. What is to be done by the poets and the publishers about thousands of Mr Littlewoods? For the writing of verse which is so blatantly decorative as Victorian wall-paper has gone out of fashion. . . . What, then, if the design should become at times too intricate for us?[16]

It was from his own experience in this context that D. G. Bridson discussed the prejudice laid on writers 'by five hundred years of conditioning by the printed page', which substituted effects of 'bookishness' and 'ambiguity' for those of 'voice'. Drama on the air restored the need for simplicity and immediacy, but, conversely, also allowed once more for the subtle 'cross-cutting of speech rhythm against the metre'. Bridson claimed this 're-conditioning process' was already discernible in the contemporary work of MacLeish, MacNeice and Christopher Fry. Similarly, MacNeice felt radio required writing less like that for stage performance and more like lyrics for music. To create subtext 'on the printed page requires constant ingenuity. . . . In radio, without sacrificing simplicity and lucidity, you can often leave the twisting to the voice.'[17] Paradoxically, resuscitating older, even pre-literary, qualities and devices would enable writers to partly overcome this perceived incompatibility between traditionalism and Modernism in the medium.

In order to appreciate Bridson's, and, later, MacNeice's achievement against the relative failure of innovative radio plays to attract a mass audience in the thirties, we also have to understand the growth of the 'feature'. This form came into its own after Features section split away from Drama in 1936, was paramount during and immediately after the Second World War (when Features became a fully-fledged Department), but then lost its own mass audience to the rise of television in the fifties. Lance Sieveking located its origins in the period 1928–32 when 'Radio began to be talked of not only as a new form of communication, but also as a potential art form.'[18] A 1933 *Listener* Editorial recalled that Sieveking's *Kaleidoscope I* 'opened up new possibilities by "mixing" scenes from separate studios, whereby artists, musicians, crowd noises and so forth were presented in a kaleidoscopic whirl which gradually fell into perspective as the noises faded into one distinct scene'. It argued form ought to be an function of the medium, because 'physical characteristics' determine the conventions of the drama of an epoch. The radio dramatist had 'to develop his power of painting word-pictures and suggesting spectacle through sound'. Similarly in 1937, Grace Wyndham Goldie argued artists had to turn the limitations of a blind medium into assets.[19] It was the feature programme's fluidity, in Sieveking's own view, that made it the 'very stuff of radio'. Its content and form varied from 'an arrangement of sounds, which has a theme but no plot' (if it had a plot it was a play) to 'a "mosaic" of poems recited between pieces of music': from an hour of 'what broadcasting would have been like in 1850': to Empire Day link-ups with the Commonwealth.[20] Gilliam's distinction that 'Features deal with Fact, Drama with Fiction' is generally accurate. As Rayner Heppenstall recalled, 'The term was used in a sense almost diametrically opposite to that which it receives in the film industry, since it primarily meant documentaries', though the feature could also be just as protean as the more experimental actuality films of the period.[21] MacNeice considered it much more than reporting in the naive journalistic sense. For him, it represented a complex transposition of the Griersonian formula of documentary 'interpretation'. Its author had to be 'much more than a *rapporteur* or a cameraman: he must select his actuality material with great discrimination and then keep control of it so that it subserves a single dramatic effect'.[22]

As one of the form's earliest pioneers. Sieveking was passionately interested in transposing cinematic techniques to sound production. Analogous effects to slow motion, close-ups, dissolves, fades, mixes and montage were all used in programmes he wrote in the late twenties to early thirties, and simultaneously theorised in his writings.[23] On the one hand, the features' 'sound pictures' were linked in discussion with movies, especially Russian avant-gardist, and, on the other, with the openness of Shakespearian theatre, because the absence of visual staging combined with poetic imagery, as Heppenstall put it, 'allowed a form of drama which was able to "cut" with ease from one location or storyline to another'. Features could dispense with the narrating 'Voice of Information', often used so clumsily in radio plays, as Grace Wyndham Goldie complained, as a means of bridging spatio-temporal shifts.[24]

Features gave particular scope to avant-garde substitutes for traditional plot structure. Sieveking conceived of himself as an 'orchestrator' or director, sitting at his dramatic control panel, coordinating elements – actors, musicians, chorus, sound effects – from different studios, and of his scripts as musical scores. Despite his experimentalism, though, Sieveking was anxious to preserve orthodox cultural hierarchies (in *Kaleidoscope I* Beethoven and Handel represent Good; the 'hot dirt' of jazz, Evil) and to refute accusations that anything 'not entirely conventional and academic' was automatically 'Bolshie'. He asserted his credentials as a 'Christian and loyal subject', but, rather contradictorily, denied Art could ever be compatible with propaganda: 'Mix them and the result is a proper bastard.'[25] However, Sieveking's projects became of value primarily because they were followed up by A. E. Harding, a fellow member of the BBC Research Unit, who shared his Modernism but combined it with a radical outlook.

Harding's features for the BBC's National Programme between 1929 and 1932 included *The Republic of Austria, Crisis in Spain* and *New Year Over Europe*. *Crisis in Spain* was particularly innovative in its use of impressionistic montage of words and music, resembling the 'symphonic' documentaries of Ruttmann and Cavalcanti, to represent the events leading up to the Spanish Republic as they were relayed over the world communications network in a kind of 'metaradio'. In Scannell and Cardiff's terms. 'By foregrounding the role of the modern media, the narrative achieved a complex cross-cutting between events taking place in Spain and their simultaneous retransmission round the world. The significance of the Spanish crisis was extended beyond its own frontiers by the formal devices of the narrative itself.' Similarly, *New Year Over Europe* replaced the usual 'bland medley' to mark events on the last day of 1932, sounding 'a more ominous and overtly political note whose underlying topic was peace or war in Europe'.[26] However, the interspersed commentary, on the amount of GNP spent on armaments in various European countries involved in the live link-up, raised a protest from the Polish Ambassador. Reith, consequently, sent Harding into the BBC's equivalent of Siberian exile in Manchester. This proved one of the lucky accidents of radio history, because Harding, who believed the capitalist system depended on silencing the majority, was instrumental in giving an under-represented part of the country a broadcast voice in its own accents.[27]

As new Programme Director to the Northern Region, Harding recruited a group of highly talented personnel. A leading member was D. G. Bridson, put in touch with Harding by Leftist journalist Claud Cockburn in 1933. This didn't mean London allowed them a free hand, however. Harding's knuckles were rapped in 1934 for interviewing hunger-marchers who bad-mouthed the National Government. Bridson was also turned down for the Northern Region Drama Producer's job for being 'politically minded' – contemporary BBC-speak for Left-wing, but they did stretch the limits of the Reithian cultural agenda sometimes to breaking-point.

Bridson had both avant-garde and demotic ambitions. His 1938 National Programme adaptation of *The Waste Land* demonstrated Eliot's text's polyphonic elements were as radiogenic, as its montage was cinematic. He was also a friend of Pound and Hugh Mac-Diarmid, who strove during the same period to assert Scots 'as a fit vehicle for philosophy'.[28] Harding, believing poetry could be used in radio as innovatively as it had been in Auden's documentary filmwork, gave Bridson his feature break in *May Day in England* (1934), a programme 'sampling' the celebration's role from ancient fertility rite to modern-day social protest. Bridson's highly Auden-esque 'Song for the Three Million' was 'snarled out' above tramping feet 'by a vigorously proletarian voice that must have rattled the coffee-cups in sitting rooms all over the country'.[29] The voice was just-recruited busker Ewan MacColl's, drawing on his own anger at an economic system (especially one that had just officially estimated the minimum needed to keep a human being alive for a week), as the son of a Glasgow steelworker who tramped to Salford in the 1920s in desperate search for work.

Bank-balance bagmen, we are getting wise
To lickspit platitude and lovestock lies. . . .

Where they make the money, you may be the guys, –
But four and three-ha'pence will scale no eyes . . .
If we sack your City, let it not be said
That makeshift shystering has made its own bed.

(*Christmas Child*, p. 43)

Above all, Harding and Bridson wanted Manchester to have a different relation to the public than the aloof National Programme, to be mutually communicative and 'put people in touch with each other, not merely to instruct or inform or even to entertain them'. Since its inception, broadcasting had been the exclusive concern of 'us', and listening the lucky privilege of 'them'. Social disproportionality and monoglossia ensured 'very few "actuality speakers" – as the BBC chose to call the vast bulk of their license payers – had yet been heard on the air'.[30] Technical difficulties apart, the practice of rigorous script-vetting suggests that the BBC also suspected actuality speakers might say 'controversial' things. Paradoxically, precisely because nearly all output was live, spontaneous speech was all but banned for the BBC's first twenty years. Similarly, despite some qualified departures from RP in the regions, it was not until 1941 that Wilfred Pickles became a 'frontline newsreader' with a voice identifiably non-standard. Even Reith himself provoked a barrage of complaints by reading election results in the most residually Caledonian tones.

Ironically, scripting had the effect of stimulating in 'actuality series', as Rodger puts it, 'an approach to composition that was closer to drama than to journalism'. As in the case of Bridson's *Harry Hopeful* series, 'programmes had to have a stated theme or precise topic for discussion and this naturally involved the device of presentation'.[31] Bridson hit upon employing a dramatic character as interlocutor. A glass-blower's assistant tramping for work, played by Frank Nicholls, was the perfect itinerant link between different localities, dialects and occupations. Though occasionally stilted and patronising and with slightly forced joviality, *Harry Hopeful* broke down the prejudice that non-standard 'Northern' couldn't be used seriously (Francis Dillon in Bristol did the same for 'Mummerset') and set a new precedent in actuality broadcasting and public access. Bridson's first script was on the Yorkshire Dales 'From Cam Houses to Tan Hill'. However, in 1935 Manchester possessed no mobile recording facilities as yet, so Bridson had to create, in Scannell's words, 'sound pictures of people and places as if they had been shot on location'. Locals ended up replaying themselves in the studio (as they often did in thirties film-documentary), but 'the sound of a live audience laughing, applauding and joining in the programme' was genuinely 'unlike anything heard on the radio at that time'. It proved broadcasting 'could create its own forms of public and participatory pleasures from the stuff of ordinary life'.[32]

Bridson's impressive historical features were also presented from the cultural margins. This was very much the case in the first predominantly verse feature ever written for radio, with songs in ballad and romance metre drawn from Walter Scott, and dramatic scenes in prose which also used the Brechtian device of actors slipping in and out of character to 'narrate themselves'. A joint Northern and Scottish Region production, about a pivotal moment in the past when the nation's future might well not have been Anglocentric if the outcome had been different, *The March of the '45* (first broadcast 28 February 1936) was the most ambitious and widely-heard of Bridson's programmes. He tried to create a Radio Panorama in Verse and Song', as it was billed, 'comparable in its way to what had been done by D. W. Griffith or Cecil B. de Mille'.[33] Guthrie called it 'a good Sound Picture on a sweeping scale' and it was acknowledged by both MacLeish and MacNeice as a seminal influence.[34] Rodger argues it marked the realisation of the 'symphonic' form Guthrie had predicted for radio drama, but Bridson wanted it to be also very much a collision between the 'here and now' and its prehistory, rather than a romanticised past event: 'The Scots were heard to march south to Derby and north again to their defeat at Culloden as if they were ghosts passing through the present.'[35] This climaxed in the lyric 'Farewell Manchester', which 'stepped right out of the period', as Bridson put it, by linking the contemporary landscape of Mancunian depression with the pre-industrial resistance of the Jacobites. For BBC 'balance' this was going too far and Bridson's disaffected 'unemployed' had to be rechristened 'corner-boys' until the Second World War:[36]

Not many joined him as it was. . . .
And traces vanish as the years lapse. . . .
Very few would join him now –
Apart from the unemployed, perhaps. . . .

Monotony tries everything once. . . .
(*Christmas Child*, p. 26)

Since putting over a new image of the North was a central concern of his work, *Harry Hopeful* and the four programmes Bridson made about the region's major industries in the next few years 'may be seen as the clearest expressions of this intention'.[37] His first big industrial feature, *Steel* (broadcast on the Regional Programme, 23 February 1937), was made soon after Manchester acquired its own Mobile Recording Unit with actuality inserts (from Hadfield's East Hecla works) possible at last. His project was influenced especially by the recent documentary film *Coalface*, but was also Ruttmannesquely billed an 'Industrial Symphony'. It combined poetic narrative, specially commissioned music and choral verse with 'sound shots' from the foundry. In a memorandum Bridson proposed it 'should build up not so much a mere recorded actuality programme as an aesthetically significant and emotionally stirring programme on a scale previously untouched by the Corporation'.[38] Lyrics such as 'Steelworks', chorused by eight male voices, were more than Griersonian romance of industry. They were also very aware of the fragile humanity at the centre of this titanic work, as the sudden focus on its reflection in a worker's protective mask suggests

> Nor all the vivid fires that fly
> Can shut the wide cyclopic eye
> That watches while convulsion wracks
> The heart of earth until it cracks.
>   (*Christmas Child*, pp. 120–1)

Similarly, 'The Forge' hinted at the crazy contradictions of armaments manufacture. About two works competing to make more impenetrable armour for battleships, on the one hand, and better armour-piercing shells, on the other, it ran 'Steel that shall in turn destroy/ The brain behind their shaping force,/ – The superhuman strength to shake/ A tottering future off its course . . .' (pp. 122 and Notes, 236).

Bridson's industrial features also launched Joan Littlewood's career as radio presenter. Littlewood, who literally tramped to Manchester from RADA, was also used by Bridson, after Frank Nicholls's death in 1938, for his other major industrial features like *Cotton People* in Oldham, *Wool* in Saltaire and *Coal* in Durham, to gather actuality material by the 'participant observation' principle of living and working with the communities concerned. It was also at this time that Littlewood and MacColl gathered together Theatre Union, the nucleus for Theatre Workshop, partly from contacts made through radio work. However, despite *Steel's* national acclaim, Bridson took local criticism to heart that all its poetry of technics and proletcult 'made the programme lack conviction', as Scannell puts it, and 'We hear nothing from the men who work in the factory'.[39] The Vulcanic rhapsody certainly went over the top – 'Oh god of terror fling open the gates of a new Hell!' – and there wasn't a single Sheffield accent in the programme.

Bridson dropped the symphonic form for future industrial features, returning to the more intimate method of *Harry Hopeful*, confining the verse and choral music to literary/historical features. His politics were also compromised by the need to find a pit for *Coal* where conditions would be credibly bad enough to generate sympathy for the miners without ruffling the owners.[40] The programme was graphically authentic for the prewar BBC in the way it left the colliers' mild expletives uncensored (one cussed in particular about the awfulness of working in 'a bloody twelve inch seam') and caught their robust wit ('The only way to be safe in a pit is to let the bloody coal stop there!'). Littlewood's commentary, like the best documentary writing on the industry, strove to give a vicarious experience that would defamiliarise a taken-for-granted commodity for her listeners: 'Anyone who uses coal ought to go down a mine at least once.' There were, however, institutional limits to Bridson's radicalism. As Scannell points out, *Coal* 'throughout its preproduction, was carefully orchestrated to avoid any possibility of antagonism between management, unions and workforce'.[41] Offence had been generated by Bridson's previous industrial feature *Wool*, which used Titus Salt's Saltaire works. Addressed in Littlewood's own words to 'you in the South and the Midlands' who might never have been in a Yorkshire mill, locals regarded the broadcast as faked because factory girls were heard 'singing as they went', expressly against works' rules. But Bridson's situation was basically dialectical. He went as far as he could politically at the BBC at that time. It's arguable, as Scannell concedes, that his industrial features 'were somewhat romantic and sentimental, shading out the harsher aspects of working-class life and presenting a docile and respectful workforce with a fatalistic view of life', but there was always a muted counter-discourse within the programmes, referring in passing to tedium, injuries and industrial diseases.[42]

Moreover, Bridson's features and those of his colleague Olive

Shapley had no equivalents elsewhere on the BBC for the way they foregrounded the lives, work and culture of ordinary people, both within the broadcasting and as a major part of their audience.[43] On the National Programme, by contrast, they featured only marginally, as 'victims' (occasional reminders of how the other half lived), or as stereotyped representatives of 'the man in the street'. Shapley's radio enquiry into Mass-Observation, *They Speak for Themselves*, presented by Harrisson and Madge, is particularly unique as an example of what M-O called 'the breaking through of the ordinary past the official' in the thirties.[44] It recorded the only serious consultation of public opinion about Munich in the British media, between the crisis itself and the war.

Bridson's *Coronation Scot* (1937) – a narrative/musical express journey from London via the North-West to Glasgow – was a notable attempt to retune the broadcast map of Britain more representatively. According to Rodger, it derived from Harding's Christmas Day 1932 programme 'in which voices from different parts of the world are assembled to report on the state of their countries'. Unlike the GPO documentary *Night Mail* (where the only change of accent comes with the switch to Edinburgh genteel at the border), no RP voice-over smoothed over the landscape's sociolinguistic contours. In Bridson's feature, such differences were registered dialogically. The train's passage was greeted 'along the way from field and factory . . . in a spectroscopic change of accent from Cockney up to the final Gorbals'. This was an alternative way of 'linking the various Regions into a composite national broadcast hook-up', coordinated from Manchester not London.[45] Even the fixed BBC studio was no longer the central point. Portable sound equipment located it on the moving train itself (by contrast, *Night Mail*'s 'on-board' scenes were recorded in a mock-up), anticipating how from the end of 1939 to May 1941, the wartime Features and Drama Department would actually move up to Manchester, bringing RP mountain, albeit briefly, to non-standard Mohammed.

THE CINEMA

The BBC's covertly compromised political independence and its social unrepresentativeness certainly constituted stumbling blocks to writers' involvements in broadcasting in the thirties, but any Leftist wishing to try cinema work ran slap into the question of big money. Day Lewis's introduction to *The Mind in Chains* argued the movies typified how 'quality of intellectual production is inevitably debased under monopoly-capitalism' cutting the writer's imagination 'to suit the purse of those who control them'. A point elaborated in Calder-Marshall's essay, 'The Cinema', 'the second-rater will be in his element working for the films: the first-rater will also be all right, provided that he will suppress the quality that makes him first-rate, his integrity'.[46] But in practice writers sometimes showed moral wobbliness about involvement with the movies as with the press or radio, except here the fascinations and temptations were even stronger. The cinema's critics spent much time in cinemas and often, eventually, in studios. Huxley, Greene, Isherwood, Priestley and Dylan Thomas for instance, wrote scripts, or had their writings filmed and consequently enjoyed lifelong movie involvements one way or other. Huxley's U-turn was arguably the biggest, beginning when he earned upwards of £1500 a week from MGM in 1938 for a screenplay of the Life of Madame Curie, soon followed by adaptations of *Pride and Prejudice* and *Jane Eyre*. Then soon after moving to California, Huxley was dining with Chaplin and in October 1940 calling *The Great Dictator* 'a major contribution to the cause of decency and sanity'.[47] So much for 'minority Culture's' highminded rearguard action against the debasing influence of 'mass-civilisation', apparently. It's possible the bile of the 'feelies' was actually brewed from another example of repressed film-mindedness. But, conversely, Huxley's adaptations made literary classics accessible to wider audiences and Chaplin's artistry had long been celebrated by intellectuals. (*The Great Dictator* was also lauded by Orwell in his brief stint as reviewer for *Time and Tide*.)

Meanwhile Greene, always unashamedly interested in popular movies, reported a 1937 'Film Lunch', hosted by 'the voice of American capital itself', Louis B. Mayer. The MGM mogul offered 'the novelist's Irish sweep: money for no thought, for the banal situation and the inhuman romance: money for forgetting how people live: money for "Siddown won't yer" and "I love, I love, I love" endlessly repeated . . . all that's asked in return the dried imagination and the dead pen.'[48] But later Greene acknowledged the prizes offered for such satanic compacts in the thirties were 'not so glittering as the popular journalists like to make out', but could make all the difference to the survival of struggling writers like himself in those lean times.[49]

The biggest problem facing thirties Leftists was ensuring some grit from actuality, as well as shred of political integrity, remained after the process of converting written text into industrial film product. Making the screen representation of the people less dispro-portional, in some way or other, was the objective of the loose association between writers, documentarists and organisations like the British Film Institute (set up in 1933, to promote the educational use of cinema) and a succession of intellectual film magazines, such as *Close Up, Cinema Quarterly* and *World Film News*. However, any Leftists involved in features inevitably found themselves making compromises within the institutional and economic framework of the contemporary industry. They could also find themselves out of step with popular tastes that were not so much post- as *pre-*Modernist, all but Victorian in their conditioned desire for senti-ment, easy morality, melodrama and escapism. Consequently, pulp writers commanded an audience they hardly tapped. The most screened texts of the decade were the thrillers of Edgar Wallace and farces of Ben Travers. There were, nonetheless, relatively successful adaptations of the works of the radical old guard, like Wells, Galsworthy and Shaw, and of contemporary 'middlebrow' social realist novels like A. J. Cronin's *The Stars Look Down* and *The Citadel*, Louis Golding's *Cotton Queen* and Winifred Holtby's *South Riding*.[50]

Perhaps the most extensive Left-of-centre involvement in thirties popular cinema was J. B. Priestley's. The film of his novel *The Good Companions* (1933) launched Jessie Matthews, one of the biggest British stars. The picaresque plot of this bestseller, about a touring concert party with its fairly realistic view of a rundown ordinary England, transferred easily into the musical-comedy format, with-out losing its parabolic social message.[51] Priestley's most popular screenplays were for Gracie Fields. His first, *Sing As We Go* (1934), was commissioned by Basil Dean, one of Britain's most powerful producers, following the success of *The Good Companions* scenario. As Richards puts it, its plot was true 'to working-class life as filtered through the music hall tradition', rather than documentary. When Greybeck Mill is closed down, 'Grace Platt' declares, 'If we can't spin, we can still sing,' leading the redundant workers out in a chorus of the title song. However, most of Gracie's escapades were shot amid the amusements of Blackpool, in what M-O called 'Holi-day Town', rather than the 'Worktown' it quickly escapes. Greybeck Mill is reopened at the end by a purely Micawberish strategy: Gracie and the mill-owner's son persuade a local tycoon to invest in a new 'miracle' process. Neither unemployment, nor its cure are contextualised. They are merely providential. So the message of Priestley's script was far from radical: 'initiative and self-reliance by the workers will work and that capitalism has a human face. . . . It has just been going through a bad patch. The answer is to "sing as we go".'[52] Priestley's next Fields script, *Look Up and Laugh*, wasn't fundamentally dissimilar. Fields' final British film, *Shipyard Sally* (1939), begins on depressed Clydebank, with Gracie playing a variety artiste's daughter, who gets up a petition to the Chairman of a commission of enquiry. This leads to a similarly miraculous, comic intercession, appealing to the good nature of the Government, transforming Gracie into a symbolic Britannia on the eve of war, when rearmament was ironically turning decline around. The film, as Greene noted (see above Chapter 2), closes with Gracie carolling 'Land of Hope and Glory' over the returning workers and a montage of ship-launchings amid waving Union Jacks. The only radical alternative figures briefly as a comic vignette of a Communist chauffeur.

Though politically equivocal, Priestley's scripting anticipated the concerns of more 'intellectual' thirties writers. By taking Gracie to Blackpool, he was ahead of M-O's fascination with the popular culture, part-modern, part-vernacular, of 'Holiday Town' (one of the principal destinations of *English Journey*) and of Orwell's interest in the potential subversiveness of working-class humour, discussed in Chapter 2. *Sing As We Go* is immersed in the carnivalesque discourses of fair and circus and the plot itself is an anthology, sampling modes of parody and pastiche. Gracie's scrapes continually highlight freakish phenomena (like the elephant doing a Chaplin impression) that would be perfect specimens for M-O's blend of Surrealism and anthropological analysis, as shown by Humphrey Spender's photographs of side-shows and amusements.[53] Gracie is a disruptive, shape-shifter too, metamorphosing into 'human spider', 'vanishing girl' and living doll, and, at one point, pursued by the police around cake-walks and helter-skelters, wearing pantomimic false breasts. She also subverts stereotypes of feminine passivity and glamour by custard-pieing a harasser at a boarding house and reducing a Busby Berkeleyesque 'water babes' sequence to chaos. However, Priestley began to have private reservations about Fields's Lancashire accent as the key to her success, and, in effect, about the rhetoric of his own cinematic populism. If *English Journey* set out to find common Englishness, Fields distilled the deceptive 'essence' of the Lancastrian working-class shrewdness, homely simplicity, irony, fierce independence, an impish delight in mocking whatever is thought to be affected and pretentious. That is Lancashire. The danger is of course, that you may miss a lot by always being in terror of seeming affected or pretentious. The common denominator is a good sound one, but too many people may be reduced to it.[54]

The 'folksiness' of Priestley's scripts, their serviceability as a formula for mass cheering-up and National Government social consensus might therefore be compared to the *Volkstümlichkeit* and *narodnost* which were also key cultural concepts for Nazi and Stalinist propaganda in the same period.[55]

Perhaps even more ironically, the screenplay of George Formby's first film for Basil Dean at Ealing, *No Limit* (1935) was actually scripted by *Love on the Dole* author Walter Greenwood (Formby also starred in a comedy about surviving unemployment, *Off the Dole*, that same year). In effect. Greenwood provided the scenario that took Formby away from his earlier Northern revue format. Just as Priestley relocated Gracie in 'Holiday Town': Greenwood situated his working-class hero in a wish-fulfilment fantasy at the Isle of Man T-T races, where he beats caddish upper-class rival and wins the glamorous girl. George's 'little man' popularity was so successful it was used virtually unmodified in wartime propaganda features. However, the equivocal thirties 'culture of consolation' – escapist films, holiday fantasies and prize-fortunes – had themselves been the subjects of *Love on the Dole*'s bitterest satire. Bookie Sam Grundy's motto is also 'The Sky's the Limit'. Harry Hardcastle and his girlfriend Helen get a romantic week at the seaside on his winnings from Sam, just before they discover she's pregnant and he loses his job. Grundy, morever, as Bounderbyish working-class-lad-made-good himself, has inside-knowledge of the desires and discontents of the community on which he battens. As Richards points out, nothing is more symptomatic of the double-standard about poverty and unemployment in thirties cinema, than the fact that *Love on the Dole* was unmakeable, while pools-winning films like *Lancashire Luck* (1937) were rife, with their message that

There is no need to act to change society – luck and love can make the necessary changes. There is no need to change the urban industrial environment – just get out of it as fast as you can. There is no need for class antagonism, but instead alliance between the upper and lower classes is the most constructive and sensible way of dealing with any problems which exist.[56]

This strategy of deflection is confirmed by the fact that the actress who played Sally in the highly-successful stage version of *Love on the Dole*, Wendy Hiller, also played the heroine in *Lancashire Luck*. The feature director who was exceptional in dealing seriously with working-class subjects was John Baxter, praised at the time by Grierson. His first shoestring film, *Doss House* (1933), depicted the homeless as victims of circumstance rather than culpable. Baxter's unpatronising movies managed to be both popularly comic and socially realistic, although unfortunately he did not forge a partnership with a radical writer before the war: it was Baxter, not a documentarist, who eventually filmed *Love on the Dole* (1941).

The 'middlebrow' social realism of Winifred Holtby's bestseller *South Riding* (1936) proved more acceptable to the BBFC's taboo on 'controversy' in the thirties and more adaptable for the feature industry's pursuit of saccharine solutions than Greenwood's novels. Holtby's was published posthumously (she died in September 1935). The obituary notice at the beginning of the film is keen to attest its faithfulness to her depiction of historical process and social conditions (even quoting her own words) – 'she strove to preserve for us a part of the changing England that is typical of the whole ... Winifred Holtby realised that local Government is not a dry affair of meetings and memoranda:– but "the front-line defence thrown up by humanity against against its common enemies of sickness, poverty and ignorance"' – but its superimposition over pastoral images of ploughing shire-horses (which also accompany the closing credits) stressed continuity not confrontation. Victor Saville (director of *The Good Companions*) bought the rights from Vera Brittain, Holtby's literary executor who, arguably, therefore, also sold out the novel's modestly collectivist values too. This was achieved in Ian Dalrymple's screenplay by selection and shift of emphasis, by 'asset-stripping' rather than total departure.

A cross-sectional, panoramic text transferred to a non-urban location, *South Riding* made the everyday socio-economic crises of the South Yorkshire community function as a microcosm of Britain. As Richards and Aldgate put it, the film (1938) resolved the novel's complex web of conflicts by 'turning them into clashes of character', making the private dominant in its interaction with the public and reducing her host of characters to six main figures. Consequently, it marginalised the social criticism at the novel's centre, foregrounding instead 'elements which are determined more by the classic dictates of mainstream narrative cinema than by anything else'. The objective then becomes 'extirpating the "evil" and disruptive forces . . . while negotiating a series of compromise solutions to bring about a consensus of opinion within the remaining "productive" forces.' Its moral is thus at odds with the novel's 'acute sense of loss and unfulfilled promise', a point also noted by the reviewer Victor Small at the time.[57] The film heroicises Councillor Carne (he's the only character whose past is fully externalised in a long flashback), a highly Baldwinlike, but bankrupted squire. In the book, he rides despairingly into the abyss, while Astell his Socialist opponent, ultimately frustrated with piecemeal constitutional politics, returns to Clydeside to preach revolution. Similarly, Sarah Burton is a crusading feminist teacher. In the film, her primary function is romantic prevention of Carne's suicide, his insitutionalised wife dying telepathically on cue instead as he drops the shotgun. The novel's intertextuality with *Jane Eyre* is self-conscious and ironic; the film's subliminal and exploitative. Burton, aided by Alderman Mrs Beddows, also mediates between Carne and Astell. The film ends in harmony, building a new road after the civic 'insider dealing' over Astell's housing reforms by middle-class businessmen, Alderman Snaith and Councillor Huggins, has been exposed by Carne's *noblesse oblige*. Its moral neatly reflects the National Government's publicity image of 'an alliance of concerned paternalistic gentry and moderate idealist reformers', Holtby unwittingly providing its definitive, feature scenario. Similarly, the film was later used as propaganda in the neutral US to project a Fabian-feudalist idyll of the 'British way of life'.[58]

In the late thirties three popular literary features appeared which set precedents for a more searching and radical representation of conditions, although it was the initiative of King Vidor at MGM, not a British company, which made the first artistic and commercial success, with A. J. Cronin's *The Citadel* (1938). This featured Robert Donat, star of films like *The Thirty-Nine Steps* (1935), as the idealistic young doctor, lending debonair appeal to Cronin's case for recognition of silicosis as an industrial disease in mining and the introduction of a National Health Service. The doctor's dynamiting of typhoid-spreading sewers to force their reconstruction could even be seen as prophetic of the reform of Britain's infrastructure necessitated by the war. This was quickly followed by another Cronin novel, *The Stars Look Down* (1939), directed by Carol Reed and adapted by Cronin himself. Greene, already warming to his future collaborator, praised the film, doubting whether the British film industry had produced a finer (see *Spectator*, 15 March 1940; *Mornings in the Dark*, p. 380). Centred on the history of conflict and pit disasters in the North East, it effectively called for state ownership on grounds of safety and the national interest in the voice of the young Michael Redgrave, over documentary images. Similarly, Pen Tennyson, Louis Golding and miner Jack Jones's screenplay *Proud Valley* (1940), from a story by Herbert Marshall and Alfredda Brilliant, combined depiction of a Rhondda coal village (somewhat marred by Etonian-Welsh accents) with an impassioned attack on racial prejudice ('Aren't we all black down the pit?'). It starred Paul Robeson as displaced American seaman and self-sacrificing human detonator 'David Goliath'. Hostilities overtook the filming so that the original ending, in which miners create their own cooperative, was exchanged for the owners' reopening the mine to assist the struggle against Fascism. In this way the 'People's War' became a much more effective *deus ex machina* for industrial problems than Gracie's ballads (*Shipyard Sally*, for example, was made when her popularity was already in sharp decline) or the football pools.

This is a brief sketch of the cultural and economic framework of literary involvement in popular features against which more stylistically adventurous radical writers, like Greene and Isherwood, chafed. Greene's involvement with cinema went back almost as far as his first broadcast. In 1927 he was already approaching British National Pictures about the possibility of scripting. Documentarist Basil Wright, Greene's immediate predecessor on *The Spectator*, considered he 'had a built-in filmic style' and that experience as a critic helped him 'intensify his cinematic approach'.[59] Greene's column provides both a detailed literary perspective on film discourse and suggests its manifold influence on his writing. However, the talkies brought new possibilities for the writer in what Greene called 'a selectivity of sound which promised to become as formal as the warning shadow'.[60] *Stamboul Train*, Greene's first 'entertainment', also brought his film-mindedness to its first fruition. With a hopeful eye to a 'treatment', it cashed in on the early thirties vogue for train films, such as Von Sternberg's *Shanghai Express* for Paramount, Michael Balcon's British *Rome Express*, and Turin's *Turksib*. Twentieth Century-Fox bought the rights for £2000, although the screenplay was not written by Greene himself. Released as *Orient Express*, the venality of his novel returned to haunt him. It was a salutary warning not to allow his writing to emulate studio blockbusters too closely lest it became indistinguishable from them: 'By what was unchanged I could judge and condemn my own novel: I could clearly see what was cheap and banal enough to fit the cheap banal film.' The box-office blurb reduced Greene's topical cross-section of trans-European politics and sexual discontents into a (literal) star vehicle: *'Two Youthful Hearts in the Grip of Intrigue. Fleeing from Life. Cheated? Crashing Across Europe. Wheels of Fate.'*[61] It was this 'reversion to type' that made Greene realise the aesthetic and ethical complexity of harnessing the vitality and reach of the popular media. By 1936 Greene was lamenting how *Stamboul Train*'s concept had already become a tiresomely stock scenario, 'now that the novelty of a thriller worked out in the cramped surroundings of a train, hotel or 'plane has worn off' (*Spectator*, 12 June 1936; *Mornings in the Dark*, p. 111.)

Greene thought it very ironic that *It's a Battlefield*, the most consciously cinematic of all his novels, was never filmed. He actually came to believe his books didn't make good films, despite what film companies thought. This suggests that the effects of the cinematic novel are peculiarly intertextual and do not necessarily translate easily back into the 'original' medium; also, possibly, that cinema's technical possibilities are sometimes more realisable in literature without the industry's peculiar commercial pressures.[62] However, as Greene later admitted, producing your own treatments and even 'shooting scripts' did not necessarily preserve the integrity of your writing: 'even if a script be followed word for word there are those gaps of silence which can be filled with the banal embrace. Irony can be turned into sentiment by some romantic boob of an actor.'[63] The collective nature of film-production meant that after the shooting script was completed, the screenwriter was inevitably excluded from the process and contemplated the progressive mutation of his individual effort with a mixture of powerlessness and guilt. The 'author is a forgotten man', until the rough cut, emerging bewildered 'at the new lines that are not his' like a witness of a crime 'afraid to speak, an accomplice after the fact' (*Mornings in the Dark*, p. 459). There was a reverse route in which the text emerged from the film concept, as with *The Third Man*. It was better to work up original material or a short story, because 'Condensation is always dangerous, while expansion is a form of creation.'[64]

Greene's involvement with popular cinema remained equivocal, even when it was a question of direct creation, not adaptation. In November 1936, Alexander Korda approached him, despite Greene's persistent attacks on his films (he even suggested Denham Studios' motto ought to be 'Abandon life all ye who enter here').[65] Greene was already on an advisory committee for TV and had produced the short *Calendar of the Year* (with Auden as assistant director), demonstrating the GPO's role in seasonal pastimes and festivals. The meeting with Korda turned out to be both a bluff-calling and a mutual recognition that writer and director could learn from each other. The result was Greene's apprentice scenario 'Four Dark Hours' (not actually released until 1940 as a 65-minute 'quota quickie' thriller, *The Green Cockatoo*, with a finished screenplay by Edward O. Berkman). Quentin Falk reckons this undistinguished beginning nonetheless contains in embryo many of the recurring themes of Greene's subsequent work, especially 'innocence threatened in an alien landscape', and was almost a 'trailer' for *Brighton Rock*, published the following year.[66] It's also likely some of the ethos of *Brighton Rock* derived from an earlier cinema source. Greene himself highlighted the sinister quality of a sequence from *Sous les Toits de Paris* which might have prompted the scene where Pinkie is set up by Colleoni under cover of a holiday crowd. It featured Préjean similarly cornered by a razor-thugs under the smoke and commotion of a railway viaduct (*Spectator*, 1 November 1935; *Mornings in the Dark*, p. 42). In *The Green Cockatoo*, a very boyish John Mills starred as the brother of Robert Newton (carved-up by the race-gang he double-crosses at a railway station); with Rene Ray as the naive waif inadvertently mixed up as a suspect, who becomes his lover and helps him to vengeance. Greene also confessed to adapting Galsworthy's 'The First and the Last' for Korda, released as *Twenty-One Days* (1937). This time his job was made virtually impossible by his old enemy, the BBFC, which gutted the plot – a suicide who frames an innocent man for his murder.[67] Nevertheless, Greene learnt enough from these misfires for his texts to be eminently draftable for the cinematic war effort and to ground himself in the skills which would make his postwar collaboration with Carol Reed so outstanding. The sole way to retain any control over a film would be scripting for an 'amicable director', like Reed, who could both sympathise with an author's anxieties and give guidance. This, according to Greene, was the secret of both *The Fallen Idol* and *The Third Man*.[68]

The most intriguing retrospective on Leftists' involvement with popular features in the thirties is Isherwood's autobiographical novel *Prater Violet* (1946). Ironically, it was Jean Ross (model for starstruck

'Sally Bowles') who brought Isherwood to the attention of Berthold
Viertel, veteran of Weimar cinema, who instantly spotted his talent
for dialogue. Viertel approached him in Autumn 1933 to script
Gaumont-British's *Little Friend* (with Margaret Kennedy), based
on Austrian Ernst Lothar's *Kleine Freundin*, in which a small girl
re-unites adulterous parents by attempting suicide. Lothar's 'old-
fashioned sentimental theme' was modernised in the studio 'by the
introduction of freudian symbols and dreams', particularly in the
vertiginously surreal opening sequence, full of metonymic objects
and forbidding adult authority figures. But Isherwood's dismissive
attitude in his autobiography underrates his own contribution.[69]
The script's almost Jamesianly subtle depiction, through a child's
eyes, of the stifling repressiveness and chicanery of heterosexual
propriety, was ironically reflected in the highly-coded treatment of
these subjects necessary for it to get through the BBFC. Sexual
ambivalence and censorship are not the only pervasive themes of
Isherwood's writing which infiltrate the movie. Rebellion against
class-privilege also features in the girl's friendship with a confec-
tioner's son: 'Mummy sometimes has friends that I don't like, so I
don't see why I can't have friends she doesn't like.'

This wasn't exactly Shirley Temple, but Isherwood's novel turned
it all into an 'unashamedly corny musical set in pre-1914 Vienna'
(such genre films being a common product of the British industry
in the thirties – even Hitchock directed one!), but filmed in England
during the 1934 Workers' Uprising.[70] This, paradoxically, made
'Prater Violet' more nauseating as 'film', but more searching as a
text analysing the ethical contortions of Leftists' involvement with
popular cinema. In *Mr Norris*, popular cinema and song transport
the citizens of Weimar to imaginary elsewheres like 'Never-Never-
Vienna' (p. 90). Conversely, Viertel's counterpart 'Bergmann', with
his family stranded in Dollfuß's Austria, symbolises Central European *angst* in a montage of fiction and hyperreal crisis: 'I knew that
face. It was the face of a political situation, an epoch.'[71] Hence *Prater
Violet* investigates the writer's ethical entanglement in various kinds
of propaganda disseminated through contemporary media. Dream-
factory escapism and totalitarian agitprop are its two extremes (it's
no coincidence 'Imperial Bulldog's' agent is called Katz, the name
of the lieutenant to German Communist Propaganda boss Willi
Münzenberg, for whom Isherwood worked in Berlin).[72] Perhaps
even more than Greene, Isherwood was highly equivocal about his
involvement, both queasy and compelled. He recalled countering

friends' criticisms by admitting 'he *was* partly responsible for the film's sentimentality', but that 'He, the arrogant dainty-minded private artist, needed to plunge his hands into a vulgar public bucket of dye ... to subdue his nature temporarily to it ... the making of *Little Friend* had been a new and absolutely necessary phase of his education as a writer.'[73] And this sense of guilty compromise is shared with Bergmann/Viertel, who says unconvincingly '"I feel absolutely no shame before you. We are like two married men who meet in a whorehouse."' (*Prater Violet*, p. 27).

In Marx's theory of reification, human labour and the web of social relations that produce exchange value disappear into the commodity as fetish. This meant the commodity was also a social hieroglyph, a kind of metonymy, from which these latent exploitative relations could be decoded.[74] It was for this reason that Benjamin viewed commercial cinema's 'realism' as apotheosising commodity production for the culture of an age of mechanical reproduction. Unlike avant-garde collision montage which revealed production processes (including its own) the highly 'finished' product of Hollywood erased the very means by which it was made, substituting a mystifying transparency:

> Its illusionary nature is that of the second degree, the result of cutting. That is to say, in the studio the mechanical equipment has penetrated into reality so deeply that its pure aspect freed from the foreign substance of equipment is the result of a special procedure, namely, the shooting by the specially adjusted camera and the mounting of the shot together with other similar ones. The equipment-free aspect of reality here has become the height of artifice; the sight of immediate reality has become an orchid in the land of technology.[75]

The Invisible Man, with its phantasmal manipulation of objects, from which human agency dis/appears, both epitomises and parodies this (see Chapter 2). Conversely, *Prater Violet* as novel reconstitutes what disappears in *Prater Violet* the movie – the space and time of studio technology.

> Within the great barn-like sound-stage, with its high, bare, padded walls, big enough to enclose an airship, there is neither day nor night: only irregular alternations of activity and silence. Beneath a firmament of girders and catwalks, out of which the cowled lamps shine coldly down, like planets, stands the inconsequent,

half-dismantled architecture of the sets; archways, sections of houses, wood and canvas hills, huge photographic backdrops, the frontages of streets; a kind of Pompeii, but more desolate, more uncanny, because this is, literally, a half-world, a limbo of mirror-images, a town which has lost its third dimension. Only the tangle of heavy power-cables are solid. . . . (pp. 72–3)

This underlying material reality is seen to vanish from the film-commodity at the same time as the good intentions of director and scriptwriter are progressively ensnarled and neutralised in the socio-economic forces that constitute it. Isherwood's fascination with self-reflexive consciousness (which, as we saw in Chapter 3, catches out the 'objective' camera-eye of *Goodbye to Berlin* in its own peripheral vision) also features subversively in what Bergmann calls ' "the Original Sin of the Talking Pictures" '. The 'mike-shadow' has to be rigorously excluded from the image, lest this tell-tale trace threaten its simulation (p. 81).

Bergmann's view of what they are involved in remains partly avant-gardist in its terms even when admitting its betrayal of radical principles:

The film is an infernal machine. Once it is ignited and set in motion it revolves with an enormous dynamism. It cannot pause. It cannot apologise. It cannot retract anything. It cannot wait for you to understand it. It cannot explain itself. It simply ripens to its inevitable explosion. This explosion we have to prepare, like anarchists, with the utmost ingenuity and malice. . . .

It also retains traces of Viertel's actual apprenticeship to Ruttmann: ' "The film is a symphony. Each movement is written in a certain key" ' (pp. 33 and 38). But the dilemma of director and scriptwriter is institutional, as is suggested when Bergmann acts out passages from the second *Brown Book of the Hitler Terror* (1934), covertly published by Münzenberg's organisation,[76] as if they were part of an alternative anti-Nazi screenplay the BBFC would never have licensed, even if it had found a backer: 'Now that Bergmann had become Dimitrov, he was obliged to abandon a great deal of his cynicism. It was no longer in character. Dimitrov had to have a Cause to fight for, to make speeches about. And the cause turned out to be *Prater Violet*' (p. 49). The censorship-circumventing allegory of Gaumont's *Jew Süss* (1934), which displaced Hitler's regime it into an eighteenth-century setting, was a rare exception, as we

saw in Chapter 1.[77] Alternatively, *Prater Violet*'s Ruritanian escapism demands the price of self-censorship – repression of their out-
rage at the bloody events unfolding in Austria. Although the
film-making consequently becomes a politicised issue, the finished
product exhibited to the public will simply distract from properly
informed else-awareness:

> All Bergmann's pent-up anxiety exploded. 'The picture! I s——
> upon the picture! . . . It is a crime. It definitely aids Dollfuss, and
> Starhemberg, and Fey and all their gangsters. It covers up the dirty
> syphilitic sore with rose leaves, with the petals of this hypocriti-
> cal reactionary violet. It lies and declares that the pretty Danube
> is blue, when the water is red with blood. . . . I am punished for
> assisting at this lie. We shall all be punished –' (pp. 96–7)

It is arguable Isherwood exaggerated the tackiness of *Prater Violet*, the movie, in order to make the battle to endow it with a radical
subtext seem hopeless from the start and to evade more complex
questions of accountability. Nevertheless, Bergmann's despair forces
Isherwood's 'narrated-I' to confront the crux of his generation's
involvement with popular cinema:

> 'Why can't they leave me alone?' I resentfully exclaimed. But the
> 'I' that thought this was both Patterson and Bergmann, English-
> man and Austrian, islander and continental. It was divided and
> hated its division.
>   . . . I knew what I was supposed to feel, what it was fashion-
> able for my generation to feel. We cared about everything: fas-
> cism in Germany and Italy, the seizure of Manchuria. Indian
> nationalism, the Irish question, the Workers, the Negroes, the
> Jews. We had spread our feelings over the whole world; and I
> knew that mine were spread very thin. . . . (pp. 104–5)

This was a conundrum which Isherwood was honest enough to
confront but failed to solve. His 'narrated-I' ends up not just a split,
but disintegrating post/modern subject, neither able to maintain a
politically active sympathy amid the multiple and simultaneous
consciousness of the media, nor to square the circle of radical content and popular form. The cultural objective inherited from the
Soviet avant-garde founders in a letter noting French workers

are all going to see *La Violette du Prater*, a horrible British picture which, besides being an insult to the intelligence of a five-year-old child, is definitely counter-revolutionary and ought to be banned. Meanwhile, in the cinema round the corner, a wonderful Russian masterpiece is playing to empty seats.

Although the Russian film is caricatured as 'the usual sex-triangle between a girl with thick legs, a boy, and a tractor' (p. 127), Isher-wood's flippancy doesn't release him from this haunting fascination and guilt. But then how much could any individual writer have influenced the aesthetic and political tendency of a multi-national industry by private revolt or smuggled subtexts? *Prater Violet* also seems to touch on the most disabling blindspot in thir-ties Leftists' ideas about the potential of the media – the lack of a coherent theory of pleasure, sometimes coupled with bourgeois–puritan disgust at the 'vulgarity' of the escapist impulse. This was perhaps the reason for the general failure to empathise with and organise a 'mass' response that might enjoy such products without losing critical consciousness. The subsequent measure of Isherwood's own abandonment of the Leftist project is indicated by his rapid return to scriptwriting as a Hollywood war refugee in 1940.

Documentary seemed to provide some thirties Leftists, Auden in particular, with the opportunity of writing for a genuinely collec-tive art, revealing 'the essentially cooperative or mass nature of society'.[78] The Griersonian kind, they came to realise, was deeply mortgaged to an establishment economic base. Alternatively, inde-pendent Leftist actuality films rarely had the funds, equipment or access to distribution circuits to achieve high standards of technical performance or even reach the limited audiences who saw GPO documentaries.[79] Auden's verse commentary for the GPO Film Unit's *Night Mail* (1936), a recitative chorus for its *Coal Face* (1935) (with Montagu Slater), collaboration with Britten on Strand Film's *The Way to Sea* (1937) and verse for the Realist Film Unit's *The Londoners* (1939) are rare examples of documentary involvements that did reach a relatively wide public (at least compared to his verse sub-titles for the London Film Society screening of Vertov's *Three Songs of Lenin*), but are also intertextual with the concerns of Auden's poetry as far as the restrictions on the medium would allow.

Night Mail maps the genuinely two-way private and commercial communications of a mass-society. Its cross-section uses the rail and postal infrastructure to bring together everyone, however 'far apart in space or the social complex', as Jameson put it. Official and informal communications – bills, invitations, receipts, gossip and news – are exchanged between banks and customers, relations and lovers, from every corner of these islands and abroad. *Night Mail* may not have been as 'heteroglot' as Bridson's *Coronation Scot* radio feature, but Auden's famous verses strive to imply the unequal political, economic and cultural relations inscribed within the materiality of literacy itself ('Clever stupid, short and long,/ The typed and the printed and the spelt all wrong') and the standard-ised written language. They ride the excitement of Grierson's visual poetry of technology and democratic civics, but also problematise it at an intricate, micropolitical level (see *English Auden*, pp. 290–1).

Auden also wrote the end commentary for Rotha's film *The Way to the Sea*, which brought together two subjects beloved of Leftists in Soviet films, railways and electrification. Again his language mapped the sociological landscape beside the London to Portsmouth line, cross-threaded by the common need for access to the coast. It concludes with visual imagery of mass beach pleasures recalling the ethos of 'Poem XXIV' of 1935 ('August for the people and their favourite islands') set in tension with the looming presence of bat-tleships (see *English Auden*, pp. 155–7). Although Auden only wrote sections of the commentary for *The Londoners*, the film was typical of the avant-garde tendency to create collective heroes out of metro-polises themselves. It also depicted London's history intertextually as a series of literary strata, quoting from Shelley, Dickens, etc. Primarily an advertisement for fifty years of the capital's local gov-ernment, it contrasted the anarchic slums of nineteenth-century *laissez-faire* individualism, with a modern rationalised transport infrastructure, sanitation, social housing and health, using plenty of visionary images akin to Auden's famous injunction in 'Poem XXIII' of 1930 to 'look shining at/ New styles of architecture, a change of heart' (*English Auden*, p. 36). Not only did the film model the post-war welfare state, it was redolent with Audenesque motifs of popu-lar pastimes, Bauhaus-style clinics and cavorting *Sonnenkinder*. Auden's chorus for *Coal Face*, sponsored by the Safety in Mines Board, recited the functions of different kinds of miners' work over images of a shift 'travelling' to the face. His song 'O lurcher-loving collier' accompanied their return to the surface. But like virtually all documentaries on mining in the thirties, this 'symphonic' coordina-tion of music and lyrics with images of muscle and machinery, despite repeated stress on the industry's heroic importance ('Coal mining is the basic industry of Britain' recurs like a refrain), hardly touched on its politically controversial history, unlike written reportage like Orwell's *Wigan Pier* or Hanley's *Grey Children*. Exceptional in this respect was Ralph Bond's *Today We Live* (1937), on the work of the National Council of Social Services, which confronted the devasting impact of unemployment in South Wales and even the inadequacy of the Council's own ameliorative measures, earning a salute from Rhondda proletarian Lewis Jones in the title of his second *Cwmardy* novel.[80]

In 1937, Greene wrote the commentary for Rotha's Strand Film on the inauguration of the Empire Air Mail, *The Future's in the Air*, under the influence of the stratospheric panopticism of Auden's early poems, but suppressing the scepticism about communication systems evident in *It's a Battlefield*. 'As the aeroplane has conquered natural barriers, so radio has conquered weather', the commentary trumpets. This is *Night Mail* on wings:

> this flying boat is waiting – waiting for thousands of letters which it will carry across the world. Letters from great office buildings, from country villages, from the depressed areas. Letters to brothers and cousins and sons and the man you met at the Cornonation. Letters posted as if they were just going next door. Letters to the far ends of the earth.

But the critical mismatch between Griersonian principles and writers' commentaries was too explicit in Auden's verses for the GPO project *Negroes* (eventually incorporated in *F6*). This was unsuprisingly aborted, since Auden embarrassed Griersonian documentary's ideological brief of Empire-into-economic-commonwealth-of-nations, by exhuming the 'acts of injustice' buried like human remains in its origins:

> Memory sees them down there,
> Paces alive beside his fear,
> That's slow to die and still here.

(And cf. *F6*, p. 96.)

Consequently, Auden's verbal and photographic in-joking about Grierson and his personnel ('And here's a shot for the chief – epic, the *Drifters* tradition') in *Letters from Iceland* vented reservations gained from experience about their 'creative interpretation of actuality'.[81] A sequence of 'rushes' ends

Well. That's the lot.
As you see, no crisis, no continuity.
Only heroic cutting could save it
Perhaps MacNaughten might do it
Or Legge.

(p. 224)

Auden reviewed Rotha's book in 1936 around the time he left the GPO and his criticisms of documentary's distrust of 'subjectivism' and 'fiction', as well as its lack of broader social appeal, were similarly informed. The movement insisted

'The private life is unimportant. We must abandon the story and report facts, i.e. we must show you people at their daily work, show you how modern industry is organised, show you what people do for their living, not what they feel.' But the private life and the emotions are facts like any others, and one cannot understand the public life of action without them.

The puritanism of this absolute division between 'reality' and 'entertainment' sometimes produced films with excellent qualities, but which 'to the ordinary film-goer were finally and fatally dull' (*English Auden*, pp. 354–5).

Undoubtedly, one problem for writers was Grierson himself, who could be both inspiring and dictatorial. Esmond Romilly, who worked briefly on a cinema and broadcasting journal run by his Film Unit summed up their feelings in his caricature 'MacIntosh', 'Like Sir Oswald Mosley he was known as "The Leader" or "The Chief".' At best, Grierson reminded Romilly of a progressive headmaster.[82] Nevertheless, despite Auden and Isherwood's emigration to America in 1939, the migration of writers into both the popular and documentary dimensions of British cinema, like radio, accelerated dramatically at the beginning of the war.

WARTIME CONDITIONS

The opportunity for Leftist involvements at the BBC and in the film industry in any numbers and for reaching mass audiences did not come about until the war, which itself initiated new technological conditions that increased the 'immediacy' of the hyperreal like the lightweight portable disc recorder. The gap between event and reproduction seemed almost to have disappeared altogether when the BBC broadcast the first of its 'War Report' series after the 9 o'clock news on D-Day, with its eye-witness commentary direct from the beaches, and in a matter of days newsreels of the same flooded in to packed cinemas. Many Leftists had also either become disillusioned by the Machiavellian tactics of Stalinist propaganda towards dissident groups during the Spanish Civil War, or broke with the Communist Party over the Nazi–Soviet Non-Aggression Pact of August 1939, which seemed like a betrayal of all that the Popular Front stood for (though from the Soviet point of view, the Munich sell-out scuppered the chances of an anti-Fascist alliance with Britain and France). The result was a drift back towards the cultural and political centre, through loss of faith in political extremism on the one hand and temporary necessity on the other. Many felt that the limited and contradictory freedoms of capitalist Britain might still furnish the basis for a social-democratic transformation, if they were defended from the far more immediate evil of Nazi invasion which threatened to wipe out any potential for future progress whatsoever. Defending 'the bad against the worse', as Day Lewis put it, now became the objective of Leftists who found themselves unexpectedly presented with the chance denied to them in the thirties. Writers were also pushed into war work because of the closure of literary magazines and the difficult situation (because of paper costs and the Excess Profits Tax) in publishing. Day Lewis's question 'Where Are the War Poets?',[83] posed soon after hostilties began, is best answered by focusing, not as in 1914, on combatants dashing off battlefront verses, but on the writers mobilised in the biggest exercise in mass-communications ever undertaken by a British government. Day Lewis himself worked as an editor for the MoI Publications Section. The *Horizon* 'War Writers Manifesto', signed in October 1941 by editor Cyril Connolly, Calder Marshall, Tom Harrisson, Koestler, Alun Lewis, Orwell, Spender and others, called for the formation of an official group with the same facilities as approved journalists, to aid the war effort by interpreting its events.[84] Though this group never became more than a loose association rather than an official 'writers brigade', on the Soviet model, individuals were in effect given this kind of opportunity by the state.

Involvement in media propaganda at last offered Leftists a genuine chance to reach a mass audience, though at a price. Unlike the documentarism of the New Deal in mid- to late-thirties America, or the earlier enthusiastic and eventually compulsory mobilisation of Soviet artists in the revolutionary and Stalinist phases of Soviet history, this was the first time British writers had the opportunity to take part in moulding the semi-official culture of the nation in artistically modernising and politically progressive terms. However, this situation came about through a series of complex, highly-inflected and, indeed, unique historical circumstances. With symptomatic intertextuality, one of the war's earliest propaganda features. *Freedom Radio*, released in 1941, but approved by the BBFC immediately after hostilities, was partly scripted by middlebrow social-realist Louis Golding. This foregrounded the role of the media and, implicitly, the writer in resisting Hitler, with its underground radio station subverting Nazi broadcasts with uncensored news. But British writers' own involvements were intimately bound up with the propaganda and censorship policies for moulding public consciousness of the Ministry of Information (MoI), as Ian Mclaine has shown in his study.[85]

It was precisely because Britain's media were so disproportionally representative in the thirties, that the MoI began the war so much in the dark, as far as finding out what people really thought about conditions and how to tailor its campaigns to them were concerned. Mass-Observation's findings about publicity and morale for Home Intelligence were not auspicious. They found public opinion still very much confused with 'the private opinion of newspaper proprietors, BBC directors and the three or four men who control the news-reels'.[86] Against this early background of uninformed ineptitude, Greene wrote 'Men at Work' (1940), satirising his own experience of working for the MoI in Senate House. Richard Skate, whose one play ran for a night in St John's Wood, personifies the literary bureauhack pushed into prominence by the time. The Ministry itself spreads exponentially to intrude into every aspect of culture: 'the huge staff of the Ministry accumulated like a kind of fungoid life – old divisions sprouting daily new sections which then broke away and became divisions and spawned in turn – the five hundred rooms of the great university block became inadequate'.[87] Cryptic initials and abbreviations were widespread in the MoI and organisations like the wartime BBC under its jurisdiction, as noted by Greene: 'It made telephone conversations as obscure as a cable in code.' Skate's situation anticipates Orwell's frustrating experience at the BBC's Eastern Service in many respects. But his work is trivial rather than sinister, unlike Winston Smith's at the Ministry of Truth: 'it was all a game played in a corner under the gigantic shadow. Propaganda was a means of passing the time: work was not done for its usefulness but for its own sake – simply as an occupation. He wrote wearily down "The Problem of India" on the agenda' (*Collected Stories*, p. 396). The MoI's early campaigns were on a crassly commercial, not totalitarian, model: Skate's immediate superior 'King' is an ex-ad man 'selling War' to the public (though as a populist he has a hunch J. B. Priestley is one of the 'the right authors' to employ for gaining its confidence) (pp. 397–8).[88] Above all, campaigns were insufficiently proactive to a ludicrous degree: 'the minutes on who should write a "suggested" pamphlet about the French war-effort were still circulating indecisively while Germany broke the line, passed the Somme, occupied Paris and received the delegates at Compiègne'. Skate's day's routine futility ends with an ironic 'distance shot': 'Far up in the pale enormous sky little white lines, like the phosphorescent spore of snails, showed where men were going home after work' (pp. 339 and 401).

In contrast to the Great War, when the MoI had been under Beaverbrook, its activities were now as much concerned with morale at home as with propaganda to neutrals. Significantly, its peace-time forerunner, set up by the Committee of Imperial Defence in 1936, was headed by Sir Stephen Tallents, recruiter of Griersonian documentarists into the EMB and GPO. The essential aim of MoI propaganda policy, as Nicholas Pronay argues, was to live down the backfiring of official slogans after the Great War, when the promised 'Land Fit for Heroes' vanished into the dreary reality of mass-unemployment, homelessness and poverty.[89] Misconceptions of the Ministry as a hotbed of revolutionary, or even social-democratic, cultural evangelism are belied by the roll-call of its heads: Lord Macmillan on the outbreak of war: Sir John Reith briefly from January 1940: Duff Cooper from May 1940 and, finally, Brendan Bracken from July 1941. Although Richard Crossman was coopted early as a token gesture towards the coalition with Labour, the Ministry's hierarchy remained an enclave, often recruited from the prewar media (Bracken himself, for example, was a Right-wing press-baronet). For the first two years the measures taken by the MoI propagandists were inept and/or patronising, blinkered by their own class and background. Its sub-Beaverbrookian 'Empire Crusade' failed to galvanise morale (no doubt partly due to uncomfortable parallels between 'enlightened' British and 'ruthless' Nazi imperialism which thirties EMB documentaries had failed to dispel).[90] Equally it failed to orchestrate a satisfactory discourse for the media as a whole. As M-O put it in 1940, the war was 'being treated by the Press and the BBC especially, very much as if it were an enormous sporting event, in which one side brings down one of the other's aeroplanes, 15 love, then there is a retaliation, 15 all'.[91] Eventually, however, after extensive methodical feedback from its Home Intelligence Division, the MoI's unprofessional frame of reference underwent a radical overhaul. Ministry *policy* came to regard the British masses 'as sensible and tough, and therefore entitled to be taken into the government's confidence'. In turn, this furnished the government with means for a more cohesive war effort. In mid-1940, the authorities had been seriously worried that the British public would simply cave in to invasion, like the disaffected French masses, if they felt the system as it was, or, more importantly, *might become*, was not worth defending.[92] The possibility of a long-drawn-out war of attrition meant hopes about the future might have a definite effect on present action. Consequently, in Daniel Lerner's phrase, propaganda sought to modify the public's 'structure of expectations'.[93] The switch to the cooperative and levelling notion of the People's War was a means by which the MoI met the aspirations of Leftists halfway in a kind of 'armed compromise'.

As Calder argues in both *The People's War* (1969) and *The Myth of the Blitz* (1991), MoI policy successfully extended peacetime techniques for managing opinion by means of a kind of 'applied' social science. Greene's 'King' was an accurate hunch since 'The advertising industry, one might say, was nationalised for the duration.' Though it might look democratic, the net effect was quite opposite: 'Having found out what people thought and how they behaved, the rulers of the country could manipulate them more efficiently.'[94] This made the situation for Leftist writers even more complex and dialectic. In March 1944, Koestler summed up the insidious twin dangers of 'internal censorship' and aesthetic devaluation writers exposed themselves to in propaganda work and warned about their possible permanent effects on the intelligentsia. It was imaginable that one day 'job' and 'private product' might become indistinguishable: 'when instead of regarding the former as a kind of patriotic hacking and the latter as the real thing, the energies become suddenly canalised into one stream'. Precisely because of the peculiar circumstances of wartime 'necessity', conformity might be a self-betrayal 'carried out with a perfectly clear conscience'.[95] Orwell feared a British 'Taylorisation of the arts', on the Stalinist model which might 'rob literary creation of its individual character and turn it into a conveyor belt process' (*Collected Essays*, III, p. 266). Connolly increasingly fought a High Cultural rearguard action against semi-official cultural production. Though 'we are at last getting a well-informed inquisitive public', war artists, the Brains Trust, journalism and the BBC could never be art. And all the Penguins, discussion groups and MoI films could never substitute for the 'independence, leisure and privacy' needed to produce it.[96] It is true, however, that much wartime media production was *both* politically compromised and aesthetically disposable, Orwell for one was to prove himself wrong when he wrote in October 1944 that writers' experience in wartime broadcasting was wasted: 'They will come out of the war with nothing to show for their labours and with not even the stored-up experience that the soldier gets in return for his physical suffering' (*Collected Essays*, III, p. 293). It was precisely his expense of spirit at the BBC that would crystallise thirties Leftists' general misgivings about the media into his brilliant postwar satires.[97] The cases of many others, within this negotiated context, would be just as productive, as we shall see.

An early MoI policy document (September 1939) suggested official information was distrusted because the public knew it to be censored and, alternatively, that the effectiveness and credibility of propaganda would be increased if delivered by Left-wing speakers allowed a degree of criticism of the Government. However, it also talked about 'pragmatic definition' of the truth and even falsification for justified ends.[98] This fundamental tension pervaded the wartime situations of writers, because as Orwell put it at the time, the concept of the 'People's War' meant propaganda simply could not be left to 'safe' Conservative populists like Ian Hay or A. P. Herbert (*Collected Essays*, II, p. 381). Significantly, it was Harold Nicolson, writer and centre-Left politician who formed the common link which shaped that 'armed compromise' at the MoI. As Nicolson wrote: 'The Germans are fighting a revolutionary war for very definite objectives. We are fighting a conservative war and our objects are purely negative. We must put forward a positive and revolutionary aim admitting that the old order has collapsed and asking people to fight for a new order.'[99] From June 1941, when Hitler's operation Barbarossa dragged the USSR into the conflict, MoI 'moral contortionism' was compounded by the need to temporarily rehabilitate a prewar bogey as an eligible ally. Consequently, it had to develop 'policies almost Byzantine in deviousness and complexity'. Within these contradictory parameters wartime's new cultural agenda took shape.[100]

The machinery of the Ministry itself was an extension and refinement of Britain's existing semi-official media controls, not a new system as such. Wartime censorship, as Orwell argued in July 1944, did not generally depart from the peacetime rule of genteel conspiracy to prevent public discussion of anything deemed uncongenial to the authorities. MoI 'vetting' of manuscripts submitted by publishers extended indirect practices by the BBFC and Press Association, etc. It hardly ever banned anything, instead 'suggesting' 'that this or that is undesireable, or premature, or "would serve no good purpose". And though there is no definite prohibition, no clear statement that this or that must not be printed, official policy is never flouted' (*Collected Essays*, III, p. 212). In the same venerable British tradition, the MoI's positive effect on print output was largely covert and 'anonymous'. Secret arrangements were struck with publishers like Penguin and Oxford University Press, with magazines like *Picture Post* (a vital forum for the question of postwar Britain), and with distributors such as Foyles. Its control over extra paper supplies and export subsidies 'considerably enhanced its ability to persuade publishers to co-operate in joint ventures' and to exercise 'hands off' censorship.[101] The MoI's indirect method was to suggest an idea to a publisher who might commision an author to work on it, or even publish a whole text written in the MoI. Alternatively 'raw material' was sometimes given to individual authors who would then seek publication.

With the recent model of Republican Spain in mind, writers and artists were to be both mobilised and promoted. Everything from Arnold to Joyce was cultural ammunition against Fascism's 'philistine' anarchy. Kenneth Clark's 1941 memorandum recommended propaganda should stress a crucial difference between the Great War when 'all the best elements of German culture and science were still in Germany and were supporting the German cause, whereas now they are outside Germany and supporting us'.[102] The opportunity for writers' involvement with the media was also vastly expanded by the MoI's influence over filmwork and broadcasting (responsibility for the BBC, for example, being transferred from the Postmaster General on the outbreak of war). Literary output itself was often as not connected with both MoI campaigns and the role of the media at home and abroad. Storm Jameson, for instance, edited an anthology, *London Calling*, with verse, prose and drama from 31 writers of 'special interest' to Americans, using the BBC's habitual mode of 'overseas' announcement in its title. A film made from a story by Greene published in *Collier's Magazine* took its name from a similar 1942 collection: *Went the Day Well?* (discussed below) was the title-poem of a volume of tributes to men and women killed in the war. In 1941, Jennings directed *Words for Battle*, in which Olivier read excerpts from English classics over patriotic visuals.[103] Greene himself was possibly involved in Rotha's MoI film *The Battle of the Books*, with its recollected scenes of Nazi book-burnings. (See *Mornings in the Dark*, p. 702.) The BBC's *Books and People* series and E. M. Forster's regular broadcasts, *Some Books*, typified radio campaigns to demonstrate that both contemporary writing and civilisation's classical/liberal-humanist literary heritage were 'on our side' and both at stake. Eric Linklater's radio dialogue *Cornerstones* (1941) featured philosophers and historical figures like Confucius. Lincoln and Lenin debating with a newly-dead British soldier to try and find common ground for opposing Hitler, probably inspiring the cosmic trial scenes in Michael Powell and Emmerich Pressburger's masterpiece, *A Matter of Life or Death* (1946).[104]

Forster's broadcasts may still have attracted largely 'highbrow' audiences, but the gravitational tendency of the time was towards a 'middlebrow' zone, in which writers and mass-public met half-way. What typified this for the popular imagination were media products like the feature *Pimpernel Smith* (1941), starring Leslie Howard as an Oxford don and classical scholar, who rescues artists and intellectuals from the clutches of the Nazis, and the *Brains Trust*'s radio popularisation of science as part of the educational war effort.[105] Angus Calder argues that because of the focus of wartime media work, a 'close knit literary community emerged . . . for the first time, perhaps, English literary intellectuals began to see themselves as a class, an intelligentsia on the Continental model' and far more open in its social outlook. By such unexpected means 'the educational ambitions of the Reith era reached astonishing fulfilment'.[106]

WARTIME BROADCASTING

Regular TV broadcasting was suspended during the war, giving radio features and drama an artificial breathing space as popular forms, enhanced by the initial closure of theatres and cinemas, and the public's confinement to homes and shelters. There is no doubt the war's demands changed the BBC enormously. The aloofness of its newscasters was enhanced by anonymity, as impersonal 'institutional voices', mere transmitters of authoritative discourse, but their identies were revealed in the invasion crisis of July 1940, as part of the measures to prevent Hitler capturing and manipulating the BBC. The BBC also grew into a global network: by the end of 1943, it was broadcasting in 47 foreign languages, compared with eight in 1939; its personnel virtually tripled and broadcast hours increased from 51 to 150 per day. Although we shouldn't overestimate the impact of pioneering radio work from the thirties in terms of access and democratisation of the BBC, the process was vastly accelerated by the war which gave radio a unique cultural opportunity. In Rodger's phrase, it 'became the national theatre', in more than one sense.[107] On the one hand, Val Gielgud's drafting of Greek tragedy and Ibsen for the MoI's 'culture on our side' campaign finally overcame the BBC's view that they were impossibly highbrow for popular audiences, but there was also a renewed affair between Features and Drama because of their temporary evacuation to Manchester (until 1941). This fused the experimental and traditional and led to the formation of the BBC's Repertory Company who now worked in both. Gilliam remained one of the catalysts of wartime Features, with their protean format of narration, actuality inserts, dialogue and music. And writers themselves played no small part in ensuring that wartime broadcasting became a great cultural force and, assisted by print rationing, the principal discussion forum for urgent social and economic topics.[108] This boom continued in peacetime, because the relatively small British film industry could not absorb all this energy and talent, and TV, though revived in 1946, was still a limited market until well into the 1950s.

Bridson's radio work continued in his prewar agitational strain. *Aaron's Field* (first broadcast on the Home Service on 16 November 1939) was partly an allegorical expression of disbelief at the BBC's 'masterly inactivity' during the Phoney War.[109] As the Author's Note puts it, 'the raw material was a collection of characters making up the post-Munich world'. Decent Aaron's natural inclination to retire from a self-interested and violent age into philosophic quietism (like the disillusioned reporter in the contemporary film *Thunder Rock* (1942)) has little chance because its hyperreal images and, ultimately, material consequences search him out. Realising his bad-faith too late, Aaron finally perishes in the vision of an air-raid:

> This field of mine, – who is Aaron
> That he should stand and say 'Alone
> Have I the right of sanctuary
> Within the boundaries of my own'?
> While there is danger, I must share it;
> While there is hardship, I can wait.
> If there is suffering, I'll bear it
> Till there is peace – or till too late.[110]

Bridson's first wartime actuality series was imperatively titled *Go to It!*, popularising the slogan of Herbert Morrison, Minister for Supply (who spoke in the first broadcast from a munitions factory) to boost desperately-needed productivity. This was followed by two highly successful series of *Billy Welcome*, a concept modelled on *Harry Hopeful*, played by Yorkshireman Wilfred Pickles, who had been appearing in Bridson's work since the late thirties. *Billy Welcome*, broadcast from canteens, workplaces and army camps, before live audiences, certainly continued to democratise venue and access for actuality programmes (although Pickles admitted loathing such cheer-up propaganda work).[111]

Bridson believed the feature form was 'admirably adapted for telling the story of Britain at war', at a time of clamorous demands in America and throughout the Commonwealth for treatment of current events. However, as the new Overseas Features editor and one of the BBC's token 'Bolshies', Bridson was rather wry about the post-1941 situation. Because of the MoI policy change to the People's War, 'left-wing loyalties suddenly assumed outward respectability'.[112] This new agenda of 'war socialism', with its visionary promise of postwar reconstruction, had the ironic effect of amplifying the agitational tenor of Bridson's writing, but also turning it into something close to official integration propaganda in the climate of the time. After the Soviet Union became subject to MoI rehabilitation, Bridson, like so many others, was heavily involved in the BBC's ensuing 'solidarity with Russia' campaign. The media were flooded by pro-Soviet propaganda. In 1943, the MoI confidently estimated the documentary *USSR at War* would be seen by 1.25 million factory workers in a couple of months. Similarly, in September, the Home Service broadcast 30 programmes with Russian content.[113] Bridson's most important feature was *Stalingrad* (first broadcast as *Salute to the USSR* on 8 November 1942), at the moment it seemed most likely to fall. A montage of typical Russian 'voices', it was also saturated by the iconography of Soviet film. This meant the BBC was freely broadcasting ideas and imagery to the ears of millions formerly forbidden to their eyes by the BBFC:

Lenin was right, Stalin was right. . . .
He saw this coming as well. . . . He planned and built,
Making the earth give us her own strength again –
Iron, steel, coal, oil. . . . Fretting the steppes
With tall pylons and taller chimneys. . . . Planning. . . .
Building. . . .
Damming the waters of the Dnieper, linking the Don
Here to the Volga. . . . Driving east to the great wastes. . . .
Founding, developing – Irkutsk, Novosibirsk,
Magnitogorsk, Chelyabinsk and the rest – forging
Hard steel in a barren province. . . . Gathering
Strong armies for the defence of the whole. . . .
Beating out the fabric of one world a better world.
                                        (*Christmas Child*, p. 111)

Wartime cooperation with US networks also enabled Bridson to capitalise on his interest in the heteroglot vitality of spoken English and the proletarian writing styles sponsored by *Partisan Review* and other American magazines. His linguistic tolerance was clearly anathema to those British commentators, including some Leftists, who believed Hollywoodspeak was corrupting standards of language and Culture. Bridson argued, conversely, idiomatic American could be artistically enriching because it was 'peculiarly suitable to spoken verse, as its rhythms and inflections are far more varied and colourful than our own'. Turning the cliché round, he denounced Standard English as monochrome to technicolor and proposed 'cinema American' might help liberate the internal diversity of British, whose poetic possibilities had been stifled by this Victorian concept: 'I am rather persuaded that we might still have been speaking vigorously and intelligently over here as well, if Dr Arnold had not clamped the dead hand of Public School Diction onto our long-suffering language' (*Christmas Child*, Notes, p. 237). Bridson's Anglo-American actuality 'hook-ups' included a series for NBC on life in wartime, *Britain to America*, narrated by the star of the propaganda thriller *Pimpernel Smith*, Leslie Howard, though the best of the series was MacNeice's *Where do We Go from Here?* Bridson also edited the three-year BBC–CBS collaboration *Transatlantic Call – People to People*. CBS's veteran Blitz-correspondent Ed Murrow felt non-standard British voices would be a democratic novelty to American listeners, irritated by RP. The broadcast from Lancashire discussed what a classless postwar Britain might be like, concluding that the epicentre of the original Industrial Revolution ought at long last to keep the fruits as well as fall-out of its labours.[114]

Bridson's US trip in June 1943 was the culmination of his interest in dialect, folk-music and the intertextuality of radio with popular film. He collaborated with Langston Hughes on 'radio's first ballad-opera', *The Man Who Went to War*. This story of an ordinary family surviving the Blitz as if it were taking place in Harlem (comparable to Humphrey Jennings's filmic transposition of occupied Czechoslovakia on to a Welsh mining town in *The Silent Village* (1943)) gave Londoners the chance to see themselves in the light of the Black GI's own struggle. It starred Ethel Waters, Canada Lee and Paul Robeson. The estimated audience was nearly ten million in Britain alone.[115] In his second ballad-opera, *The Martins and the Coys*, Bridson collaborated with American folksong experts, Alan and Elizabeth Lomax, to depict a parochial Appalachian feud, laid to rest in common cause against global Fascism and starring Burl Ives, Woody Guthrie, Pete Seeger and Will Geer (from the film of Erskine Caldwell's *Tobacco Road*).

Douglas Montgomery, the American pilot based in Britain in Anthony Asquith's *The Way to the Stars*,[116] played the lead in Bridson's *This Was an American* (broadcast on the Home Service in May 1945 in tribute to the US Army). This was another montage of voices and sound-flashbacks with 'Joe', an 'unknown American' talking from beyond, as the factor uniting everybody he had met and known. Unashamedly idealistic (Joe's death is only futile if the world reverts to prewar conditions) it still managed to deal openly with problems like friction between American troops and Eastenders. Bridson also reminded audiences of the pervasive thirties concern that mediated facts fail to latch on to mundane life. As Joe says:

War didn't mean very much, somehow, – coming up as the latest
    bulletin,
After the dinner bell had brought us from the fields,
And the food was there, steaming hot on the table. . . .

The war was there alright – over the radio –
Crackling like static when the lightning flickers ·
Somewhere over towards Cherokee. . . . Just like that, – just
Something out of the next county. . . . Never right there.
(*Christmas Child*, p. 125)

All that changes with the bulletin about Pearl Harbor, of course.

The 'structure of expectations' became increasingly prominent in Bridson's programmes, as in so much of the culture of the time. However, despite the social-democratisation of official propaganda policy, he ran into MoI censorship with his 1943 New Year's Day production, another modern parable, *The Builders*. Inspired by the Beveridge report and intended to highlight lack of official commitment to it, *The Builders* showed the stagnation to which postwar Britain might revert, without forward planning and with media-shortened public memory. An 'unknown' soldier returns to the 'hopeless twilight life he had known back in the thirties', in Bridson's words.[117] Politician and Economist plot to get rid of this inconvenient reminder of broken promises by walling him up, though he is saved by a neighbours' revolt. The MoI allowed *The Builders* to be broadcast only in Australia, in case it undermined morale by questioning Governmental good faith. Later Bridson took a more upbeat line on actual reforms in *Johnny Miner* (first broadcast on the Home Service, 23 December 1947). Another ballad-opera, drawing on the industry's rich vein of song and lore to remind audiences of its grim history of exploitation and resistance in lyrics like 'Slump', 'Union' and 'Pit Disaster':

> Hundreds of years his pick has won us
> Warmth and comfort here by the fire.
> What has it done for him, you ask, –
> Does Johnny Miner thrive on his hire?
> (*Christmas Child*, p. 185)[118]

The last lyric, 'Nationalisation', in Durham dialect, was a high-point of departure from the Reithian agenda by 1947, in which Bridson played no small part, as well as the rallying call for a period of common ownership that would last over forty years:

> *Gan on doon to the pit, man,* Johnny will say,
> *Gan in-bye an' cut the Cooal that's your oawn!*

The pit is oors at lasst, man, – oors forivver. . . . !
The pit an' Cooal that's in it are oors alooan. . . . !

(p. 195)

Obvious similarities in form and content between *The Builders, Johnny Miner* and Theatre Workshop's retrospectives on the thirties and the war years (like their story of the fishing industry, *The Ballad of Johnny Noble*) show how closely intertextual Littlewood and MacColl's drama remained with radio features.

Bridson's optimism about the post-1945 world, slithering into Cold War, was precarious, as *The Christmas Child* (Home Service 19 December 1948) demonstrated. With the Nativity displaced to contemporary Oldham, Mary is visited by Depression casualties Johnny Miner, Billy Spinner and Tom Shepherd. But birthday blessings by allegorical wise men (Statesman, Economist and Sociologist) are interrupted by the broadcast voice of an atomic Herod announcing the coming holocaust of innocents. Although in Bridson's original 1939 draft Herod's voice was supplied by one of Hitler's radio speeches, Bridson felt its final form was 'more depressing'. (See Bridson's note TCC, p. 240.) Ironically, postwar advances in communications seemed as inextricable from weapons technology as Orwell thought they were in the thirties.

Following in Bridson's footsteps during the war, it was Louis MacNeice, as Drakakis argues, who 'above all . . . managed to achieve a sustained critique of radio drama without having to resort to the special pleading that characterises so many accounts', referring specifically to MacNeice's introduction to *Christopher Columbus* (1944).[119] Perhaps even more so than Bridson, MacNeice's commitment to radio was as an experimenter. Drama was basically 'a very artificial thing', so Naturalism tended to contradict its own premises: 'Why should people who live in rooms with only three walls talk just like you and me'?[120] MacNeice argued that radio expanded drama's Modernist possibilities even more than cinema because it carried less diegetic baggage. You could take greater liberties with time and space, provided you made your transitions clear, jumping 'from India to the Arctic and from 1066 to 1943'. For impressionistic verisimilitude, the burden of visualisation was thrown back on the listener's imaginative cooperation. Features, particularly, could create effects 'of up-to-the-minute actuality . . . as vivid as a running commentary'. However, MacNeice also believed radio could rejuvenate devices from pre-Naturalistic and Classical drama, like 'allegorical speakers or choruses'.[121] The two basic patterns of his wartime work, the Morality and the Quest, were both very thirties and very parabolic, as epitomised by Auden's poetry. MacNeice insisted that the argument that the radio dramatist inevitably needed to be vulgar and 'write down' was based on a patronising misconstruction of what the average listener might be capable of. Like Greene on the cinema, he believed popularity could be achieved without compromising artistic integrity with the right formula: 'what is primitive is not *ipso facto* crude or false'. It might preclude symbolist nuances, but still express basic emotions in the 'broader forms of poetry' (Introduction to *Christopher Columbus*, pp. 8–10).[122]

MacNeice, whose broadcasting experience in the thirties comprised only a few readings and discussions, began his long and distinguished career as 'air-borne bard' (*Autumn Sequel, Collected Poems*, p. 344), scriptwriter and producer, as an attempt to do something 'agin the Govt and still support the war', like so many Leftists.[123] In *Autumn Sequel*, 'Harrap' (A. E. Harding) tells him his role will be supplying

> The tall transmitters with hot news – Dunkirk,
> Tobruk or Singapore, you will have to set
> Traps for your neutral listeners, Yank or Turk,
>
> While your blacked-out compatriots must be met
> Half-way – half-reprimanded and half-flattered,
> Cajoled to half-remember and half-forget.
> <div align="right">(<i>Collected Poems</i>, pp. 345–6)</div>

MacNeice's aesthetic negotiations with propaganda's pressures were dexterous and subtle, contriving, as Ian MacDonald puts it, to 'meet and resist' them simultaneously. For example, Gilliam, according to Coulton, encouraged MacNeice to write a strident celebration of the D-Day landings, 'in the spirit of the speech at Harfleur in Shakespeare's *Henry V*'. MacNeice actually produced a piece which was, in Rodger's words, 'low key and contemplative', portraying a soldier's private thoughts (very much as in *He Had A Date* (broadcast the same month, June 1944), discussed below). Similarly, because a play's objective 'must be more devious', than mere exhortatory rhetoric, it is not surprising MacNeice 'came to favour the use of allegory and parable' for presenting events.[124]

MacNeice's output was prolific on a number of media-fronts (he also replaced Greene as *Spectator* film critic and wrote for *Picture*

Post). By the time he became a permant BBC staff member on 26 May 1941, MacNeice had already written a substantial number of scripts, comparing this volume production to film-editing in *Autumn Sequel*:

> To work. To my own office, my own job,
> Not matching pictures, but inventing sound,
> Pre-calculating microphone and knob
>
> In homage to the human voice. To found
> A castle in the air requires a mint
> Of golden intonations and a mound
>
> Of typescript in the trays.
> (Collected Poems, p. 344)

Above all it was in Features at Savoy Hill and later Portland Place that MacNeice's talents were primarily employed. He made a crucial contribution to the daily *War Report* series following the nine o'clock news, showing an eye for the intimate, even surreal details of ordinary people's experience of war, reminiscent of the films of Humphrey Jennings:

> The nightly rush of people cascading into the shelter of the tube stations: the nightly huddle of tin-hatted wardens in blacked-out Civil Defence posts; gin-rummy among the ambulance crews till the first call outs brought them racing out for their vehicles; the sweltering work of the firemen picked out in silhouette against the flames of the blazing buildings; the morning sweeping-up of the broken glass, tinkling like Japanese gongs in a high wind – these were the things which he could report dispassionately.[125]

Features often entailed fieldwork and MacNeice went literally half across the Atlantic gathering material on the convoys for *Freedom's Ferry – Life on an ex-American Destroyer* (16 July 1941) to drama-tise maritime supply-lines and the Lend-Lease programme. Like Bridson's, much of his work was designed to encourage mutual else-awareness between the British public and its allies of their distinctive efforts in a common struggle. MoI campaigns aimed to combat myths about the forces stationed in Britain and MacNeice wrote a Board of Education pamphlet, *Meet the US Army*, which dealt, among other matters, with racism against black troops.[126] He was particularly irked by how media stereotypes constructed in the thirties created psychological obstacles during the war. In 'Touching America', he argued greater international understanding was vital, but English films still made Americans think of 'an unspeakably caste-ridden nation consisting entirely of stuffed shirts and resigned drudges', while Hollywood still made the British think of 'a whirl of millionaires, hard-boiled business men, simple-minded toughs and free-living blondes – all of them housed in chromium. Though he was as outraged by the poor quality of America's commercial radio as the sadism of its police, his broadcasting, like Bridson's, worked hard to represent both cultures more accurately and proportionately.[127] As such they were both typical of the contemporary Leftist belief that the key image in war propaganda must be of a functioning democracy. In a 'London Letter' to the American periodical *Common Sense* in April 1941, MacNeice discussed his own feature-scripts in exactly this way.[128] Before the US entered the war in December 1941, he scripted the series, *The Stones Cry Out*, on historic buildings as monumental symbols of democracy and lone defiance against the Luftwaffe, helping prepare American opinion. No. 30 in the series was on the Plymouth Barbican, narrated by a personification of the city with Devon-accented inserts from Drake's own writings and dramatised scenes about the Pilgrim Fathers, to show Americans that in this Blitzed, seafaring city a common history was alive and kicking.[129] MacNeice also scripted in support of other countries sucked into the widening maelstrom, as in his Russian features.

The stiffening of Soviet resistance was famously celebrated in his Eisenstein-influenced feature history *Alexander Nevsky* (8 December 1941), with Prokofiev's film-score performed by the BBC choruses and orchestra. Preceded by an address from Ambassador Maisky, it was strategically rebroadcast after speeches by Roosevelt and Churchill on 9 December, only two nights after Pearl Harbor. *Nevsky* exemplified radio drama's intertextuality with film, its dramatisation following Eisenstein's screenplay closely, in a lavish, high-profile production, with movie-idol Robert Donat. As a philologist, MacNeice realised the oral qualities of Homeric and Icelandic epics were revivable on radio, but especially by using Soviet film as a narrative model. Broadcast drama could 'only reach its heights when the subject is slightly larger, or at least simpler, than life and the treatment is to some extent stylised'. (See Introduction to *Christopher Columbus*, p. 15.) His *Nevsky* was the rebirth of 'story', in this sense, as well as a late offspring of thirties Leftists' romance with Russian cinema. But MacNeice's practice was also conditioned by the political circumstances of wartime propaganda broadcasting which 'justified' the use of fabular simplicity. Eisenstein's 1938 film about the medieval Russian hero was a patriotic vehicle, gearing up Stalin's regime against invasion. Its most famous *coup de cinéma*, the final destruction of the Teutonic Knights by the sudden break-up of a frozen lake, as if the Russian landscape itself were repelling the enemy, was also incorporated in MacNeice's programme which followed its imagery quite closely, especially the advancing inhuman helmets and black crosses silhouetted against the snow, by using the highly radiophonic classical device of a blind seer. As he wrote, although the film 'disappointed some English intellectuals because of its lack of subtlety in characterisation, its complete innocence of psychological conflict, its primitive pattern of Black versus White', these were the very reasons it was readily adaptable for a particular kind of broadcast (*Christopher Columbus*, p. 15). MacNeice's drama is certainly epic in tone but not dramatically unsophisticated or psychologically two-dimensional, reversing the scenario of MacLeish's *Fall of the City* to show how the political apathy and cynicism which paralyses the will to resist could be overcome under more representative leadership. Although the return of Nevsky is certainly an allegory for the rousing of Russia during the winter of 1941–42, the contemporary parallel with 'the moneybags' who exiled him and collaborated with the Teutonic Knights is ambiguously applicable, either to capitalist appeasers or Stalin's Non-Aggression Pact with Hitler (the medieval invaders break a similar treaty with Novgorod). Similarly, Nevsky's speeches talk anachronistically about the Germans 'violating the rights of Man', a charge equally applicable to the Soviet regime. At one point the Grand Master of the Teutonic Knights scoffs at the political naivety of his enemies in proto-Orwellian terms: 'These Russians are stupid. They believe that two and two make five.' Though he is warned not to underestimate them (or, allegorically, Stalin's leadership), 'give them a broken reed and they will use it as a spear'. MacNeice's other pro-Russian scripts included the 'feature-biography' *Sunbeams in his Hat* (first broadcast as *Dr Chekhov* on the Home Service, 6 September 1941), in which the dying writer recollects his past as an interlocking series of flashbacks and dream sequences. There was also *The Nosebag*, a topical version of the folktale 'Death and the Soldier' (Home Service, 13 March 1944), saluting the immortal Russian infantryman, especially in concluding dialogue about defeated invasions throughout Russian history.[130]

To mark the 450th anniversary of the 'discovery' of the New World, MacNeice wrote the *pièce d'occasion, Christopher Columbus*, broadcast simultaneously on both sides of the Atlantic, to a sensational reception. His first full-length verse radio play, it was performed with Laurence Olivier in the title role, co-starring Margaret Rawlings, and with original music by William Walton, on 12 October 1942. Bridson considered it 'probably the most memorable programme written during the war' and Gielgud, 'the highest achievement to date of pure Radio Drama'.[131] Whatever the contingent merits of his *Alexander Nevsky, Christopher Columbus* seems very different now outside the midwar climate. The original broadcast was largely intended as an affirmation of allied solidarity, implying that America's past and future identity was also at stake in defending the visionary 'Old World' humanism which had 'civilised' it in the first place. As the protagonist proclaims:

> I am Columbus, the bearer of Christ,
> I am the Dove that travels the world,
> And the words that I speak are the words that I hear
> And the words that I hear are the words of God.
> I am the last apostle. Let them give me a ship
> And I will carry Christ to the world that no one knows,
> I will remake the maps and I will remake
> The destinies of the human race. Give me a ship
> And I will pass the gates of the West and build
> A bridge across the Future.
>
> *(Christopher Columbus*, pp. 31–2)

Columbus seems a navigational St Peter, triumphantly presenting the keys of a 'New World' to Renaissance Spain. However, the production for the recent Columbus quincentenary (26 January 1992, BBC Radio 3) highlighted a more ambivalent thread in MacNeice's text, making him as much an ancestor of Hitlerian missionary irrationalism, as of Rooseveltian social democracy. Indeed, MacNeice vented his own misgivings off-air in the Appendix to the published text, writing of his impulse 'to debunk the Columbus legend' (see pp. 89–90). In 1992 there was a symptomatic shift away from Olivier, who played the role in a way comparable to the charismatic *Henry V* of his 1944 film.[132] But Columbus, like Henry in Kenneth Branagh's post-Falklands version, can also be seen as romantically dubious, demagogic. When played by Anglo-Indian Ben Kingsley, 1942's transatlantic hero, Columbus, was recast for our post-colonial, New Historicist, age – a proto-Fascist megalomaniac, fashioning an ideology to sanction conquest and genocide. The fact the text was revivable in this alternative reading testifies to how MacNeice's wartime drama managed to negotiate formal and political constraints without fatally compromising artistic integrity.

MacNeice continued to break new ground throughout the war by the sheer formal diversity of his output. His 'feature-portrait', *The Story of my Death* (8 October 1943), for example, about Lauro de Bosis (a young poet whose plane disappeared over Rome in 1931 while scattering anti-Fascist leaflets) concluded with a Yeatsian internal monologue, representing the airman's feelings and memories alone before death. MacNeice also wrote the life and times of 'Tom Varney', based on his friend Graham Shephard, killed serving on the Atlantic convoys (commemorated more explictly in 'The Casualty' (see *Collected Poems*, pp. 245–8). *He Had a Date Or, What Bearing?* undoubtedly owes much to Guthrie's pioneering radio drama, especially *The Flowers Are Not For You to Pick.*[133] 'Tom Varney', an announcer informs, meditates on 'a private newsreel of his life' (*Selected Plays*, p. 75), trying to make sense of it against the crosscurrents of the public events of the time (the same historical task, as we saw in Chapter 3, brooded on by MacNeice's own persona in his poem 'The News-Reel'). The 1949 Author's Introductory Note, 'Portrait of a Modern Man', discusses how Varney escaped the 'moulding process of his class', but even in his final phase, when he comes close to finding himself 'on the lower deck', he 'remains confused and inconsistent'. The programme was particularly experimental in that it applied the feature format to a fictitious character. Basically, it consisted of a series of elliptical flashbacks, exfoliating from the moment of a torpedo's fatal impact to the cradle and back to the bridge again, with missing years both 'spotlighted and separated by the popular songs of the day' (opening with Varney whistling 'Himno de Riego' from the Spanish Civil War), as a kind of chorus evoking poignancy and ironic distance. (See *Selected Plays*, pp. 71–2.)

Varney's response to the officer's suggestive phrase 'what bearing?' is that it 'Might apply to anything. Life, death, your life, mine' (p. 76). His personal past is replayed in a way which foregrounds the role of the media in creating false consciousness. The public school ideology of fair play is shattered for him when a striker points out the economic reality perpetuated by his jolly but ignorant scabbing. Later he loses his cub reporter's job for factual inaccuracy (he makes up a concert notice), but on a paper which systematically distorts truth on a grand scale and depresses the popular IQ. The media were particularly indicted for giving the impression that events which would cause the global horror of 1939 were all taking place at the time in far-away countries about which the public need care nothing, as when Varney tells his wife he's volunteered:

MARY Spain! Why?
TOM There's a war in Spain.
MARY Oh, that Civil War of theirs.
TOM A civil war of ours.
(p. 96)

As a generational type, Varney's experiences in Spain pastiche accounts of the political education of several of its literary combatants. Like Orwell, he is baffled by the rash of initials and 'rich men going round in overalls', hinting at murky factionalism and counterrevolutionary forces lying low, as in *Homage to Catalonia*. The book barricade, behind which he snipes at Madrid's University city, is the same symbol of the value of abstract ideology in a life-or-death situation used in Cornford's letters. (See *Selected Plays*, pp. 97–8.)[134] But the feature's most ironic moment is Varney's recollection of fulsome coverage of Chamberlain's Appeasement and the virtually idolatrous public reaction caused by such apparently good tidings. A recording of the Heston airport speech is montaged over his mother's 'I don't mind saying I knelt down in this room and I thanked God for our Prime Minister. For bringing us peace in our time. And then when I saw him on the news-reel and heard him recounting' (p. 100).

MacNeice's classical training also came in handy for *A Roman Holiday*, which used the carnivalesque Saturnalia tradition to satirise contemporary Britain and point up the need for sweeping reforms (10 January 1945). Though it's undoubtedly true, as Robert Hewison points out, that 'the BBC had more influence on popular culture' with *It's That Man Again* than with *Christopher Columbus*, MacNeice's *The March Hare Resigns* (1945) and *Salute to All Fools* (1946) coupled his interest in parable with a revue format influenced by Tommy Handley's madcap wartime comedy to survey the scene on the eve of the peace. (From its first broadcast, on 19 September ITMA had been lampooning inept bureaucracies, such as the 'Ministry of Aggravation', a compound of Agriculture and Information, empowered to 'confiscate, complicate and commandeer'.)[135]

By the end of the war MacNeice was moving still further away from literary Naturalism: 'pure "realism" is in our time almost played out'.[136] *The Dark Tower* (broadcast in 1946), taken from Browning's poem, was also the culmination of the Audenesque morality and quest structures, whose wide use in wartime broadcasting can be largely credited to MacNeice and Bridson. Set in an ambiguous world, both medieval and contemporary, the play cast a warning shadow across postwar optimism – the hero can only reach his objective by surviving the 'Desert of Hopes'. From 1943, MacNeice produced nearly all his own scripts, gaining a measure of control over their performance few theatre playwrights ever obtain. Through tape and other postwar technical innovations, his method would also move ever closer to film.[137]

The war boosted the credibility of radio news commentary enormously at a time of awesomely confusing events. This new status of the BBC at home and in occupied Europe, as a source of informational resistance, was partly in response to the impact of German propaganda stations and, in particular, of 'Lord Haw Haw', or William Joyce's broadcasts. Rumours of Haw Haw's omniscience about the homefront were rife and gleefully fanned in his commentaries, although both public confidence and paranoia were somewhat misplaced. The BBC was not always truthful or well-informed by the MoI and German intelligence-gathering in Britain was relatively poor. Calder calls Lord Haw Haw the 'first new radio personality of the war'. His ironic popularity filled the vacuum created by the BBC's initial ineffectiveness (in Autumn 1939, six million tuned in regularly, and three times that number occasionally).[138] However, Left-of-centre, middlebrow writer J. B. Priestley was crucially involved in both countering the panic spread by Haw Haw and in recuperating the BBC's popular credibility by his non-standard tones. Home Intelligence continually advised the MoI that ordinary people 'find wireless voices too impersonal and language too academic to affect them personally'.[139] The Reithian register had, moreover, been both hijacked and, perhaps, parodied by Joyce's braying, upper-class tones, from which his nickname derived. German black propaganda also attempted to use the BBC's linguistic *gravitas* against it by enlisting the very regional resentments fuelled by its cultural metropolitanism. Their New British Broadcasting Station, supposedly based under cover in Northern England, exemplifies this. On the other hand, posh accents became associated in wartime culture with incompetence and even fifth-columnism.

Priestley, who broadcast a popular commentary on current events as early as 1933 called *I'll Tell You Everything*, concluded from already long experience in 1940 that the medium made virtually any other method of communication 'seem like the method of a secret society'. The BBC was as important as any branch of the forces. The only people who didn't realise this were the Cabinet. Moreover, Priestley, like Bridson, advocated ditching RP condescension once and for all: the war broadcaster 'must talk as if he were among serious friends', not like the 'head of an infant's school'. Like Greene too, as we shall see, he felt it was useless handing out 'a lot of dope left over from the last war'.[140] As Calder argues in *The Myth of the Blitz* (1992), Priestley's wartime broadcasts drew up a political and cultural precedent others would build on to reconstruct the nation's self-image.[141] The pattern for this was already set by Priestley before his *Postscripts* in *New English Journey* (23 April 1940), produced by Bridson. Intertextual with his classic reportage, this programme set out to assess changes in conditions since 1933 in Britain's internal war between 'decency and poverty'. It revisited the West Country to record belligerent dialect conversations in Bristol pubs and agricultural regeneration in the Cotswolds (a 'depressed area' since the medieval wooltrade). Although the Blitzkrieg could hardly deface the Black Country landscape any further, its industry remained indispensable to the war effort, for which its own social-democratic reconstruction would be the reward. From the West Riding town of 'Braddleford', to the Potteries, Tyneside, Hull and Lincoln, the story was the same. Lancashire lasses were being re-engaged by warcotton and postwar expectations, alongside Central European refugees in Manchester. The ending of the original *English Journey* was updated with a call to keep future peacetime production on wartime priorities to finally right the Industrial Revolution's injustice: 'We shouldn't rest until every wrong done to the lovely face of this country, and to the kindly, decent patient folk of this country is put right. . . . A nobler framework of life must be constructed. And the vistas of mean little streets, and the ruined landscapes, the humiliation of bad housing, the heartbreak of long unemployment must vanish like an evil dream.'

Priestley also did considerable broadcasting to the USA (where his influence was exceeded only by CBS's Ed Murrow, who made the historic commentary from the roof of Broadcasting House during an air-raid, and with whom Priestley was given top billing in a radio 'tour' of the blackout, *London After Dark* (24 August 1940))[142] and the Commonwealth, but his charismatic populism was most crucial in propagating the 'People's War' through his Home Service *Postcripts*. The first series was broadcast after the 9.15 p.m. Sunday news during the fall of France and onset of the Blitz, from June until October 1940. They initially counterattacked Lord Haw Haw's etherial raids, but acquired their own impetus, eventually rating audiences virtually as wide as Churchill's,[143] however, with the difference that Priestley argued Fascism could only be defeated by simultaneously reforming Britain, potently mixing patriotism and millenarian social democracy. For this reason, Orwell credited Priestley's broadcasting with as much influence in building the consensus that made the Welfare State possible as *Picture Post* (see *Collected Essays*, II, pp. 112 and 118). Greene too finally apologised for *Stamboul Train's* caricature 'Quinn Savory': 'When this war is over we may argue again about his merits as a novelist: for those dangerous months, when the Gestapo arrived in Paris, he was unmistakably a great man.' Similarly, for MacNeice, Priestley proved 'radio has brought us back to the conditions of the Greek City State, where the man who can hold the people's ear . . . will acquire the most astonishing influence'.[144] None of his *Postscript* successors (except perhaps the American correspondent, Quentin Reynolds) had anything like this clout, though Priestley didn't altogether relish his media-inflated reputation, which he compared to being lashed to a barrage balloon.[145]

His first *Postscript* (5 June 1940) played a major part in mythologising the Dunkirk evacuation. Abject defeat became glorious enterprise, postponing victory but confirming its inevitability. Priestley's rhetoric strained to rescue national self-esteem: 'This is not the German way. They don't make such mistakes (a grim fact that we should bear in mind) but also they don't achieve such epics. . . . That vast machine of theirs can't create a glimmer of the poetry of action which distinguishes war from mass murder' (*Postscripts*, pp. 1–2). It is easy now to object that his radicalism was

compromised by a mystique of essential Englishness that sometimes came close to the racist ideology it intended to resist.[146] Similarly, in the 1990s, distinctions between 'the poetry of action and
. . . mass murder' seem themselves exactly like illusions constructed
by media strategies. However, though symptomatic of the contradictions of the time, his broadcasts were a highly effective thrust in
the campaign by Leftists of many shades to 'Defend the bad against
the worse'. Priestley was well aware of what was at stake in such
apparent necessity and was up against an establishment reluctant
to realise political compromise was vital to its own survival in the
face of the most powerful external threat it had ever encountered.
The fact the MoI allowed him prime airtime at all testifies to its
desperation during the invasion crisis and the pressure that finally
'shoved him off the air', in Orwell's phrase, after he suggested con-
fiscating the property of rich people who fled the country (see
Collected Essays, II, p. 118), testifies to the difficulty of his position.
We can never be certain to what extent writers' wartime involvements, exemplified by Priestley's, sponsored a genuine people's
initiative – a kind of British 'velvet revolution' – or were merely
allowed to create the appearance of one, by the very establishment
against which it was aimed, for its galvanising effect.

The Dunkirk broadcast was also typical in the way Priestley
manipulated associations inherited from the twisted skein of thirties media and politics. The motley flotilla of little ships were turned
into a metonym for the ordinary civilian's heroic potential: 'Among
those paddle steamers that will never return was one that I knew
well, for it was the pride of our ferry service to the Isle of Wight –
none other than the good ship "Gracie Fields".' It was as if *Shipyard
Sally* had stalwartly intervened in history itself, a role which could
be imitated by her fans (*Postcripts*, p. 3). Allusion to a film that
provided an imaginary solution to the problems of the Depression
helped found the myth of the People's War. Wartime's highly
intertextual culture was, in effect, a hyperreal conscripting of the
population by mediating the war as if the collective fate depended
on the energy and initiative of anonymous individuals. Hence the
disclaimer of the film of *Love on the Dole* (finally released in 1941),
that the thirties must never happen again, and the cross-breeding of
documentary and feature forms in film propaganda which 'empowered' the ordinary person, as in *Millions Like Us* (1943). Priestley
took care to emphasise that distinctions between non/combatants
no longer held in modern, total war: 'we're not really civilians any

longer but a mixed lot of soldiers – machine-minding soldiers, milk-men and postmen soldiers, housewife and mother soldiers – and what a gallant corps that is – and even broadcasting soldiers' (8 September 1940, p. 68). He defamiliarised not only class- but also sex-roles. Broadcasting and the Luftwaffe made the Blitz a domestic front, by definition: 'total war is right inside the home itself, emp-tying the clothes cupboards and the larder, screaming its threats through the radio at the hearth, burning and bombing its way from roof to cellar' (22 September 1940, p. 78). The rapidly increasing numbers of women employed outside the home in factories and offices faced battlefront dangers everyday. All this logically entailed, of course, that the projected postwar would reward mothers, house-wives and working-women with better conditions. Consequently, the concept of the wartime radio soap, *The Robinsons,* or 'Front-Line Family' owed something to Priestley's ideas.

Priestley also invoked popular literary intertextuality to construct an image of the Home Guard as a cross-section of English rural life which 'made me feel I'd wandered into one of those rich chapters of Thomas Hardy's fiction in which his rustics meet in the gather-ing darkness on some Wessex hillside' (16 June 1940, p. 9). His Londoners-who-can-take-it were equivalent reach-me-down fic-tional types, redoubtably chirpy Samuel Weller cocknies. (See 15 September 1940, pp. 71–5.) However, what's striking about Priestley's broadcasts compared to more 'serious' wartime writers, says Orwell, is not so much their differences as their common agenda, albeit designed for consumption by different audiences. 'Common decency' and 'essential Englishness' are key concepts for the *Post-scripts* and texts like *The Lion and the Unicorn* (1941). In this way, war propaganda became another 'version' of Empsonian pastoral, cross-breeding the urban iconography of thirties Proletcult with the rural concept of 'Deep England'.[147] The People's War became a question not of competing national ideologies, but of the 'natural', Hardyesque-rural or Dickensian-urban, versus 'unnatural' Nazism, uncomfortably echoed by Hitler's own deployment of Nature as a metaphysical alibi. However, Priestley also insisted Nazism was extreme tribalism and that rabid fear of 'otherness' was potential in *any culture.* Historical circumstances had caused an apocalyptic outbreak in Germany, but the Appeasing international community, he reminded listeners, was also complicit: the concentration camps were 'the shame of the whole watching world' (23 June 1940, pp. 15–16).

Guilo Douhet, the theorist of terror-bombing, predicted it would cause mass-panic, social collapse and defeatism.[148] Priestley believed rather it would create pressure for reform by shifting power away from an establishment exposed as incompetent, that the national character of the people would wrest control over the war – from 'them':

> all of us ordinary people – are on one side of a high fence, and on the other side ... under a buzzing cloud of secretaries, are the official and important personages: the pundits, and mandarins of the Fifth Button. And now and then a head appears above the fence and tells us to carry our gas masks, look to our blackouts, do this and attend to that. (30 June 1940, p. 19)

Priestley helped reverse the prewar, media-sponsored 'else-awareness' which disconnected mundane life from collective processes: 'Already the future historians are fastening their gaze upon us, seeing us all in that clear and searching light of the great moments of history' (p. 23). It was this that made Greene remark that Priestley the dramatist never experimented with time so effectively as Priestley the broadcaster.[149] Priestley continued to foster the emergent social-democratic consensus by agitating for a clear definition of war aims to counter the Nazis' 'New Order' for Europe (21 July 1940, p. 38). Like Orwell (see discussion below), he insisted it was vital to conducting hostilities with maximum commitment and efficiency. His answer to Rightist criticism was put up or shut up: 'We should mean what we say.' Fighting for democracy also meant attempting to discover 'the deeper causes of this war and to try and find a remedy for them', lest the passing of a high mood meant regression to the kind of world that made Nazism possible (20 October 1940, p. 98). Priestley also answered charges of mawkishness and oversimplification from the Left, and from Communists (still toeing the pre-June 1941 line that this was an 'imperialist war') in particular, by admitting that his seven-minute programmes were designed to appeal to the widest audience not to 'lecture on all possible political, economic, and social developments' (25 August 1940, p. 57).

At the end of the first *Postscript* series (20 October 1940), Priestley denied the BBC dismissed him, but indicated he was pressurised by the MoI.[150] Though it was intended as counter-propaganda, it is true the Nazis did sometimes use it as ammunition. On 7 October 1940,

Deutschlandsender gloated over his exposé of poverty and class as proof of Britain's rottenness. However, Priestley insisted social-democratisation was not subversion, but a national obligation:

> I've been getting some very fierce and angry [letters] telling me to get off the air before the Government 'puts you where you belong' – the real Fascist touch. Well obviously, it wouldn't matter much if I were taken off the air, but it would matter a great deal, even to these Blimps, if these young men of the RAF were taken off the air: and so I repeat my question – in return for their skill, devotion, endurance and self-sacrifice, what are we civilians prepared to do? (28 July 1940, pp. 42–3)[151]

After the end of his second series, he continued to campaign through the influential 1941 Committee, a think-tank linked with *Picture Post*'s 'Plan for Britain', drumming up support for Beveridge. It was indicative of Priestley's irrevocable status as household 'voice', that the Committee became known as 'a sort of Leftist Brains Trust', which had begun broadcasting that year.[152]

Priestley emerged from his broadcasting involvement feeling it was, on the whole, progressive and enlightening. In contrast, during the war Orwell realised the contradictory potentials of radio for abolishing geographical frontiers only to reinforce mental ones. It created the prospect of exclusive 'states' of hyperreal containment: 'The result is that each national radio is a sort of totalitarian world of its own, braying propaganda night and day to people who can listen to nothing else' (*Collected Essays*, III, pp. 173–5); (see also Chapter 2 above). Orwell's inside knowledge of the relationship between propaganda and the media, the documentary fabrication of history, was based not only on firsthand experience of Stalinist witchhunting in Spain, but also on his own BBC broadcasting, as the transcripts of his radio war confirm.[153]

The propaganda, *volte-face* and 'doublethink' ('block thinking' was the term used by opinion managers at the time) which could corrupt even a Just War were by no means a totalitarian monopoly. The official campaign to rehabilitate the prewar Bolshevik bogey as 'Uncle Joe' was at its height in 1942 when Orwell wrote of the media's expedient overriding of historical contradictions under the MoI's shadowy supervision: 'the extraordinary swings of opinion which occur nowadays, the emotions which can be turned on and off like a tap, are the result of newspaper and radio hypnosis' (*Col-*

lected *Essays*, II, p. 288). MoI 'feeding' and censorship of the BBC similarly help to explain the development of Orwell's position between his pre- and postwar writing, situated in the white tower of Senate House in Malet Street, like MINITRU, with its telegraphic name MINIFORM and headed, from 1941, by Brendan Bracken, known to subordinates as 'B.B.' Consequently, W. J. West's argument that pro-Soviet propaganda was the result of Communist infiltration of the MoI and BBC (for example, by Guy Burgess) ignores the fact it was official policy (and so 'open' that even Harrods was bedecked with hammers and sickles).[154]

To pretend that Oceania's alternation between alliance and war with either of the other superstates (while preserving the illusion of continuity with ideological principles) only satirises the Russo-German Pact is grotesque. As the transcripts of Orwell's broadcasts show, this was only part of the contemporary skein of compromise and Doublethink which Orwell become entangled in himself at the BBC. Similarly, MoI attempts to prevent publication of Orwell's *Animal Farm* (1945) not to offend an ally were also part of this expedient strategy.[155] Orwell was fully aware of the ironies of all this. Though 'the pinks' might deprecate criticism of the USSR 'on the ground that it "plays into the hands of the Tories"' the Tories seemed temporarily 'the most pro-Russian of the lot' (*Collected Essays*, III, p. 224). Wartime pro-Stalinism was also duly disseminated by the Right-wing press, as in the case of Rothermere's *Sunday Dispatch* – 'one of the very worst of the gutter papers (murders, chorus-girls' legs and the Union Jack' – which, as we saw, had been pro-Nazi (II, p. 267). Prewar Appeasers had in 'their clumsy way' been 'playing the game of Machiavelli, of "political realism"' (II, pp. 363–6). Wartime pro-Stalinism was simply another round: 'This disgusting murderer is temporarily on our side, and so the purges etc. are suddenly forgotten. So also with Franco, Mussolini etc., should they ultimately come over to us' (II, p. 461, and cf. pp. 478–9).

At the onset of the Cold War in 1947–48, the Soviet image was reversed again. Orwell's later texts, which, as I have shown, were rooted in thirties Leftist suspicions about media power, would ironically themselves be hijacked into its mythology and its process of organised forgetting. In 1944, he attacked the doublethink of 'denouncing war while wanting to preserve the kind of society that makes war inevitable' and suggested prophetically that propaganda campaigns conducted in a society nominally at peace would be more damaging than the actual conflict itself, psychological attrition against imaginative sympathy with what is 'other' to the system: 'By shooting at your enemy you are not in the deepest sense wronging him. But by hating him, by inventing lies about him and bringing children up to believe them . . . you are striking not at one perishable generation, but at humanity itself' (III, pp. 215 and 233). Fear about the real danger of fascism would be displaced into a hyperreal postwar menace, providing an alibi for internal repression.

Joining as a BBC Talks Assistant and going on to become a Producer, Orwell made weekly news summaries and cultural broadcasts for its Eastern Service, countering the Axis offensive from Berlin by Subhas Chandra Bose's (1897–1945) Radio Azad Hind ('Free India'). He aimed at India's opinion-forming intelligentsia, to sustain the provisional allegiance of nationalists and, especially, two million Indian troops. Despite this apparent contradiction with his anti-imperialism, Orwell believed firmly that 'India is compelled to be with Britain' because Axis victory would postpone independence 'far longer than the most reactionary British Government'.[156] The ambivalence of his involvement was symbolised by his on-air identity. Pseudonymous 'George Orwell', had written the seditious *Burmese Days*, still banned in wartime India. Not until the end of 1942 did Eric Blair broadcast using his *nom-de-plume*, because the MoI realised his dissident *bona fides* would be more marketable to the Indian public. (See Introduction to *War Broadcasts*, pp. 42–4.) Orwell negotiated conditions to safeguard his reputation, though they were ultimately inadequate. The news commentaries, assembled from transcriptions of Axis broadcasts and MoI press releases, ran from December 1941 until he resigned in August 1943, feeling like 'an orange that's been trodden on by a very dirty boot' (*Collected Essays*, II, p. 349).

Radio propaganda was a long-range psychological weapon operated behind enemy lines. As Grierson wrote in 1942, by the thirties nations were 'fighting for command of the international ether'. The 'strategy of position', which made 1914–18 the war of the trenches, had been rendered obsolete.[157] As West notes, besides land campaigns, Orwell reported those 'in worlds without frontiers', at sea and in the air, but all suffused by the etherial conflict (Introduction to *War Commentaries*, pp. 16–17). Perhaps Orwell's single most significant technical experience at the BBC was with wartime experiments in C. K. Ogden's Basic English. Had Orwell stayed in the Indian section, he might even have been in Empson's position, translating news into Basic. Basic, which used only 850 words, seems initially to have appealed to Orwell's interest in clear communication, but *Nineteen Eighty-Four*'s prescriptive, thought-policing 'Newspeak' also seems to have originated as a parody of it. Orwell realised Basic extended the objectivist myth about language into an ultimately privileged, 'monoglot' medium – a 'deviceless' discourse, reporting facts with apparent neutrality. Basic was the perfect official *'News*-speak'. Like its dystopian counterpart, it abolished alternative signifiers and constituted reality in an orthodox form, hypostatising the routine process of conceptual categorisation and factual selection implicit in the media. Orwell's broadcasting involvement bridges his pre- and postwar writing in other important respects. The idea of invulnerable autarchic superstates locked in permanent attrition may well have evolved from Nazi projections of a 'fortress Europe', while the Pacific theatre was known as 'Oceana'. Orwell also commissioned a series of topical and cultural talks from leading scientists and thinkers called *A.D. 2,000*, which fed his hypotheses about how media technology might shape the near future. His own features scripts (which must have felt a bit like literary production line-work), such as his adaptation of Ignazio Silone's beast allegory 'The Fox', and the collective 'Story by Five Authors', contributed any amount of formal influences, plot details and atmosphere.[158]

The War Commentaries similarly demonstrate how even this proverbially honest Leftist became entangled in ethically questionable practices, albeit largely by sins of omission and emphasis. For example, Orwell bucked the MoI line on Gandhi as, in West's words, 'a backward-looking pacifist and Petainist', but could not broadcast his own opinion because of script-vetting and switch-censorship, though he did manage to slip some subversive views on Burma past. Orwell was also obliged to vet and alter his own talkers' scripts, though he was thrown by Ellen Wilkinson's extemporising. (See *War Commentaries*, pp. 19, 52–3 and 184.) Having to continually justify Allied actions to sceptical Indian nationalists must have intensified his awareness of the ironies of linguistic chicanery. He derided Nazi euphemisms like 'rationalising' for retreating, but soon had to invent 'strategic sacrifice of territory' for Russian setbacks. (See 20 December 1941, p. 26, and 11 July 1942, p. 112.) Doublethinking slogans like 'War is Peace', 'Freedom is Slavery' might easily have orginated in Japan's stated mission to 'liberate by conquest'.

Equally it is hard to tell if Orwell was simply naive or disingenuous when necessary. On 10 January 1942, he denied Axis claims that 'Britain and Russia have agreed to carve up the world between them', and trustingly followed the official MoI version of Allied peace aims, guaranteeing universal national self-determination (*War Commentaries*, p. 34, and cf. Orwell on Anglo-Soviet Treaty, 13 June 1942, pp. 106–7). Similarly, he lambasted Axis atrocity-mongering while sometimes doing the same himself, although he, like many others, was probably not told the truth by the MoI about Bomber Command's deliberate targeting of German cities which would culminate in the Dresden fire-storm of February 1945: 'These attacks . . . are not wanton and are not delivered against the civilian population, although non-combatants are inevitably killed in them' (6 June 1942, pp. 102–3). Though the MoI was also reluctant to publicise it before 1945, as we shall see, hard evidence from the death-camps was of an entirely different order to traditional horror stories. Orwell discussed the same Polish Government in Exile report Koestler came under flak for: 'this kind of cold-blooded, systematic cruelty, utterly different from the violences committed in battle, brings home to us the nature of Fascism' (12 December 1942, pp. 187–8; and cf. 17 December, p. 192).[159] Like a telescreen announcer, Orwell heroicised British morale – ordinary people never grumbled about rationing, and were 'even heard to say that they would welcome greater sacrifices' – and fanfared 'truly staggering' Ministry of production figures (14 February 1942, p. 53, and 13 June 1942, p. 109). Like other Leftists, he sincerely tried to broadcast socio-economic changes at home as proof of a genuine 'velvet revolution' that would democratise Britain and dismantle imperialism, but the censor was quick to obliterate references portraying the struggle against inequality with embarrassing explicitness, indicating how expedient MoI 'People's War' fervour actually was (14 March 1942, p. 64).

On 17 January 1942 Orwell stated 'propaganda is an actual weapon, like guns or bombs, and to learn how to discount it is as important as taking cover during an air raid'. But his rule for achieving immunity to it, by comparing what Axis broadcasts 'say they will do with what they are actually doing', is disarmingly simple (pp. 37–8). Though apparently asserting the superiority of empirical over hyperreal 'truth', it ignores the fact that Indians could only receive alternative accounts of what was going on in occupied Burma or China through Allied channels. This wasn't consciously misleading, but it shows the informational double-bind emerging from the post/modern condition of Orwell and his Leftist contemporaries. Sometimes Orwell's broadcasts unconsciously foreshadow how studiously superficial reading of *Nineteen Eighty-Four* gave Cold Warriors a formula for highlighting Soviet propaganda, while begging the question of the Western media's entitlement to pose as touchstones of actuality. He advocated (to borrow Milan Kundera's phrase) 'the struggle of memory against forgetting'[160] to his Indian audience, but his own attempts to remind them of British Appeasement were censored. (See 16 May 1942, pp. 94–5.) Mulk Raj Anand's talk for Orwell's *History of Fascism* series was similarly banned (see *War Broadcasts*, p. 44.) One of the main principles of Axis propaganda, identified by Orwell on 25 July 1942, could be extended into a general theory of the facilitation of doublethink by media control. Because 'very few people are interested in knowing what is being done or said in other parts of the world than their own', it was not only enemy propagandists who 'can contradict themselves grossly without much danger of being detected'. Axis promises of liberation to the colonised on the one hand, and racial supremacy to the Afrikaaners on the other, need to be read in the light of Orwell's own prewar essay 'Not Counting Niggers', which pointed out the basic contradiction in Britain's role as defender of world freedom and democracy. Axis propaganda against the Raj was not simply lies, but 'lying with the truth', to use Orwell's own paradox (*War Commentaries*, p. 119, and *Collected Essays*, II, p. 465).

Orwell certainly stretched MoI limitations, after the Japanese threat to India receded in 1943, and had probably already decided to resign, resisting the pressure to police his own thoughts like his fictional persona, Winston Smith at the Ministry of Truth.[161] However, for Orwell, one thing worse than propaganda was inefficient propaganda, lacking coherent policy, and hampered by shadowy interventions (See *Collected Essays*, II, p. 489.) He implied that responsibility lay primarily with the MoI, exonerating the Reithian principle of public-service broadcasting, while condemning political meddling with its independence:

in my experience the BBC is relatively truthful and, above all, has a responsible attitude towards news and does not disseminate lies because they are 'newsy'.

Of course, untrue statements are constantly being broadcast . . . But in most cases this is due to genuine error, and the BBC sins more by simply avoiding anything controversial than by direct propaganda. (*Tribune*, 21 April 1944; *Collected Essays*, III, p. 155)

Orwell's wartime features work was also crucial to his literary development. The perspective he cultivated in *Through Eastern Eyes* intensified his defamiliarising style and interest in the micropolitically symptomatic aspects of everyday British life and culture that figures so strongly in his 'As I Please' column. The general idea of the series was 'to interpret the West, and in particular Great Britain, to India ... from the Houses of Parliament to the village pub' (*War Broadcasts*, p. 286). Orwell's very first involvement in broadcasting was a talk about proletarian writing with Jack Common for Desmond Hawkins's Home Service series, *The Writer in the Witness Box* on 6 December 1940 (*Collected Essays*, II, pp. 54–61), and his cultural propaganda to India must have sharpened his awareness of the politics of literature. As a Producer Orwell commissioned series like *Books that Changed the World* and *English Poetry since 1900*, in line with the MoI's promotion of the critical liberal-humanist tradition and against political orthodoxy. *Voice*, Orwell's pioneering broadcast literary magazine was popularisingly 'middlebrow', but featured some of the most innovatory writers and texts of the time. It thus broke the BBC's unwritten rule that, as Desmond Hawkins put it, 'living poet' was a contradiction in terms. Orwell defended *Voice* 'at a moment when, quite literally, the fate of the world is being decided by bombs and bullets' from charges of dilettantism: 'it is exactly at times like the present that literature ought not to be forgotten'. The 'business of pumping words into the ether' had a deadly serious side (11 August 1942; *War Broadcasts*, p. 80). Orwell's motives for signing the *Horizon* 'War Writers' Manifesto', his views about literature's role in sustaining and amplifying humane consciousness, were expounded in *Voice* No. 2's discussion of the question 'Where are the War Poets?', using J. M. Tambimuttu's anthology as a way in for the Indian audience: 'there can be an actual enthusiasm for war when it's for some cause such as national liberation. I mean one can feel the war is not merely a disagreeable necessity, but that it is spiritually better than peace – the kind of peace you have in Vichy France, for instance.' Conversely, writers, like Pound, who broadcast for the Axis, were war criminals as much as if they had taken up arms (18 September 1942, pp. 85–7). (Also see *Collected Essays*, III, pp. 105–6.)

Orwell's ambivalence about his own involvement climaxed in his midwar features. In the talk 'Money and Guns', he was optimistic about rising standards of cultural and political awareness, in which enormous sales of Penguins and other cheap literary editions played a significant part, but which also reacted on the media, 'making them more serious and less sensational' (20 January 1942, p. 73). However, Orwell's scepticism re-erupted in 'Jonathan Swift an Imaginary Interview', putting popular enlightenment under the scrutiny of the most savage of satirists as his alter-ego:

> ORWELL: ... But don't you find that the mass of the people are more intelligent than they were, or at least better educated? How about the newspapers and the radio? Surely they have opened people's minds? There are very few people in England now who can't read?
> SWIFT: That is why they are so easily deceived. Your ancestors two hundred years ago were full of barbarous superstitions, but they would not have been so credulous as to believe your daily newspapers. (2 November 1942, p. 115)

This suggests how Orwell's suspicions of the abuse of the media's power would win out over his belief in their positive potentials in his postwar writing.

WARTIME CINEMA

Picture-houses had immediately been closed in September 1939 for fear of air-raids, but gradually began to reopen, and there is no doubt the increased number of British films screened were a considerable asset in the war effort. Even in America their reputation – low with rare exceptions – was established at last by a distinctive fusion of drama and documentary in features. As James Agee, reviewer for *Time* and *The Nation* wrote. 'The thing that so impresses me about the nonfiction films which keep coming over from England is the abounding evidence of just such a universal adulthood, intelligence, and trust as we lack.'[162]

Both critics and public acknowledged a tremendous rise in quality, a veritable Renaissance funded largely by Rank. This shouldn't be exaggerated, however. Hollywood escapism remained Britain's staple viewing and the quota was reduced from 20 to 15 per cent.[163] Mass-Observation found the impact of the Crown Film Unit, for

example, distinctly limited: not only were its audiences still relatively small, but they often did not respond as the MoI intended
they should. Lord Taylor considered the Film Unit a 'nice little flash
in the cultural pan' which served only to keep documentary film-
makers happy.[164] In part this was a question of old habits dying
hard. The conditioning of a generation could produce some bizarre
paradoxes. As M-O noted, wartime filmgoers sometimes sat through
actuality footage of ordinary people like themselves surviving the
Blitz from day to day supremely unmoved, while they might weep
copiously at patently specious projections of the same experience in
features like *Mrs Miniver* (1941).[165]

Conversely, even the new realism couldn't eschew what Paul
Fussell calls 'cinema's instinct for "effects" and sentimental misrepresentation'. Agee thought the British Army Film Unit's *Desert Victory* 'the first completely admirable combat film', for its serious
attempt to make audiences participate in actuality, in contrast to
American propaganda which used 'films to illustrate the rotten
words we worship'.[166] However, much 'real' desert combat footage
was in fact faked at base depot, it was revealed by the cameraman
in 1981. Even though the genuine article was in plentiful supply,
action has to 'be rendered in the received clichés' (Fussell's phrase),
of the feature idiom, otherwise it looked inauthentic to civilians.
Keith Douglas, who fought at El-Alamein, also suspected, correctly,
that the film's lack of precise locations was as much for purposes of
simulation as military secrecy. Even his own regiment had obligingly played themselves on occasions, putting 'their tanks through
various evolutions for the camera'.[167]

The concept of 'The People's War' necessitated coming to closer
terms with conditions than had been possible in thirties features.
Studios like Ealing recruited both radical writers and documentarists,
in Richards's words, 'to give entertainment films a new authenticity
of form and content . . . in dramatising the lowering of class barriers, depicting the heroism of ordinary folk and creating a mood of
promise.' However, there was a downside. Pronay points out that
some wartime labour conditions, glossed over in such films, were
precisely those which trades unions had fought against in peacetime.[168] Nevertheless, exceptional wartime films like Humphrey
Jennings's *London/Britain Can Take It* (1940) and *Fires Were Started*
(1943) did expose larger audiences to the documentary methods
and modified Surrealist techniques of Mass-Observation, transferring them successfully from text to screen.[169] William Whitebait,

writing in the *New Statesman* on 23 May 1942, characterised this hybrid form. Reality and fiction films no longer 'flowed along opposite sides of the street', meaning British directors were finally reaching the technical standards of their Soviet mentors' dramatisations of historical events.[170]

Leftist writers involved in cinema helped create this wartime cultural agenda, as much if not more than those involved in radio work, which, in turn, renegotiated the events and texts of the thirties. Again, cinema was inextricably linked with MoI bureaucracy.[171] Its Films Division and Ideas Committee produced or, more often, 'suggested' themes and subjects for, features, documentaries and newsreels, 'inviting' cooperation from the industry as a whole and revamping the GPO Film Unit into the Crown Film Unit in 1940. The 'Programme for Film Propaganda', like its broadcasting policy, was not specifically Left, but made similar practical use of Leftist personnel and ideas.[172] Calder Marshall, one of cinema's most acerbic prewar critics, as we have seen, worked as an MoI production specialist and was instrumental in getting backing for Pat Jackson's Atlantic Convoy picture *Western Approaches* (1944), (Agee considered this Crown Film Unit classic greatly superior to Noël Coward's 1942 naval feature *In Which We Serve*.)[173] He thought it a better morale-raiser than an 'undramatised' documentary; his memorandum of 15 July 1942 epitomises how Leftists seized the potential of features for popularising their ideas about the war. Films like *Western Approaches* intensified the cinematic, cooperative vision of thirties texts. Unlike a conventional feature

the amount of footage given to the various operations guided or recorded by the operations room does give one a feeling of a message at a second level – which is that in the war, or in fact in life today – the history of the individual is intimately tied up with the history of all sorts of other people.[174]

Calder Marshall also helped produce Frank Capra-like 'Why We Fight' film-propaganda aimed at America, such as *World of Plenty* (1943) on global food strategy, appealing to the spirit of New Deal politics, and himself scripted a film about refugee resettlement, *The Star and the Sand* (1945).[175]

Cinema's social democratic 'opening shot in the People's War', as Miles and Smith put it, was the 1941 film of *Love on the Dole*, adapted by Greenwood himself from the stage version.[176] The novel's *saeva indigatio* was finally allowed full vent – intensification in some respects – on the screen by the wartime BBFC. The film opens with an aerial panorama of an industrial townscape, gradually zooming in on the morning scene in the Hardcastle household, in which a single breakfast egg is being shared out. Outside the shadow of the pawnshop lies, literally, over the street. The 'culture of consolation' is no less indicted, despite Greenwood's own scripting for Formby. Crowding faces stare rapturously as Grundy counts out Harry's winnings. But his betting ticket later merges into an admission to Blackpool's Tower Ballroom tossed in a Hanky Park backstreet gutter, all that remains of two week's escape. Floating down the same gutter will be headlines announcing economic collapse, which quickly cut to the labour exchange grille. The film avoids distraction by the exceptionality of individual circumstances. Collective events continually intercut the storyline. Redundancy and Means Test headlines, or rows of stopped machines are superimposed over characters' faces, to emphasise the typicality of their individual predicaments. But there are also subtle changes which shift the agenda away from the novel's confrontational stance. Larry Meath's speeches explaining Capital or pointing out that its victims 'made this Government and its conditions', now contain ominous references to a 'coming catastrophe', suggesting that the current situation will be transformed by the very war to which it is leading. Similarly, in the protest march scene, police brutality is played down by showing them reluctantly intervening in a riot caused by a minority of yobs, egged on by bully-boy Ned Narkey (in the novel Narkey had *joined* the police ranks). Conflict is also reduced by having Larry, who tries to prevent the disorder, accidentally killed by a rearing police horse, thus creating a martyr for the moderate constitutional socialism that might one day cooperate with the authorities for the common good. There are more obvious interpolations too. An opening caption framed the story's pastness, rather than burning topicality:

> The film recalls one of the darker pages of our industrial history. On the outskirts of every City, there is a region of darkness and poverty: where men and women forever strive to live decently in face of overwhelming odds, never doubting that the clouds of depression will one day be lifted. Such a district was Hanky Park in March, 1930.

The film breaks the novel's remorselessly cyclical structure, because the last scene does not simply repeat the first with a new generation. Instead it concludes with Mrs Hardcastle, eyes misting into a middle-distance future, 'where people'll begin to see what's been "appenin"' and 'there'll be no Hanky Park anymore'. It also carried a closing statement by a Labour Minister, A. V. Alexander, First Lord of the Admiralty, in the Wartime Coalition: 'Our working men and women have responded magnificently to any and every call made upon them, their reward must be a new Britain. Never again must the unemployed become the forgotten men of the peace.'[177] John Baxter, *Love on the Dole*'s director, also filmed popular texts, designed to encourage productivity, like Priestley's *Let the People Sing* (1942), set in an aircraft factory and featuring Alistair Sim. Charles Frend's *The Foreman Went to France*, was also based on a topical short story by Priestley and starred radio comic Tommy Trinder. Priestley's peacetime partnership with entertainers continued into wartime, but he also continued to bring more 'highbrow' subjects to popular audiences. Priestley had written the screenplay of the *The Old Dark House* for James Whale, director of *The Invisible Man,* in 1932, two years before his first for Gracie Fields. This revealed a more haunted, Expressionistic strain in his writing (it even featured a murderous Caligariesque nightstalker). The young Charles Laughton starred as a self-made Yorkshireman, marooned with other socially-allegorical types in a Gothic mansion symbolising the anachronistic, decaying state of contemporary Britain. Similarly, his Shavian 'play of ideas' *They Came to a City* was adapted by Ealing in 1944. In this a cross-section of lost individuals are given the chance of entering an invisible Utopia of the postwar future.[178]

Wartime movie adaptations reprojected the social crises of thirties texts both explicitly and implicitly. As we shall see, the 'new patriotism' was epitomised by *Went the Day Well* (based on Greene's pivotal 1940 story 'The Lieutenant Died Last'), in which a quisling squire was played by Leslie Banks, erstwhile upper-class hero of *Sanders of the River* (Greene deplored that film's shameless imperialism in 1936 (see *Mornings in he Dark*, p. 402). In his *Spectator* column, Greene advocated a defamiliarising, demotic formula for effective film propaganda, like that pursued in broadcasting by Priestley and Bridson. Screening Britain as Grierson's 'functioning democracy' meant ditching BBC-accented voice-overs and concomitant social attitudes.[179] Greene advocated using radical documentaries like Hemingway and Ivens's *Spanish Earth* and Elton and Anstey's

Housing Problems as models for a 'different conception of news'. The old patronising commentary was out of place in a people's war. America was more likely to listen sympathetically 'to the rough unprepared words of a Mrs Jarvis, of Penge, faced with evacuation, blackouts, a broken home, than to the smooth-handled phrases of personalities' (29 Sept. 1939; *Mornings in the Dark,* p. 331). Everything he objected to was encapsulated in *The Lion Has Wings,* based on the Kiel Canal raid, especially in Merle Oberon's closing statement about defending 'Truth, and beauty, and fair play, and kindliness'. As a declaration of war aims, Greene felt, 'this leaves the world beyond Roedean still expectant' (3 November 1939; *Mornings in the Dark,* p. 42). Greene's viewpoint was widely shared by Leftists. The scenario and casting of *Mrs Miniver,* declared William Whitebait ('George Stonier'), made the Blitz seem only 'the best people's war.' RP remained socially dominant through the thirties, but Tom Harrisson recalled the 'sort of phonetic nausea' now induced in wartime audiences by its supercilious 'uplift'.[180] Demands for change were disseminated and developed by the *Documentary News Letter* group which gained considerable influence on MoI policy.

In practice, though, Greene's documentary scripting was disappointing. His MoI short *The New Britain* (1941) extolled prewar British history as uninterrupted social progress and prosperity, as if the Depression had never happened and the Welfare State was already in place, threatened only by continuous intercutting of contrasting developments in Nazi Germany. This screen pageant avoided the very domestic issues he criticised prewar Griersonian documentaries for omitting. Its patriotic sentiments resemble the opening sequences of *The Lion Has Wings* and were much more fulsome than, for example, those of Priestley's GPO short *Britain at Bay.* This cinematic analogy to the *Postscripts* was at least plausibly democratised by his Yorkshire accent, skilful editing and practical demand for a citizens' army.[181]

The popular appeal of Greene's writing was employed with greater success in wartime features. Fritz Lang transcribed Greene's *The Ministry of Fear* (1943) to the screen almost as the novel was coming off the press. A metaphysical thriller, with an anti-Nazi message, Greene's text seems, in turn, to owe much to his longstanding admiration for the director's work (discussed above in Chapter 3). Morton Dauwen Zabel considers the world of Greene's novel as much that of Lang, Murnau, Renoir and Hitchcock as 'putsches, pogroms, marches and mobilisations'.[182] Lang's 1941 adaptation of Geoffrey Household's transatlantic best-seller *Rogue Male* (as *Man Hunt*) seems to have been a specific influence. Greene's own high expectations of the allegorical method of *Man Hunt*'s fantasy supports this theory (especially his remarks in a 1941 radio talk for the BBC Spanish Service about the symbolism of the closing sequence in which the protagonist parachutes from a bomber with a big-game rifle, 'now that such a large number of young Englishmen fly over Germany every night following, so to speak, the scent of the Führer' (*Mornings in the Dark*, p. 520)). Shot with Expressionistic menace, fraught with 'warning shadows', that were Lang's trademark, *Man Hunt* explored the psychologically murky pressures and susceptibilities that constitute the 'enemy within', in both a Freudian and geopolitical sense, which might paralyse the will to resist. Besides the pursuit across Britain by enemy agents, there are other telling symmetries with Greene's novel. In *Man Hunt*, the hero discovers the will to resist only when he can finally admit his prewar 'sporting stalk' of Hitler was actually an unconscious wish to avenge his victims: his own persecution by the Gestapo forces him to confront his self-evasion and moral cowardice. In Greene's text, the hero turns and destroys his pursuers when no longer self-pityingly guiltridden for mercy-killing his terminally-ill wife: the Nazi agents no longer appear sanctioned furies, but murderous fanatics.

Ironically, Greene himself was bitterly disappointed by the tangible fruit of his admiration for Lang. He considered the film of *The Ministry of Fear* one of the execrably bad adaptations of his work (the director had much more success collaborating with Brecht the same year on the propaganda thriller *Hangmen Also Die*). Lang himself eventually apologised. A contract trapped him into making the best of a ready-made, psychologically two-dimensional script which gutted the novel's central part, especially crucial mental clinic sequences – a classic testimony to how the institutional power of Hollywood could hamstring even the sympathetic directors with whom Greene felt he could work (see 'Guardian Film Lecture', 3 September 1984; *Mornings in the Dark*, pp. 543–4).

Perhaps the best wartime feature from Greene's work was *Went the Day Well?*, directed by documentarist Cavalcanti for Ealing and released in October 1942. Official, in the sense of carrying the MoI stamp of approval, this film of his short story 'The Lieutenant Died Last' is a good example of how long-standing propaganda campaigns were taken up by the cinema. 'If the Invader Comes' was the title of a pamphlet circulated from mid-June 1940 (it plops through the average family's letterbox in *Millions Like Us*) and the ruthlessness and brutality of the film's Nazis also shows the way the MoI's 'Anger Campaigns' were reinforced on screen.[183] *Went the Day Well?* was designed to jolt midwar complacency, by imaginatively transferring the experience of conquered populations to the Orwellian doze of that 'Deep England' constructed in so much wartime propaganda as the nation's heartland. Greene's orginal text was set in 'Potter', a non-descript 'Metroland' newtown; the film, in pastoral Buckinghamshire. The MoI had been involved right from conception. 'The Lieutenant Died Last' was originally published in *Collier's Weekly*, 29 June 1940,[184] as part of the MoI's strategy to convince neutrals of Britain's dogged belligerence and functioning democracy, by arranging 'unofficial' contributions to overseas publications. *Collier's* was an appropriate platform: its London correspondent was the highly sympathetic Quentin Reynolds, known to Americans especially as the voice-over in *London Can Take It* (1940) (released here as *Britain Can Take It*). Freely adapted by John Dighton, Diana Morgan and Angus MacPhail (by then Greene was in Africa for MI6), the film also exemplifies how texts could be taken out of writers' hands and depersonalised in becoming official projects.

Went the Day Well? had particular impact by identifying successful resistance with the collective heroism of citizens' initiatives and *de facto* social revolution. It begins with the verger of 'Bramley End' looking back from a hypothetical postwar future to 48 hours in May 1942. This encapsulates the double strategy to reassure about eventual victory while attacking complacency in the pivotal year of the war. German parachutists, disguised as Royal Engineers (another of the film's additions), take over the village to disable radar defences for full-scale air- and seaborne invasion. Another MoI pamphlet (June 1940) put forward the shocking possibility of treachery by individuals regarded as pillars of society in the thirties should invasion occur. Evidence was drawn from the collaboration of the authorities in Vichy France (though the Channel Islands might have been more worrying), many of whom had been Rightist fellow-travellers:

> Anyone who thinks . . . it 'can't happen here', had simply fallen into the trap laid by the fifth column itself. For *the first job of the fifth column is to make people think that it does not exist*. In other countries the most respectable and neighbourly citizens turned out to be fifth columnists when the time came.[185]

The film furnishes an MoI object-lesson in alertness. Suspicions are aroused by a continental Seven and a bar of 'Schokolade Wien', though the villagers are temporarily deceived by the Squire (a German agent) who lies that these are Mass-Obervation 'plants' to test public reaction (M-O, in fact, regularly gauged responses to MoI campaigns for Home Intelligence). The most crucial shift in class terms went further than Greene's story. The film focuses not on the cussed individualism of poacher Bill Purves, but the solidarity of the community as a whole. Action is initiated by a socially representative cross-section; a sailor on leave organises the villagers' take-over of the manor; the elderly postmistress axes a guard; young Thora Hird becomes a sniping Landgirl; a cockney boy-evacuee gets through to the outside world. The climactic scene with the manor 'functioning diagrammatically as a map of "England" under attack, is one of the most intense in all British war films'.[186]

The feature thus went further than what had become, by midwar, ritual indictment of 'the rigmarole of blimp and bullshit', as *Picture Post* editor Tom Hopkinson called it,[187] although, as Aldgate points out, hierarchy is not fundamentally abolished. It suggested the persistence of élitism was potentially treasonous, but, could also, on the other hand be seen as reinstating its values: it's the Vicar's daughter who steels herself to shoot the squire.[188] There's no doubt though that simplistic anti-Germanism was averted by the equivocal otherness of Fascists in British uniforms, making a richer, more disturbing poetic subtext available. The reception of *Went the Day Well?* in Britain was controversial on both aesthetic and political grounds. Similarly, Agee thought Jennings's *The Silent Village* on Lidice a better film, because its characters were not crude literary-social types, but interestingly, also though it the on-screen climax of thirties writers' forebodings. He considered it a near-surreal defamiliarisation of Britain's polite civic structures, symbolising the division, corruption and violence lurking beneath:

> As the audience watches from a hill, with the eyes at once of a helpless outsider, a masked invader, and a still innocent defender, a mere crossroads imparts qualities of pity and terror which . . . it seldom shows except under tilted circumstances. And at moments, when the invaders prowlingly approach through the placid gardens of the barricaded manor in the neat morning light, the film has the sinister, freezing beauty of an Auden prophecy come true.[189]

Other war features from Greene's work also indicate how key issues in the texts of thirties writers were equivocally renegotiated. For example, Greene stated that *A Gun for Sale* (1936) marked a point when patriotism seemed utterly discredited by the Great War and tabloid jingoism:

> An early hero of mine was John Buchan, but when I re-opened his books I found I could no longer get the same pleasure from the adventures of Richard Hannay. More than the dialogue and the situation had dated: the moral climate was no longer that of my boyhood. Patriotism had lost its appeal, even for a schoolboy, at Passchendaele, and the Empire brought first to mind the Beaverbrook Crusader, while it was difficult, during the years of the Depression, to believe in the high purposes of the City of London or of the British Constitution. The hunger marchers seemed more real than the politicians. It was no longer a Buchan world.

A commission enquiring into arms-dealing exposed another pillar of the thirties establishment, Sir Basil Zaharoff, as, in Greene's words, 'a more plausible villain for those days' than the one in *The Thirty-Nine Steps* 'who could "hood his eyes like a hawk"'.[190] However, the success of Hitchcock's screen version of Buchan's novel, though lambasted by Greene in *The Spectator*, suggests ethically uncomplicated nationalism was also far from dead in the Britain of 1935. Furthermore, Hollywood's relocation of Greene's own novel in post-Pearl Harbor America as *This Gun for Hire* (1942) jettisoned its attack on multi-nationals for straight anti-Japanese propaganda. Greene's psychological cripple Raven was hired by bosses with no allegiance but profit, to assassinate a statesman and trigger off world war. Their subsequent double-crossing of him makes Raven realise the horror of what he has done, and prompts him to seek revenge and avert Armageddon. In the filmscript by W. R. Burnett and Albert Maltz, Greene's 'Midland Steel' became the conventionally treacherous 'Nitro Chemical Corporation', supplying poison-gas specifically to America's enemies. Consequently, Raven, played by Alan Ladd, is converted to conventional loyalties. If this wasn't unqualified regression to Buchanism as such, it did sacrifice the novel's ethical complexity to the political demands of the time.

In the light of Greene's views on the BBFC's cinematic Appeasement, it is also ironic that Herman Shumlin's 1945 adaptation of the

The Confidential Agent (1939) was allowed to make his text's anti-fascist, Spanish Civil War background explicit in a way impossible at its time of publication. The novel originated as a prewar screenplay for Korda, although it became too politically hot to handle (see *Mornings in the Dark,* p. 701). Agee rightly scoffed that the 1945 version's 'intrepidity in calling Sp-n, and even F-sc-sm, by their full right names would have been easier to appreciate in 1938 or so', though he acknowledged its relative success in tackling 'Greene's somewhat mawkish metaphysic of universal mistrust'. Most intriguingly, Agee felt it failed to approximate what was fundamentally cinematic in Greene's style: 'the look and effluence of places, streets and things'. Though in a sense Greene did not write novels at all, 'but verbal movies' he might also have proved that certain kinds of movies 'are better on the page than they can ever be on the screen'.[191]

The intertextuality of wartime film and thirties Leftist writing was pervaded by historical ironies. A British cinematic indictment of the 'Guilty Men' – the appeasing politicians and fellow-travelling media barons (represented by the *'Daily Argus'*) – was *Thunder Rock* (1942), adapted from the play by Robert Ardrey. But the film's retrospective praising of anti-fascist writers and journalists who tried to alert Britain, but were largely denied access to the most effective mass-media channels for communicating with it, was doublethink to Agee. The fundamental historical lesson was missed through smugness: 'horribly late approval anaesthetises us against an awareness of matters which, ten years from now, will become material for bold, bitter, instructive pieces of surefire hindsight'.[192] Filmwork also extended the journalistic activities, of the authors of *Guilty Men* themselves, Michael Foot and Frank Owen alias 'Cato'. They scripted the satire of Mussolini, *Yellow Caesar* (1941), a montage of actuality clips with a mocking commentary, and Cavalcanti's *Young Veteran* (1941), about a raw recruit based on the *Daily Express* character 'Young Bert'. Foot was just as misinformed by the MoI as Orwell in his Indian broadcasts about RAF raids on non-military targets. Foot's commentary for the documentary *The Biter Bit* (1943) justified Allied area bombing, with its 'merely accidental' impact on population centres, by contrasting it with the deliberate action of the Luftwaffe against civilians, using excerpts from the Nazi film used to terrorise neutrals early in the war, *Feuertaufe* ('Baptism of Fire').[193]

Besides the restrictions on writers' media involvements imposed by the MoI as official taskmaster, censor and source of facts, its policy's democratisation of wartime culture has to be seen as limited. Even MoI-sponsored films aimed at working-class audiences did not employ proletarians as scriptwriters in great numbers, but tended to recruit those with traditional, albeit renegade, public-school credentials and contacts. Jack Hilton, author of *Caliban Shrieks*, for example, praised by Orwell for writing in the 'authentic accents' of the working man, tried but failed to get film or broadcast work.[194] A notable exception was Jack Common's *Tyneside Story* (1943) which perhaps explains MoI reluctance to hire writers who might probe potential sorepoints of the 'People's War' agenda too deeply in accents that reflected its audience's scepticism too closely. Nominally part of a drive to recruit redundant shipworkers back into the industry, Common's script closed with a Tynesider doubting the establishment's expedient change of heart would be maintained without vigilant political pressure after the war:

> Aye, but wait a minute. Tyneside is busy enough today, old uns and young uns hard at work makin' good ships, but just remember what the yards looked like five years ago: idle, empty, some of 'em derelict, and the skilled men that worked in them scattered and forgotten. Will it be the same again five years from now?

Conversely, even 'difficult' non-proletarian writers like Dylan Thomas were enlisted in the cinematic war effort. Thomas's output was quite prolific. He worked on the (1942) Council for the Encouragement of Music and the Arts short about democratising culture – concerts in factories and exhibitions in industrial towns – and *Balloon Site 568* about the WAAF. Thomas even wrote a locally-accented poetic commentary for *Wales – Green Mountain, Black Mountain* (1943), with the now-standard message of no-return to the conditions of the thirties. He traded his exuberant crypticism for accessibility 'worthy of Mayakovsky at Agitprop', as Pronay puts it:[195]

> Remember the procession of the old young men,
> From dole queue to corner and back again.
> From the pinched back street to the peak of slag,
> In the bite of the winter and with shovel and pack,
> With a droopy fag and a turned back collar,
> Stamping for the cold on the ill-lit corner.
> Dragging through the squalor with their hearts like lead,
> Staring at the hunger and the shut pit head.

Nothing in their pockets, nothing home to eat,
Lagging from the slag heap to the pinched back street.
Remember the procession of the old young men,
It shall never happen again.

Thomas also wrote verse for *These Are the Men* (1943) and *Our Country* (1945). The former indicted Nazi leaders with recut material from Riefenstahl's Nürnberg Parteitag film, ironically juxtaposing the triumphalism of 1934 with its catastrophic consequences for the German people themselves. The latter was a panoramic seaman's journey around Britain near D-Day. Rex Warner similarly abandoned fantastic allegories to write a commentary for *The Great Harvest* (1942), a documentary about agricultural regeneration. Even pre-thirties literary veterans were mobilised. E. M. Forster, hitherto uninvolved with film, wrote the commentary in *Diary for Timothy* (1945), one of Jennings's finest films (although Forster was unhappy about Jennings's retention of educational privilege, among other things, which diluted the radicalism of this projection of postwar Britain).[196]

As Orwell suggested, perhaps the most culpable underuse of literary talent by the MoI was in the case of ex-Communist Arthur Koestler, with his unmatchable experience in Münzenberg's multi-media western propaganda organisation (see *Collected Essays*, II, p. 435). Though Koestler did script *Lift Your Head Comrade* (from the title of a concentration camp song by a murdered poet) for the Films Division, concerned with the work of the Fifteenth Alien Company of the Pioneer Crops, it was considered too sensitive a subject in 1940. 'Premature' anti-fascists were still suspected and, ironically, often interned as enemy aliens until Hitler's breaching of the Non-Aggression pact with Russia. The film was finally directed three years later by Michael Hankinson. Its refugees were German, Austrian and Russian. Many, like Koestler, were Jewish. As the narrating officer says, 'for them the War started in 1933 when Hitler came to power'. The film then flashes-back to compare their condition in 1939, noting, reassuringly, that 'The past is the past. You're in a free country now.' Many of these intellectuals and writers, like Koestler himself, were only trusted to do donkey work and the suspension of the film-making constitutes a chapter of the secret history of censorship that contradicted a once-Appeasing Britain's officially clean conscience about the war's causes, conduct and aims. The MoI's notorious 'silence' on the Holocaust was also an aspect of this. Koestler was even requested to tone down survivors' accounts of their experiences in the concentration camps, partly because it was felt the public would disbelieve mere 'atrocity-mongering', although the film's incorporation of identity papers with shaven heads and a Dachau inmate's recollection of being hung by the wrists seems small beer now. More importantly, the Government had already received conclusive proof of the *Endlösung* as early as 1942. It didn't want to foreground the Jews' special status as victims, for fear of fanning the embarrassing increase in British anti-semitism during the war.[197]

As it turned out, rare documentaries like *Lift Your Head Comrade*, which attempted to confront the truth about Nazi ideology and its logical implications met with incomprehension. The public were virtually unprepared for the sudden materialisation of the full horror when footage of liberated death camps began to be screened in 1945. For some writers, this event burst the limits of rationality and representation, damaging both the humanistic discourse of literature and the media's technological reproduction irreparably. The shock of these images, at once irrefutably actual, yet appearing to issue from a parallel dimension all but impossible to integrate with 'normative' experience, was unprecedented (as James Young and other commentators on the holocaust have argued).[198] They finally wrenched open an 'unimaginable real', truly Postmodern in its epistemological dysfunctionality, dislocation of meaning and challenge to liberal-humanist concepts of historical progress, though, as Home Intelligence's reports on the increase in wartime anti-semitism suggest, it still had definite, albeit distanced, roots in the uninformed reality of everyday prejudice and apathy.

CODA

The Holocaust jolted many writers into a condition of self-reflexive *angst* about the duplicity of discourse and the philosophical recessiveness of reality. At the same time, wartime's mobilisation of human and material resources vastly intensified and extended the technological and economic force-field in which they would henceforth write. The post-1945 world is irreversibly saturated with the forms and pressures of media propaganda. Holocaust images co-exist in our culture with simulations that censored and sanitised the full horror of a 'Good War' at the time, concealing its blunders to safeguard its fightability, and conditioning its aftermyth. As Fussell argues, what was projected 'almost had to be fictional, an image of pseudo-war and pseudo-human behavior not too distant from the familiar world of magazine advertising and improving popular fiction'. Consequently, the postwar media's power 'to determine what shall be embraced as reality' is a continuation of the success of wartime morale culture.[199]

This was a two-way process. The war's events were screened and managed, and at the same time the media discourses into which they were transfigured conditioned even the consciousness of those directly involved in them, shaped how they saw their actual experience to an extent impossible in the Great War, where the ironic differential between frontline reality and domestic propaganda was blatant to anyone familiar with both states. That differential was still very much there in the Second World War, but technological change made determining the truth of it much more complex. A young poet, particularly aware of how battlefield experience was transfigured into media discourse, and how that discourse was projected cognitively back into it, was Keith Douglas. The Battle of El Alamein was the first occasion on which BBC news commentary employed regular disc recording from the field, using *Belinda*, its new mobile sound van. Douglas's writing about the same action suggests the hyperreal had so thoroughly interpenetrated warfare itself as to alter cognition of it irrevocably. He grew up in the culture of the thirties; his account of the North African desert campaign, *Alamein to Zem Zem*, is a fascinating coda to its media preoccupations and, equally, a suggestive anticipation of more fully Postmodern literary responses to war, like Joseph Heller's *Catch 22*, Michael Herr's *Dispatches* or Swift's *Out of this World*. Douglas's text foregrounds the 'multiple and simultaneous consciousness' inherent in tank warfare coordinated by wireless or airborne combat by radar. In a way, it picks up the question left hanging by Greene's ironisation of Kinglake's Crimean soldiers, imprisoned in their empirical cells by the foggy chaos of a collective event.

A keen photographer and talented graphic artist, Douglas was continuously imaging his own subjective reality. Photogenically wounded, he half-jokingly 'looked vainly round for someone from the Army Film and Photographic Unit' to record it.[200] His account sports a battery of camera-eyed ways of seeing, alternating unflinching documentary close-ups of the dead with dreamlike footage of the minimalist desert landscape. His text suggests a condition of media containment, both external and internalised, something to both look *at*, and *out of*. Douglas even equated motorised warfare with being caught up inside the visual dynamic of a movie, as if actuality and spectacle are now cognitively indivisible:

> The view from a moving tank is like that in a camera obscura or a silent film – in that since the engine drowns all the other noises except explosions, the whole world moves silently. Men shout, vehicles move, aeroplanes fly over, and all soundlessly: the noise of the tank being continuous, perhaps for hours on end, the effect is of silence. It is the same in an aircraft. . . .

However, this technological kind of seeing didn't necessarily guarantee the reality of his impressions: 'think it may have been the fact that for so much of the time I saw it without hearing it, which led me to feel that country into which we were now moving as an illimitably strange land, quite unrelated to real life, like the scenes in *The Cabinet of Doctor Caligari*' (*Alamein to Zem Zem*, p. 28). Conversely, in battlefield circumstances sound became paramount for practical reasons. Wartime civilians became familiar with running combat commentaries after the first aerial dog-fights over South-East England. By D-Day, sound equipment was portable enough for radio crews to broadcast events virtually as they took place, but Douglas was nonetheless dependent on vicarious contact even at the frontline. Netted into the tank's internal and external radio system, he understood his own relation to collective events in the same aural mode:

> Anyone who takes part in a modern battle in a tank, which is equipped with a wireless, has an advantage over the infantry-man, and over all the soldiers and generals of earlier wars. Before his mind's eye the panorama of the battle is kept, more vividly even than before. . . . He hears a continuous account of the battle through these earphones.

This particular overlap of the real and hyperreal presented itself to Douglas as a kind of extended dialogue between avant-garde art and the popular media. The mix of secret codes and improvised regimental banter alternated between 'the mysterious symbolic language . . . of a wildly experimental school of poets' and the stilted absurdity of 'the conversation of the two Englishmen in *The Lady*

Vanishes' (pp. 108–9).[201] Despite expanding consciousness, this informational net could sometimes get tangled and opaque. It multiplied the confusion and horror of mere sensory experience when transmissions could not be decoded, broke down or were intercepted. Sometimes, it even relayed the grisly moment at which an enemy shell impacted on the crew of a distant tank with which Douglas was in radio contact. Tantalising, scrappy and inconclusive though Douglas's poetic insights were (he would die at Normandy), they heralded a new phase in the ongoing struggle by writers, inherited from the thirties, to rationalise changes in perception and culture wrought by the power of media technology.

Conclusions

Bergonzi may or may not be right that thirties writers 'were the first literary generation in England to have to face mass civilisation directly', but it is certainly the case that their encounter with it through the discourses and effects of mass-media power is 'a major determinant of the literature of the time'.[1]

Spender blamed the fatal political paralysis of the thirties on the lack of a properly informing media that might have roused the public conscience and 'forced Britain, France, and perhaps even the United States, to take the necessary stand to prevent war'.[2] However, implicit in that judgement was a sense of Leftist writers' own failure to sponsor more widespread alertness against a vastly powerful media's simulated realities and subliminal agendas. Similarly, Orwell's broadcast alter-ego, the shade of Swift, would seem to endorse Michael D. Biddiss's conclusion that undemocratic media promoting 'half-knowledge' prevent 'Sceptical good sense, the best of the Enlightenment tradition', from winning a mass audience.[3]

M-O found the war did globalise ordinary Britons' awareness because their own fate depended on information about far-off events, like Roosevelt's re-election in November 1940.[4] Conversely, wartime media propaganda, as writers like Orwell found, also desensitised and depleted language at the moment of most imperative need for new modes of representation adequate to the reality of the deathcamps. As Calder notes, propaganda robbed words of force and obliterated their finer shades of meaning. Orwell's Newspeak partly derived from the MoI-sponsored sloganising of the British media, as well as Ogden's Basic. *All* combatant nations had been infiltrated by 'the vocabulary of totalitarianism', because of the demands of technology and total warfare and the cultural conditions they created.[5]

Orwell thought wartime bureaucratisation pressurised the writer and artist into 'a minor official working on themes handed to him from above and never telling what seems to him to be the whole truth' (*Collected Essays*, IV, p. 82). But the necessity and scale of the campaign to disseminate the People's War myth also meant 'the existing intelligentsia had to be utilised' which modified 'the tone and even to some extent the content of official propaganda' accordingly. This process had some positive implications for future dialectical resistance to the mediation of reality by official and/or commercial monopolies. The modern state's need for artists to feed its ideological apparatuses was a kind of minimal saving grace. The bigger this machinery became, 'the more loose ends and forgotten corners there are in it', and the more opportunity would arise for subverting it from within with products that were 'all wrong from the bureaucratic point of view' (*Collected Essays*, II, pp. 381–2). However, isolated pearls produced by bits of grit in the machinery were no substitute for the huge changes that would be needed to bring about more truly proportional political representation and cultural progress. As Orwell concluded, the media's 'immense educational possibilities' could only be realised when they were 'freed once and for all from vested interests' (*Collected Essays*, III, p. 54). He reconsidered the Leavisite mass-civilisation and minority culture split in 'Poetry and the Microphone' (1943). The danger in accepting the separation between popular media commodities and art's defamiliarisation of forms and ideas was that 'a breach of this kind tends to widen simply because of its existence, the common man becoming more and more anti-poetry, the poet more and more arrogant and unintelligible', until the cultural divorce between them became naturalised (*Collected Essays*, II, p. 378). For Orwell, the postwar writer's struggle had the same essential aim as the common Leftist project of the thirties: to objectify changes in perception wrought through media power by mobilising his/her own art against the challenge they presented.

In some respects thirties Leftists understood the workings of the contemporary media only too well and historical research (drawn on extensively in this study) bears them out. In other respects, their standpoint could be reductive and/or prone to gender- and class-induced blindspots. Sometimes this meant they failed to recognise the media's potentially positive effects. The proletarian novelist Jack Common, in his study of mass-society from the inside, *The Freedom of the Streets* (1938), argued that precisely because of mass-production everybody in contemporary society, regardless of class, was a consumer and 'in relation to it you are one of the masses'. It was because this situation was unwilled, 'an imposed degradation', that the denial of the individual in the mass was a negative thing. It could be reversed if 'we learn to take pleasure in the new contiguity, to realise the enormous imaginative possibilities which our own situation has once we accept it and begin to use its opportunities'. Common concluded that to an historian of the future the underlying duplicity of the mass-civilisation/minority Culture split would be glaring, that this split was indeed a symptom not a cure:

> He would see individualist art retreating into Bloomsbury, growing ever more chilly and interbred and analytic of its own tradition and popular culture left to showmen and cheapjacks, themselves with no newer faith to go on. He would see how everybody was content to live by mass-production and was also content to see that production needlessly tawdry and actually disguised in individualist symbols.[6]

Bourgeois Leftists tended to assume they somehow stood outside mass-culture and its 'mystified subject'. Their viewpoint was sometimes unqualified by empathy and acknowledgement of their own unconscious dependencies and conditioning. They could fall into displaced snobbery, on the one hand, and deny their own susceptibility to powerful seductions, on the other. Consideration, for example, of the complex parameters conditioning relations between the cinema and its far from monolithically responsive mass-audiences did not get beyond a certain point for precisely such reasons, although the equivocal role played by cinema in mediating modernity, particularly in terms of the reinvention of gender roles, was portrayed by some working-class writers. In *Love on the Dole*, for example, there is a real sense of excitement about the part the Saturday-night ritual of the 'flecky parlour' plays in the youth culture of Marlowe's apprentices and their girlfriends, to set against Helen Hawkins's outburst against its narcosis. Greenwood also acknowledges that the pictures are, albeit fleetingly, a liberating and expressive space for the generation of single girls disgorging from the mill-gates.

> A few still held to the picturesque clogs and shawls of yesterday, but the majority represented modernity: cheap artificial silk-stockings, cheap short-skirted frocks, cheap coats, cheap shoes, crimped hair, powder and rouge; five and a half days weekly in a spinning mill or weaving shed, a threepenny seat in the picture theatre twice a week, a ninepenny or shilling dance of a Saturday night, a Sunday afternoon parade on the erstwhile aristocratic Eccles Old Road which incloses the public park, then work

again, until they married when picture theatres became luxuries and Saturday dances, Sunday parades and cheap finery ceased altogether. (p. 42)

Similarly, unhampered by some of the prejudices of her male middle-class contemporaries, Winifred Holtby's *Women and a Changing Civilisation* (1934) argued that a media-saturated condition was inevitably refiguring gender identities in a complex dialectic the effects of which might be unpredictable and inconsistent, but by no means all regressive: 'A woman, Mrs. Hamilton, is director of the British Broadcasting Corporation, though the first attempt to employ a woman announcer was soon abandoned.' The responses of the sexes to the new media were made both similar and manifestly different by cultural pre-conditioning. She cited a census of topics of conversation among factory girls:

Cinema stars, men friends and private gossip came out at the top of the schedule. . . . Young women, then are not much interested in the valuation of the dollar, the future of democracy, or the exploration of the stratosphere. Neither are the young men. But the women are affected by a discouragement which does not afflict their brothers. From childhood upward they hear the cry that 'Men hate a clever woman.' Baby-faced blondes, the Jean Harlows and Clara Bows of film-fame, are the models of those whom gentlemen prefer.[7]

Male Leftists favoured serious Russian movies, generally despising or ignoring commercial Priestleyesque musicals and the 'women's picture'. But the sympathetic hunches of writers like Woolf, Holtby and Bowen sketched the possibility of more informed feminist critical positions on popular culture that would take shape from the sixties. There was a tension within Hollywood's focus on the self-image of women themselves, who were the largest portion of features' audiences. The cinema was one of the first places of entertainment where unaccompanied women could go without the automatic assumption of sexual availability. On the regressive side, cinema's preoccupation with gender furnished a way of negotiating a modernity, in which all women had the vote from 1930 and an unprecedented degree of social independence (made possible by economic and technological change, birth-control and education), while preserving the Victorian domestic stereotype of an essential or 'natural' femininity. More progressively, as recent feminist rereadings of the genre have suggested, the women's picture was also a source of potential empowerment, foregrounding the very crisis of gender identity it attempted to stabilise. This is very much the point made by Jeanine Basinger, building on the work of Christine Gledhill and Tania Modleski, among others. As Julie Wheelwright puts it, 'In the much-maligned women's film, the eternal, female dilemma of juggling professional ambitions, matrimony and maternity, was writ large.'[8] And although that dilemma was almost invariably solved with traditional moralism, the fact of its projection so frequently meant alternative possibilities were simultaneously aroused as well as denied in its audiences. The position actually occupied by the spectator was not necessarily identical to the hegemonic one constructed by filmmakers and the BBFC any more than for nineties TV soaps. The lack of awareness among Leftists of the micropolitical implications of such features and of the individual indeterminacy of 'mass' audience responses was rivalled only by their lack of any coherent or positive theory of pleasure.

Even Orwell's most historically acute diagnoses of the changes wrought by what Lewis Mumford called the 'neotechnic age' of petrochemicals and electricity[9] are occasionally tinged with social ambivalence. What Priestley called the 'third England' was created out of the spread of broadcasting, as much as suburbia, cars and the southward shift of industry. Orwell noted in 1941 that it had significantly eroded or redrawn social and cultural boundaries. For the first time, there were people who could not be positioned within the traditional class-system. Choosing the same pivotal year as the Modernist Woolf, Orwell attributed a similar sea-change to technology as she did to Post-Impressionist art.[10]

In 1910 every human being in these islands could be 'placed' in an instant by his clothes, manners and accent. This is no longer the case. . . . The place to look for the germs of the future England is in the light-industry areas and along the arterial roads. In Slough, Dagenham, Barnet, Letchworth, Hayes. . . . There are wide gradations of income, but it is the same kind of life that is being lived at different levels, in labour-saving flats or council houses, along the concrete roads and in the naked deomcracy of the swimming pools. It is a rather restless, cultureless life, centring round tinned food, *Picture Post*, the radio and the internal combustion engine. (*The Lion and the Unicorn, Collected Essays*, II, p. 98)

For Orwell the radio engineer epitomised the new 'classless' professions. But this passage's distinctly patrician regret for the disappearance of culture with a 'C' (a muted echo of Betjeman's snobbish poetic Blitzing of Slough) offsets its welcoming of new mobilities. Lack of obvious political signposts in Orwell's topography, beyond *Picture Post's* populist Left-of-Centrism, is also significant. *Picture Post* itself would disappear in 1955, of course, when this apparently egalitarian landscape emerged from the millenarian climate of postwar welfare-state building to become the heartland of Macmillan's neo-Conservativism, when distinctions in income and consumption would begin to figure more than accent in the index of caste markers.

Over in Hollywood, Isherwood as a postwar expatriate scriptwriter had inside knowledge of the next wave of 'Americanisation' which would sweep the Atlantic during the McCarthy era (itself a counter-attack on the cultural legacy of the New Deal, especially in the medium of film). In his view, the only way to survive Cold War capital's brave renewed consumerism was to maintain critical vigilance against its media and public relations industries, to refuse to accept the fake subjectivity they proferred as the genuine article:

> To live sanely in Los Angeles (or, I suppose, in any other large American city) you have to cultivate the art of staying awake. You must learn to resist (firmly but not tensely) the unceasing hypnotic suggestions of the radio, the billboards, the movies and the newspapers: those demon voices which are forever whispering in your ear what you should desire, what you should fear. . . .

This chorus of interpellating voices wove a complete ideology: 'they have planned a life for you – from the cradle to the grave and beyond – which it would be easy, fatally easy, to accept'.[11]

Under such internal and external pressures, the distinctive qualities and forms of Britain's wartime media, shaped so much by Leftist writers, could not outlast their unique circumstances unchanged. A conspicuous example was the popular ground wartime radio broadcasting would soon be surrendering to the resumption of television. The two scripts of 1946 most influential on future developments in radio were MacNeice's *The Dark Tower* and Douglas Cleverdon's adaptation of David Jones's *In Parenthesis*. Until the development of portable tape, actuality features continued to depend on literary structure for some time. But as Gielgud puts it, the story of the radio play 'that "Cinderella of the Drama"' reached its wartime ending too late, so that 'Television snatched the glass slipper, and married the Prince' soon afterwards.[12]

Postwar radio was in fact set for a rapid expansion of literary opportunity, but with specific drawbacks. The idea of a three-tiered programme service had been mooted in the thirties, but was inaugurated only in 1946. Director-General Sir William Haley felt that the cultural range offered by the two main wavelengths, Home Service and Light Programme, was too narrow, and that a further channel was needed, devoted to serious music and drama. However, there was much debate at the time about the advisability of removing the literary output from the mixed diet offered by the established channels. Reith objected and got a surprising amount of support from many who had most sought to challenge his vision of public broadcasting in the thirties. Ironically, this was because the Third Programme was seen by some Leftists not as the solution to, but the termination of, their circle-squaring ambitions. Arguably, the old mass-civilisation/minority Culture split was reasserting itself in a new guise, showing it was only temporarily sutured by the 'middlebrow' circumstances of enlightened wartime programming. Bridson, for example, stressed the etymology of 'broadcast' means to disseminate widely and 'to confine the best in radio to one exclusive wavelength could only result in disseminating it most narrowly'.[13] The division of the BBC into a series of specialised 'Programmes' catering for different audiences and with little dialogue between them meant 'ghettoising' the innovative and challenging. In Heppenstall's words, the merit of wartime work was 'that one communicated with a large, mixed audience, whom one might induce to accept what it would never have sought'. The Third Programme 'would separate-off and spoon-feed just that part of the audience which was most capable of procuring its own artistic pleasures', while the Light Programme (an extension of the Wartime Forces Programme), confined itself to 'easy listening'.[14] Heppenstall's caution seems even more relevant to the multiplication of television channels from the sixties and 'niche-marketed' satellite broadcasting in the nineties, haunted though it is by the ghost of 'improving' cultural authoritarianism. However, as Kate Whitehead's admirable study demonstrates, the Third Programme did at least ensure a national platform for the kind of radio experiment that only found a limited home, largely in Features, in the thirties.[15]

Change in postwar broadcasting accelerated so rapidly that MacNeice introduced the 1963 edition of *Columbus* by looking back on his own heyday in the forties as the 'innocent but quaint and archaic period' of '"steam radio"'. This once bang-up-to-date medium matured and aged virtually as quickly as the silent film in the twenties. That ultimate medium for Naturalistic representation, the 'juggernaut of television', restored the power of image over word and, in the process, the hegemony of a transparent realism which broadcast dramatists like MacNeice and Bridson had so strenuously eschewed.[16] But, on the other hand, the avant-garde tradition got wired into fifties television too, largely thanks to the influence of Roland Cartier, who continued the pattern of involvement by Central European producers and directors, which had been so crucial to the British film and drama in the thirties. Cartier productions such as the television adaptation of *Nineteen Eighty-Four* and the *Quatermass* series soon showed writers that the small screen could be a popular and artistic medium as much as the big. In the sixties the floodgates would open. New writers, epitomised by Dennis Potter, would make TV their principal medium and continue to erode cultural boundaries. Potter himself would revisit the thirties in his seventies masterpiece *Pennies from Heaven*. This recycled the songs and movie clichés of the period, for its dialogic form, blending popular culture and radical, anti-Naturalistic experiment, in a way that thirties Leftists believed was possible, but which proved unrealisable under the conditions of their time. Similarly, James Barke's leading question about Molly Bloom and Mae West has found a literary answer in Angela Carter's carnivalesque feminist fictions, especially *Wise Children* (1991), in which Joycean monologuing recounts the Hollywood of Max Reinhardt's all-singing, all-dancing *Midsummer Night's Dream*, while Salman Rushdie draws on 'Bollywood's' reverse cultural colonisation to Easternise *The Wizard of Oz*. The thirties struggle with socially-divided cultural identities and passion for the aesthetically popularising possibilities of cinema also continue to reverberate strongly in the style and content of poems by Tony Harrison and Carol Ann Duffy.

I hope I have succeeded in demonstrating some of the energising but perplexing formal and political effects which intertextuality with the mass-media had on Leftist writers in the thirties. This was, above all, a symptom of their transitional post/modern consciousness. I have endeavoured to historicise the complex origins and working-out of a cultural process that resulted in their encounter with modes of production and audiences outside the traditional Literary domain. It was in this encounter that the decade's reinflection of the doubts raised by Modernism about concepts of authenticity and truth reached their crisis of epistemological strain and semiotic complexity. Moreover, this anticipates crucial topoi of the postwar era's fully Postmodern fiction and theory – the dissection of naive belief in the 'transcribability' of the actual, in 'hyperreality' ever giving direct access to objective facts. The return of diegesis in writing at the beginning of the thirties certainly signalled some kind of anti-modernist reaction. Cultural fusion between the modern media and Marxist theory promised to reorientate the human subject politically by equipping it with a working cognitive map of a traumatically mutated world. This may have turned out to be a panoptic fantasy, but, on the other hand, the questions raised by its very failure have certainly not gone away. On the contrary, they are posed with multiplying urgency by our present condition of global internetting and hallucinatory virtual reality technology. The easy options remain: retreat into that increasingly delapidated tower of 'Cultural standards', or the 'beguiling relativity', to use Julian Barnes's phrase,[17] of unpoliticised Postmodernism. The thirties offer a paradigm of rightly antagonistic, but also mutually enriching, intertextuality between literary art and the popular media in an age of perilous transition, making this neglected moment vital to our understanding of the prehistory of today's cultural dilemmas.

Notes

Preface

1. *Mornings in the Dark: The Graham Greene Film Reader*, ed. David Parkinson (Manchester: Carcanet, 1993), Intro. p. xi.
2. 'Ministry of Truth' was coined by E. H. Robinson in his *Broadcasting and a Changing Civilisation* (London: John Lane, 1935), pp. 151–2 (see also below, Chapter 2). The same year Robinson also published the prospective *Televiewing, etc.* (London: Selwyn and Blount, 1935) which may have sowed the imaginative seeds of Orwell's two-way Telescreen.
3. See my unpublished thesis 'Reportage in the Thirties' for the Oxford D.Phil., 1991.

Introduction: Obituaries of History and the Thirties Sublime

1. Graham Swift, *Out of This World* (Harmondsworth: Penguin, 1988), p. 189.
2. See Chapter 2 below, 'Press'.
3. See Jean Baudrillard, 'The Reality Gulf' *The Guardian* (11 January 1991) and 'La Guerre du Golfe n'a pas en lieu', *Liberation* (29 March 1991). Also Christopher Norris, *Uncritical Theory: Postmodernism, Intellectuals and the Gulf War* (London: Lawrence and Wishart, 1992), especially pp. 11–31 and 192–6.
4. Jean Baudrillard, *Selected Writings*, ed. M. Poster (Cambridge: Polity Press), pp. 145–7.
5. Jean-François Lyotard, *The Postmodern Condition: A Report on Knowledge* (Manchester: Manchester University Press, 1981), p. 45. Also Terry Eagleton, 'Capitalism, Modernism and Postmodernism', *New Left Review* (1985), repr. in David Lodge (ed.), *Modern Criticism and Theory: A Reader* (London: Longman, 1988), p. 387.
6. Julian Barnes, *A History of the World in 10½ Chapters* (London: Jonathan Cape, 1989; repr. Picador, 1990), pp. 245–6.
7. See Philip M. Taylor, *War and the Media: Propaganda and Persuasion in the Gulf War* (Manchester: Manchester University Press, 1992).
8. George Orwell, 'Looking Back on the Spanish War' (1994), *Collected Essays, Journalism and Letters*, Vol. II, p. 294. Henceforth all page references to Orwell's *Collected Essays* will be given in brackets in the text.
9. See Baudrillard, 'Simulacra and Simulations', in his *Selected Writings*, pp. 166–84. Also Hayden White, *Metahistory: The Historical Imagination in Nineteenth-Century Europe* (Baltimore and London: Johns Hopkins University Press, 1973), pp. 39–40.
10. See Fredric Jameson, *Postmodernism, or, The Cultural Logic of Late Capitalism* (London and New York: Verso, 1991), especially Chapter 1.

241

11.   See Chapter 6, 'Forms', of Raymond Williams, *Culture* (Glasgow: Fontana, 1981), pp. 148–80.

12.   Jameson, *Postmodernism*, p. 6.

13.   Jameson, ibid., p. 18. Also Guy Debord, *The Society of the Spectacle* trans. from the French (Detroit: Black and Red, 1983), section 34.

14.   See, respectively, Walter Benjamin, 'The Work of Art in the Age of Mechanical Reproduction' (1936), in *Illuminations*, ed. Hannah Arendt (London: Fontana, 1973), pp. 219–53; Orwell, *Collected Essays*, Vol. IV, pp. 312–13; Stephen Spender, 'Guernica', *New Statesman* (15 October 1938), p. 568.

15.   F. T. Marinetti, in Umbro Apollonio (ed.), *Futurist Manifestos* (London: Thames and Hudson, 1973), pp. 96–7.

16.   Benjamin, *Illuminations*, p. 252.

17.   Benjamin, ibid., p. 234. Also *Brecht on Theatre* ed. and trans. John Willett (London: Eyre Methuen, 1978), p. 135.

18.   Benjamin, *Illuminations*, p. 253, note. Donald Albrecht, by tracing the use of the new architecture on screen in the twenties and thirties, shows the alternative method by which Western commercial cinema absorbed Modernist aesthetics, to dilute their philosophical complexity and condition a conservative 'mass' response. In its most positive projections, Modernist design tended to be used for superficial optimism, the faintest visual echo of the Utopian social agenda of movements like the Bauhaus. When featured in the form of 'Art Deco', Modernism was transformed into a chic 'streamlined' symbol of wealth and privilege, as in many Hollywood musicals. On the negative side, it was associated with dehumanising urbanism, as, most famously, in the Futurist city of Fritz Lang's *Metropolis* (1926). See Donald Albrecht, *Designing Dreams* (London: Thames and Hudson, 1988).

19.   Jameson's phrase in *Postmodernism*, p. 25.

20.   Cecil Day Lewis, *Revolution in Writing* (London: Leonard and Virginia Woolf, 1935), p. 9.

21.   Valentine Cunningham, *British Writers of the Thirties* (Oxford: Oxford University Press, 1988), p. 279.

22.   Stephen Spender, 'Poetry and Revolution' in Michael Roberts (ed.), *New Country: Prose and Poetry by the Authors of* New Signatures (London: Leonard and Virginia Woolf/Hogarth, 1933), pp. 62–71, especially p. 64. (Also repr. in Spender's *The Thirties and After: Poetry, Politics, People (1933–75)* (Macmillan, 1978), pp. 48–53, p. 48.)

23.   Jameson, *Postmodernism*, p. 47.

24.   Ibid., pp. 37–8. Cf. Eagleton, 'The Marxist Sublime' in his *The Ideology of the Aesthetic* (Oxford: Blackwell, 1990) and Norris, *Uncritical Theory*, Chapter 4.

25.   Christopher Isherwood, *Lions and Shadows: An Education in the Twenties* (1938: repr. London: Methuen, 1979), pp. 121–2.

26.   Jorge Luis Borges, *A Personal Anthology*, ed. and with a foreword by Anthony Kerrigan (New York: Grove Press, 1967), pp. 138–54, especially p. 147. The Aleph becomes a device for mapping the Postmodern universe of computer data or 'cyberspace' in William Gibson's novel

Mona Lisa Overdrive (London: Gollancz, 1986) and for the new cartographics in Edward W. Soja, *Postmodern Geographies: The Reassertion of Space in Critical and Social Theory* (London: Verso, 1989), Preface and Chapters 8 and 9.

27. See *Kino-Eye: The Writings of Dziga Vertov*, ed. Annette Michelson, trans. Kevin O'Brien (Berkeley and Los Angeles: University of California Press, 1984), pp. 50 and 66.

28. *The English Auden: Poems, Essays and Dramatic Writings 1927–1939*, ed. Edward Mendelson (London: Faber, 1977), p. 46. Henceforth all page references to *English Auden* will be given in brackets in the text.

29. See 'Francois Mauriac' (1945), Graham Greene, *Collected Essays* (London: Bodley Head, 1969), pp. 115–21. Also 'The Explorers' (1952), p. 316.

30. *Selected Literary Criticism of Louis MacNeice*, ed. Alan Heuser (Oxford: Clarendon, 1987), p. 2. Also 'The Poet in England Today: A Reassessment' (1940), p. 114.

31. See the opening section of 'Memorial for the City' for Auden's postwar recantation in his *Collected Poems*, ed. Edward Mendelson (London: Faber, 1976), p. 450.

32. See Cunningham, *British Writers*, pp. 78–9. 'In the Cage' is in Vol. X of *The Complete Henry James* (London: Rupert Hart Davis, 1964), pp. 15–138. It is also significant that the discarded title for *The Waste Land*'s 'A Game of Chess' section was taken from James's story and cf. MacNeice's reference to Auden's 'poem-telegrams' in a 1931 review (*Selected Literary Criticism*, p. 1).

33. Graham Greene, *It's A Battlefield*, p. 7. Henceforth all page references to *It's A Battlefield* will be given in brackets in the text.

34. Rex Warner, *The Wild Goose Chase* (London: Boris Wood, 1937), pp. 224–5. Henceforth, page references to *The Wild Goose Chase* will be given in brackets in the text.

35. See 'Panopticism' in *A Foucault Reader*, ed. Paul Rabinow (Harmondsworth: Penguin, 1991), pp. 206–13.

36. Cunningham, *British Writers*, p. 10.

37. Jameson, *Postmodernism*, pp. 47–8. Also Benjamin, 'Theses on the Philosophy of History', *Illuminations*, pp. 253–64.

38. Lance Sieveking, *The Stuff of Radio* (London: Cassell, 1934), p. 63.

39. Cecil Day Lewis, *Revolution in Writing*, p. 15.

40. Graham Greene, 'Wings Over Wardour Street', *Spectator* (24 January 1936), repr. in *Mornings in the Dark*, p. 487. (Henceforth all page references to *Mornings in the Dark* will be given in brackets in the text.) Also Day Lewis, *Revolution in Writing*, p. 15.

41. Jameson, *Postmodernism*, p. 48.

42. Foreword to Readers' Union edition of Charles Davy (ed.), *Footnotes to the Film* (London: Lovat Dickson, 1938), pp. v–vi.

43. See F. R. Leavis, *Mass-Civilization and Minority Culture* (Cambridge: Minority Press, 1930).

44. Cunningham, *British Writers*, p. 296.

45. Ortega y Gasset, *The Revolt of the Masses* (1930 Spanish; English trans. London: Allen and Unwin, 1932), p. 59. Also Charles Madge, 'Press,

Radio and Social Consciousness', in Cecil Day Lewis (ed.), *The Mind in Chains: Socialism and the Cultural Revolution* (London: Frederick Muller, 1937), p. 154.

46.   J. B. Priestley, *English Journey* (London: Heinemann, 1934: repr. Harmondsworth: Penguin, 1987), p. 375. Henceforth all page references to *English Journey* will be given in brackets in the text.

47.   Peter Miles and Malcolm Smith, *Cinema, Literature and Society: Elite and Mass Culture in Inter-War Britain* (London: Croom Helm, 1987), p. 82.

48.   Q. D. Leavis, *Fiction and the Reading Public* (1932: repr. Penguin, 1979), p. 78.

49.   Quoted in Bernard Waites *et al.* (eds), *Popular Culture: Past and Present: A Reader* (London: Croom Helm, 1982), p. 163.

50.   See Philip M. Taylor, 'Propaganda in International Politics 1919–1939', in K. R. M. Short (ed.), *Film and Radio Propaganda in World War Two* (London: Croom Helm, 1983), p. 9.

51.   Winifred Holtby, *South Riding* (London: Collins, 1936), p. 18. Henceforth all page references to *South Riding* will be given in brackets in the text.

52.   Claude Cockburn *The Devil's Decade* (London: Sidgwick and Jackson, 1973), p. 103. Also Paddy Scannell and David Cardiff, *A Social History of British Broadcasting*, Vol. I, *1922–1939* (Oxford: Blackwell, 1990–), pp. 298–9.

53.   Stephen Tallents, 'Fleet Street and Portland Place', quoted in Asa Briggs, *A History of Broadcasting in the United Kingdom*, Vol. II, *The Golden Age of Wireless* (London: Oxford University Press, 1965), p. 160.

54.   See Walter Lippmann, *Public Opinion* (London: Allen and Unwin, 1929), pp. 14–19.

55.   W. H. Auden and Christopher Isherwood, *The Ascent of F6* and *On the Frontier* (London: Faber, 1958), p. 153.

56.   *World Within World: The Autobiography of Stephen Spender* (1951: repr. London: Hamish Hamilton, 1964), pp. 190–1. Also *Collected Poems* (London: Faber, 1955), p. 109. Henceforth all page references to *Collected Poems* will be given in brackets in the text.

57.   Cunningham, *British Writers*, p. 281.

1   A Twisted Skein: The Media Background

1.   Taylor, in Short (ed.), *Film and Radio Propaganda*, p. 21.

2.   Keith Middlemas, *Politics in Industrial Society: The Experience of the British System since 1911* (London: Deutsch, 1979), p. 337.

3.   Introduction to Short (ed.), *Film and Radio Propaganda*, p. 3.

4.   Nevile Henderson, *Failure of a Mission* (London: Hodder and Stoughton, 1970), p. 71.

5.   See John Stevenson, *British Society 1914–45* (Harmondsworth: Penguin, 1984), p. 48.

6.   Madge in Cecil Day Lewis (ed.), *The Mind in Chains*, pp. 147–9.

7.   See Introduction to Part I, 'Media and Public Opinion' of James Curran, Anthony Smith and Pauline Wingate (eds), *Impacts and*

Influences: Essays on Media Power in the Twentieth Century (London: Methuen, 1987), p. 7. Gramsci's view of the hegemonic function of the media is elaborated by Stuart Hall in 'Culture, the Media and the "Ideological Effect"', in James Curran *et al.* (eds), *Communication and Society* (London: Edward Arnold/Open University, 1979), pp. 315–48.

8. A. J. Cummings, *The Press and a Changing Civilisation* (London: John Lane/The Bodley Head, 1936), p. 1.
9. Ibid., p. 41.
10. Stephen Spender, *Forward from Liberalism* (London: Gollancz, 1937), p. 125.
11. Curran *et al.* (eds), *Impacts and Influences*, p. 8. Also Calder-Marshall, *The Changing Scene: Essays on Contemporary English Society* (London: Chapman and Hall, 1938), p. 17.
12. Cummings, *The Press*, p. 47.
13. Cummings, ibid., pp. 20 and 26–9. Also Arthur Ponsonby, *Falsehood in Wartime: Containing an Assortment of Lies Circulated Throughout the Nations during the Great War* (London: Allen and Unwin, 1928), pp. 102–13.
14. For details of the ownership and circulation of both Right and Left (based on newspapers' own figures for the summer of 1936), see Jane Soames, *The English Press: Newspapers and News* (London: Lindsay Drummond, 1936), pp. 54–7. Also cf. 'The Era of the Press Barons', in James Curran and Jean Seaton, *Power Without Responsibility: The Press and Broadcasting in Britain*, fourth edn (London: Routledge, 1991), pp. 52–8.
15. See Taylor, in Short (ed.), *Film and Radio Propaganda*, p. 32.
16. Cummings, *The Press*, p. 80.
17. Tom Jeffery and Keith McClelland, 'A World Fit to Live In: The *Daily Mail* and the middle classes 1918–39', in Curran *et al.* (eds), *Impacts and Influences*, pp. 28 and 41.
18. See A. J. P. Taylor, *Beaverbrook* (London: Hamish Hamilton, 1972), pp. 223–4 and cf. D. G. Boyce, 'Crusaders Without Chains: Power and the Press Barons 1896–1951', in Curran *et al.* (eds), *Impacts and Influences*, p. 106. Also Scannell and Cardiff, *A Social History of British Broadcasting*, Vol. I, p. 26.
19. Richard Griffiths, *Fellow Travellers of the Right: British Enthusiasts for Nazi Germany 1933–39* (Oxford: Oxford University Press, 1983), p. 163 and cf. Benny Morris, *The Roots of Appeasement: The British Weekly Press and Nazi Germany during the 1930s* (London: Frank Cass, 1991), pp. 67 and 110. Also George Orwell, *Homage to Catalonia* (London: Secker and Warburg, 1937; repr. Harmondsworth: Penguin, 1989), p. 190.
20. *Sunday Dispatch*, quoted in Noreen Branson and Margot Heinemann *Britain in the Nineteen Thirties* (London: Weidenfeld and Nicholson, 1971: repr. Frogmore: Granada, 1973), p. 307.
21. Cummings, *The Press*, p. 34.
22. Ibid., pp. 77–8.
23. Stevenson, *British Society*, p. 405.

24. Guglielmo Marconi, quoted in J. Hale, *Radio Power: Propaganda and International Broadcasting* (London: Elek, 1975), p. xiii.
25. Taylor in Short (ed.), *Radio and Film Propaganda*, pp. 30–1. See also D. C. Watt, 'The Naure of the European Civil War, 1919–39', in his *Too Serious a Business* (London: Temple Smith, 1975).
26. Cummings, *The Press*, p. 123. Sieveking referred to the BBC militaristically as 'another "Air Force"'. (See *The Stuff of Radio*, note to the illustration facing page 18.)
27. A. J. P. Taylor, *English History 1914–1945* (Oxford: Oxford University Press, 1965: repr. Harmondsworth: Penguin, 1975), p. 385.
28. Scannell and Cardiff, *A Social History of British Broadcasting*, Vol. I, pp. 14–15.
29. Ibid., pp. 3, 361 and 369.
30. John Reith, *Broadcast Over Britain* (London: Hodder and Stoughton, 1924), p. 19. See also Briggs, *A History of Broadcasting*, Vol. I, *The Birth of Broadcasting* (London: Oxford University Press, 1961), p. 235.
31. John Reith, *Into the Wind* (London: Hodder and Stoughton, 1949), p. 136.
32. See Madge, in Day Lewis (ed.), *The Mind in Chains*, pp. 156–9.
33. Quoted in Scannell and Cardiff, *A Social History of British Broadcasting*, Vol. I, p. 33. Also below.
34. Briggs, *A History of Broadcasting*, Vol. I, p. 371.
35. Scannell and Cardiff, *A Social History of British Broadcasting*, Vol. I, p. 39.
36. Ibid., pp. 23–4.
37. John Reith quoted by Nicholas Pronay in 'Rearmament and the British Public: Policy and Propaganda', in Curran *et al.* (eds), *Impacts and Influences*, p. 70.
38. Scannell and Cardiff, *A Social History of British Broadcasting*, Vol. I, p. 56.
39. Scannell and Cardiff, ibid., p. 58. For Reith's response to MacDonald below, see pp. 65–6.
40. Ibid., p. 71.
41. See *A Social History of British Broadcasting*, Vol. I, pp. 81–2, and Pronay on newsreels.
42. Pronay suggests that Reith's failure to cooperate in checking 'pinkish' tendencies may well have been behind his transfer. *Impacts and Influences*, pp. 69–70.
43. Scannell and Cardiff, *A Social History of British Broadcasting*, Vol. I, p. 100.
44. *Britain by Mass-Observation*, arranged and written by Tom Harrisson and Charles Madge (Penguin, 1939; repr. London: Century Hutchinson, 1986), p. 25.
45. Scannell and Cardiff, *A Social History of British Broadcasting*, Vol. I, pp. 101–2.
46. Ibid., p. 129.
47. John Reith, *Into the Wind* (London: Hodder and Stoughton, 1949), p. 101.

48. For Mikhail Bakhtin's concept of 'monoglot' or 'unitary' language and its striving to maintain hegemony over other dialects, see 'Discourse in the Novel' in his *The Dialogic Imagination: Four Essays*, ed. Michael Holquist (Austin: University of Texas Press, 1981), p. 271.

49. R. W. Postgate, *The Listener*, Vol. III, No. 57 (12 February 1930), p. 284.

50. Ian Rodger, *Radio Drama* (London: Macmillan, 1982), p. 40.

51. Scannell and Cardiff, 'Broadcasting and National Unity' in Curran *et al.* (eds), *Impacts and Influences*, pp. 164–5.

52. Scannell and Cardiff, ibid., p. 169.

53. Scannell and Cardiff, *A Social History of British Broadcasting*, Vol. I, pp. 245 and 250.

54. Rodger, *Radio Drama*, p. 41.

55. Scannell and Cardiff, *A Social History of British Broadcasting*, Vol. I, p. 255.

56. R. S. Lambert, *The Listener*, Vol. III, No. 53 (15 January 1930), p. 100.

57. Cardiff and Scannell, *A Social History of British Broadcasting*, Vol. I, p. 380.

58. Ibid., p. 334.

59. Asa Briggs, *The History of Broadcasting in the United Kingdom*, Vol. II, *The Golden Age of Wireless* (London: Oxford University Press, 1965), pp. 35 and 54. Cf. alternatively, Scannell and Cardiff's table of programming costs and hours for London's programming in 1934 and 1937 (*A Social History of British Broadcasting*, p. 240).

60. Val Gielgud, *British Radio Drama 1922–1956: A Survey* (London: Harrap, 1957), p. 36.

61. Rodger, *Radio Drama*, pp. 34–5 and 52.

62. Rayner Heppenstall, *The Intellectual Part* (London: Barrie and Rockliff, 1963), p. 35. Also below, p. 37.

63. Gielgud, *British Radio Drama*, p. 31.

64. The 'script' of Sieveking's *Kaleidoscope II* (1929) is partly reproduced in Appendix A, 'Extracts from Plays too purely Radio to be printed for reading', of his *Stuff of Radio*, pp. 383–8. Appendix B describes how the Dramatic Control panel was 'played' (pp. 397–404). See also below Chapter 4.

65. Gielgud, *British Radio Drama*, p. 163.

66. Briggs, *A History of Broadcasting*, Vol. II, p. 161.

67. See Sieveking, *Stuff of Radio*, p. 51.

68. Scannell and Cardiff, *A Social History of British Broadcasting*, Vol. I, p. 134.

69. See Baudrillard, *Selected Writings*, p. 145.

70. *The Listener*, Vol. XVII, No. 461 (11 November 1937), p. 1035. Presumably the BBC did not intend the public's participation to be quite as active as to interrupt the broadcasting of the 'two minutes silence' as a protestor did that year, puncturing the illusion of national consensus on the 'motives which led to this country joining in the Great War'. (See 'Two Minute Story', in *Britain by Mass-Observation*, arranged and written by Tom Harrisson and Charles Madge (1939: repr. London: Cresset, 1986), p. 199.

71. Sieveking, *Stuff of Radio*, p. 63.

72. For audience sizes, see Paul Swann, *The British Documentary Film Movement, 1926–1946* (Cambridge: Cambridge University Press, 1989), especially pp. 70–3.

73. See Paul Rotha, *Documentary Film* (London: Faber, 1935; third edn, 1952), pp. 52–7. Cf. Jeffrey Richards, *The Age of the Dream Palace: Cinema and Society in Britain 1930–1939* (London: Routledge, 1984; pbk 1989), pp. 11–12.

74. Taylor, *English History*, p. 392.

75. See Benjamin, *Illuminations*, p. 234 and Miles and Smith, *Cinema, Literature and Society*, p. 181. Also Richards, *Dream Palace*, p. 34, for details of 'Money behind the Screen'.

76. Alexander Korda on 'British Films: To-Day and To-morrow', in Davy (ed.), *Footnotes to the Film*, p. 164.

77. Korda in ibid., p. 163. Also p. 168.

78. Charles Davy, 'Conclusion: Are Films Worth While?', in Davy (ed.), *Footnotes to the Film*, pp. 279–80.

79. Richards, *Dream Palace*, p. 35.

80. Richards, ibid., p. 136.

81. Ibid., p. 44.

82. Ibid., p. 89 and cf. Anthony Aldgate, 'Ideological Consensus in British Feature Films 1935–47', in K. R. M. Short (ed.), *Feature Films as History* (London: Croom Helm, 1981), pp. 94–112.

83. Clive Coultass, *Images for Battle: British Film and the Second World War 1939–1945* (Newark and Toronto: University of Delaware/ Associated University Presses, 1989), p. 13. Also James C. Robertson, *The British Board of Film Censors: Film Censorship in Britain 1896–1950* (London: Croom Helm, 1985).

84. Pronay in Curran *et al.* (eds), *Impacts and Influences*, p. 71. For other examples, see Richards *Dream Palace*, pp. 101–7 and Robertson, *British Board of Film Censors*.

85. BBFC, 'Censorship in Great Britain', quoted by Hardy in Davy (ed.), *Footnotes to the Film*, p. 267. Hardy's own comment is on pp. 268–9.

86. Richards, *Dream Palace*, pp. 113–14.

87. *Sunday Pictorial* (1 June 1941). The BBFC 1936 report on *Love on the Dole* is quoted by Richards, *Dream Palace*, pp. 119–20. As Greenwood's parenthetical translations of Salford dialect suggest, his novel was primarily aimed at the 'opinion-forming' Southern middle-class. Similarly, Ronald Gow's 1934 stage adaptation did not run into censorship problems, even though the Lord Chamberlain's jurisdiction could be equally as severe as the BBFC's, because theatregoing was also more of a 'bourgeois' habit than film-going and, therefore, safer.

88. Forsyth Hardy, 'Censorship and Film Societies', in Davy (ed.), *Footnotes to the Film*, p. 265.

89. Richards, *Dream Palace*, p. 121.

90. Ibid., p. 125.

91. Ibid., p. 133.

92. D. A. Spencer and H. D. Waley, *The Cinema Today* (London: Oxford University Press, 1940), p. 153.

93. Richards, *Dream Palace*, p. 156. Also below, p. 158.
94. Michael Korda, *Charmed Lives* (London: Allen Lane, 1980), p. 123.
95. Richards, *Dream Palace*, p. 289.
96. Russell Ferguson, 'Armaments Rings, Assassins and Political Madmen: Our Major National Problems as Seen in British Films', *World Film News*, Vol. II, No. 5 (August 1937), p. 4. But cf. the Payne Trust's findings on the socio-economically disproportional image of the US projected by Hollywood in the 1930s, as discussed by John Grierson, *Grierson on Documentary*, ed. Forsyth Hardy (London: Faber, 1946; repr. 1966), p. 174.
97. Pronay, 'Rearmament and the British Public: Policy and Propaganda', in Curran *et al.* (eds), *Impacts and Influences*, pp. 53–96.
98. Pronay, in ibid., pp. 73–4.
99. Ibid., pp. 76–7. Also below, p. 83.
100. See Leslie Halliwell, *The Filmgoer's Book of Quotes* (London: Hart-Davis MacGibbon, 1973), p. 86. For further commentary on *Wedding Rehearsal*, see Richards, *Dream Palace*, p. 313.
101. Arthur Marwick, *Class, Image and Reality in Britain, France and the USA since 1930* (London: Collins, 1980), p. 22.
102. Jeffrey Richards and Anthony Aldgate, *Best of British: Cinema and Society 1930–1970* (Oxford: Blackwell, 1983), p. 4.

2 Refractions: The Media as Subject Matter

1. Aldous Huxley, 'Writers and Readers', *The Olive Tree and Other Essays* (London: Chatto and Windus, 1936), p. 8.
2. Madge, in Day Lewis (ed.), *Mind in Chains*, p. 150.
3. Madge, in ibid., pp. 161–3.
4. Ibid., pp. 154–5.
5. Cummings, *The Press*, p. 35. Madge also quotes p. 36 of Cummings's book in his *Mind in Chains* essay (p. 152), which seems to have been considerably influenced by Cummings's ideas, as well as Norman Angell's *The Press and the Organization of Society* (Cambridge: Cambridge University Press: 1922; repr. 1933). Angell, the most outspoken critic of the tabloid press in this period, had actually worked for Northcliffe's *Daily Mail* for eight years.
6. Calder-Marshall, *The Changing Scene*, pp. 139–40. And see Spender in Introduction. Also below, *The Changing Scene*, pp. 122 and 125.
7. Louis MacNeice, *Collected Poems*, ed. E. R. Dodds (London: Faber, 1966), p. 140. Henceforth all references to MacNeice, *Collected Poems* will be given in brackets in the text.
8. Auden modelled *The Courier* on *The Helensburgh and Gareloch Times*, a local Scottish paper from his time as a minor public schoolmaster while composing *The Orators*. (See Stan Smith, 'Remembering Bryden's Bill: Modernism from Eliot to Auden', *Critical Survey*, Vol. VI, No. 3 (1994).
9. *The Complete Poems of Cecil Day Lewis* (London: Sinclair Stevenson,

1992), pp. 101–2. Henceforth, all page references to *The Complete Poems of Cecil Day Lewis* will be given in brackets in the text.

10. W. H. Auden and Christopher Isherwood, *The Ascent of F6 and On the Frontier* (London: Faber, 1958; repr. 1968), pp. 20–2. Henceforth, all page references to *F6* will be given in brackets in the text.

11. F. L. Stevens, *On Going to Press* (London: Methuen 1930), p. 63.

12. Hillel Bernstein, *Choose a Bright Morning* (London: Gollancz, 1936), pp. 70–1. Henceforth, all page references to *Choose a Bright Morning* will be given in brackets in the text.

13. Stephen Spender, *Vienna* (London: Faber, 1934), p. 13. Also John Lehmann, *Evil Was Abroad* (London: Cresset, 1937), pp. 75–6. Henceforth all page references to *Evil Was Abroad* will be given in brackets in the text.

14. Spender, *World Within World*, p. 130.

15. Day Lewis, *Revolution in Writing*, p. 40.

16. Christopher Isherwood, *Mister Norris Changes Trains* (London: Hogarth, 1935; repr. London: Granada, 1978), p. 90. Henceforth, all page references to *Mister Norris* will be given in brackets in the text.

17. See Christopher Caudwell writing as 'Christopher St John Sprigge', *Fatality in Fleet Street* (London: Eldon Press, 1933).

18. W. H. Auden and Christopher Isherwood, *On the Frontier*, p. 157 (see note 10 above). Henceforth, all references to *On the Frontier* will be given in brackets in the text.

19. Samuel Hynes, *The Auden Generation: Literature and Politics in England in the Nineteen Thirties* (London: Faber, 1976; pbk 1979), p. 237.

20. W. H. Auden and Christopher Isherwood, *The Dog Beneath the Skin or Where is Francis?* (London: Faber, 1935; repr. 1968), pp. 40 and 41. Henceforth, all page references to *Dog Beneath the Skin* will be given in brackets in the text.

21. W. H. Auden and Christopher Isherwood *Journey to a War* (London: Faber, 1939; repr. 1986), p. 20. Henceforth, all page references to *Journey to a War* will be given in brackets in the text.

22. Anthony Powell, *Venusberg* (London: Duckworth, 1932; repr. Penguin pbk, 1961), p. 9.

23. Graham Greene, *England Made Me* (London: Heinemann, 1935; Pan pbk, 1954), p. 63. Henceforth, all page references to *England Made Me* will be given in brackets in the text.

24. Lewis Grassic Gibbon, *Grey Granite* (1934; repr. in *A Scots Quair* (London: Pan pbk 1982), p. 63. Also pp. 145 and 201. Henceforth, all page references to *Grey Granite* will be given in brackets in the text.

25. Walter Brierley, *Sandwichman* (London: Methuen, 1937; repr. Merlin, 1990), p. 254. Henceforth, all page references to *Sandwichman* will be given in brackets in the text.

26. See Calder-Marshall, *The Changing Scene*, p. 124.

27. Harold Heslop, *Last Cage Down* (London: Wishart, 1935; repr. Lawrence and Wishart, 1984), p. 235. Henceforth, all page references to *Last Cage Down* will be given in brackets in the text.

28. *Jew Boy* (London: Jonathan Cape, 1935; repr. Lawrence and Wishart, 1986), p. 241. Henceforth, all page references to *Jew Boy* will be given in brackets in the text.

29. John Cornford, *Collected Writings*, ed. Jonathan Galassi (Manchester: Carcanet, 1986), p. 26.

30. Quoted by Jeffrey and Keith McClelland in 'A World Fit to Live In: *The Daily Mail* and the Middle Classes 1918–39', in Curran *et al.* (eds), *Impacts and Influences*, p. 49.

31. George Orwell, *Homage to Catalonia* (London: Secker and Warburg, 1938; repr. Harmondsworth: Penguin, 1989), p. 64.

32. Calder-Marshall, *The Changing Scene*, p. 97, footnote.

33. See the numerous sections on public reaction to this in *May the Twelfth: Mass-Observation Day Surveys 1937* by Two Hundred Observers, ed. Humphrey Jennings, Charles Madge *et al.* (London: Faber, 1937; pbk 1987).

34. Calder-Marshall, *The Changing Scene*, pp. 100–1.

35. Welles had already played a similar commentator in Archibald MacLeish's 'metaradio' drama, *The Fall of the City* (1937). He also used the same device for adapting Shakespeare's *Julius Caesar* for transmission, with veteran news broadcaster, H. V. Kaltenborn.

36. Calder-Marshall, *The Changing Scene*, pp. 102, 29 and 32, respectively.

37. See Chapter 1 and this chapter, pp. 27 and 61 above.

38. See Briggs, *A History of Broadcasting*, II, p. 154. Also Scannell and Cardiff, *A Social History of British Broadcasting*, I, p. 118.

39. Louis MacNeice, *Out of the Picture* (London: Faber, 1937), p. 46. Henceforth, all page references to *Out of the Picture* will be given in brackets in the text.

40. Rex Warner, *The Wild Goose Chase* (London: Boriswood, 1937), pp. 18 and 202–3. Henceforth, all page references to *Wild Goose Chase* will be given in brackets in the text.

41. Calder-Marshall, *Changing Scene*, p. 100.

42. Katherine Burdekin, *Swastika Night* (London: Gollancz, 1937; repr. Lawrence and Wishart, 1985), p. 16. Henceforth, all page references to *Swastika Night* will be given in brackets in the text.

43. Storm Jameson, 'The Novel in Contemporary Life' (1937), in her *Civil Journey* (London: Cassell, 1939), p. 57.

44. Christopher Isherwood, *Exhumations: Stories, Articles, Verses* (London: Methuen, 1966; pbk 1984), pp. 25–7, especially 27.

45. See this chapter, 'The Cinema'.

46. James Barke, *Major Operation* (London: Collins, 1936), p. 375. Henceforth, all page references to *Major Operation* will be given in brackets in the text.

47. See Robert Skelton (ed.), *Poetry of the Thirties* (Harmondsworth: Penguin, 1964).

48. Graham Greene, 'Twenty-four Hours in Metroland' (1938), in his *Reflections*, ed. Judith Adamson (London: Reinhardt, 1990; Harmondsworth: Penguin, 1991), pp. 73–4. Henceforth, all page references to *Reflections* will be given in brackets in the text.

49. Louis MacNeice, *I Crossed the Minch* (London: Longman, 1938), p. 40.
50. *A Social History of British Broadcasting*, Vol. I, p. 206.
51. Calder-Marshall, *Changing Scene*, p. 85.
52. Henry Green, *Living* (London: Hogarth, 1929), p. 118. Henceforth, all page references to *Living* will be given in brackets in the text.
53. Walter Greenwood, *His Worship the Mayor: or 'It's Only Human Nature After All'* (London: Jonathan Cape, 1934), p. 127. Henceforth, all page references to *His Worship the Mayor* will be given in brackets in the text. Scannell and Cardiff discuss the gender-specific habits of early listeners in *A Social History of British Broadcasting*, Vol. I, pp. 357–8.
54. James Hanley, *Grey Children: A Study in Humbug and Misery* (London: Methuen, 1937), p. 226.
55. Cunningham, *British Writers of the Thirties*, p. 317.
56. See John Sommerfield, *May Day* (London: Lawrence and Wishart, 1936), pp. 50–1. Henceforth, all page references to *May Day* will be given in brackets in the text. Also Chapter 1, Note 70 above, and Madge, in Day Lewis (ed.), *Mind in Chains*, pp. 156–9.
57. Briggs, *History of Broadcasting*, II, p. 134, who also quotes Gardiner above.
58. Rex Warner, *The Professor* (London: Boriswood, 1938; repr. Lawrence and Wishart, 1986), pp. 184 and 197. Henceforth, all page references to *The Professor* will be given in brackets in the text.
59. William L. Shirer, *Berlin Diary: The Journal of a Foreign Correspondent 1934–1941* (London: Hamish Hamilton, 1941), p. 94.
60. Robinson, *Broadcasting and a Changing Civilisation*, pp. 55–6. T. H. Pear also devoted several chapters of his *Voice and Personality* (London: Chapman and Hall, 1932) to radio 'presence'.
61. See below, Chapter 4.
62. Cunningham, *British Writers of the Thirties*, p. 290.
63. Aldous Huxley, *Brave New World* (1932; repr. London: Chatto, 1960), pp. 136–7.
64. Winifred Holtby, *Mandoa, Mandoa!* (London: Collins, 1933; repr. Virago, 1982), p. 21. Henceforth, all page references to *Mandoa, Mandoa!* will be given in brackets in the text.
65. Huxley, 'Writers and Readers', in *The Olive Tree*, pp. 39–40.
66. Christopher Cauldwell, *Illusion and Reality* (London: Macmillan, 1937 repr. Berlin: Seven Seas Verlag, 1977), p. 122.
67. Dylan Thomas, *Collected Poems 1934–52* (London: Dent, pbk 1971), pp. 13–14. Henceforth, all page references to *Collected Poems* will be given in brackets in the text.
68. Calder-Marshall, 'The Cinema' in Day Lewis (ed.), *Mind in Chains*, pp. 59 and 65. Also Calder-Marshall, *The Changing Scene*, p. 79.
69. Calder-Marshall, in Day Lewis (ed.), *Mind in Chains*, p. 71.
70. Victor Small, *Left Review* (April 1938), p. 935.
71. Grierson quoted by Judith Adamson in 'Graham Greene as Film Critic', *Sight and Sound* (Spring 1972), p. 104.

72. V. I. Pudovkin's essays were also collected at the time in his *Film Technique*, trans. Ivor Montagu (London: Galloway, 1929; expanded edition, Newnes, 1933).

73. Greene, *Ways of Escape* (London: Bodley Head, 1980; Harmondsworth: Penguin, 1981), p. 47. 1930s Hollywood pretensions to historical authenticity were regularly parodied by the *Daily Express*'s Beachcomber in his caricature director 'Sol Hogwasch'.

74. 'Subjects and Stories' first appeared in Davy (ed.), *Footnotes to the Film*.

75. Greene's sense of irony was vindicated by the fact that some features with serious social concern about British issues, like *The Citadel*, had to be made by Hollywood (see Chapter 4).

76. Graham Greene, *The Confidential Agent* (London: Heinemann, 1939; repr. Harmondsworth: Penguin, 1971), p. 149. Henceforth, all page references to *Confidential Agent* will be given in brackets in the text.

77. Greene's *Wee Willie Winkie* review was in *Night and Day* (28 October 1937). His own account of the trial is in *Ways of Escape*, pp. 48–50.

78. Greene described the same Pavlovian response, jaundiced by Pinkie's sexual disgust, in *Brighton Rock* (London: Heinemann, 1938; repr. Harmondsworth: Penguin, 1970), p. 179.

79. Anthony Powell, *Agents and Patients* (London: Duckworth, 1936; repr. Harmondsworth: Penguin, 1962), p. 110. Henceforth, all page references to *Agents and Patients* will be given in brackets in the text.

80. Miles and Smith, *Cinema, Literature and Society*, p. 171.

81. Christopher Isherwood, *Goodbye to Berlin* (London: Hogarth, 1939; repr. Triad/Granada pbk 1977), pp. 50, 72 and 75. Henceforth, all page references to *Goodbye to Berlin* will be given in brackets in the text.

82. Elizabeth Bowen in Davy (ed.), *Footnotes to the Film*, p. 213.

83. Bowen in ibid., p. 212.

84. Quoted in John Danvers Williams, 'The Menacing Movie Machine', *New Theatre* (September 1939), p. 11.

85. Louis MacNeice, *Zoo* (London: Michael Joseph, 1938), pp. 29 and 40. Henceforth, all page references to *Zoo* will be given in brackets in the text.

86. Jean Rhys, *Good Morning Midnight* (London: Constable, 1939; repr. Deutsch, 1967), p. 176. Also *Voyage in the Dark* (London: Constable, 1934; repr. Harmondsworth: Penguin, 1969), pp. 92–3.

87. Louis MacNeice, *The Strings Are False: An Unfinished Autobiography* (London: Faber, 1965), p. 138.

88. Louis MacNeice, 'In Defence of Vulgarity', *Selected Prose*, ed. Alan Heuser (Oxford: Clarendon, 1990), pp. 43 and 45.

89. W. H. Auden and Louis MacNeice, *Letters from Iceland* (London: Faber, 1938), p. 247. Henceforth, all page references to *Letters from Iceland* will be given in brackets in the text.

90. Bowen in Davy (ed.), *Footnotes to the Film*, pp. 205–19, pp. 205 and 207.

91. Bowen in ibid., pp. 208–9.

92. Sidney L. Bernstein 'Walk Up! Walk Up! – *Please'*, in Davy (ed.), *Footnotes to the Film*, pp. 224–5.
93. George Orwell, *Keep the Aspidistra Flying* (London: Gollancz, 1936; repr. Harmondsworth: Penguin, 1963), p. 80.
94. E. W. Bakke, *The Unemployed Man: A Social Study* (London: Nisbet, 1933), p. 182.
95. George Orwell, *The Road to Wigan Pier* (London: Gollancz, 1937; repr. Harmondsworth, Penguin, 1989), pp. 74 and 81–2. Henceforth, all page references to *Wigan Pier* will be given in brackets in the text.
96. See Miles and Smith, *Cinema, Literature and Society*, pp. 171–3.
97. Bowen, in Davy (ed.), *Footnotes to the Film*, pp. 216–17.
98. Ewan MacColl, Introduction to Howard Goorney and Ewan MacColl (eds), *Agit-Prop to Theatre Workshop: Political Playscripts 1930–50* (Manchester: Manchester University Press, 1986), p. xlix. Henceforth, all page references to *Agit-Prop to Theatre Workshop* will be given in brackets in the text.
99. In March 1938, the 'Bolton Questionnaire' asked over 500 ordinary 'Worktown' cinemagoers, among other things, whether they saw 'people like themselves' on the screen. The overwhelming majority neither expected nor wanted to. (See Jeffrey Richards and Dorothy Sheridan (eds), *Mass-Observation at the Movies* (London: Routledge and Kegan Paul, 1987), pp. 92–4).
100. Oddvar Holmesland, *A Living Vision: A Critical Introduction to Henry Green's Novels* (London: Macmillan, 1986) is the most extensive study of the cinematic influence in his writing.
101. Tennessee Williams, *The Glass Menagerie*, Scene 6 (New York: Random House, 1945; repr. 1949), p. 76.
102. Holtby's review was in *Time and Tide* (11 March 1933; repr. in Paul Berry and Alan Bishop (eds), *Testament of a Generation: The Journalism of Vera Brittain and Winifred Holtby* (London: Virago, 1985), pp. 285–9). She also mentioned *Cavalcade* in *Mandoa, Mandoa!*, p. 82. Victor Small similarly thought *Cavalcade* 'far more effective nationalist propaganda than anything emanating from Conservative head office' (see *Left Review*, April 1938, p. 935).
103. Miles and Smith, *Cinema, Literature and Society*, pp. 29–30. Also cf. Priestley's use of Fields's reputation to heroicise Dunkirk, discussed in Chapter 4 below.
104. See Richards, *Dream Palace*, pp. 169–90.
105. See Studs Terkel, *Hard Times: An Oral History of the Great Depression* (New York: Random House, 1970; repr. 1986), pp. 19–21. Also Robert Graves and Alan Hodge, *The Long Weekend: A Social History of Great Britain 1919–1939* (London: Faber, 1940), p. 298.
106. Richards, *Dream Palace*, p. 171.
107. Ibid., p. 177. But cf. Priestley's unease after *Look Up and Laugh* (1935) in Chapter 4, below.
108. Bowen in Davy (ed.), *Footnotes to the Film*, p. 209.
109. See Richards, *Dream Palace*, pp. 64–6, and Peter Stead, 'Hollywood's Message for the World: the British Response in the Nineteen

Thirties', *Historical Journal of Film, Radio and Television*, I, No. 1 (1981), pp. 19–32. Also Bert Hogenkamp, *Deadly Parallels: Film and the Left in Britain 1929–1939* (London: Lawrence and Wishart, 1986) and Stephen G. Jones, *The British Labour Movement and Film 1918–1939* (London: Routledge, 1986).

110. See, for example, Priestley's view in *World Film News*, Vol. I, No. 8 (November 1936), p. 3.

111. See Richards, *Dream Palace*, pp. 191–206, and cf. Orwell in *Wigan Pier*, p. 163: 'It is doubtful whether anything describable as proletarian literature now exists – even the *Daily Worker* is written in standard South English – but a good music-hall comedian comes nearer to producing it than any Socialist writer.'

112. Angela Carter, 'Titillation', *Nothing Sacred: Selected Writings* (London: Virago, 1982), p. 151.

113. See Richards, pp. 296–7 and cf. Greenwood's script for Formby's *No Limit*, discussed in Chapter 4, below.

114. The comparable interest of Modernist sects like the Surrealists, especially Salvador Dali, in Mae West as a popular-cinema icon is well known (see for example his sofa designed in the shape of her lips). For a definition of 'dialogics', see Tzvetan Todorov, *Mikhail Bakhtin: The Dialogical Principle*, trans. Wlad Godzich (Manchester: Manchester University Press, 1984), p. 110. Also 'Word, Dialogue and the Novel' in Toril Moi (ed.), *The Kristeva Reader* (Oxford: Basil Blackwell, 1986), p. 37. For a discussion of Modernism and the carnivalesque in 'mass' culture, see R. B. Kershner's *Joyce, Bakhtin and Popular Literature* (Chapel Hill: University of North Carolina Press, 1989).

115. Richards, *Dream Palace*, p. 171.

116. Thom Thomas, *Their Theatre and Ours*, repr. in Raphael Samuel, Ewan MacColl and Stuart Cosgrove (eds), *Theatres of the Left 1880–1935: Workers' Theatre Movements in Britain and America* (London: Routledge and Kegan Paul, 1985), pp. 142–4. Henceforth, all page references to *Theatres of the Left* will be given in brackets in the text.

117. Walter Greenwood, *Love on the Dole* (London: Jonathan Cape, 1933; repr. Harmondsworth: Penguin, 1969), p. 65. Henceforth, all page references to *Love on the Dole* will be given in brackets in the text.

118. Bernard Bergonzi, *Reading the Thirties: Texts and Contexts* (London: Macmillan, 1979), p. 129.

119. Alick West, *One Man in his Time: An Autobiography* (London: Allen and Unwin, 1969), p. 97.

120. Spender, *World Within World*, pp. 132–3. See also Philip French and Ken Wlaschin (eds), *The Faber Book of Movie Verse* (London: Faber, 1994), note, p. 57.

121. Spender's reminiscences of Weimar Sonnenkinder making and watching amateur films of themselves feature in both *World Within World*, p. 111, and his rejected 1929 autobiographical novel, *The Temple* (London: Faber, 1988; repr. pbk 1989), pp. 44–5. 'Joachim Lenz', in the latter, continually visualises his experience through the perspective of a cameraman/director.

122. MacColl, in Goorney and MacColl (eds), *Agitprop to Theatre Workshop*, pp. xv–xvi. Also Bowen in Davy (ed.), *Footnotes to the Film*, p. 211.
123. Tom Wintringham, 'The Immortal Tractor', *Storm: Stories of the Struggle*, Vol. I, No. 1 (February 1933), pp. 17–18.
124. Spender, *World Within World*, p. 132.
125. Day Lewis, in Roberts (ed.), *New Country*, p. 29.
126. Bowen, in Davy (ed.), *Footnotes to the Film*, p. 213.
127. *Grierson on Documentary*, pp. 116–17.
128. Calder-Marshall, in Day Lewis (ed.), *Mind in Chains*, pp. 74–5.
129. Calder-Marshall, *Changing Scene*, pp. 38–9 and 82.
130. See Hogenkamp, *Deadly Parallels*, especially p. 45.
131. George Barker, *Collected Poems* (London: Faber, 1987), p. 58. Henceforth, all references to Barker, *Collected Poems* will be given in brackets in the text.
132. Calder-Marshall, in Day Lewis (ed.), *Mind in Chains*, p. 73.
133. Ibid., pp. 73–4.
134. See David Mellor, 'Brandt's Phantoms', in *Bill Brandt behind the Camera: Photographs 1928–1983* (New York: Aperture, 1985), p. 93. Also Paul Rotha, *Documentary Diary: An Informal History of the British Documentary Film 1928–1939* (London: Secker and Warburg, 1973), pp. 102–4.
135. See *Grierson on Documentary*, pp. 202 and 250.
136. Calder-Marshall, *Changing Scene*, p. 46.
137. Ibid., p. 14.
138. For a contemporary account, see Chetwode Crawley, *From Telegraphy to Television: The Story of Electrical Communications* (London and New York: Frederick Warne, 1931), p. 179.
139. See Bertolt Brecht, *The Life of Galileo*, trans. John Willett (London: Methuen, 1986), Scene 13, p. 98.
140. Stephen Spender, 'Guernica', *New Statesman* (15 October 1938), p. 568.
141. Robert Hughes, *The Shock of the New* (revised and enlarged edn: London: Thames and Hudson, 1991), p. 110.
142. See Karl Radek, 'Contemporary World Literature and the Tasks of Proletarian Art', in A. Zhdanov *et al.*, *Problems of Soviet Literature: Reports and Speeches at the First Soviet Writers's Congress 1934*, ed. H. G. Scott (London: Martin Lawrence, 1935; repr. Lawrence and Wishart, 1977), pp. 73–182, especially 141–4. For the wording of the Soviet Writers' Union statute, see Ronald Hingley, *Russian Writers and Soviet Society 1917–1978* (London: Methuen, 1981), p. 198.
143. Stephen Spender, *Trial of a Judge: A Tragedy in Five Acts* (London: Faber, 1938), pp. 29 and 94–5.
144. Robinson, *Broadcasting and a Changing Civilisation*, pp. 151–2.
145. J. W. Dunne, author of *Experiment with Time* (1927) and *The Serial Universe* (1934), theorised paradoxical time pheneomena like precognition, previsional dreaming, etc. under the influence of Henri Bergson. His ideas prompted Greene in *Ways of Escape*, Chapter 3, to consider if novelists might unconsciously draw symbols from the future as well as the past.

146. 'A Little Place off the Edgware Road', Graham Greene, *Collected Stories* (London: The Bodley Head/William Heinemann, 1972), pp. 412–19, especially pp. 412–13 and 414. The atmosphere and themes of this tale overlap with the 'screen dreams' in Greene's *A World of My Own* (1992). 'Edgware Road' itself was reworked as the unmade 1947 film-script 'All But Empty' (1947).
147. Day Lewis, *Revolution in Writing*, pp. 34 and 43–4.
148. Edgell Rickword, in Day Lewis (ed.), *Mind in Chains*, p. 13.

3 Responses: The Mass-Media as Formal Influences

1. *Britain by Mass-Observation*, p. 10.
2. Davy (ed.), *Footnotes to the Film*, pp. 287–8.
3. See Colin Chambers, *The Story of Unity Theatre* (London: Lawrence and Wishart, 1989), p. 27.
4. Howard Goorney and Ewan MacColl (eds), *Agit-prop to Theatre Workshop: Political Playscripts 1930–50* (Manchester: Manchester University Press, 1986), p. xxvi.
5. Although Goorney and MacColl attribute the *Newsboy* adaption to 'G.' Blumenfeld, that it was actually by the novelist and *Left Review* editor Simon is confirmed by Chambers (see *Unity Theatre*, p. 41).
6. Hodge worked with another taxi-driver, Rob Buckland, to produce the topical satire *Where's That Bomb?* (1936). Its pantomime, allegorical and dream techniques were expanded in *Cannibal Carnival* (1937) and Hodge's satire on newspaper publishing, *Strike Me Red*, performed by Merseyside Left Theatre in 1940. Hodge gave radio talks in the late thirties from the point of view of *The Man in the Street*, comparable to Priestley's *Let Me Tell You* series. Unity got a radio boost when Hodge broadcast a programme on the theatre in 1939 during its run of *Harvest in the North*, about unemployment in the Lancashire mills, by proletarian playwright James Lansdale Hodson. See Herbert Hodge's autobiography *It's Draughty in Front* (London: Michael Joseph, 1938) and Chambers, *Unity Theatre*, pp. 70–4 and 179.
7. Chambers, *Unity Theatre*, pp. 142–3.
8. Maureen Bell *et al.* (eds), *Unity Theatre, Busmen and Living Newspaper from America: One Third of a Nation* (Nottingham: Nottingham Drama Texts, 1984), p. 30. Arthur Arent's contemporary 1938 article 'The Technique of the Living Newspaper' was reprinted in *Theatre Quarterly*, No. 4 (October–December 1971), pp. 57–9.
9. Chambers, *Unity Theatre*, p. 144.
10. See Chambers, ibid., p. 98 for a list of media-connected plays, among others, performed by local groups.
11. See Hogenkamp, *Deadly Parallels*, p. 202.
12. The Lord Chamberlain did not grant a licence for *Crisis* and, consequently, it could not be published. The script is held in the British Theatre Association Library.
13. For a full account of *Babes*, see Chambers *Unity Theatre*, pp. 170–5.
14. Peter Black, *The Biggest Aspidistra in the World: A Personal Celebration of Fifty Years of the BBC* (London: BBC, 1972), p. 37.

15. Introduction to John Drakakis (ed.), *British Radio Drama* (Cambridge: Cambridge University Press, 1981), p. 5.

16. Drakakis in ibid., p. 7. Cf. E. H. Robinson's summary of that 'basic grammar' in contemporary terms in his *Broadcasting and a Changing Civilisation*, pp. 57–8.

17. Rodger, *Radio Drama*, p. 51.

18. Scannell and Cardiff, *A Social History of British Broadcasting*, Vol. I, p. 374.

19. See Christopher Holme, 'The Radio Drama of Louis MacNeice', in Drakakis (ed.), *British Radio Drama*, p. 43. Also Chapter 1, 'The Early Years' of Barbara Coulton, *Louis MacNeice in the BBC* (London: Faber, 1980). The broad appeal and journalistic acuteness of MacNeice's features were no doubt also assisted by his regular writing for *Picture Post* during the war.

20. R. D. Smith, 'Castle on the Air', in Terence Brown and Alec Reid (eds), *Time Was Away: The World of Louis MacNeice* (Dublin: Dolmen Press, 1974), p. 88. Also Walter Allen, introduction to MacNeice's *Modern Poetry* (1938: repr. Oxford: Clarendon Press, 1966), p. xiv.

21. MacNeice, 'The Play and the Audience' (1938) in his *Selected Literary Criticism*, pp. 87 and 91–2.

22. MacNeice, *Modern Poetry*, p. 196.

23. See F. D. Klingender, 'Content and Form in Art' in Herbert Read, F. D. Klingender, Eric Gill, A. L. Lloyd, Alick West, *5 on Revolutionary Art* (London: Wishart, 1935), pp. 37–8.

24. MacNeice, *The Strings are False*, p. 177.

25. MacNeice, *Selected Prose*, pp. 86 and 166.

26. MacNeice, *Selected Literary Criticism*, p. 153.

27. See W. H. Auden, *Complete Poems*, ed. Edward Mendelson (London: Faber, 1976), p. 630.

28. George Orwell, *Coming Up for Air* (London: Gollancz, 1939: Harmondsworth: Penguin, 1962), pp. 223–4.

29. MacNeice, *Selected Literary Criticism*, pp. 161–2.

30. Evelyn Waugh, 'Felix Culpa' (1948), *The Essays, Articles and Reviews of Evelyn Waugh*, ed. Donat Gallagher (London: Methuen, 1983), p. 362. Waugh's essay backs up the impression that Greene's camera was 'God-held'.

31. Grahame Smith, *The Achievement of Graham Greene* (Brighton: Harvester, 1986), pp. 211–12. See also Tony Pinkney's Introduction to Raymond Williams, *The Politics of Modernism: Against the New Conformists* (London: Verso, 1989), p. 10. The cinematic qualities of Joyce's writing were evident as early as *A Portrait of the Artist as a Young Man* (1916). Neil Sinyard calls its opening chapters' 'free movement between time and space ... one of the finest examples of montage in fiction'. See his *Filming Literature: The art of screen adaptation* (London: Croom Helm, 1986), p. viii.

32. 'Conclusion: Are Films Worth While?', to Davy (ed.), *Footnotes to the Film*, pp. 285–6. Also Virginia Woolf, *The Years* (London: Hogarth, 1937; repr. 1990), p. 76. Davy proceeds to translate the whole quoted passage into sequences of screen images (see *Footnotes*, pp. 286–7).

33. *Daily Worker* (9 May 1936).
34. See Zhdanov *et al.*, *Problems of Soviet Literature*, p. 153.
35. Ezra Pound, *The Dial* (January 1922).
36. Alick West, *Crisis and Criticism* (London: Lawrence and Wishart, 1937), pp. 163–4.
37. Calder-Marshall, *Changing Scene*, p. 72.
38. 'Handling the Camera', in Davy (ed.), *Footnotes to the Film*, p. 39. Also Allardyce Nicoll, *Film and Theatre* (London: Harrap, 1936), pp. 187–9.
39. This intertextuality was considered to work both ways, as the rendering of contemporary film theory in linguistic terms by others as well as Spottiswoode shows. For example: 'you can regard the standard long-shot of an object as the noun. Pans, changes of angle and distance, trick shots or what you will, these are the verbs, adjectives, adverbs, prepositions and so on which put altogether make up a coherent sentence' (Wright, in Davy (ed.), *Footnotes to the Film*, p. 51).
40. See Raymond Spottiswoode, *A Grammar of the Film: An Analysis of Film Technique* (London: Faber, 1935), p. 51. Spottiswoode also lists a whole series of sub-divisions of montage: primary, simultaneous, rhythmical, secondary, implicational and ideological.
41. Philip Henderson, *Events in the Early Life of Anthony Price* (London: Boriswood, 1935), pp. 149–51.
42. See *Left Review*, Vol. II, No. 8 (May 1936), p. 403.
43. For further discussion of cinematic documentary fiction in the 1930s, see, among others, Stuart Laing, 'Presenting "Things As They Are": John Sommerfield's *May Day* and Mass-Observation' in Frank Gloversmith (ed.), *Class, Culture and Social Change: A New View of the 1930s* (Brighton: Harvester, 1980), pp. 142–60. Also Andy Croft, 'Returned Volunteer: The Novels of John Sommerfield', *London Magazine* (April/May 1983), pp. 61–70, and his *Red Letter Days: British Fiction in the 1930s* (London: Lawrence and Wishart, 1990), pp. 254–65.
44. Croft, *London Magazine* (April/May 1983), pp. 64–5.
45. Croft, *Red Letter Days*, pp. 259–60.
46. Laing in Gloversmith (ed.), *Class, Culture and Social Change*, p. 149.
47. Ibid.
48. Storm Jameson's definition of the basic function of documentary film and writing in 'Documents', *Fact*, No. 4 (July 1937), pp. 17–18.
49. Helga Geyer-Ryan's formulation of the artist's dilemma after Modernism. See her 'Counterfactual Artefacts: Walter Benjamin's Philosophy of History' in Edward Timms and Peter Collier (eds), *Visions and Blueprints: Avant-Garde Culture and Radical Politics in Early Twentieth-Century Europe* (Manchester: Manchester University Press, 1988), p. 66.
50. An overlapping sequence is also discussed by Croft in *London Magazine* (April/May 1983), pp. 63–4.
51. See Ken Worpole, *Dockers and Detectives: Popular Reading: Popular Writing* (London: Verso, 1983), pp. 94–108.
52. *Grierson on Documentary*, pp. 82–3.

53. Ashley Smith, *A City Stirs* (London: Chapman and Hall, 1939), pp. 55, 40 and 107.
54. Graham Greene, *The Lawless Roads* (London: Heinemann, 1939; Harmondsworth: Penguin, 1981), p. 218.
55. See Note 44 above.
56. A letter of 21 March 1927 announces he's off to the opening night of *Metropolis* in London and an appointment with 'Maxwell, managing director of British National Pictures', though nothing seems to have come of this (See *Mornings in the Dark*, p. xvi).
57. See Part Four of Katherine Burdekin (pseudonym 'Murray Constantine'), *Proud Man* (London: Boriswood, 1934).
58. See Smith, *The Achievement of Graham Greene*, pp. 211–12. Neil Sinyard, in his discussion of Greene and Hitchcock comes to similar conclusions, despite Greene's disclaimers (see Sinyard, *Filming Literature*, pp. 107–11).
59. See Graham Greene, *A Sort of Life* (London: Bodley Head, 1971; Harmondsworth: Penguin, 1972), p. 151. The cross-sectional film of Vicki Baum's novel, *Grand Hotel* (1932), set in Weimar Berlin (which also made Garbo's name) is another probable influence.
60. Greene, *Ways of Escape*, pp. 25 and 29.
61. Christopher Isherwood, *Christopher and His Kind* (London: Eyre Methuen, 1977), p. 90. Swingler's poem is repr. in French and Wlaschin (eds), *Faber Book of Movie Verse*, p. 283.
62. Isherwood's foreword to the 1958 edition is repr. in his *Exhumations*, pp. 91–3.
63. See above Chapter 2, Note 120. Also Paul Piazza, *Christopher Isherwood: Myth and Anti-Myth* (New York: Columbia University Press, 1978), pp. 117–26.
64. See Benjamin, *Illuminations*, pp. 237–9.
65. Christopher Isherwood, *Lions and Shadows: An Education in the Twenties* (London: Hogarth, 1938; repr. Methuen pbk 1979), pp. 52–3. Henceforth, all page references to *Lions and Shadows* will be given in brackets in the text.
66. Davy (ed.), *Footnotes to the Film*, pp. 300–1. On p. 317. Davy also makes an interesting point about film comedy and Freud's *Psychopathology of Everyday Life*, and cf. Humphrey Jennings's ideas about surrealism and 'unconscious optics' in Kevin Jackson (ed.), *The Humphrey Jennings Film Reader* (London: Carcanet, 1993), especially pp. 219–20 and 229–30.
67. David Lodge, *The Modes of Modern Writing: Metaphor, Metonymy and the Typology of Modern Literature* (London: Edward Arnold, 1977; pbk 1979), p. 214.
68. See Alfred Hitchcock, 'Direction', in Davy (ed.), *Footnotes to the Film*, p. 8.
69. Brian Finney, *Christopher Isherwood: A Critical Biography* (London: Faber, 1979), p. 117. Also see below, Chapter 4, for Isherwood's fictionalisation of his scripting experience.
70. Cf. discussion of the opening sequence of the film *Little Friend* in Chapter 4 below.

71.   See *Christopher and His Kind*, pp. 135–6. Roland Barthes's distinction between 'readerly' (i.e. inert) and 'writerly' (i.e. interactively produced texts) is in his *S/Z*, trans. Richard Miller (London: Jonathan Cape, 1975), pp. 4–6.

72.   Sally Carson, *A Traveller Came By* (London: Hodder and Stoughton, 1938), p. 8. And cf. Croft, *Red Letter Days*, p. 322.

73.   See Derek Paget, *True Stories? Documentary Drama on Radio, Screen and Stage* (Manchester: Manchester University Press, 1990), pp. 112–13.

74.   Hynes, *Auden Generation*, p. 356. Also Piazza, *Christopher Isherwood*, p. 117. For Isherwood's views on commentators who failed to suspect his camera-eye was a persona, see *Christopher and His Kind*, p. 49.

75.   See Storm Jameson, 'Documents', *Fact*, No. 4 (July 1937), pp. 15–16.

76.   Cunningham, *British Writers of the Thirties*, pp. 197–8.

77.   Sergei M. Eisenstein, *The Film Sense* trans. J. Leyda (London: Faber, 1943; pbk 1986), p. 24.

78.   Keith Cohen, *Film and Fiction: The Dynamics of Exchange* (New Haven and London: Yale University Press, 1979), pp. 75–6.

79.   The sexual orientation of stage and screen adaptations of Isherwood's Berlin writings is discussed in Chapter 2, 'Good Heter Stuff: Isherwood, Sally Bowles and the Vision of Camp', in Linda Mizejewski's *Divine Decadence: Fascism, Female Spectacle and the Makings of Sally Bowles* (Princeton NJ: Princeton University Press, 1992), pp. 37–84. The difficulty of publishing texts with any overt homosexual content at this time was a genuine problem, as the 1929 rejection of the manuscript of Spender's *The Temple* shows.

4   Involvements: Writing for the Mass Media

1.   For Huxley's other broadcasting, see *The Hidden Huxley: Contempt and Compassion for the Masses 1920–1936*, ed. David Bradshaw (London: Faber, 1994).

2.   Day Lewis, *Revolution in Writing*, p. 11. This talk, which became Part One, The Revolution in Literature', was nonetheless published in *The Listener*, Vol. XIII, No. 324 (27 March 1935), pp. 511–12 and 537.

3.   Cunningham, p. 292.

4.   John Grierson, Preface to Paul Rotha, *Documentary Film* (London: Faber, 1935), pp. 8–9.

5.   Sieveking, *Stuff of Radio*, p. 15. Also Paddy Scannell, '"The Stuff of Radio": Developments in Radio Features and Documentaries before the War' in John Corner (ed.), *Documentary and the Mass Media* (London: Edward Arnold, 1986), p. 24.

6.   D. G. Bridson, *Prospero and Ariel: The Rise and Fall of Radio: A Personal Recollection* (London: Gollancz, 1971), p. 41. The association of politically and linguistically radical texts with Caliban was not uncommon at the time as in, for example, Jack Hilton's contemporary proletarian autobiography *Caliban Shrieks* (1935), praised by Orwell for using the 'authentic accents' of the working man (see *Collected Essays*, I, p. 173).

7. Rodger, *Radio Drama*, p. 16.
8. Tyrone Guthrie, 'The Future of Broadcast Drama', *BBC Yearbook* (London: BBC, 1931), pp. 185–90, especially p. 189.
9. Tyrone Guthrie, Introduction to *Squirrel's Cage and Two Other Microphone Plays* (London: Cobden Sanderson, 1931), pp. 8–10.
10. Rodger, *Radio Drama*, pp. 20–1. Also Richard Hughes, Introduction to Sieveking, *Stuff of Radio*, p. 7.
11. Gielgud, *British Radio Drama*, p. 68.
12. Rodger, *Radio Drama*, pp. 24–5.
13. See Erik Barnouw, *A Tower in Babel: A History of Broadcasting in the US*, Vol. II (New York: Oxford University Press, 1966–70), pp. 66–70. Also Archibald MacLeish, Foreword to *The Fall of the City: A Verse Play For Radio* (New York: Farrar and Rinehart, 1937), pp. ix–xiii.
14. Rodger, *Radio Drama*, pp. 11 and 39.
15. Sieveking, *Stuff of Radio*, p. 48.
16. *The Listener*, Vol. XVII, No. 433 (28 April 1937), p. 829.
17. D. G. Bridson, Foreword 'On Spoken and Written Poetry', *The Christmas Child* (London: Falcon Press, 1950), pp. 1–12. Henceforth, all page references to *The Christmas Child* will be given in brackets in the text. Also Louis MacNeice, Introduction to *Christopher Columbus: A Radio Play* (London: Faber, 1944), p. 8.
18. Lance Sieveking, *Stuff of Radio*, p. 2.
19. Editorial, 'Reviving Radio Plays' *The Listener*, Vol. IX, No. 218 (15 March 1933), p. 400. Also Grace Wyndham Goldie, 'Technique of the Radio Play', *The Listener*, Vol. XVII, No. 425 (3 March 1937), p. 408.
20. Sieveking, *Stuff of Radio*, pp. 25–6.
21. Gielgud, *British Radio Drama*, p. 48. Also Rayner Heppenstall, *Portrait of the Artist as a Professional Man* (London: Peter Owen, 1969), p. 26.
22. MacNeice, *Christopher Columbus*, p. 12. Cf. the 'Introductory Note' to MacNeice's 'feature-biography' on Chekhov, *Sunbeams in his Hat*, which indicated the range inherent in wartime propaganda features in his *The Dark Tower and Other Radio Scripts* (London: Faber, 1947), p. 69.
23. See Sieveking, *Stuff of Radio*, pp. 33–43. In another chapter, 'And Then Take the Movies', Sieveking compared radio with film. Among other things, he discussed Pudovkin's ideas against his own play *Intimate Shapshots* (broadcast on 22 November 1929; script on pp. 279–307), also radio's temporal equivalent of spatial effects and excerpting of actuality. He argued there was feedback the other way too. The talkies suggested mass-movement/ironic simultaneity by using 'sound-montage'. In *Gabriel Over the White House* (1993), 'the loud speaker . . . was giving the unemployed leader's speech, while the President and his nephew talked through it and played games' (*Stuff of Radio*, p. 41).
24. Heppenstall, *Portrait of the Artist As a Professional Man*, p. 26. Grace Wyndham Goldie, 'Technique of the Radio Play', *The Listener*, Vol. XVII, No. 425 (3 March 1937), p. 408.

25. Sieveking, *Stuff of Radio*, pp. 22–3, and 31–2.
26. Scannell in Corner (ed.), *Documentary and the Mass-Media*, pp. 5–6. Also, *A Social History of British Broadcasting*, Vol. I, p. 139.
27. See Bridson's account in *Prospero and Ariel*, p. 20.
28. Rodger, *Radio Drama*, p. 47.
29. Bridson, *Prospero and Ariel*, p. 34. Bridson's 'Song for the Three Million' has affinities with the metre and voice of Auden poems such as 'A Communist to Others' or 'Song for the New Year'.
30. Bridson, *Prospero and Ariel*, pp. 51–3.
31. Rodger, *Radio Drama*, pp. 44–5 and 46.
32. Scannell, in Corner, *Documentary and the Mass-Media*, pp. 15 and 26. Also in *A Social History of British Broadcasting*, Vol. I, p. 341.
33. Bridson, *Prospero and Ariel*, p. 57.
34. For Guthrie and MacLeish's responses, see Rodger, *Radio Drama*, p. 48. Also MacNeice, *Christopher Columbus*, p. 15.
35. Rodger, *Radio Drama*, p. 47.
36. See Bridson, *Christmas Child*, notes on pp. 231–2. Also Bridson, *Prospero and Ariel*, p. 59.
37. Scannell in Corner (ed.), *Documentary and the Mass-Media*, p. 16.
38. Quoted in above, p. 38.
39. See Scannell, in Corner (ed.), *Documentary and the Mass-Media*, p. 17. Also *A Social History of British Broadcasting*, Vol. I, p. 342.
40. Brancepath Colliery, Wilmington, Co. Durham was eventually chosen. *Coal* was broadcast on 17 November 1938. (See account in Scannell and Cardiff, *A Social History of British Broadcasting*, Vol. I, p. 353.
41. Ibid., p. 354.
42. Ibid.
43. For Shapley's features, see Scannell, in Corner (ed.), *Documentary and the Mass-Media*, p. 22, and *A Social History of British Broadcasting*, Vol. I, pp. 344 and 349.
44. *Britain by Mass-Observation*, p. 210. Much of this study was concerned with analysing the change in public response to Chamberlain's pact with Hitler once the cost of 'peace' to the Czechs became known.
45. Bridson, *Prospero and Ariel*, p. 61. Also Rodger, *Radio Drama*, p. 49.
46. Day Lewis (ed.), *Mind in Chains*, pp. 14–15. Also Calder-Marshall, in ibid., p. 63.
47. Letter to Frieda Lawrence (7 October 1940) in *Letters of Aldous Huxley*, ed. Grover Smith (London: Chatto and Windus, 1969), p. 459. And cf. David King Dunaway, *Huxley in Hollywood* (London: Bloomsbury, 1991), pp. 154–5.
48. Greene, *Collected Essays*, pp. 425–6.
49. Greene, 'The Novelist and the Cinema: A Personal Experience' in William Whitebait (ed.), *International Film Annual* (New York: Doubleday, 1958), p. 54.
50. See Richards, *Dream Palace*, p. 315.
51. Ibid., p. 181.
52. Ibid., p. 183.

53. Numerous examples are reproduced in, among others, *Worktown: Photographs of Bolton and Blackpool Taken for Mass-Observation 1937–38* (Brighton: Gardner Centre Gallery, 1987). For examples of M-O's interest in popular seaside culture, see *Worktowners at Blackpool: Mass-Observation and Popular Leisure in the 1930s*, ed. Gary Cross (London: Routledge, 1990).

54. Priestley, *English Journey*, p. 252.

55. See Hingley, *Russian Writers*, pp. 199–200, and Frank Whitford, 'The Triumph of the Banal: Art in Nazi Germany' in Collier and Timms (eds.), *Visions and Blueprints*, pp. 252–69.

56. Richards, *Dream Palace*, p. 303.

57. See 'The Age of Consensus: *South Riding*', in Jeffrey Richards and Anthony Aldgate, *Best of British* (Oxford: Blackwell, 1983), pp. 29–42, especially p. 34. Also Victor Small, *Left Review* (April 1983), p. 936: 'The Holtby story has everything that makes for good cinema, but as usual it was realised that the social significance of the story could not be allowed on the screen unaltered.'

58. Richards, *Dream Palace*, p. 321. See also Anthony Aldgate and Jeffrey Richards *Britain Can Take It: The British Cinema in the Second World War* (Oxford: Basil Blackwell, 1986), p. 38.

59. Basil Wright, *The Long View* (London: Secker and Warburg, 1974), p. 94.

60. Greene in Whitebait (ed.), *International Film Annual*, p. 56.

61. Graham Greene, *Journey without Maps* (London: Heinemann, 1936), p. 24. Also cf. *Ways of Escape*, pp. 22–3.

62. See Greene's own remarks to Marie-François Allain in *Conversations with Graham Greene* (Harmondsworth: Penguin, 1991), p. 146. Cf. also this Chapter, below, James Agee's point about the film of *The Confidential Agent* being 'less cinematic' than the book.

63. Greene in *International Film Annual*, p. 61.

64. Interview, 'The Screenwriter' from *The Making of Feature Films: A Guide* by Ivan Butler (Pelican, 1971), pp. 71–2, p. 523). The published version of *The Third Man* was a in fact a 'treatment' not a screenplay or final shooting script. The only one of the latter Greene did was for the film of *Brighton Rock* (1947).

65. See Greene, *Ways of Escape*, p. 50.

66. For a detailed description of Greene's 1936 improvisation and the resulting film, see *Ways of Escape*, p. 50, and Quentin Falk, *Travels in Greeneland: The Cinema of Graham Greene* (Quartet, 1984; revised pbk, 1990), p. 12.

67. Greene rubbished it himself while acknowledging his own culpability (See *Spectator*, 12 January 1940; *Mornings in the Dark*, p. 363).

68. See the Preface to *The Third Man and the Fallen Idol* (London: Heinemann, 1950), pp. 145–6.

69. Isherwood's account is in *Christopher and His Kind*, Chapter 9, pp. 115–31. For Viertel's influence on British cinema, see Günter Berghaus, *Theatre and Film in Exile: German Artists in Britain, 1933–1945* (London: Berg Publishers, 1989), especially Kevin Gough-Yates, 'The British Feature Film as a European Concern: Britain and the

Emigré Film-Maker, 1933–45, pp. 135–66. In real life, Jean Ross was far from naively starstruck and had radical film credentials of her own. Married to Claud Cockburn, editor of the exposé journal *The Week*, she became *Daily Worker* film critic, 'Peter Porcupine' and secretary to the Workers' Film and Photo League.

70. Isherwood, *Christopher and His Kind*, p. 117. The plot of 'Prater Violet the movie' was pastiched by John van Druten, who, arguably, later also saccharined *Goodbye to Berlin* to a certain extent as a (1951) stage play. (See Chapter 3, 'The Cold War Against Mummy': Van Druten's *I Am a Camera* in Mizejewski, *Divine Decadence*, pp. 85–119.)

71. Christopher Isherwood, *Prater Violet* (London: Methuen, 1946; Harmondsworth: Penguin, 1961), p. 20. Henceforth, all page references to *Prater Violet* will be given in brackets in the text.

72. See *Christopher and His Kind*, p. 91.

73. Ibid., p. 131.

74. See Chapter 3, 'Money or the Circulation of Commodities', of Karl Marx, *Capital*, trans. Ben Foukes (Harmondsworth: Penguin, 1990), pp. 189–244.

75. Benjamin, *Illuminations*, p. 233. Cf. Vertov, *Kino-Eye*, pp. 34–5. Grierson on Documentary, pp. 135–8, for their accounts of how film could reverse the disappearance of production into commodities.

76. See *The Reichstag Fire Trial: The Brown Book of the Hitler Terror* (London: Editions du Carrefour, 1934), produced by 'The World Committee for the Relief of the Victims of German Fascism', a front for Münzenberg's German Communist propaganda machine, then operating in exile in Paris.

77. It was not only a rare exception, but an internationally successful film, as the Nazi's *Staatsauftragfilms* counter-version of it, *Jud Süss* (1940), suggests.

78. Grierson, quoted in Cunningham, *British Writers*, p. 329.

79. See Hogenkamp, *Deadly Parallels*, p. 106.

80. Lewis Jones, *We Live: The Story of a Welsh Mining Valley* (London: Lawrence and Wishart, 1939; repr. 1978).

81. Grierson's own definition of documentary (see his article 'The Documentary Producer', *Cinema Quarterly*, Vol. II, No. 1 (1933), p. 8.

82. Esmond Romilly, *Boadilla* (London: Hamish Hamilton, 1937; repr. with an intro. and notes by Hugh Thomas by Macdonald, 1971), pp. 22–3.

83. Day Lewis, 'Where Are the War Poets?', *Collected Poems*, p. 228.

84. 'Why Not War Writers', *Horizon*, Vol. IV (October 1941), pp. 236–9.

85. Ian McLaine, *Ministry of Morale: Home Front Morale and Ministry of Information in World War II* (London: Allen and Unwin, 1979).

86. Mass-Observation, *War Begins at Home*, ed. and arranged Tom Harrison and Charles Madge (London: Chatto and Windus, 1940), p. 13.

87. Graham Greene, *Collected Stories* (Vol. VIII of the *The Collected Works*) (London: Bodley Head/Heinemann, 1972), p. 395. Henceforth, all references to *Collected Stories* will be given in brackets in the text. Cf. Waugh's similar experience-based satire of MoI ineptitude in *Put Out More Flags* (London: Chapman and Hall, 1942).

88.   See Orwell's remark that the Government could not rely simply on
       'safe' Right-wing popular novelists like Ian Hay and A. P. Herbert
       to produce effective wartime propaganda, in *Collected Essays*, II, p.
       381.

89.   Pronay, in Short (ed.), *Film and Radio Propaganda*, p. 52.

90.   For the 'Empire Crusade', see McLaine, *Ministry of Morale*, pp.
       223–4.

91.   M-O, *War Begins At Home*, p. 270. A BBC reporter, Charles Gardner,
       set the precedent for this kind of 'sporting' coverage by a sponta-
       neous on-the-spot coverage of an early aerial dog-fight above Do-
       ver as if it were a cricket match. See Angus Calder, *The Myth of the
       Blitz* (London: Jonathan Cape, 1991), p. 31.

92.   McLaine, *Ministry of Morale*, pp. 10–11.

93.   See Daniel Lerner, 'Effective Propaganda' in his (ed.) *Propaganda in
       War and Crisis: Materials for American Policy* (New York: G. W. Stewart,
       1951).

94.   Angus Calder, *The People's War: Britain 1939–45* (London: Jonathan
       Cape, 1969), p. 471. Cf. Orwell's comments on how the space occu-
       pied by MoI posters was gradually taken over by advertising again
       as the war neared its end (*Collected Essays*, III, pp. 217–18).

95.   Arthur Koestler, 'The Intelligentsia', *Horizon* (March 1944), repr. in
       The Yogi and the Commissar (London: Jonathan Cape, 1945), p. 83.

96.   Cyril Connolly, 'Comment', *Horizon*, Vol. VI (December 1942),
       p. 371.

97.   Not only did Orwell put his own media experiences to good liter-
       ary use, but probably his wife's as well: Eileen Blair wrote copy for
       the Ministry of Food programme *Kitchen Front*, likely source of some
       of the covering up of shortages and the *ersatz* nature of the basic
       quality of life under Ingsoc. (See Bernard Crick, *George Orwell: A
       Life* (London: Secker and Warburg, 1980; repr. Harmondsworth: Pen-
       guin, 1982), p. 434.)

98.   McLaine, *Ministry of Morale*, p. 28. A perfect example of the MoI's
       softening up of a potentially hostile public was its recruitment of
       Orwell to broadcast to India. (See below, this chapter.) An instance
       of its deception would be the continuous denial that civilian popu-
       lation centres were never deliberately targeted in Bomber Com-
       mand mass raids. (See McLaine, pp. 156–66, and below, this chapter,
       for examples of how writers involved in the media, like Orwell and
       Michael Foot, were misinformed by the MoI about this.)

99.   Harold Nicolson, diary entry (3 July 1940), *Diaries and Letters*, Vol.
       II (London: Collins, 1967), p. 99.

100.   McLaine, *Ministry of Morale*, pp. 194–5.

101.   See McLaine, ibid., p. 48. *Picture Post*, *The Daily Worker* and *The Week*
       were all, in effect, banned at home and/or for export by such means
       at various stages of the war.

102.   Quoted in McLaine, *Ministry of Morale*, p. 156.

103.   'Went the Day Well?' was itself the title of a poem written by John
       Maxwell Edmonds for the Great War Graves Commission. See the
       Introduction to French and Wlaschin (eds), *Faber Book of Movie Verse*,

p. 7. For the script of *Words for Battle*, see Jackson (ed.), *Humphrey Jennings Film Reader*, pp. 17–23.

104. See Rodger, *Radio Drama*, p. 60.

105. *Pimpernel Smith* is said to have inspired the 'Swedish Schindler', Raoul Wallenberg. Howard's impact on writers was acknowledged in Maurice Lindsay's poetic epitaph, 'Elegy for an Actor Drowned in Time of War' (repr. in French and Wlaschin (eds), *Faber Book of Movie Verse*, pp. 232–3) and in Priestley's BBC memorial broadcast (6 June 1943).

106. Calder, *People's War*, pp. 513 and 364, respectively.

107. Rodger, *Radio Drama*, p. 54.

108. See Rodger, ibid., p. 69.

109. See Bridson, *Prospero and Ariel*, p. 72.

110. Bridson *Aaron's Field* (London: Pendock Press, 1943), pp. 41–2 and p. 34. (Also repr. in *Christmas Child*, pp. 54–91.)

111. See Wilfred Pickles's autobiography, *Between You and Me* (London: Werner Laurie, 1949), p. 126.

112. Bridson, *Prospero and Ariel*, pp. 80 and 84.

113. McLaine, *Ministry of Morale*, p. 203.

114. Bridson, *Prospero and Ariel*, p. 97, and cross-ref. The (particularly linguistically) democratising war propaganda called for by Greene, *The Documentary Newsletter* group and *Horizon* 'War Writers Manifesto' was especially important in the US.

115. See *Prospero and Ariel*, pp. 109–10.

116. The reading in this feature of 'Reported Missing' by Bridson's fellow radio producer-poet, John Pudney, made it 'for a while, the best known poem of World War Two'. (See French and Wlaschin (eds) *Faber Book of Movie Verse*, p. 9.)

117. Bridson, *Prospero and Ariel*, p. 94.

118. *Johnny Miner* was dedicated to colliers' leader and writer A. L. Loyd, himself editor of a collection of folklore, *Come All Ye Miners: Ballads and Songs of the Coalfields* (London: Wishart, 1952).

119. Drakakis (ed.), *British Radio Drama*, p. 31.

120. MacNeice, *Modern Poetry*, pp. 193–4.

121. MacNeice, Introduction to *Christopher Columbus: A Radio Play* (London: Faber, 1944), p. 12 (repr. in Peter MacDonald and Alan Heuser (eds), *Selected Plays of Louis MacNeice* (Oxford: Clarendon, 1993) as Appendix 1, pp. 393–402). Henceforth, all page references to *Christopher Columbus* will be given in brackets in the text. MacDonald draws attention to the importance of classical and morality play elements in MacNeice's radio drama in his introduction to the *Selected Plays*, p. xiii. The Doubt/Faith chorus in *Christopher Columbus*, for example, seems to have been influenced by T. S. Eliot's earlier attempts to resuscitate such devices in *The Family Reunion* (1939).

122. There is evidence that MacNeice's esteem for the 'ordinary listener's' intellectual astuteness rose even higher during the war. In MacNeice's feature *Four Years at War* (3 September 1943) a sceptical 'listener's voice' constantly interrupts the official triumphalism to make claims for his own efforts, to shape the programme and to call

for a 'Battle of the Peace' when it is over. Compare this to his more naive counterpart in *Out of the Picture*.

123. For an example of MacNeice's thirties broadcasts, see 'Tendencies in Modern Poetry: Discussion between F. R. Higgins and Louis MacNeice, broadcast from Northern Ireland', in *The Listener*, Vol. XXII, No. 550 (27 July 1939), pp. 185–6. MacNeice's ambivalent attitude to war work is quoted in Coulton, *Louis MacNeice in the BBC*, p. 47.

124. See MacDonald's introduction to *Selected Plays of Louis MacNeice*, p. xi. Coulton's account of the writing of the D-Day piece is in her *Louis MacNeice at the BBC*, p. 67. Also Rodger, *Radio Drama*, pp. 66 and 151.

125. Bridson, *Prospero and Ariel*, p. 81.

126. See McLaine, *Ministry of Morale*, pp. 264 and 271–2.

127. MacNeice, *Horizon*, Vol. III, No. 15 (March 1941) repr. in *Selected Prose*, pp. 92 and 94.

128. Ibid., pp. 106–11.

129. Cf. MacNeice's script for another feature in the same series, *A Cook's Tour of the London Subways*, *The Listener*, Vol. XXV, No. 640 (17 April 1941), pp. 554–60.

130. See Louis MacNeice, *The Nosebag* in his *The Dark Tower and Other Radio Scripts* (Faber: London, 1947), pp. 132–3.

131. Bridson, *Prospero and Ariel*, p. 81. Also Gielgud *British Radio Drama*, p. 69. Besides MacNeice's own acknowledgement of the influence of Bridson's *March of the '45*, *Christopher Columbus* also used a running commentary in verse over triumphant processional music recalling MacLeish's *Fall of the City*.

132. A performance of the Agincourt scene from *Henry V* was among the first wartime propaganda broadcasts and Olivier's film was also influenced by Eisenstein's *Nevsky*. Calder argues Churchill's morale-boosting aristocratic populism also played up to Shakespeare's idea of a 'little touch of Harry in the night' (see *People's War*, p. 94).

133. Guthrie's influence was acknowledged in MacNeice's 1949 Introduction (see MacNeice, *Selected Plays*, p. 72). Henceforth, all page references to *Selected Plays* will be given in brackets in the text. *He Had A Date* also has a similar structure to other 'radiogenic' retrospectives on the thirties like Bridson's *Johnny Miner* and Theatre Workshop's *Johnny Noble*, etc.

134. See Orwell, *Homage to Catalonia*, pp. 188 and 2–3, respectively. Also Cornford, *Collected Writings*, p. 188.

135. Robert Hewison, *Under Siege* (London: Weidenfeld and Nicolson, 1977: repr. in paperback by Quartet, 1979), p. 160. Also Ted Kavanagh, *Tommy Handley* (London: Hodder and Stoughton, 1949), pp. 116–17, and cf. Calder, *People's War*, p. 65.

136. MacNeice, Introductory Note to *The Dark Tower*, p. 21.

137. See General Introduction to *The Dark Tower*, pp. 9–17.

138. For BBC truthfulness and German intelligence see McLaine, *Ministry of Morale*, pp. 80–1. For Haw-Haw's 'ratings', see Calder, *People's War*, p. 65.

139. McLaine, *Ministry of Morale*, p. 99.
140. J. B. Priestley, *Postscripts* (London: Heinemann, 1940), pp. vi and vii. Henceforth, all page references to *Postscripts* will be given in brackets in the text.
141. For the impact of Priestley's broadcasts see Angus Calder, *The Myth of the Blitz*, especially pp. 196–204.
142. Cf. Priestley's parallel to Murrow's voiceover for the film *London/Britain Can Take It*, in *Britain at Bay* (both of 1940).
143. According to Briggs, on average 31 per cent of the adult population listened in. (See *A History of Broadcasting*, Vol. III, *The War of the Words* (London: Oxford University Press, 1970), p. 210.)
144. Greene, 'Review of *Postscripts*', Spectator (13 December 1940; repr. in *Reflections*, pp. 87–8). MacNeice, 'London Letter' to *Common Sense* (May 1941), repr. in *Selected Prose*, p. 115.
145. See J. B. Priestley, *Margin Released* (London: Heinemann, 1962), p. 221.
146. This is ironically confirmed by the wall-poster Priestley wrote for the MoI's 'Anger Campaign' called *The Secret Beast* (see McLaine *Ministry of Morale*, pp. 146–7). Such crudity was mercifully not very frequent in propaganda from Leftist writers.
147. For Empson's theory that proletarian art displaced pastoral into class terms, see Chapter 1 of his *Some Versions of Pastoral* (London: Chatto and Windus, 1935). For the cultural history of 'Deep England', Calder, *Myth of the Blitz*, especially pp. 182–3.
148. General Guilo Douhet's *Il dominio dell' aria* was published in 1921. For British attitudes to his theory, see Tom Harrisson, *Living Through the Blitz* (London: Collins, 1976; repr. Harmondsworth: Penguin, 1990), pp. 21–4.
149. See Greene, *Reflections*, p. 87. Priestley had begun exploring the dramatic possibilities of J. W. Dunne's ideas in *Time and the Conways* (1937) (see Note 145 to Chapter 2, above).
150. Priestley gave a later account of typical buck-passing bureaucratic chicanery. The MoI told him the decision was the BBC's; the BBC finally told him it was an MoI directive. (See his *Margin Released*, pp. 221–2.) Richard Maconachie, Talks Director, was also known to be unhappy about the 'controversial' politics of the *Postscripts*. (See Briggs, *History of Broadcasting*, III, p. 211.)
151. The Nazi broadcast is quoted in Briggs, ibid., p. 232. In Powell and Pressburger's 1943 film *The Life and Death Colonel Blimp*, Blimp is scheduled to give a BBC talk, but finds himself replaced by Priestley.
152. The second series began on 26th January 1941 and almost immediately provoked protests from the Tory 1922 Committee to the Minister of Information, Duff Cooper, who thereafter restricted Priestley to six programmes in rotation with others. (See Briggs, *History of Broadcasting*, III, pp. 322 and 619.) For Priestley's ideas about the 1941 Committee, see his *Out of the People* (London: Heinemann, 1941).
153. For Orwell's wartime film reviews in *Time and Tide*, see Crick, *George Orwell*, pp. 383–4.

154. See George Orwell, *The War Commentaries*, ed. W. J. West (London: Duckworth, 1985; repr. Harmondsworth: Penguin, 1987), especially the MoI special issue report quoted by West on pp. 20–2.

155. *Animal Farm* was officially muzzled until it became *equally expedient* among the British and American Right to promote it. (See *Collected Essays*, III, p. 212 and IV, pp. 433–4.) As MacLaine shows, the MoI advised publishers to reject it (see *Ministry of Morale*, p. 203).

156. Orwell, *War Commentaries*, p. 93. (Orwell's views on Indian independence were set out extensively in *The Lion and the Unicorn* (1941, repr. in his *Collected Essays*, II, pp. 122–4). Henceforth, all page references to the *War Commentaries* will be given in brackets in the text.

157. *Grierson on Documentary*, p. 101.

158. See George Orwell, *The War Broadcasts*, ed. W. J. West (London: Duckworth, 1985; repr. Harmondsworth: Penguin, 1987), pp. 139–48 and 95–111. Henceforth, all page references to *War Broadcasts* will be given in brackets in the text.

159. For Koestler's attempts to broadcast evidence of the Endlösung brought back by an agent of the Polish Government in Exile in 1942 and the public response, see his 'On Disbelieving Atrocities', *Yogi and the Commissar*, pp. 94–9 and *The Invisible Writing: The Second Volume of an Autobiography* (London: Collins/Hamish Hamilton, 1954; repr. Hutchinson pbk 1969), pp. 521–2. See also discussion later in this chapter of Koestler's MoI filmscript on the concentration camps.

160. Milan Kundera, *The Book of Laughter and Forgetting*, trans. Alfred A. Knopf (London: Faber, 1982), p. 3.

161. See, for example, Orwell's diary entry for 21 June 1942 (*Collected Essays*, II, pp. 489–90).

162. Agee singled out *I Was a Fireman, Before the Raid, ABCA, Psychiatry in Action* among others. (See *Agee on Film*, Vol. I, *Reviews and Comments by James Agee* (London: Peter Owen, 1963), pp. 33–4, and cf. pp. 57–8).

163. See Calder, *People's War*, p. 369.

164. See the Section on MoI shorts in *Mass-Observation at the Movies*, pp. 424–60 and Tom Harrisson, 'Films and the Home Front' in Pronay and Spring, *Propaganda, Politics and Film* (London: Macmillan, 1982), pp. 234–48. Also Taylor quoted in McLaine, *Ministry of Morale*, p. 279.

165. See *Mass-Observation at the Movies*, pp. 15–16. However, Paul Fussell shows audiences were growing impatient with *Mrs Miniver* by 1944. (See his *Wartime: Understanding and Behavior in the Second World War* (New York and Oxford: Oxford University Press, 1989), p. 189.)

166. Fussell, *Wartime*, p. 190. Also Agee, *Nation* (1 May 1943), repr. in *Agee on Film*, pp. 33–4.

167. Fussell, *Wartime*, p. 190. Also Keith Douglas, *Alamein to Zem Zem* (London: Editions Poetry, 1946; repr. Faber, 1992), p. 18.

168. Richards, *Dream Palace*, p. 309. Also Nicholas Pronay, "The Land of Promise": The Projection of Peace Aims in Britain', in Short (ed.), *Radio and Film Propaganda*, pp. 51–77, especially p. 67.

169. See *Humphrey Jennings Film Reader*, especially pp. 6–10, 38–55 and 302.

170. William Whitebait, quoted in Aldgate and Richards, *Britain Can Take It*, p. 109.

171. Aldgate and Richards, ibid., p. 4.

172. See Nicholas Pronay and Jeremy Croft, 'British Film Censorship and Propaganda Policy during the Second World War', in James Curran and Vincent Porter (eds), *British Cinema History* (London: Weidenfeld and Nicolson, 1983), pp. 155–63). Also Aldgate and Richards, *Britain Can Take It*, pp. 248–9.

173. See *Agee on Film*, pp. 222–4.

174. Calder-Marshall, quoted in *Britain Can Take It*, pp. 256–7.

175. See Coultass, *Images for Battle*, pp. 137 and 183.

176. Miles and Smith, *Cinema, Literature and Society*, p. 244.

177. For a full account of the filming, see S. Constantine, '*Love on the Dole* and its Reception in the 1930s', *Literature and History*, Vol. VIII, No. 2 (Autumn 1982), pp. 232–47.

178. The screen pattern for urban regeneration was set in the documentary scripted by Dylan Thomas, *New Towns for Old* (1942). Its 'structure of expectations' hardly anticipated the dreadful design errors and non-consultation of some postwar rehousing schemes.

179. See Paul Swann, *The British Documentary Film Movement 1926–1946* (Cambridge: Cambridge University Press, 1989), p. 139.

180. William Whitebait, *New Statesman*, Vol. XXIV, No. 595 (18 July 1942), p. 42. Also Harrisson in Pronay and Spring (eds), *Propaganda, Politics and Film*, p. 239.

181. Coultass, *Images for Battle*, p. 45.

182. Morton Dauwen Zabel, 'The Best and the Worst', in Samuel Hynes (ed.), *Graham Greene: A Collection of Critical Essays* (Englewood Cliffs, New Jersey: Prentice Hall, 1973), p. 31.

183. See McLaine, *Ministry of Morale*, p. 48. Also Penelope Houston, *Went the Day Well?* (London: British Film Institute, 1993) and Aldgate and Jeffrey Richards, *Britain Can Take It*, pp. 17 and 133. This MoI multimedia campaign is a possible source of the daily 'Two Minutes Hate' in Orwell's *Nineteen Eighty-Four*.

184. Repr. along with Greene's *Liberty Radio*-like tale about the subversion of Nazi broadcasting, 'The News in English', in *The Last Word and Other Stories* (London: Reindardt, 1990), pp. 46–59 and 19–31, respectively.

185. Quoted in McLaine, *Ministry of Morale*, p. 75.

186. Charles Barr, *Ealing Studios* (London: Cameron and Taylor/David and Charles, 1977), pp. 32–3.

187. Tom Hopkinson *Of This Our Time: A Journalist's Story 1905–50* (London: Hutchinson, 1982), p. 74.

188. See Aldgate and Richards, *Britain Can Take It*, p. 131. Also cf. Barr *Ealing Studios*, pp. 31–2, and Raymond Durgnat, *A Mirror For England: British Movies from Austerity to Affluence* (London: Faber, 1970), pp. 15–16.

189. For the British pro and anti reviews, see Houston, *Went the Day Well?*, pp. 53–5. Also Agee, *Nation* (15 July 1944), repr. in *Agee on Film*, p. 104.

190. Greene, *Ways of Escape*, pp. 54–5.

191. *Nation* (10 November 1945), *Agee on Film*, pp. 178–9.

192. *Nation* (4 October 1944), *Agee on Film*, p. 122.

193. For further commentary on all these films, see Coultass, *Images for Battle*, pp. 57, p. 61 and pp. 144–5. Also Aldgate and Richard's chapter on *Thunder Rock*, 'Signs of the Times', in *Britain Can Take It*, pp. 168–86.

194. For biographical information, see Clive Fleay, 'Voices in the Gallery: George Orwell and Jack Hilton' and other contributions to *The Itch of Class: Essays in Memory of Jack Hilton, Middlesex Polytechnic History Journal*, Vol. II, No. 1 (Spring 1985), pp. 55–81.

195. Pronay in Short (ed.), *Film and Radio Propaganda*, p. 65 (Pronay also quotes Thomas's script). And cf. Coultass's account of Thomas's involvement with wartime cinema in *Images for Battle*, pp. 94 and 117.

196. See Coultass, *Images for Battle*, p. 189. Some of the script of *Diary for Timothy* is repr. in the *Humphrey Jennings Film Reader*, pp. 96–100.

197. See Note 159 above, and Coultass *Images for Battle*, pp. 133–5. For Home Intelligence's reports on the wartime increase in British anti-semitism, see McLaine, *Ministry of Morale*, pp. 166–8.

198. See, among others, James E. Young, *Writing and Rewriting the Holocaust: Narrative and the Consequences of Interpretation* (Bloomington: Indiana University Press, 1988); also his *The Texture of Memory: Holocaust Memorials and Meaning* (New Haven: Yale University Press, 1993).

199. Fussell, *Wartime*, p. 164.

200. Keith Douglas, *Alamein to Zem Zem*, p. 131. Henceforth, all page references to *Alamein to Zem Zem* will be given in brackets in the text.

201. Douglas referred to the stolidly absurd, but unflappably English characters created by Frank Launder and Sidney Gilliat in their script for Hitchcock's covertly anti-fascist thriller *The Lady Vanishes* (1938), so popular that they reappeared in the wartime morale-booster *Night Train to Munich* (1940).

CONCLUSIONS

1. Bergonzi, *Reading the Thirties*, p. 143.

2. Spender, *World Within World*, p. 202.

3. Malcolm Biddiss, *The Age of the Masses: Ideas and Society in Europe since 1870* (Harmondsworth: Penguin, 1977), pp. 16–17.

4. Calder, *People's War*, p. 230.

5. Ibid., pp. 500–1.

6. Jack Common, *The Freedom of the Streets* (London: Secker and Warburg, 1938), pp. 3–4 and 29.
7. Winifred Holtby, *Women and A Changing Civilization* (London: Longmans, 1934; repr. Chicago: Academy Press, 1978), pp. 83 and 121–2.
8. Jeanine Basinger, *A Woman's View: How Hollywood Spoke to Women 1930–1960* (London: Chatto and Windus, 1993) reviewed by Julie Wheelwright, 'The Pancake Factory', *Guardian* (5 January 1994), pp. 8–9. See also Christine Gledhill (ed.), *Stardom* (London: Routledge, 1991) and Tania Modleski, *Loving with a Vengeance: Mass produced Fantasies for Women* (New York and London: Routledge, 1990).
9. See Lewis Mumford, *Technics and Civilization* (London: Routledge, 1934), pp. 212–14.
10. See Virginia Woolf, 'Mr Bennett and Mrs Brown' (1924), in her *Collected Essays*, ed. Leonard Woolf, Vol. I (London: Hogarth, 1966), p. 320.
11. Isherwood, 'Los Angeles' (1947), *Exhumations*, p. 320.
12. Gielgud, *British Radio Drama*, p. 7.
13. Bridson, *Prospero and Ariel*, p. 179.
14. Heppenstall, *Portrait of the Artist as a Professional Man*, pp. 36–7.
15. See Kate Whitehead, *The Third Programme: A Literary History* (Oxford: Clarendon, 1987).
16. MacNeice Introduction to 1963 edition of *Christopher Columbus* repr. in his *Selected Plays*, pp. 3–4.
17. See Introduction, above, pp. 2–3.

Index

Aaron's Field 189–90
abuse of public trust invested in print 50
Acton, Harold 151
advertising revenue in newspapers 24
aestheticisation of militarism 6
Afternoon Men (Powell) 131
Agee, James 106, 215
Agents and Patients (Powell) 78, 95
agitprop 115–19
Alamein to Zem-Zem (Douglas) 229
Aldgate, Anthony 46, 169
Aleph, The (Borges) 9, 12
Alexander Nevsky (film and radio feature) 197–8
All the Conspirators (Isherwood) 143
American entertainment 17
American Federal Theater 116
Animal Farm (Orwell) 209
Arent, Arthur 116
Army Bureau of Current Affairs 119
Ascent of F6, The 51–2, 54, 122–3
Associated British Picture Corporation 39
Astor family 23
Auden, W. H. 1, 10, 50–1, 51–2, 54, 62, 69, 72, 97
    influence of cinema 125–7, 178–81
    Journey to a War 56–7, 101, 109
    Letters from Iceland 81–2, 99, 104, 107
    Night Mail 178–9
    radio 152
audience research by BBC 27
Autumn Journal (MacNeice) 50, 67, 69, 70, 80, 107, 128

Babes in the Wood (Unity Theatre) 119
Baird, John Logie 37
Bakhtin, M. M. 90
Bakke, E. W. 83
Baldwin, Stanley 68–9
Band Waggon (radio programme) 33
Barke, James 63, 90, 93, 120, 132, 135
Barker, George 102, 105
Barnes, Julian 2
Battleship Potemkin (film) 41, 42, 95–6
Baudrillard, Jean 1, 2, 4, 18, 37, 62
Baxter, John 169, 219
BBC 25–6
    Advisory Committee of Spoken English 31
    Charter 26, 27, 67
    crisis for broadcasting 29–30
    documentaries 36
    drama 35–6, 153–7
    evolution of narrative drama 155
    features 157–64
    first radio play 153
    foreign correspondents 30
    impermanence of radio 153
    intrusiveness 64–6
    jingoism 32
    Leftist writers in Thirties 152
    Listener Research Department 33
    Microphone Serials 154
    Music and Variety 32
    'national culture' 31–2, 160–4
    National Programme 34, 160, 164
    news commentary credibility 202–6
        see also Priestley, J. B.
    news reporting style 28

BBC – *continued*
  outside broadcasts 36
  and politics 67
  pronunciation 30–1, 63, 160–4
  Regional Programmes 34, 160–4
  Repertory Company 189
  social mix of audience 65,
    155–6, 160
  Talks Department 28, 151
  television 37
  wartime broadcasting 188–215
Beaverbrook, Lord 50, 51
Benjamin, Walter 5, 6
  on cinema 6, 38, 143–4, 175
Bernstein, Hillel 52, 57, 67
Bernstein, Sidney L. 82–3
Black, Peter 121
Blair, Eric *see* Orwell, George
Blumenfeld, Simon 59, 66, 77, 84,
  96, 116, 135
Borges, Jorge-Luis 9
Bottomley, Horatio 54
Bowen, Elizabeth 79–80, 81, 83, 89
  on Soviet films 97, 98
Bower, Dallas 14
Bracken, Brendan 184
Brandt, Bill 106
Brave New World (Huxley) 13, 48,
  70–1, 152
Brecht, Bertold 109
Bridson, D. G. 121, 153, 156,
  159–64, 189–92
Brierley, Walter 58, 66
Briggs, Asa 27, 34, 67
British Board of Film Censors
  (BBFC) 40–1, 77, 101, 224
British Film Institute 166
British Union of Fascists 23
Britten, Benjamin 152
broadcasting 25–36, 61–70
  influence of 120
  Thirties 151–64
  see also BBC
*Broadcasting and a Changing
  Civilisation* (Robinson) 68, 112
Brooke-Wilkinson, Joseph (BBFC)
  40
Brown Book of the Hitler Terror
  (1934) 176

Builders, The (radio) 193
Burdekin, Katherine 63, 104, 140
Bury the Dead (Shaw) 115
Busmen (Allen, Slater & Hodge)
  116–17

Calamiterror (Barker) 102
Calder, Angus 185, 188, 203
Calder-Marshall, Arthur 22,
  49–50, 59, 61, 62, 63, 64–5, 73,
  99–100
  Dead Centre 131
  and films 217
  Great War (1914–18) 107
  on narrative structure 130–1
  newsreels 102
  'The Cinema' 165
'camera-eye' techniques of writers
  10–13, 133–6, 145–50
Capa, Robert 104
Cardiff, David 25, 27, 29, 30,
  31–2, 33, 36, 158
Carson, Sally 146
Carter, Angela 90
Caudwell, Christopher 14, 53, 72
Cavalcade (Coward film) 86
censorship in cinema 40–2
Chamberlain, Neville 23, 28, 29,
  39, 45, 46, 108, 118
Chaplin, Charles 98
Chiang Kai-shek, General 109
Choose a Bright Morning (Bernstein)
  52, 57, 67, 106–7, 110
Christmas Child (Bridson) 191,
  192–3, 194
Christopher and his Kind
  (Isherwood) 142–3
Christopher Columbus (MacNeice)
  194–5, 199
cinema 37–46, 70–106, 164–81
  anti-Nazi films 42
  architecture of 79–80
  and attempts at actuality 85
  attendances at 37–8
  British upturn in 39
  censorship 40–2
  changes in consciousness
    brought about by 104, 109
  cooperation with politicians 39

cinema – *continued*
  cultural dislocation 71–2, 98
  deprived areas and 84
  documentaries 99–101, 178
  effect on jobless 83–4
  escapism 43, 87, 178, 215
  European 95–9
  Hollywood effect on British
      85–6, 115, 215
  influence on fiction 128–50
  influence on poetry 125–8
  narrative with poetic subtext
      142
  and Nazis 96
  newsreels 44–6, 102–4
  as opiate for the people 72–3, 80
  photography 104–6
  popularity of 70, 81, 164–71
  propaganda in 101–6, 108
  publicly acceptable prurience
      76–9
  refractions of 70–106
  split subject in seductiveness
      78–9
  star cult 43, 91
  wartime 215–31
  and working class 72–3, 80–1,
      87
  working-class stars' popularity
      89–95, 166–9
cinematic effects 125
cinematic intertextuality 129–30,
    138–9, 144
cinematic techniques applied to
    radio 157–8
Cinematograph Act (1927) 39, 42
Citadel, The (Cronin) 170
City Stirs, A (Ashley Smith)
    135–6
Clark, Kenneth 187
class loyalties in reading
    newspapers 48–9
Clergyman's Daughter, A (Orwell)
    120
Cockburn, Claude 17, 159
Cohen, Keith 149–50
Comedians (Griffiths) 90
commodification (Marx) 6
conceptualising media function 21

Confessions of a Nazi Spy (film)
    101
Confidential Agent, The (Greene)
    70, 76, 78, 225
Connolly, Cyril 186
Conservative Party Film
    Association 39
Conservative Party Research
    Department 108
Constructivism in former USSR 8
consumerism 24
Cooper, Duff 184
Coultass, Clive 40
Coward, Noel 86
Crisis and Criticism (West) 130
Croft, Andy 132–3, 146
Cronin, A. J. 166, 170
Crossman, Richard 184
Crown Film Unit (formerly GPO
    Film Unit) 178, 216–17
'Culture, Progress and the English
    Tradition' (Rickword) 113
Cummings, A. J. 21–3, 24, 49
Cunningham, Valentine 7, 12, 15,
    19, 66, 69, 152
Curran, James 21

Daily Express 23, 24
Daily Herald 23, 24, 49, 59
Daily Mail 23, 24, 49, 60
Daily Mirror 24, 49
Daily Worker 59
Danger (Hughes) 153
Dark Tower, The (MacNeice) 202
Davy, Charles 14, 38–9, 114, 129,
    144
Day Lewis, Cecil 7, 14, 51, 53,
    97–8
  'Newsreel' 103, 127
  on poetry 113
  radio 152
Dead Centre (Calder-Marshall) 131
Dean, Basil 166, 168
Debord, Guy 5
Delderfield, R. F. 34
Der Angriff 53
Deutsch, Oscar 39
dialectics 15
Dimbleby, Richard 30

disproportionate representation in media 107, 183
documentaries *see* BBC, cinema
documentary novels of Thirties 146
Dog Beneath the Skin, The (Auden & Isherwood) 1, 55–6, 57–8, 59, 92
Donat, Robert 170
double-thinking 211–12
Douglas, Keith 216, 229–31
Douhet, Guilo 207
Drakakis, John 121, 194
drama 114–23
 Soviet travelling shows 116
dramatic control panel technique 121
Du Garde Peach, L. 34
Dunkirk evacuation 204–5
Dunne, J. W. 112
Dzigan, Yefim 139

Eagleton, Terry 2
Ealing Studios 216
economics and film potential 74
Eisenstein, Sergei 41, 130, 149
Eliot, T. S. 8, 126, 152, 159
Empire Marketing Board 17
England Made Me (Greene) 57, 120, 141–2
English Auden 62, 92, 99, 104, 126
English Journey (Priestley) 54, 70
European Civil War of 1920s & 1930s 25
Evans, Walter 106
Events in the Early Life of Anthony Price (Henderson) 131–2
Evil Was Abroad (Lehmann) 53
Experiment with Time (Dunne) 112

Fall of the City (MacLeish) 109, 154–5
Fatality in Fleet Street (Caudwell) 53
Federation of Workers' Film Societies 102
Ferguson, Russell 44
Fiction and the Reading Public (Q. D. Leavis) 16

fiction influenced by cinema 128–50
Fields, Gracie 87–9, 166–7
film, potential for psychoanalysis 143
Film and the Theatre 114
film distributors 40
film techniques imitated by writers 18
films
 British anti-establishment 44
 influence on textual form 124
 mainstream British 43–4
 see also cinema
Finney, Brian 145
First World War *see* Great War
Flanagan, Hallie 116
Flowers Are Not For You To Pick, The (Guthrie) 121, 153
footage-faking 101
Footnotes to the Film (Davy) 14
Ford, Ford Madox 74
foreign policy and cinema censorship 42
Foreman Went to France, The (film) 219
Formby, George 89–90, 168
Forster, E. M. 188
Foucault, Michel 12
freedom of the Press 22
Freedom Radio 183
Freund, Karl 140
Fussell, Paul 216
Future's in the Air, The 100, 180

Galsworthy, John 166
Gardiner, A. C. 67
Gaumont-British Picture Corporation 39
General Strike 27, 28
Germany, Nazi 18, 29, 42
Gibbon, Lewis Grassic 58, 94
Gielgud, Val 34, 35, 154
Gilliam, Laurence 154, 157
Glass Menagerie, The (Williams) 86
global totality represented in British writing 9–12
Goebbels, Josef 45, 51

Goldie, Grace Wyndham   157, 158
Golding, Louis   166
Good Companions, The (Priestley)
    88, 166
Good Morning Midnight (Rhys)   80
Good Soldier Schweik, The   115
Goodbye to Berlin (Isherwood)   78,
    104, 143, 144–9
GPO Film Unit (later Crown Film
    Unit)   178
Grammar of the Film, A
    (Spottiswoode)   131
Grassic Gibbon, Lewis *see* Gibbon,
    Lewis Grassic
Great War (1914–18)   20–1, 184
Green, Henry   65, 85
Greene, Felix   28
Greene, Graham   10, 14, 41
    'A Little Place off the Edgware
        Road'   112
    broadcasting   151–2
    cinema   70, 74–7, 112, 129, 131,
        136–42, 165, 171–3, 180
        see also Mornings in the Dark
    England Made Me   57, 120,
        141–2
    Green Cockatoo   84
    Heart of the Matter   128
    It's a Battlefield   11–12, 48, 55,
        56, 57, 67, 70, 77, 91, 110,
        134, 137–8, 172
    Ministry of Information (MoI)
        183–4, 220
    Mornings in the Dark   74–5, 77,
        84–5, 86–7, 98, 112, 129
    on Russian films   98–9
    Stamboul Train   137, 141, 171–2
    Third Man, The   112, 138
    wartime features   221–5
Greenwood, Walter   65, 94, 135,
    168
Grey Children (Hanley; and film)
    91–2
Grey Granite (Grassic Gibbon)
    58, 65, 94–5, 135
Grierson, John   17, 37, 63, 98–100,
    152, 210
Griffis, Stanton   80
Griffiths, Richard   23

Griffiths, Trevor   90
Grigson, Geoffrey   14
Guernica (Picasso)   110
Gulf War, Second (1991)   1, 2, 3
Guthrie, Tyrone   121, 153–5, 161

Hands of Orlac, The   140
Hanley, James   91–2
Harding, A. E.   158–9, 195
Hardy, Forsyth   40–1
Hay, Ian   186
Heart of the Matter, The (Greene)
    128
Heartfield, John   124
Henderson, Nevile   20
Henderson, Philip   131–2
Heppenstall, Rayner   35, 157–8
Herbert, A. P.   186
Heslop, Harold   59, 65
Hiller, Wendy   169
His Worship the Mayor
    (Greenwood)   65, 135
History of the World in 10½ Chapters
    (Barnes)   2–3
Hitchcock, Alfred   140–1, 144
Hitler, Adolf   20, 69
Hogenkamp, Bert   89
Hollywood
    competition with   39
    domination of British film
        culture   42, 85–6, 115
    escapism of   17
    see also cinema
Holocaust, influence on writers
    228
Holtby, Winifred   16, 55, 66, 71,
    77, 86–7, 108, 166, 169–70
Homage to Catalonia (Orwell)
    103–4
Howard, Bryan   151
Hughes, Langston   192
Hughes, Richard   153
Huxley, Aldous   48, 72, 101, 152,
    165
Hynes, Samuel   147
hyperreality   1–2, 11, 20, 108,
    181–2
    and film   37
    and radio   62

I Crossed the Minch (MacNeice) 64
Illusion and Reality (Caudwell) 72
Information, Ministry of *see*
  Ministry of Information
international understanding, radio
  as aid to 67
intertextuality
  cinematic 129–30, 138–9
  of visual and verbal media 149
  in wartime 205–6
intrusiveness of radio 64
Invisible Man, The (Wells; and
  film) 108–9, 175
Isherwood, Christopher 1, 8,
  142–3, 145
  Ascent of F6 51–2
  and the camera-eye 147
  Goodbye to Berlin 78, 104
  Journey to a War 56–7, 101, 104,
    109
  Mr Norris Changes Trains 53
  On the Frontier 54, 69, 109
  Prater Violet 83, 173–8
  on *The Grapes of Wrath* 63
It's a Battlefield (Greene) 11–12,
  48, 55, 56, 57, 67, 70, 77, 91,
  110, 134, 137–8, 172
It's That Man Again (ITMA) 201–2

Jameson, Fredric 4, 5, 8, 13
Jameson, Storm 63, 134, 148, 188
Jennings, Humphrey 192, 216
Jew Boy (Blumenfeld) 59, 66,
  77–8, 84, 96, 135
Jew Süss (film) 42, 176–7
Johnny Miner (radio) 193–4
Jones, Stephen G. 89
journalists, integrity of 55–7
Journey to a War (Auden &
  Isherwood) 56–7, 101, 109
Joyce, James 120, 129
Joyce, William ('Lord Haw-Haw')
  202–3

Kaleidoscope I (Sieveking) 121, 157
Kantian Sublime 8
Keep the Aspidistra Flying (Orwell)
  83
Klingender, Francis 124

Koestler, Arthur 185, 228
Korda, Alexander 38, 39
Kristeva, Julia 90

Laboratory Theatre, New York
  116
Laing, Stuart 133
Lambert, R. S. 33
Lancashire Luck (film) 168
Lang, Fritz 72, 140
language, newspaper 53, 58
Last Cage Down (Heslop) 59, 65,
  66, 125
Last Edition 117–18, 122
Leavis, F. R. 14, 15, 152
Leavis, Q. D. 14, 16
Left Book Club 118
Left Review 14
Leftists
  attempts to demystify films
    92–3
  attempts to detoxify working-
    class film addicts 93
  attitude to BBC 61–3, 66
  cinema writing 164–81
  concern to expose falsity 101–3
  cultural production of 114
  culture 15–16, 16–18, 33
  culture and film 38
  documentaries 178
  fear of the press 51
  and Five Year Plan films 97
  incursion into mass media 151
  quest for modernised neo-
    realism 130
  radio 152
  refractions of media in the
    Thirties 106–13
  theatre 119–20
  themes 50
  wartime involvement with
    media 181–3
  writing and mass media in the
    Thirties 46
Lehmann, John 53, 125
Let the People Sing (Priestley)
  88, 219
Letters from Iceland (Auden &
  MacNeice) 81–2, 99, 104, 107

Lewis, Wyndham 152
Life of Galileo (Brecht) 109
Linklater, Eric 188
Lions and Shadows (Isherwood) 149
Lippmann, Walter 17
Listener, The 33, 37, 152, 156
Listener's Commentary (Postgate) 31
literature and the media 7
Little Friend (film) 174
'Little Place off the Edgware Road, A' (Greene) 112
Littlewood, Joan 119, 121–2, 162–3
Litvak, Anatole 101
Living (Green) 65, 85
Living Newspaper, British 116–18
Lloyd-James, Arthur 31
Lodge, David 144
Look Up and Laugh (film) 87, 167
Lorre, Peter 140
Love on the Dole (film) 41–2, 94, 168, 217–19
Lyotard, Jean-François 2

MacColl, Ewan 97, 115–16, 119, 122, 159
MacLeish, Archibald 109, 154–5
Macmillan, Lord 184
MacNeice, Louis 10–11, 24–5, 62, 64, 194–5
  on Auden 126
  Autumn Journal 50, 67, 69, 70, 80, 107, 128
  and BBC 123
  on BBC Features 157
  broadcasting 194–202
  Christopher Columbus 194–5, 199–200
  on Eliot 126
  Letters from Iceland 81–2, 99, 107
  'News-Reel' 128
  Out of the Picture 91, 105, 123
  on radio drama 156
  Zoo 80, 104
Maconachie, Richard 29

Madge, Charles 15, 21, 27, 49–50, 62
Mais, S. P. B. 28
Major Operation (Barke) 63, 90, 93–4, 120, 132, 133, 135
Man of Aran (film) 99
Manchester and broadcasting 160–2
Manchester Theatre of Action 116
Mandoa, Mandoa! (Holtby) 55, 71
March of Time, The (newsreel) 42, 102, 117
Marinetti, F. T. 5–6
Marshall, Howard 28
Marwick, Arthur 46
Marxism 4–5, 175
  and media technology 9
Mass Civilisation and Minority Culture (F. R. Leavis) 15
mass media
  discussions on 14–17
  as formal influences
    drama 114–23
    fiction 128–50
    verse 124–8
  wartime conditions 181–8
  writing for the 151
  see also propaganda and media
mass perceptions in cinema 109–10
Mass-Observation (M-O) 17, 29, 82, 114, 117, 118, 124, 164, 167, 183, 216
Matheson, Hilda 28
Matrimonial News (Guthrie) 153–4
Matter of Life or Death, A (film) 188
May Day in England (Bridson) 159
May Day (Sommerfield) 54–5, 93, 132–4
May the 12th (Mass-Observation survey) 117
media
  consciousness in the Thirties 5, 6–8, 46, 112
  dependence on 17–18
  disproportionately representative 107, 183

media – *continued*
  general 106–13
  and Great War 107
Mein Kampf (Hitler) 20
metonymy
  in broadcasting 205
  in film 144
Metro-Vickers trial, Soviet 21, 42
Metropolis (film) 72
Middlemas, Keith 20
Miles 38, 78, 84
Mind in Chains (ed. Day Lewis)
  73, 165
Ministry of Fear (Greene) 220
Ministry of Information (MoI) 28,
  40, 70, 183–8, 220, 222
Mitchell, Robert 119
'mobilising', meanings of the term,
  ix
Modern Times (film) 98
Modernism 4–5, 11
Modernist novel and broadcasting
  120
Modernists
  and cinema 130–2, 142–3
  English-writing 7
montage
  radiogenic 121, 122
  in Thirties novels 131–5
  in verse 126
morals and cinema censorship
  41, 43
Mornings in the Dark (Greene)
  74–5, 77, 84–5, 86–7, 98, 101,
  112, 126, 129, 131, passim
Mosley, Oswald 23
movies *see* cinema
Mr Deeds Goes to Town (film) 73
Mr Norris Changes Trains
  (Isherwood) 53, 56
Murrow, Ed 30, 192, 204
Mussolini, Benito 69
Myth of the Blitz, The (Calder)
  185, 203

narrative with poetic subtext in
  films 142
narrative radio drama, evolution
  of 155

National Publicity Bureau 108
National Unemployed Workers'
  Movement (NUWM) 45
Naturalism in theatre 115
Nazi ideology, attempts to
  confront 228
New Way to Win, A (Slater) 115
News Chronicle 21
news and reality 101
news reporting style of BBC 28
'News-reel' (MacNeice) 128
newspapers
  capitalist 49
  in fiction 50–61
  working-class loyalties 48–9
Newsreel Association of Great
  Britain 45
'Newsreel' (Day Lewis) 103, 127
newsreels 37, 44–6
  see also cinema: newsreels
Nicoll, Allardyce 114, 131
Night Mail (Auden) 178–9
Nineteen Eighty-Four (Orwell) 108,
  211, 213
Norris, Christopher 1
Northcliffe, Lord 22, 51
novel, thirties 128, 166
Nuremberg Rally (1934) 20

Observer 23
O'Connor, T. P. 40
Odeon cinema circuit 39
Odets, Clifford 115
Ogden, C. K. 210–11
On Going to Press (Stevens) 52
On the Frontier (Auden and
  Isherwood) 54, 69, 109,
  110–11
Orwell, George 3–4, 14, 23, 24,
  60–1, 69, 83, 84, 185–6
  on broadcasting in wartime
  208–15
  Clergyman's Daughter 120
  Homage to Catalonia 103–4
  Nineteen Eighty-Four 108, 211,
  213
  Road to Wigan Pier 84, 107–8
  War Commentaries 211
  on working-class humour 89–90

Ostrer, Isidore 39, 44–5
Out of the Picture (MacNeice) 62, 91, 105
Out of this World (Swift) 1
Oxford Outlook 74

Paget, Derek 147
panopticism *see* camera eyes of writers
panoramic effects in fiction 135–6, 169
Paramount News 45
People's War, The (Calder) 185, 205
performativity principle 2, 4
Phelan, Jim 135
photographic images and realism 104–6, 124
photomagazines 37
photomontage 124
see also montage
Piazza, Paul 143, 147
Pickles, Wilfred 31, 64, 190
Pimpernel Smith (film) 188, 192
poetry *see* verse
'Poetry by Wireless' (Greene) 151
political violence reported in the press 59–60
post-television theatre, ideas for 14
Postgate, R. W. 31
Postmodernism 1–4, 9
Postmodernism (Jameson) 4
Postscripts (Priestley) 204, 205, 207
Pound, Ezra 130, 152
Powell, Anthony 57, 78, 95, 131
Prater Violet (Isherwood) 83, 173–8
Press 21–5
critical refractions of the 48–61
integrity of the 55–9
international effects of the 53
and politics 48
Press and a Changing Civilisation (Cummings) 21
Priestley, J. B. 54, 70, 87, 88, 121, 166–8, 202–8
Professor, The (Warner) 67

Professor Mamlock (film) 98
Pronay, Nicholas 45, 184
propaganda
in film 101–6, 108
German 202
Spanish Civil War 110
propaganda and media 20, 23–4, 28, 52
Nazi 43, 67–8
newspapers 51–4
newsreels 44–6
radio 25
wartime 181–208
see also BBC, cinema
Proud Man (Burdekin) 140
Proud Valley (film) 171
psychoanalytic revelations in film 143
public service and BBC 30
Pudney, John 121, 152
Pudovkin, V. I. 75, 140

Radek, Karl 130
radio *see* BBC, broadcasting
Radio Drama (Rodger) 122
radio production, basic grammar of 121
radio serials 121
radio-dependence of working classes 66
radios, first mass-produced 25–6
Rains, Claude 108
Rank, J. Arthur 215
'real', notion of the 2, 4, 101
Red Megaphones group 115
Reed, Carol 142
Reflections (ed. Davy) 75, 76, 98, 140, 151–2
Reith, Lord (formerly Sir John) 16, 26–8, 30, 36, 65, 184
Remote People (Waugh) 50
reportage, cult of 17
Rhys, Jean 80–1
Richards, Jeffrey 39, 46, 89, 168, 169
Rickword, Edgell 113
Road to Wigan Pier, The (Orwell) 84, 107–8
Robeson, Paul 171

Robinson, Ernest H.   68, 112
Rodger, Ian   31, 122, 155, 160, 161
romans fleuves, cinematic   132–3
Romm, Mikhail   98
Roosevelt, Franklin D.   69
Rotha, Paul   37, 100, 106, 179
Rothermere, Lord   22, 23, 51, 60
Roughton, Roger   64
Russia, Stalinist   18
Ruttmann, Walther   131, 135–6

Salford Workers' Film Society   97
Sandwichman (Brierley)   58–9,
   63–4, 66
satire on newspapers *see*
   newspapers in fiction
Scannell, Paddy   25, 27, 29, 30,
   31–2, 33, 36, 158, 163
Scoop: A Novel about Journalists
   (Waugh)   50
Second World War (1939–45)
   151, 181–2, 215–31
Shapley, Olive   121, 163–4
Shaw, George Bernard   166
Shaw, Irwin   115
Sherriff, R. C.   108
Shipyard Sally (film)   87, 89, 167
Shirer, William L.   30, 68
Siepmann, Charles   28
Sieveking, Lance   35, 37, 121, 153,
   156–8
Silent Village, The (film)   192
Sing As We Go (film)   87–8, 89, 166
Slater, Montagu   115
Small, Victor   73–4
Smith   38, 78, 84
Smith, Ashley   135–6
Smith, Grahame   128–9
social aspects of broadcasting
   32–4
Socialist Film Council   102
Society of the Spectacle (Debord)   5
socio-economic revelations in film
   143
Sommerfield, John   54, 66, 93, 132
Son of the Sheik (film)   112
Song of Ceylon (Wright)   99
South Riding (Holtby)   16, 66, 77,
   79, 87, 169–70

Soviet Union
   films   95–6, 139–40, 178–9
   wartime attitude towards
      190–1, 209–10
Soviet Writers' Union Congress
   (1934)   130
Spanish Civil War   3, 27, 30, 122,
   124, 158
speech in broadcasting   30–1
Spencer, D. A.   43
Spender, Stephen   7, 18, 22, 53, 97
   on Guernica   110
   photography   104, 105
   on Russian films   96, 143
   Trial of a Judge   111
   Vienna   53, 106, 109
Spottiswoode, Raymond   126, 131
Squirrel's Cage (Guthrie)   121, 153
Stamboul Train (Greene)   137, 141,
   171
Stars Look Down, The (Cronin)
   170–1
Stead, Peter   89
Stevens, F. L.   52
stream of consciousness effects in
   radio   121
subjective consciousness of
   fictional characters   11–12
Sunday Dispatch   23
Sunday Pictorial   41
Swastika Night (Burdekin)   63,
   104–5
Swift, Graham   1
synecdoche in film   144

tabloid format   24
taboos in broadcasting   34–5
Tallents, Stephen   17, 33, 184
Taylor, A. J. P.   25, 38
Taylor, Philip M.   3, 20
technology and criticism   8
television   37
Temple, The (Spender)   96
Ten-a-Penny People (Phelan)   135
Thaelmann (film)   42
theatre
   epic   115
   see also drama
Theatre Union   115, 122, 163

Theatre Workshop   163
Theatres of the Left (Blumenfeld)
   116, 118
Their Theatre and Ours (Thomas)
   92–3, 102–3, 115
They Came to a City (film)   219
Third Man, The (film)   112, 138–9
'Thirties Sublime'   8–9
Thirty-nine Steps, The (film)   141,
   170
This Gun for Hire (film)   224
Thomas, Dylan   73, 105, 120
Thomas, H. B. (Thom)   92, 102, 115
Thunder Rock (film)   189, 225
Time to Spare (documentary)   28–9
Times, The   23
*Transatlantic Call – People to
   People*   192
transatlanticism of popular culture
   15–16
Traveller Came By, A (Carson)   146
Travers, Ben   166
Trial of a Judge (Spender)   111
truth-telling in media   112
Tyrrel, Lord (BBFC)   40

Ulysses (Joyce)   120, 130
Uncritical Theory (Norris)   1–2
Under Milk Wood (Thomas)   120
Unemployed Man, The (Bakke)   83
unemployment   15, 28–9
Unity Theatre, North London
   116–19
US radio networks in wartime
   191–3

Venusberg (Powell)   57
verse, influence of cinema on
   125–8
Vertov, Dziga   9, 124, 131, 147
Victoria the Great (film)   86
Vidor, King   170
Vienna (Spender)   53, 109
Viertel, Berthold   174, 176
Vietnam war   3
Vile Bodies (Waugh)   50
voice of the people, newspapers as
   22

'voice-overs' technique   120
Voyage in the Dark (Rhys)   81

Waiting for Lefty (Odets)   115
Waley, H. D.   43
Wallace, Edgar   166
War Commentaries (Orwell)   211
War of the Worlds, The (radio
   broadcast)   61
Warner, Rex   12, 62, 67, 107
Waste Land, The (Eliot)   8, 126, 159
Waugh, Evelyn   50, 128
Waugh in Abyssinia (film)   101
Way to the Sea (film)   179
Way to the Stars, The (film)   192
We from Kronstadt (Dzigan)   139
Weimar Sonnenkinder, films of
   96–7
Wells, H. G.   108, 166
Went the Day Well? (Greene)   188,
   219
West, Alick   95, 130
Western Approaches (film)   217
When We Are Married (Priestley)
   121
Whitebait, William   216–17
Wilcox, Herbert   41
Wild Goose Chase, The (Warner)
   12, 63, 107
Williams, John Danvers   80
Williams, Raymond   4–5
Williams, Tennessee   86
Wintringham, Tom   97
Wolf, Friedrich   98
Woolf, Virginia   129
Workers Film and Photo League
   89
Workers' Theatre Movement   92,
   102, 115–16
Workers' Uprising (1934)   174
World of Plenty (film)   217
Worpole, Ken   135
Wright, Basil   99, 131, 171

Years, The (Woolf)   129

Zinoviev Letter (1924)   23, 51
Zoo (MacNeice)   80, 104